FREE GRACE
SOTERIOLOGY

FREE GRACE SOTERIOLOGY

THIRD EDITION

DAVID R. ANDERSON, PhD

Free Grace Soteriology Third Edition

Copyright © 2018 by Grace Theology Press. Published by Grace Theology Press.

All rights reserved. No part of this publication may be reproduced, stored in a retrieval system, or transmitted in any form by any means, electronic, mechanical, photocopy, recording, or otherwise, without the prior permission of the publisher, except as provided for by USA copyright law.

First Printing 2018

Unless otherwise indicated, Bible quotations are taken from the New King James Version of the Bible, © 1982 by Thomas Nelson Publishers.

ISBN-13: 978-0-9884112-1-0
ISBN-10: 988411210

Special Sales: Most Grace Theology Press titles are available in special quantity discounts. Custom imprinting or excerpting can also be done to fit special needs. Contact Grace Theology Press at info@gracetheology.org.

Table of Contents

Preface to the Third Edition vii
Preface to the Revised Edition ix
Preface to the First Edition xi
Dedication xv
How Augustine's Change in Eschatology Has Shaped
Christian Soteriology 1
The Sinfulness of Man 33
Salvation in the Old Testament 55
The Cross of Jesus Christ 74
Justification 99
The Order of Salvation ("Ordo Salutis") 118
Repentance 125
Faith 166
Eternal Security 191
Assurance of Salvation 208
Regeneration 229
Lordship Salvation 258
Infants and "Heathen" 287
Divine Sovereignty and Human Responsibility 297
Universalism 324

APPENDIX A
Sōzō and the Hermeneutical Circle 351

APPENDIX B
Another "Tale of Two Cities" 375

Further Reading: Selected Bibliography 403

Subject–Author Index 411

Scripture Index 425

Preface to the Third Edition

From what began as a set of class-notes to the first revised edition a lot of changes were needed. Since that first revised edition a number of other suggestions have made it necessary to revise *Free Grace Soteriology* once again. Many have said that Appendix A should come at the beginning of the book. It shows how the teachings of Augustine set forth the ultimate and final requirement for anyone to spend eternity with God: perseverance of the saints. According to him, a person can be regenerated, saved, and be a genuine believer, but still not be elect if he does not persevere faithfully in his Christian walk until the end of his life. That's what the Catholics teach today, but it's also what the Calvinists teach, and that's also what the Arminians teach. According to the Calvinists, if a person does not persevere faithfully until the end of his life, he never was elect. And according to the Arminians, if a person does not persevere faithfully until the end of his life, he loses his salvation. So, all three groups park their cars in the Vatican parking lot. And that represents about 99% of Christianity. It's so important to understand this commonality among Catholics, Arminians, and Calvinists that we have moved Appendix A from the first and second editions to the front of the book in this edition.

Since the writing of the first edition almost twenty years ago, a number of theological issues have popped up on the radar screen that were not there at that time. One of those is the subject of universalism. More and more Christian pastors (Rob Bell) and philosophers

(Thomas Talbott and Gregory MacDonald) have thrown their hats into the ring of universalism. So, we thought it necessary to address that issue.

Finally, the fog covering the relationship between faith and works gets thicker and thicker. Some authors, who have graduated from conservative, evangelical schools, have concluded that justification is by faith plus works (Alan Stanley and Matthew Bates). Still others have made perseverance part of the essence of saving faith (D. A. Carson). While we agree that consistency demands that the theology of these men should lead to justification by faith and works, twenty years ago they were not admitting it. Now they are. So, we want to address some of these works as well.

As always, we never pretend to have the last word in theology. That belongs to God. But we continue to search for the system which has the greatest degree of consistency, comprehensiveness, congruency, and coherence. We are presenting the soteriological slice of that theological pie in this book.

David R. Anderson, PhD
June, 2018

Preface to the Revised Edition

The First Edition of *Free Grace Soteriology* has been well-received. With the capable help of my editor, Jim Reitman, the Revised Edition corrects a number of minor irregularities of grammar, style, font use, reference citation, and theological content that were detected in the First Edition. These were due mainly to variation in the text of the teaching notes and articles from which the material for the book was drawn. To this end the manuscript has been extensively edited, updated, and re-typeset, with new Scripture and Subject Indexes to facilitate cross-referencing.

Issues of content that have been updated include the following:

- In the Preface to the First Edition, Free Grace is now noted to be the outflow of premillennialism, rather than dispensationalism *per se*.

- In the chapter "The Sinfulness of Man," the Federal Headship view of Romans 5:12 is no longer held, and this section has been revised to harmonize with our exposition of Romans 5–8 in our new book, *Portraits of Righteousness: Free Grace Sanctification in Romans 5–8* (Liberty University Press, in press).

- In the same chapter, the section on "The Unregenerate Mind" has been revised to: (1) reflect the updated view that the *natural* man in 1 Cor 2:14 (as contrasted with the *spiritual* man) represents the unbeliever rather than a *soulish* category of Christian; and (2) distinguish between the conscience of the unbeliever and that of the believer.

- The chapter "Regeneration" now includes our response to a recently presented specious argument from 1 John 5:1 that regeneration precedes faith in the *ordo salutis*.
- The chapter "Infants and Heathen," under the heading "Heathen," has been revised to better reflect the continuity of God's plan of salvation in progressive revelation.

David R. Anderson, PhD
May, 2012

Preface to the First Edition

Soteriology is nothing new. It is just the study of salvation, usually thought of in terms of how one lives forever with his Maker. But what is "Free Grace" soteriology? In fact, surely it is redundant to put the word "free" next to the word "grace." What is the point of qualifying "grace" as "free," if indeed the word "grace" means an *undeserved* favor?

Apparently, the Holy Spirit understood that all Christian groups would utilize the word *grace* in their theology. Few Christian theologians have written more about grace than Augustine (d. 431), who formed the backbone of Roman Catholic theology. And if we divide the Reformers between the Arminians and the Calvinists, both groups claim salvation by grace without works. But a Protestant does not want to be called a Catholic, and a Calvinist is insulted if you label him Arminian. So, there are very real and serious differences in these streams of Christianity. Nevertheless, all of them lay claim to grace. Therefore, in order to clarify what He means by *grace*, the Holy Spirit Himself qualified the term by saying it is *free*.

Perhaps the most well-known example of this qualification can be found in Ephesians 2:8-10. There, we read that we are saved *by grace* through faith. If grace were a completely clear concept to his readers, Paul would not have continued with his qualifications. But he does continue. On the negative side, he says this salvation by grace through faith is "not of yourselves." But on the positive side, he says it is "the gift" of God. This word for gift is one of several found in the NT. Its special emphasis is that this gift is *free*.

For example, if one were to offer a gift to a policeman who had stopped him for speeding, we have another word for this *gift*. It is the word *bribe*. If the policeman receives the gift, the driver is expecting the policeman to do something for him in return. That would not be the kind of gift meant by the word chosen in Ephesians 2:9. This word (*dōrean*) is found in its adverbial form twice in Revelation in connection with receiving eternal life. Revelation 21:6 says, "I will give of the fountain of the water of life *freely* to him who thirsts." That adverb has the same root as the noun we find in Ephesians 2:9. The only difference is that one is an adverb (Rev 21:6) and the other is a noun (Eph 2:9). This adverb is used again in Revelation 22:17: "Whosoever desires, let him take of the water of life *freely*." The free aspect of this water must be much imbedded in John's thinking because this adverb is found in noun form in John 4:10 where Jesus talks about the free gift (*dōrean*) of God symbolized by the water which would slake one's thirst forever. So, in Ephesians 2:8-10, Paul qualifies grace by saying it is a *free gift*. A free gift has no strings attached on the front end (or it becomes a wage) and no strings attached on the back end (or it is a bribe).

Over and over, Paul tries to make this distinction. That is why he mentions the "gift of grace" in Ephesians 3:7, where, once again, the word for gift is *dōrean*. And in Romans 5, he juxtaposes "grace" and "free gift" over and over, using this word for "free gift" (*dōrean*) three times (5:15, 16, and 17). In Romans 5:17, Paul even speaks of the "free gift" of righteousness. Thus, the concept of "free" grace is a very biblical concept. If modern teachers of Free Grace can be accused of redundancy, then so could Paul and John. "Free" or "freely" is a qualifier to make sure no one attached any strings to God's wonderful grace. It is absolutely free.

Who teaches Free Grace? Lots of people do, though they may not go out of their way to distinguish their message as a "Free Grace" message. Free grace is an outflow of premillennialism. Only premillennialism has a judgment seat for believers some time before the thousand-year reign of Christ (in Jerusalem on earth) and a judgment seat for unbelievers after this one-thousand-year reign. Which judgment seat a person appears before is determined not by his works, but by his faith in Christ or lack thereof. At each judgment seat a person is judged for his works, but not to determine his destiny in eternity. That has already been determined by his faith (with God forever) or lack of faith (apart from God forever). The judgment for his works is to determine his rewards, not his destiny. When the thousand year reign of Christ on earth is removed (which all amillennialists do), then the two judgment seats collapse into one judgment for believers and unbelievers simultaneously. Since these people (believers and unbelievers) are judged for their works at this single judgment seat, the basis for salvation can become muddled very quickly.

Because Augustine changed his eschatology (doctrine of future things) from premillennial to amillennial, he also had to change his understanding of the requirements for election. The ultimate requirement became to persevere in faithfulness until death (Matt 24:13). That was his *sine qua non* for election. The Reformers did not challenge this requirement since they did not challenge Augustine's eschatology. For both the Arminians and the Calvinists, one must persevere faithfully until the end of his life or he does not go to heaven. The Arminians claim that the one who does not remain faithful loses his salvation, while the Calvinists claim that one who does not remain faithful never had salvation. In either case, faithfulness until the end of one's life is the ultimate litmus test for one to spend eternity with God. When a faithful life is made a requirement for salvation, teachers of Free Grace claim that works have been appended to faith, turning God's so great salvation into more of a bribe than a gift. It turns the Christian life into a "have to" life rather than a "thank you" life, which is often the difference between a job and a joy.

In this volume, we attempt to develop a view of soteriology which is consistent with the Free Grace emphasized by John and Paul. By doing so, we hope to establish that only through Free Grace theology can one legitimately have the assurance of one's salvation in this life and the peace and joy which accompany such assurance. As Augustine himself taught, if one must persevere in faithful living until the end of his life in order to demonstrate his election, he can never know if he is elect until he dies. That is another way of saying that assurance in this life is impossible for anyone adopting Augustine's view of perseverance. We offer an alternative that is consistent with John's claim that believers can *know* they have eternal life before they die based on what they believe instead of how they behave (1 Jn 5:13). Along the way, we will categorically deny that this is "cheap" grace, while heralding without equivocation that it is "free" grace.

Dedication

I wish to dedicate this volume to all my students through the years who have held fast to the wonderful doctrines of Free Grace. May your joy abound as you share this incredible message to a dying world which can never live up to God's standard of holiness.

How Augustine's Change in Eschatology Has Shaped Christian Soteriology

In a recent article[1] we introduced the concept of "Spread Sheet Theology" by suggesting that this might be an alternative way to describe Systematic Theology. A good system is unified, comprehensive, consistent, and everything "fits." That means if we make a significant change in one part of the system, it may well affect other parts of the system. We made the claim that Augustine's choice to do away with premillennial eschatology is a case in point. That is, when Augustine became amillennial, this major change in his eschatology affected other parts of his theology, namely his soteriology. The purpose of this chapter will be to demonstrate how Augustine's change to amillennialism still has ripples in soteriology today. In order to do this, we will develop the study in four parts: the Eschatology of Augustine, the Soteriology of Augustine, the Soteriology of John Calvin, and the Soteriology of today. Admittedly, each of the subtitles could contain volumes. What we are trying to do in this chapter is to show how Augustine's change in eschatology affected not only his soteriology, but the soteriology of Western Christianity from the Medieval Period until today.

---

[1] David R. Anderson, "Regeneration: a Crux Interpretum," *Journal of the Grace Evangelical Society* (Fall, 2000):43-65.

Though pretribulational, premillennial eschatology is often criticized as a "recent" development in theology, such is simply not the case. That chiliasm was the norm in eschatology up until roughly A.D. 400 is no debate among church historians.[2] So we can safely say the church fathers were premillennial. But were they pretribulational?

The primary defense for a pretribulational approach to the rapture is the early church's view of imminency.[3] If one is premillennial and believes in a rapture such as that described in 1 Thessalonians 4, then the only chronological option for this rapture which is consistent with imminency is a rapture before the beginning of the Tribulation.[4] Thus, a stronger argument can be made for the early

---

[2] In the *Dialogue with Trypho*, 7 and 8, Justin Martyr (d. 165) explains: "I and *every other completely orthodox Christian* feel certain that there will be a resurrection of the flesh, followed by a thousand years in the rebuilt, embellished, and enlarged city of Jerusalem, as was announced by the Prophets Ezechiel, Isaias and the others" (italics mine). The great apologist Irenaeus of Lyons (d. 200) in his anti-Gnostic work, *Adversus haereses*, gives evidence of his belief in a Tribulation which would precede Christ's millennial reign (V, 28, 3): "For in as many days as this world was made, in so many thousand years shall it be concluded.... For the day of the Lord is as a thousand years.... [When] this Antichrist shall have devastated all things in this world, he will reign for three years and six months, and sit in the temple at Jerusalem; and then the Lord will come from heaven in the clouds, in the glory of the Father, sending this man and those who are following him into the lake of fire; but bringing in for the righteous the times of the kingdom, that is, the rest, the hallowed seventh day." Interestingly, Irenaeus was known as the "man of Tradition" because of his teaching on the Apostolic Tradition, and he claimed to teach only what he had heard as having been proclaimed from the beginning.

[3] A belief in imminency is obvious from the *Didachè*: "Watch over your life; your lamps must not go out, nor your loins be ungirded; on the contrary, be ready. You do not know the hour in which Our Lord is coming." And Clement (*I Clement*, XXIII) exhorts the Corinthians: "Take a vine: first it drops its leaves; then a shoot comes, then a leaf, then a flower, after that the sour fruit, then the fully ripe grapes. You see that in a short time the fruit of the tree reaches maturity. In truth his will shall be fulfilled quickly and suddenly.... He shall come quickly and not linger, and the Lord will come suddenly to his temple...."

[4] As the quote from Irenaeus above demonstrates, those who believed in a literal millennium on earth also believed in a literal Tribulation, which would

Fathers being pretribulational and premillennial than any other eschatological position with regard to Christ's Parousia.[5] With the notable exception of Origen of Alexandria, this was the prevailing approach to eschatology when Augustine came on the scene.

Augustine's Eschatology

It may shock some to realize that Augustine was not only premillennial[6] in his early eschatology, but he was also dispensational. Of course, if we understand Spread Sheet Theology and Dispensationalism as a system (spread sheet) of theology, this should not be a surprise. A literal millennium on earth is of the essence of dispensational theology. Augustine held to a traditional seven-age (dispensational) model which coordinated periods in biblical history with humanity's spiritual progress toward redemption. The initial five stages correlated to Old Testament history and were demarcated by Adam, Noah, Abraham, David, and the Exile.[7] The two New Testament dispensations, according to Augustine and practically all

---

immediately precede this millennium, as described by Daniel and Revelation. If the Rapture were to occur any time during this Tribulation, then any concept of imminency associated with Christ's Second Coming would be destroyed, since both Daniel and Revelation tell us how many days are in the Tribulation. If the Rapture took place during the Tribulation, one could easily calculate the exact day of His Second Coming. But this would contradict Christ's statement that no one knew the day nor the hour except His Father.

[5] See Craig L. Blomberg, The Posttribulationism of the New Testament: Leaving the "Left Behind" Behind, in *A Case for Historic Premillennialism: An Alternative to "Left Behind" Eschatology*, ed. by Craig L. Blomberg and Sung Wook Chung, (Grand Rapids, MI 2009) 31. This chapter and the book overall is a defense for the Posttribulational rapture view assumed to be found in the early church.

[6] Augustine, City of God, 20.7,1; see also G. Folliet, "La typologie du *sabbat* chez Saint Augustin. Son interpretation millénariste entre 386 et 400," *REAug* 2 (1956): 371-90.

[7] Though dispensationalists disagree somewhat on the different administrative periods (economies) in the OT, there is general agreement that a dispensation is a distinguishable economy in God's administration of His redemptive plan for mankind.

dispensationalists, were the Church Age and the Millennial Kingdom, "the Sabbath Rest" of the saints on earth.[8]

But three factors converged in northern Africa which influenced Augustine to take a new approach to the Millennium. The first was his revulsion over the bacchanal celebrations of the Donatists. The Catholics were the intruders in N. Africa, the "Bible Belt" of the Mediterranean world. They were the minority right up through the fourth century. But the Donatist Church, which separated from Rome over the issue of rebaptism of the *traditores* who succumbed to the pressure from Diocletian to burn their holy books, had the upper hand. And they were fervent. The Donatists were the "church of the martyrs," the faithful who would not compromise no matter how fierce the persecution. They honored their dead by burying them in wet plaster so as to preserve every detail of the body's outline—all the better to anticipate the resurrection of said body to reign in the physical Millennium to come. So, they had a concept of reigning as a reward for faithfulness.

But it was the drunken feasts celebrated by the "cult of the dead" which offended Augustine. He associated this kind of behavior with the Jewish apocalyptic emphasis on grand feasts of celebration during the kingdom of the saints on earth. His platonic leanings influenced him to view such materialistic gorging with a jaundiced eye. Augustine's revulsion at his own pre-Christian debauchery left him with an ascetic bent. For example, married men who indulged in sexual pleasure after procreation were guilty of venial sins.[9] For Augustine this revelry for the dead was *carnalis ingurgitatio*. Through Plato's eyes he understood the material flesh to be flawed, imperfect, defective—especially when compared to the spiritual world with its perfect forms and ideals. The human spirit is tortured in its carnal prison; it longs to be set free. The pilgrim can hasten its release by fleshly self-denial. Therefore, along with his growing disdain for the

---

[8] Augustine, *Sermon 259,2*. See also Paula Fredriksen, "Apocalypse and Redemption in Early Christianity," *Vigiliae Christianae* 45 (1991): 163.
[9] Augustine, *On Marriage and Concupiscience*, 1.3.

carnal *laetitia* (joy) of the saints was an increasing desire to understand the Millennium in a spiritual instead of a material light.

A second factor which frustrated the Bishop of Hippo was the growing excitement of millenarians as they saw A.D. 500 approaching. The seven days of creation from Genesis 1 were used as figures for many concepts, including the "cosmic week."[10] The seven days of creation were combined with Ps 90:4/2 Pet 3:8 (a day is with the Lord as a thousand years and a thousand years as a day) and the thousand years of Revelation 20 to establish the ages of the world. Just as the Lord had created the earth in six days and rested on the seventh, so the world would exist for six ages of one thousand years each, but would find rest during the seventh age of a thousand years when Christ returned to rule from Jerusalem. Therefore, one could figure out when Christ would return simply by figuring out the age of mankind.

Hippolytus and Julius Africanus (early third century) calculated that Jesus was born in the 5,500th year since creation. Obviously then, He would return to set up His Kingdom in A.D. 500. This date did not stir up the readers in the days of Julius and Hippolytus, but as A.D. 400 rolled around, anticipation of the coming Millennium added to the ardor and excitement of the Donatists in their celebrations. Augustine's anti-materialism motivated him to deflate this millennial balloon of material emphasis. He could do this if he could use the Scriptures to prove that the Millennium was spiritual instead of physical, and if he could discredit the "cosmic week" chronology so widely accepted in his day. And this leads us to the third factor which combined with the other two to enable Augustine to erase millenarianism from the main stream of Catholic doctrine. It was the hermeneutics of Tyconius.

Origen of Alexandria is often credited with influencing Augustine to use allegory as a tool to do away with a literal, physical millennium. This is not the case. It is true, of course, that Origen was a scholar of such immense giftedness and influence that his allegorizing of Scripture became a popular approach to interpretation. But his

---

[10] J. Daniélou, "La typologie millenariste de la semaine dans le christianisme primitif," *Vigiliae Christiane* 2 (1948):1-16.

influence was nothing new when Augustine became a Christian. Rather it was the influence of a lay theologian named Tyconius, who first touched Augustine in the 390s. According to Paula Fredriksen,

> [I]t is Tyconius who stands at the source of a radical transformation of African—and thus, ultimately, of Latin—theology, and whose reinterpretation of his culture's separatist and millenarian traditions provided the point of departure for what is most brilliant and idiosyncratic in Augustine's own theology. And it is Tyconius, most precisely, whose own reading of John's Apocalypse determined the Western church's exegesis for the next eight hundred years.[11]

The primary tool of Tyconius was not allegory; it was typology. He used typology to avoid the ahistoricism of allegory while insisting that the time of the End could not be known. Through the use of the seven rules of Tyconius,[12] Augustine was able to turn numbers into symbols, to bind Satan in the sixth age of a thousand years rather

---

[11] Fredriksen, "Apocalypse," 157.

[12] Ibid., 157-58. Rule 1: *mysticae*—compositional principles encoded within the text of Scripture which obscure or hide its meaning; Rule 2: *de Domini corpore bipertito*—the body of the Lord, the church, is divided between both the good and the wicked; Rule3: *de promissis et lege*—the Bible contains both law and promise, the former arousing faith in the latter among the saints; Rule 4: *de specie et genere*—simple reference to particular persons and events can convey general truths; Rule 5: *de temporibus*—numbers in Scripture defy calculation because they are elastic with an infinite number of interpretations; Rule 6: *de recapitulatione*—what appears to be sequence may actually be recapitulation; Rule 7: *de diabolo et eius corpore*—references to the devil in Scripture might actually be referring to his unrighteous followers. With these rules Tyconius could assign historical value but obscure the eschatological significance of the millenarian/apocalyptic passages in the Bible. It is easy to see the influence of the these rules in Augustine and subsequent eschatology throughout the centuries of church history: 1) "Future figures" like Gog and the Son of Man appear in present time rather than the future; 2) Millenarian references can be recapitulatory rather than sequential (Rev 20); 3) Persecution does not identify the righteous of the Great Tribulation since the good and wicked coexist in the present church age; 4) Apocalyptic numbers of former significance

than the seventh, and to have saints rule with Christ spiritually in the sixth age rather than the seventh. The miracles of the saints proved that they were reigning with Christ in the Church Age, the sixth dispensation. He found the Antichrist, Gog and Magog, and the first resurrection—all in the age in which he lived.

Augustine eschewed any sort of *Heilsgeschichte* which was linear. For him it was a tragic waste to try to superimpose a time line on God's redemptive plan, if for no other reason than the fact that Christ Himself did not know when it would end. God's medium of salvation was not history, but rather the individual. Individuals will be raised with corporeal bodies, but these bodies will live in the heavens, not in some kingdom on earth. There will be no food, no procreation, no social relations in God's kingdom. Instead, perfected beings in their thirties will stand around gazing at God. What, then, is the seventh age of a thousand years for Augustine? Although the first six ages were indeed historical, the seventh age is the saints themselves: "After this present age God will rest, as it were, on the seventh day; and he will cause us, who are the seventh day, to find our rest in him" (*De Civ. Dei* XXII.0,5).

The success of Tyconius and Augustine can be measured by the Catholic commentary tradition, which followed their lead step by step. By the time the Reformers appear on the stage of history, eschatology was a dead issue. No scholar had avowed millenarianism for centuries. But the influence of Augustine reached far beyond the eschatological. His most profound influence may have been soteriological. But before we can assess his influence in the soteriology of the Roman Catholic Church, the Reformers, and beyond, we must first understand how his eschatological change affected his own soteriology.

Augustine's Soteriology

Two salient features of Augustine's soteriology are standard fare in any text book discussion on this most influential of Church

---

(1,000; 144,000; 1260 days; 42 months) are stretched any number of ways with vertiginous ease; 5) Realized eschatology.

Fathers. His approach to the depravity of man emasculated man's ability to pull himself up by his own bootstraps to the portals of heaven. Without God's grace it would be impossible for anyone to be eternally saved. Total depravity and human ability stood as antipodes in the soteriological debates, but grace stood out as the corollary of depravity. Depravity underscored the exigency of grace. God's grace was man's only hope for eternal salvation. For these Siamese truths both Catholics and Protestants are indebted to Augustine.

In centuries to come the differences would arise from disagreements over grace. How was God's grace to be obtained? Could one deposit of grace open the doors of heaven to a fallen sinner, or were daily deposits throughout one's life required? Could salvific grace be earned, or was it completely unmeritorious? Could venerable saints like the Virgin Mary also dispense God's grace, or was saving grace the proprietary property of Almighty God alone? And so it goes.

Among these discussions on obtaining God's grace, it is often pointed out that Augustine's scant knowledge of Greek caused him to misunderstand *dikaioō* (δικαιοω), translating it in its present infinitive form, "to *make* righteous,"[13] as opposed to the defining truth of the Reformers that this word meant "to *declare* righteous." The distinction was enough to cause a schism in Western Christianity. Whereas the former meaning signified a change of *character*, the latter meaning referred to a change of *standing*. "To make righteous" looked to one's experience in life, but "to declare righteous" looked to the court room of heaven. The temporal significance of the distinction in meanings was monumental. Augustine saw justification (the making of righteous character) as a life-long effort, whereas Luther understood that one could be "declared righteous" in God's court at a moment in time.

Initially, the forensic view of justification ("to declare righteous") was not illumination given to Martin Luther. His issue when he tacked his ninety-five theses to the door at Wittenburg was the sale of indulgences. It was his fellow colleague and language teacher, Philipp

---

[13] Augustine, *On the Spirit and the Letter*, 45.

Melanchthon, who persuaded Luther of the truth and implications of forensic righteousness some ten years after the Reformation officially began (1517). But when Luther did understand the significance of "court room" justification, he penned a truth perhaps no one since Paul himself clearly understood: *simul iustus et peccator* (just and a sinner at the same time). This apparent contradiction—that one could be declared righteous (justified) in his position or standing before God, but still be sinful in his character and condition in his temporal body— was a truth never comprehended by Augustine. He was convinced that the character of Christ needed to be infused into the character of the sinner from regeneration at water baptism (usually of infants) until death in order for the person to be *made righteous* (justified) enough to enter God's heaven. Even the vast majority of God's elect would not pass muster, so they would be consigned to Purgatory[14] until the final vestiges of sin could be eliminated from their character. Only then could they march confidently through heaven's gates. So, for Augustine justification was a life-long process. In fact, Purgatory was a provision of God for those in whom the process had not been completed. These elements of Augustine's soteriology have been sifted through by more scholars than we can number.

However, the connection between Augustine's understanding of justification and his understanding of eschatology has not, to my knowledge, been previously explored. As we have already seen, Augustine's exposure to the hermeneutics of Tyconius occurred in the early 390s. By A.D. 400 Augustine had already become a variation of what we would call today amillennial (no literal, physical thousand-year reign of Christ on earth). He had also set his sights to destroy millenarianism in Western Christianity. Yet the vast majority of his writings occurred post A.D. 400. Almost all of his writings pertaining to soteriology were written after this point. And in the soteriological writings of Augustine, one verse has center stage. This verse is essentially the point of departure for Augustine's understanding of soteriology. It occurs in his writings more times than John 3:16 or

---

[14] Nik Ansell, "Hell: the Nemesis of Hope?" in *Her Gates Will Never Be Shut* by Bradley Jersak (Eugene, OR: Wipf & Stock, 2009), 203.

Ephesians 2:8–9 or any verse or passage from Romans 3–8. This verse is none other than Matthew 24:13: "But he who endures to the end shall be saved."

According to the millenarian understanding of the Olivet Discourse, the meaning of "saved" in the Olivet Discourse referred to physical deliverance from death at the hands of the Antichrist or from the horrendous plagues at the end of the Tribulation Period. The following quote from Chrysostom, a contemporary of Augustine, typifies the view of the premillennial church fathers of the day and would have harmonized with Augustine's own views:

> "And except those days should be shortened, there should no flesh be saved; but for the elect's sake those days shall be shortened." . . . If, saith He, the war of the Romans against the city had prevailed further, all the Jews had perished (for by "no flesh" here, He meaneth no Jewish flesh) . . . But whom doth He here mean by the elect? The believers that were shut up in the midst of them. For that Jews may not say that because of the gospel, and the worship of Christ, these ills took place, He showeth, that so far from the believers being the cause, if it had not been for them, all had perished utterly. For if God had permitted the war to be protracted, not so much as a remnant of the Jews had remained, but lest those of them who had become believers should perish together with the unbelieving Jews, He quickly put down the fighting, and gave an end to the war. Therefore He saith, "But for the elect's sake they shall be shortened."[15]

Of course, Chrysostom is looking back at A.D. 70 instead of a future Tribulation, but it is his understanding of "saved" we want to observe. Here he equates "saved" with not perishing physically. This would have been Augustine's view when he held to a future Tribulation followed by a literal Millennium on earth. But getting rid of the literal Millennium also forced him to reassess the meaning of "saved" in Matthew 24:13. In all his writings after A.D. 400 he equates "saved"

---

[15] Chrysostom, *Homily 76*, Number 2.

with eternal, spiritual salvation. There are over 250 such references to persevering unto the end (of one's physical life) in order to be saved (eternally). Here are a couple references to clarify his thought: "Who could be ordained to eternal life save by the gift of perseverance? And when we read, 'He that shall persevere unto the end shall be saved;' with what salvation but eternal?"[16] In another treatise he reiterates the same thought: "Who could be ordained to eternal life save by the gift of perseverance? And when we read, 'He that shall persevere unto the end shall be saved;' with what salvation but eternal?"[17] No longer does Augustine understand "saved" in this context to refer to physical salvation. Now it is spiritual salvation.

For Augustine, Matthew 24:13 becomes the *sine qua non* of eternal salvation. One can genuinely believe, but not be elect: "It is, indeed, to be wondered at, *and greatly to be wondered at* (italics mine), that to some of His own children—whom He has regenerated in Christ—to whom He has given faith, hope, and love, God does not give perseverance also . . . "[18] One can be regenerated, but not be elect: "Some are regenerated, but not elect, since they do not persevere; . . . ."[19] The only way to validate one's election was to persevere until the end of his physical life on earth. This was the ultimate sign of the elect:

> We, then, call men elected, and Christ's disciples, and God's children, because they are to be so called whom, being regenerated, we see to live piously; but they are then truly what they are called if they shall abide in that on account of which they are so called. But if they have not perseverance,—that is, if they continue not in that which they have begun to be,—they are not truly called what they are called and are not; for they are not this in the sight of Him to whom it is known what they are going to be,—that is to say, from good men, bad men.[20]

---

[16] Augustine, *On Rebuke and Grace*, 5.10.
[17] Augustine, *On Perseverance*, 4.10.
[18] Augustine, *Rebuke and Grace*, 5.18.
[19] Ibid., 5.17.
[20] Ibid., 5.22.

Of course, with this approach to soteriology, Augustine did not think anyone could know that he was elect until he died. No matter how righteous and pious a life the believer might be living today, he could always fall away from the faith before he died (1 Cor. 10:12). Such a falling away would prove that this former believer was never elect to begin with, and it would also prove that any assurance derived from the righteousness of his former life was false assurance indeed.

No one can be certain until death:

> Therefore, it is uncertain whether any one has received this gift so long as he is still alive. For if he fall before he dies, he is, of course, said not to have persevered; and most truly is it said. How, then, should he be said to have received or to have had perseverance who has not persevered?[21]

Can the connection between Augustine's change in eschatology and his soteriology be made? It should be obvious. As a pretribulational, premillennial dispensationalist, Augustine would understand the salvation of Matthew 24:13 in a physical sense, especially when two previous uses of "the end" (24:3, 6) and an immediately subsequent use (24:14) both refer to "the end of the age," not the end of one's life. But when Augustine changed his eschatology, that is, when he negated any literal, physical Millennium on earth, which would be preceded by a time of Tribulation such as the world has never seen nor shall ever see again (Matt 24:21), then his options for understanding Matthew 24:13 were narrowed considerably. No longer could "saved" have a physical meaning, and no longer could "the end" mean the end of the age. The only interpretive option open to him was a spiritual one, so he understood the verse to mean only those believers who persevere in their Christian lives until the end of their physical lives will be able to go to heaven (saved).

With this understanding of Matthew 24:13 as the driving force behind his soteriology, Augustine also had reason to believe that justification must be a life-long process. No one could know if he were

---

[21] Augustine, *On the Gift of Perseverance*, 5.1.

justified until his physical death, since no one could know if he would persevere in the Christian faith and practice until his physical death. Thus, even today, members of the RCC still have no assurance that they will go to heaven when they die. There is never any knowledge if their life of perseverance is actually good enough to be accepted by God.

One consequence of this approach to soteriology is a life of self-denial and asceticism so as to help ensure that the believer has not been seduced from the straight and narrow by the sirens of this world. Such self-denial then becomes a requirement for eternal salvation. As Augustine said, "Self-denial of all sorts, if one perseveres to the end of his life, will bring salvation."[22] If one loves his wife, parents, or children more than Christ, he is not elect.[23] To the unbiased observer this kind of "self-denial salvation" is none other than a works approach to eternal life. But no, Augustine solves the apparent contradiction between self-denial and grace by falling back on verses like Philippians 2:12–13 to prove that the power to persist comes from God, not man.[24] Hence, perseverance to the end is a product of God's grace, since He is the one who graciously gives a baptized, regenerated believer the power and the desire to do His good pleasure.

Of course, Augustine is still left with a conundrum. Why is it that God graciously gives some baptized, regenerated believers the gift of perseverance to the end but does not give it to others? Now there is only one fallback position left in this labyrinth of soteriological sophistry: it is a mystery. When the theologian can transform obvious contradictions into mysteries, one can easily explain the inexplicable, solve the insoluble, and unscrew the inscrutable! No wonder Philip Schaff concludes that the soteriology of Augustine is both gloomy and full of contradictions.[25]

---

[22] Augustine, *Reply to Faustus the Manichaean*, 5.9.
[23] Augustine, *City of God*, 21.26.
[24] Augustine, Homily 8; *On the Gift of Perseverance*, 33.
[25] Philip Schaff, "Prolegomena," in *St. Augustine: Confession, Life, Life and Work*, ed. Philip Schaff, vol. 1, *Early Church Fathers*, CD-Rom (Dallas, Galaxie Software, 1999).

The point here is that a change in eschatology has effected a change in soteriology. Changing from premillennial to amillennial caused Augustine to reinterpret Matthew 24:13. Completely ignoring the three near references to "the end" which undeniably refer to the end of the age (vv. 3, 6, 14), he chose to interpret "the end" as the end of one's physical life and "saved" as eternal salvation. With this understanding only those baptized, regenerate believers who remained faithful to Christ until the end of their lives were elect. Faulty biblical theology can lead to faulty systematic theology.

But one might say, "So what? Augustine wrote sixteen hundred years ago. He may have influenced the RCC, but the Reformers broke away from the RCC. My legacy is Reformed, not Roman Catholic." To which we should reply, "Ah, my friend, you do not understand the influence of Augustine upon the Reformed tradition."

The Soteriology of John Calvin

As we have already noted, the concept of *simul iustus et peccator* was passed on to Martin Luther by Philipp Melanchthon, and John Calvin hitch-hiked with Martin Luther. When John Calvin first published his *Institutes* in 1536, there were only six chapters. He defended forensic justification by faith alone from Romans 4.[26] He understood that one could be declared righteous at a moment in time when a sinner's faith intersected with God's offer of the free gift of eternal life through His Son Jesus Christ. As such, no sins past, present, or future could bar the sinner-turned-saint from entrance to God's Kingdom.

So much for *iustus* (being just). What about *peccator* (being sinful)? How can the sinner-turned-saint be declared just by God when in his character he is still so far short of God's holiness, that is, still sinful? Initially, the Reformers saw a divorce between what they called justification and what many theologians today call progressive sanctification. Justification took place at a moment in time in heaven's court room; sanctification was the transformation of one's character

---

[26] John Calvin, *Calvin's New Testament Commentaries*, (Grand Rapids, Michigan: Eerdmans Publishing, 1975) vol. 8, 73, 83.

and walk to conform to that of Christ. But justification did not guarantee sanctification.

However, the Council of Trent formed in 1545 as the rebuttal of the RCC to the doctrine of the Reformers. This Council continued to meet until 1563. They attacked the Reformers' doctrine of justification as preaching license. To tell people their future sins are already forgiven in Christ is to tell them they can live any way they want and still go to heaven when they die. This kind of preaching will promote loose living, the Council accused. These attacks needed answers. So John Calvin continued to write. When he finished his *Institutes* in 1559, there were eighty chapters. And under pressure from the Council of Trent, Calvin remarried justification and sanctification. "You cannot possess Christ without being made partaker in his sanctification. . . . in our sharing in Christ, which justifies us, sanctification is just as much included as righteousness."[27] What was Calvin's basis for this remarriage? The influence of Augustine.

Yes, the long arms of Augustine reached right across the "Dark Ages"[28] (411-1000) into the Medieval Period of church history in the West (1054-1500). After the Dark Ages, the medieval scholars went back to the Fathers. In the West it was natural to go to the Latin writers. Hence, the starting point for most medieval thinkers was to ponder the writings of Augustine. The "Great Schism" (1378-1418) was a time of competition between Rome and Avignon in France for the seat of the papacy, and during this time the writings of Augustine and Ambrose became a focus of study in the universities in and surrounding Paris.

Peter Lombard produced the *Four Books of Sentences* for his students in Paris in 1140. It was a topical listing of verses and patristic quotes. His assignment, to solve the apparent inconsistencies in the Bible and the Fathers with plausible answers, caused his students to wrestle with the thinking of Augustine. Lombard's book was the most important publication of his age. Every theologian was required to comment on

---

[27] John Calvin, *Institutes*, III.16.1; 11.1.
[28] The "Dark Ages" are thought to be the period between the defeat of Rome (A.D. 410) by Alaric up to A.D. 1000.

it. And, in time, the University of Paris became the most important center for learning in Europe. College de la Sorbonne became known as "the Sorbonne" and synonymous with the University of Paris. This college produced Erasmus and John Calvin.

By 1500 Augustinian thinking was pervasive in the scholastic circles of Europe. Erasmus helped facilitate this with his editorial work on the writings of Augustine. But even before Erasmus the "Augustinian School" had developed in Great Britain as well as Paris. Thomas Bradwardine reacted to the Pelagian approach to justification at Oxford. He retreated to the teachings of Augustine for support. There was not much cross current between England and the Continent because of the Hundred Years War. But Gregory of Rimini at the University of Paris was Bradwardine's counterpart in Europe. He was a member of the Augustinian order, which claimed Martin Luther some years later.

All this to say when John Calvin developed his *Institutes,* he could claim that his theology was thoroughly Augustinian. But if Calvin's theology is thoroughly Augustinian, what can we say about his soteriology? Certainly Calvin's understanding of forensic justification was a major departure from the life-long process of justification advocated by Augustine. Or was it? Unfortunately, under pressure from the RCC via the Council of Trent John Calvin felt forced to come up with an answer to the accusation of license stemming from his "moment in time" justification.

The RCC had adopted Augustine's doctrine of lifelong justification wholesale. At the Council of Trent the RCC defined justification as the *process* of becoming righteous, but even justification had to be augmented if one wanted to get to heaven.[29] A mortal sin could cancel out any accrued justification, but through penance one could be restored. And the RCC continued in Augustine's belief that it is not possible to know if one is going to heaven before death: "No one can know with the certitude of faith, which cannot admit of any error, that he has obtained God's grace."[30] The best one can attain to in this life

---

[29] Council of Trent, X.
[30] Ibid., IX.

is hope mixed with "fear and apprehension." God rewards the good works of His saints even though He is the power source behind these works, and these rewards help pry open the gates of heaven.[31]

The Council of Trent put a curse on anyone saying justification is not increased by good works.[32] A further curse was put on anyone who believed good works were not meritorious for entrance to heaven.[33] The concept of "imputed" righteousness was believed to be a serious threat to moral effort. Bruce Demarest sums up the RCC approach when he says:

> Traditional Roman Catholics, in other words, trust in God's infusion of a new nature and plead the worth of their God-enabled works. Justification in Catholic theology is a comprehensive term that includes, among other things, what Protestants understand by regeneration and sanctification. For Rome, justification is not divine-wise an objective pronouncement of righteousness but is human-wise a lifelong process of becoming righteous.[34]

With this kind of pressure Calvin needed plausible answers to the accusers of antinomianism. His defense was to claim that one truly justified in God's court room at a moment in time would most certainly go on to maturity in Christ (progressive sanctification), given sufficient time in this world before physical death to do so. In other words, justification guaranteed sanctification—or, Matthew 24:13. Only those who persevere in the faith to the end of their physical lives will be eternally saved. Once again, Augustine's understanding of Matthew 24:13 became the bench mark of the elect. If one was truly elect, he would persevere; if he did not persevere, he was not elect.

Of course, this drove Calvin into the same kind of contradictory casuistry Augustine developed. What are we to say of those believers who have all the characteristics of genuine Christianity, but they fall

---

[31] Ibid., XVI.
[32] Ibid., Canon 24.
[33] Ibid., Canon 32.
[34] Bruce Demarest, *The Cross and Salvation* (Wheaton, IL: Crossway, 1997), 350.

away from the faith before they die? Many evangelicals today would simply use the "professing but not possessing" retreat. They profess to be believers, but, indeed, their faith is not saving faith because it is only intellectual assent. Thus, these professing believers are not genuine believers at all. They profess faith but do not possess faith. But this is not what Augustine did. Nor Calvin.

Augustine said the non-elect can have genuine faith. Augustine said the non-elect can be legitimately regenerated by the Holy Spirit. But because they have not received that most necessary of all gifts, the gift of perseverance, these regenerated believers are non-elect[35]. Forget the fact that the Scriptures never suppose that one who is regenerated is not also elect (cf. 1 Pet 1:1, 3 and Tit 1:1; 3:5). When pressed on this matter, as previously stated, Augustine explained this contradiction as "a mystery."

Calvin fell into a similar trap. Pressed into a remarriage[36] of justification and sanctification, he had to have a way of explaining how some can bear all the good fruit of the elect yet prove they were not elect because they did not persevere to the end of their lives on earth. His answer was "temporary faith." He based his understanding of temporary faith on his interpretations of the parable of the sower, the warning of Hebrews 6, and the warning to the people saying, "Lord, Lord . . . " in Matthew 7.[37] Here, for example, is what Calvin said concerning Hebrews 6:4-5:

> I know that to attribute faith to the reprobate seems hard to some when Paul declares it (faith) to be the result of election. This difficulty is easily solved. For . . . experience shows that the reprobate are

---

[35] *The Works of Aurelius Augustine*, vol 15, *Anti-Pelagian Works* (ed. M. Dods; T and T Clark, 1876). The Latin title is *De Dono Perseverantiae*, "On the Benefit of Perseverance." 21.8.

[36] We call this a remarriage because the original marriage took place in the theology of Augustine with his view of life-long justification, a justification which would obviously subsume sanctification.

[37] Joseph Dillow, *Reign of the Servant Kings* (Hayesville, NC: Schoettle, 2002), 254.

sometimes affected by almost the same feeling as the elect, so that even in their own judgment they do not in any way differ from the elect.[38]

Hence, the people in Hebrews 6 could have been enlightened, have tasted the Word of God, the heavenly gift and the power of the age to come, but still fall away and prove they were never elect. Calvin called this operation of the Spirit an "ineffectual" calling, "an inferior operation of the Spirit."[39]

Calvin seemed to think that allowing the reprobate such full experiences of God justified His rejection of them for eternity. Dillow explains:

> The central claim of this teaching is that God imparts supernatural influences to the reprobate which approximate, but do not equal, the influences of effectual calling. He is illuminated, he tastes, he grows, and he has similar feelings as the elect. However, it seems God is deceiving this man into believing he is elect so that God can be more than just in condemning him when he finally falls away. After all, the man had these "tastes."[40]

Apparently, such deep experiences with God make the reprobate all that much more inexcusable when they do not *really* believe. At least this theodicy goes a step beyond Augustine's standard cop-out for an inexplicable contradiction: "mystery."

But imagine the implications of a statement like this for assurance: "Experience shows that the reprobate are sometimes affected in a way so similar to the elect, that even in their own judgment there is

---

[38] Calvin, *Institutes*, 3.2.11.
[39] Calvin, *Commentary*, Lk 17:13; *Institutes*, 3.2.12; 3.2.11.
[40] Dillow, *Reign*, 254. See Also Paul Tanner, "Hebrews 6:4-6 and the Question of Christian Perseverance: A Case for Christian Rebellion Met by Temporal Judgement and Loss of Reward," in *A Defense of Free Grace Theology: With Respect to Saving Faith, Perseverance, and Assurance*, ed. Fred Chay (USA: Grace Theology Press, 2017), 239.

no difference between them." So, here we have two groups of people who look like the elect, and both groups "in their own judgment" are elect. However, according to Calvin, some of those who look like the elect (meaning they have the same fruit as the elect) and think they are elect, are not in fact elect and will prove this fact by falling away some time before they die. This poor class of people is comprised of the reprobate, who think they are elect but are self-deceived. Can it be more transparent? With such a teaching no one could know he was one of the elect until he dies. Of course, that is precisely what Augustine taught, and Calvin would have admitted the same had he been consistent within his own system. Alas, he was not.

Because of the terrible possibility that one might actually be one of the reprobate when he thought he was one of the elect, Calvin says, "Meanwhile, believers are taught to examine themselves carefully and humbly, lest carnal security creep in and take the place of assurance of faith." [41] So now we have a distinction between "carnal security" and "assurance of faith." Calvin is now stretching as far as he can to maintain the Reformed doctrine of instantaneous justification in an amillennial system of theology, which says the just must persevere until the end or they were never just in the first place. "In the elect alone He implants the living root of faith, so that they persevere even to the end."[42]

Apparently, Calvin even thought some of those in the parable of the sower who produced fruit were not elect: " . . . just as a tree not planted deep enough may take root but will in the process of time wither away, though it may for several years not only put forth leaves and flowers, but produce fruit."[43] He must have realized the implications of some of his teachings because he sprinkles his writings with answers to supposed objections which only confuse the issue more. Take this one, for example:

---

[41] Ibid.
[42] Ibid.
[43] Ibid.

Should it be objected that believers have no stronger testimony to assure them of their adoption, I answer that there is a great resemblance and affinity between the elect of God and those who are impressed for a time with fading faith, yet the elect alone have that full assurance which is extolled by Paul, and by which they are enabled to cry, Abba, Father.[44]

That really helped. How is the believer (whether real or imaginary) to know whether he has *full* assurance? Maybe his assurance is only part assurance, but how is he to know? R. T. Kendall recognizes the problem here when he writes:

And if the reprobate may experience "almost the same feeling as the elect," there is no way to know finally what the reprobate experiences. Furthermore, if the reprobate may believe that God is merciful towards them, how can we be sure our believing the same thing is any different from theirs? How can we be so sure that our "beginning of faith" is saving and is not the "beginning of faith" which the reprobate seem to have?[45]

Calvin digs an even deeper hole by speaking of an inner assurance given by the Spirit to the elect, and then says the reprobate can have a similar sensation. With this kind of teaching one could never have assurance of his salvation. He could only know he is elect when he dies. The pressure from the RCC trapped Calvin into the very same fear of the eternal future inherent in the Catholic system that he was trying to escape. Dillow hits the nail on the head when he observes:

In the final analysis Calvin has thrown away the possibility of assurance, at least until the final hour. When he grants that the only certain difference between the faith of the elect and the faith of the

---

[44] Ibid.
[45] R. T. Kendall, *Calvin and English Calvinism to 1649* (Oxford: Oxford University Press, 1979), 24.

reprobate is that the faith of the former perseveres to the end, he makes assurance now virtually impossible.[46]

To summarize, we are trying to demonstrate what we might call Spread Sheet Theology. To change one ingressed doctrine in a system will most likely change other ingressed doctrines in that very system. When Augustine changed his eschatology, it affected his soteriology—drastically. Matthew 24:13 (perseverance in the faith to the end of one's physical life as a requirement for eternal salvation) became the cornerstone of his salvation system. Purgatory developed as a figment of his logic based on Matthew 24:13 (what to do if one does persevere to the end of his life in the faith but still has vestiges of sin in his character—*voila*, Purgatory). The RCC bought into Augustine's theology, both in terms of eschatology and soteriology.

The Reformers like Calvin retained the eschatology of Augustine (amillennial), but tried to change the soteriology (forensic justification). But that was like pouring new wine into old wineskins. "Declared righteousness" could not waltz with Augustine's understanding of Matthew 24:13. The latter won out. The remarriage between justification and sanctification, which Luther and Zwingli had fought hard to resist, took place in Geneva. And with the Geneva Academy, which trained pastors in the Reformed tradition, the errors of Augustine and Calvin have been perpetuated until today. Augustine's understanding (an amillennial understanding) of Matthew 24:13 continues to be a fly in the ointment of modern soteriology, which undermines one's assurance of salvation at the least and teaches a works-oriented salvation at the most.

The Soteriology of Western Christianity Today

The soteriology of Western Christianity today obviously falls into two categories: Roman Catholic soteriology and Protestant soteriology. The former has completely absorbed Augustine's approach to justification, leaving the election of a professing believer in question

---

[46] Dillow, *Reign*, 258.

until his death. The "making righteous" of the elect person continues through his life and even in Purgatory after death, if necessary. As discussed under "Augustine's Soteriology," persevering in the faith until the end of one's life based on an amillennial understanding of Matthew 24:13 was the basis for this approach to soteriology in general and justification in particular.

In Protestant circles John Calvin set the tone with the Geneva Academy, which did more to disseminate doctrine into the West than any other influence. With their amillennial stance and spiritual understanding of Matthew 24:13, the modern industry of spiritual fruit inspecting flourished. The fruit inspecting of Theodore Beza, William Perkins, and the English Calvinists has been well documented by R.T. Kendall.[47] All of these adopted the "temporary faith" solution to the warning passages in Hebrews suggested by Calvin, when interpreted according to their understanding of Matthew 24:13. If one has the fruit of the elect and the faith of the elect but does not persevere in the faith until the end of his physical life, then God must have given the believer only "temporary faith." It must be noted that this is neither fake faith nor spurious faith. It is genuine faith, but alas, it is *temporary*. As such, the one who possesses genuine but temporary faith is non-elect.

Such reliance on Matthew 24:13 as the *sine qua non* of eternal salvation leaves very little difference between the Arminians and the Calvinists as it relates to the bottom line for getting into heaven. R. T. Kendall echoes this sentiment when he says that when it comes to perseverance, the Calvinists of the Puritan persuasion and Arminians have the same position:[48]

> If Perkins holds that the recipient of the first grace must obtain the second (perseverance) or the first [initial faith] is rendered invalid, there is no practical difference whatever in the two positions. If the

---

[47] Kendall, *Calvinism*.
[48] Ibid., 143.

believer does not persevere (whether Arminius or Perkins says it), such a person proves to be non-elect.[49]

As the fruit inspecting industry crossed the ocean to America, there is a familiar ring. C. Hodge typifies this group:

> Election, calling, justification, and salvation are indissolubly united; and, therefore, he who has clear evidence of his being called has the same evidence of his election and final salvation . . . The only evidence of election is effectual calling, that is, the production of holiness. And the only evidence of the genuineness of this call and the certainty of our perseverance, is a patient continuance in well doing.[50]

Or, as J. Murray put it, "The perseverance of the saints reminds us very forcefully that only those who persevere to the end are truly saints."[51]

And how does this understanding of perseverance differ from "the churches of Christ"? R. Shank, one of their chief spokesmen writes: "Obviously, it can be known only as one finally perseveres (or fails to persevere) in faith. There is *no valid assurance* of election and final salvation for any man, *apart from deliberate perseverance in faith.*"[52] But Shank is a pure Arminian, who left the Southern Baptist Convention over the issue of eternal security. It is strange how alike aspects of these two systems become (Calvinism and Arminianism), when one studies their doctrines of perseverance based on an amillennial interpretation of Matthew 24:13.

Yet surely the modern advances of exegesis under the scrutiny of the grammatical-historical method have cleared away the brush hiding the inconsistency of interpreting "the end" of Matthew 24:13

---

[49] Ibid., 144.
[50] C. Hodge, *St. Paul's Epistle to the Romans* (1860; reprint ed., Grand Rapids: William B. Eerdmans Publishing Co., 1950), 212 (emphasis added).
[51] Quoted by Dillow, *Reign*, 259.
[52] R.Shank, *Life in the Son: A Study of the Doctrine of Perseverance* (Springfield, MO: Westcott, 1961), 293 (emphasis added).

differently from "the end" of Matthew 24:3, 6, and 14. So let us take a contemporary NT scholar who teaches at a respected, conservative seminary as a case in point: Scot McKnight.

In a 1992 article McKnight addressed the warning passages of Hebrews.[53] The first question he had to settle was whether the recipients of the epistle were believers or unbelievers. Like a prospector panning for gold he sifted through the evidence very carefully. Page after page of research amassed the evidence and concluded the obvious—these are actual believers, not fake believers or professors/not possessors. He does not like the implications connected with Calvin's solution of "temporary faith," so he searches for another explanation as to how actual believers can wind up in hell (his conclusion).

McKnight is to be commended for not allowing his Reformed approach to perseverance to cause him to declare these recipients unbelievers. However, because he is convinced that only believers who persevere to the end of their lives are elect, he must make categories among those who have actually believed. So he distinguishes between "genuine, true, real, or saving" faith and what he calls *phenomenological* faith.[54] Those who are *phenomenological* believers are those who, from the human perspective, have been observed to have all the fruits of genuine faith, but from an ontological standpoint may have fallen short of the same.[55] Because these believers have genuinely experienced the Holy Spirit, the powers of the age to come, the taste of God's Word, and so on, they have enjoyed spiritual *phenomena* which are genuine spiritual experiences shared by the elect.[56] But, alas, they are not elect. How do we know? Because they do not persevere in the faith until the end of their lives, and Matthew 24:13 tells us that people who do not

---

[53] Scot McKnight, "The Warning Passages of Hebrews: A Formal Analysis and Theological Conclusions," *Trinity Journal* 13(Spring 1992):22-59.
[54] Ibid., 24, n. 12.
[55] Ibid., n. 10.
[56] McKnight recognizes these believers as regenerate, but for him regeneration does not necessitate perseverance and is, by his definition, a life-long process. So, much like Augustine, these believers can be regenerated but fall away from the faith and be eternally damned.

persevere until the end cannot be saved (notice that Hebrews never uses such terminology).

McKnight's entire article is a classic study in circular reasoning. He assumes what he is trying to prove. He assumes (from Matt 24:13) that anyone who does not persevere in the faith until the end of his life cannot go to heaven. But the evidence he amasses from Hebrews demonstrates the readers to be believers. Now the only way to keep these believers out of heaven is to say they lose their salvation (an Arminian option), they go to purgatory for further cleansing (a Catholic option), or there must be different categories of believers (his final option). On this basis, he understands only Joshua and Caleb from the redeemed "Egyptian" generation of Israelites to be with the Lord today (see below). How Moses appeared with the Lord at the transfiguration he does not explain. Why Michael the archangel contended with the devil over the body of Moses (Jude 9) remains a mystery.

Yes, McKnight recognizes the recipients of Hebrews as believers, but they may be only *phenomenological* believers who wind up in hell because of apostasy. He uses the severe language in the warning of Hebrews 10:26ff to determine (by analogy of faith) that all the warning passages in Hebrews are alluding to the danger of hell-fire if one does not persevere:

> The following logic is at the heart of the author's exhortations: if willful disobedience and apostasy in the Mosaic era brought discipline and prohibited entrance into the Land (a type of the eternal rest), then surely willful disobedience and apostasy in the new era will bring eternal exclusion from the eternal rest.
>
> In light of the final sense of several of these expressions (cf. especially the harsh realities of 10:30–31, 39) and the use of imagery in Hebrews that elsewhere is used predominantly of eternal damnation, it becomes quite clear that the author has in mind an eternal sense of destruction. The author of Hebrews makes it unambiguously clear that those who do not persevere until the end will suffer eternal punishment at the expense of the wrath of God. There is no escape; like the children of Israel who disobeyed, those who shrink back will

be destroyed. The consequences for those who apostasize [sic] are eternal damnation and judgment; therefore, the author has exhorted his readers to persevere until the end.[57]

Never mind the fact that the words "hell," "lake of fire," "eternal," "everlasting," "forever," "damnation," and the like never occur in any of these warning passages. He is convinced the language of 10:26-39 is so severe it must refer to eternal damnation. Does he conclude the same for Deuteronomy 4:24 (LXX) where ἀπωλείᾳ ἀπολεῖσθε (utterly destroy) and ἐκτριβῇ ἐκτριβήσεσθε (utterly destroy) are even more emphatic than the ἀπώλειαν (destruction) of Hebrews 10:39?[58] Not likely. The curses in Deuteronomy are temporal curses. God's covenants with Abraham and David ensure an eternal relationship with Israel. The issue in Deuteronomy 4 and 30 is fellowship, not relationship. Then could the same not be said of the Hebrew Christians of Hebrews, especially when drawing on the warnings of temporal judgment given in Deuteronomy 32 (32:35 and 36 are quoted in Heb 10:30), the language of which is even more graphic than that of Hebrews 10:26ff.?

McKnight concludes that those who do not persevere until the end cannot go to heaven, since that is the "single condition"[59] for final

---

[57] Ibid., 35-36. His view of "fire" and "burning" is limited to hell-fire. But note Deuteronomy 4:24 and the consuming fire, the jealous God, and the utter destruction (the LXX uses ἀπωλείᾳ ἀπολεῖσθε to emphasize the *utter* destruction to come upon Israel if she is unfaithful, and this is the same term used in Heb 10:39). Malachi 4:1 also points to the fire, and this fire will destroy the Jews in the land. They will not prolong their days in the land. Interpreters who object to the warning in Hebrews 10 as being a temporal judgment instead of eternal speak of the much worse judgment to come upon believers in Christ who apostatize as opposed to the judgment which came upon the unfaithful Israelites at Kadesh-Barnea. However, they overlook the fact that a judgment which affects one's rest in the Millennium (1,000 years) is much worse than a judgment which affects one's rest in the land for forty years.

[58] When a verb in Hebrew or Greek is preceded by a noun with the same root as the verb, the action of the verb is being emphasized.

[59] Ibid., 59.

salvation (whatever happened to believing in Jesus?). With the circle complete he warns his own readers that we should not be hasty in giving assurance of salvation to people who look like genuine believers. Why? Because they may only be *phenomenological* believers.

How can one know if he is a *phenomenological* believer instead of a genuine believer, since the observable fruit for each category is the same until the former falls away somewhere before the end of his life? Obviously, one cannot know which category he belongs to until the end of his life. Again, McKnight is to be credited for some consistency. That is, he warns us that no one can have assurance of his salvation in this life.

But is this not the very conclusion of Augustine and Calvin? Augustine never espoused assurance of salvation before death. Calvin did, but only initially. Assurance was of the essence of faith in his early writings, but not after his interaction with the Council of Trent. It would seem the apple does not fall very far from the tree.

Conclusion

Once again, this has been a study in Spread Sheet Theology. By this nomenclature we refer to a system which has a high level of consistency, comprehensiveness, congruity, and coherence. Changing one doctrine ingressive to the system will most likely cause changes in other parts of the system as well. We have chosen the theology of Augustine as a case in point.

Though Augustine was a pretribulational, premillennial, dispensationalist in his early theology, a change in his eschatology resulted in a change in his soteriology. When he reacted to the eschatological feasting of the Donatists and their obsessive preoccupation with the dating of Christ's return to set up His kingdom on earth, Augustine used the hermeneutics of Tyconius to eliminate any future, physical, kingdom of Christ on earth. In this sense he became amillennial (though he did see a thousand-year reign of Christ in heaven).

This change in his systematic theology caused a reinterpretation of some of Augustine's biblical theology. He no longer interpreted

Matthew 24:13 as a promise of physical salvation leading into the Millennium (since there was not going to be a physical Millennium in his new approach to eschatology). Now he saw Matthew 24:13 as a promise of spiritual salvation. In his mind a new test for soteriology was born: one must endure in his Christian faithfulness until the end of his life. This verse became the driving force and final arbiter in Augustine's soteriology.

When the Reformers came along over a thousand years later, a revival in the study of Augustine's writings had been in vogue for over a hundred years. His eschatology (amillennial) still held. But the Reformers sought to make a change in soteriology. Justification could be declared in the court room of heaven at an instant in time. One could be declared righteous by God in his position, yet still retain sin in his condition: *simul iustus et peccator*. This was a monumental change in soteriology, enough to effect the Reformation. If they had followed through on a good system of theology, the Reformers would have examined their eschatology to see how their new approach to soteriology might cause changes in their understanding of the future. But they did not develop a good system. Instead they tried to amalgamate Augustine's theology with their own. The result was an alloy of contradictions.

John Calvin, who began teaching assurance as of the essence of faith, wound up teaching no man could tell if he were elect or reprobate until he died. Matthew 24:13 remained a cornerstone of the soteriology of the Reformers. Fruit inspecting flourished among the followers of Calvin. It came to America through the Puritans. Writers like John Owen wrote tomes on how to know if one was among the elect.[60] All of this was driven by an amillennial interpretation of Matthew 24:13.

It might be argued that there were certainly other passages than Matthew 24:13 which were marshaled to support the doctrine that

---

[60] J. Owen, *The Works of John Owen*, 16 vols., vol. 3: *A Discourse concerning the Holy Spirit* (1677; reprint, Edinburgh: Banner of Truth, 1965), 45-47, 226-28. This particular volume was over 650 pages dedicated, according to Owen, to helping professors of Christ determine if they were possessors of Christ.

one must persevere to the end in order to be saved. True. But Matthew 24:13 remained the cornerstone on which the other passages were built because it is the only verse which includes both the word "saved" and the word "end."

Scot McKnight's article on the warning passages in Hebrews was offered as a case study in the effect a "spiritual salvation" understanding of Matthew 24:13 can have on interpreting an entire book. His understanding of Matthew 24:13 (endure until the end of one's life in order to go to heaven) as the "single" (and surely he must mean the single most important) spiritual condition which must be met in order to separate the sheep from the goats guides him throughout the maze of twists and turns in Hebrews.

Rather than allowing his interpretation to emerge from the words of the text, McKnight uses a point of reference (Matt 24:13) outside the text of Hebrews to determine his understanding of Hebrews itself. His "phenomenological believer" concoction, in which the epistle is addressed to actual but not genuine, observable but not ontological believers must stand as one of the all-time examples of creatively "forcing" the text when one comes to the end of an exegetical cul de sac. How much simpler to change one's eschatology back to the pre-Augustinian days of premillennialism when Matthew 24:13 could have a physical reference and the "rest" in Hebrews could refer to the Millennium (as the early Fathers taught) rather than the eternal state.

The appeal of this study is really a warning. It is dangerous to mix theological systems. By definition, mixing systems will create contradictions. We must be careful when we pick and choose that which seems appealing from one system and try to fit it into the constructs of another system. Those who claim to be Dispensationalists should be careful not to introduce ingressive doctrines from Reformed theologians into their system and vice-versa. These are two mutually exclusive systems. This author agrees with R. C. Sproul when he claims there is no such thing as a "four point" Calvinist, when the points are defined by classic Dortian Calvinism.[61] One is either a "five

---

[61] R. C. Sproul, *Willing to Believe* (Grand Rapids: Baker, 1997), 193.

point" Calvinist or none (although being a "no point" Calvinist does not make one an Arminian). Dortian Calvinism is a system. To pull just one point out of the system destroys the entire system.

On the other hand, to incorporate one point from Dortian Calvinism into Dispensationalism can also destroy the entire system.[62] If the Dortian view of perseverance of the saints is correct (the view taught by Augustine), then the spiritual view of Matthew 24:13 is also correct. If the spiritual view of Matthew 24:13 is correct, then amillennialism is true. If amillennialism is true, then there is no distinction between Israel and the Church. If there is no distinction between Israel and the Church, then Dispensationalism is false.

We applaud the emphasis on Biblical Theology in recent decades.[63] This approach to theology accentuates the strength of grammatical-historical exegesis. However, let us not lose sight of the fact that Biblical Theology stops with what the text said to its original recipients, as opposed to Systematic Theology, which starts with the original audience but does not stop there. A good systematic theologian must not only contextualize; he must also decontextualize and recontextualize. That is, he must find out what the text said to its original recipients, look for the timeless truths which transcend cultures and centuries, and transfer those timeless truths into the respective contexts of differing modern societies. Systematic Theology speaks to us today.

Furthermore, Systematic Theology incorporates Historical Theology in its quest to understand how the theology of today developed. Both Biblical and Historical Theology feed like tributaries into the river of Systematic Theology. When we focus on one of the tributaries to the neglect of the other or of the main river itself, we get

---

[62] It must be pointed out that dispensationalists like L. Sperry Chafer redefine the "points" of Dortian Calvinism to fit their system. Chafer, for example, limited the perseverance of the saints to eternal security in his *Systematic Theology*, vol. 3 (Grand Rapids: Kregel, 1976), 267-354. For the sake of clear communication, it might be better to stay consistent in our definitions.

[63] G.K. Beale, *A New Testament Biblical Theology*, (Grand Rapids MI. Baker Academic, 2011)

stuck in St. Louis when we are trying to go down the Mississippi to the Gulf of Mexico.

Finally, let us remember, Systematic Theology is like a spread sheet. Changes in one of the major points of the system will most likely cause changes in other points of the system as well. This could be good. It could lead to a new system with a greater degree of consistency, coherence, congruity, and comprehensiveness. But if it leads to increased contradictions or fails to incorporate all the evidence, perhaps the proposed change is invalid. We believe that Augustine's eschatological change from premillennialism to amillennialism led him and his followers into a theological labyrinth of contradictions in soteriology which persists until today.

The Sinfulness of Man

Although saving man from the lake of fire is the greatest event in his life, there is much more that God wants to save or salvage from his life than just his presence with Him forever. In our course of study, we will examine three main aspects of His so great salvation: salvation from the penalty of sin (our justification in the past), salvation from the power of sin (our sanctification in the present), and salvation from the presence of sin (our glorification in the future). But before we focus the lenses of our study on salvation, it is important to understand what we are being saved from, that is, our depravity. Man is fallen. But what does that mean? Not until we have some grasp on the scope of our depravity are we able to understand the extent of our salvation. So we need to review some anthropology and hamartiology. How did sin come into the world, and what were its effects on the human race?

Some Anthropology

Scripture tells us that man was made as a tripartite being: body, soul, and spirit (1 Thess 5:23). The word *psychē* is used in four primary ways in the NT. Only a handful of the 104 uses refer to the immaterial part of man, which enjoys heaven or suffers in hell. Most of the time, the word refers either to our time on earth (our life) or to our inner self as a unique combination of mind (with one *psychē* striving together—Phil 1:27), emotions (Mk 14:34—my *psychē* is exceedingly sorrowful), and will (doing the will of God from the *psychē*). It is this latter use (the inner self), that fits the context of 1 Thessalonians 5:23.

Many think part of the *imago Dei* (image of God) in man, if not the primary understanding, is this tripartite make-up.[1] In the original creation, Adam and Eve were one with the Lord, had immortal physical bodies, and had the undiminished capacity to enjoy His love, interact with His thoughts, and obey His will. But the Fall affected all aspects of man.

In a sense, evil did not come into the world through Adam. Satan was already on planet earth before the creation of Adam. He brought evil into the world, in that Satan is the personification of evil. Adam and Eve did not have sinful natures. But they did have corruptible natures just like the angels. God cannot sin because it is not in His character or make-up. His nature is incorruptible. That is why Jesus could not sin.[2] Because he was undiminished deity and perfect humanity in one person, his human nature could be legitimately tempted, but his divine nature could not sin. As a unique combination of God and man, he simply could not sin. But Adam was fully man. He had a corruptible nature. And it was corrupted.

When Adam sinned, all aspects of his humanity were corrupted. His body became mortal. His spirit was separated from God (spiritual death) as fellowship was broken for the first time since his creation. And every part of his *psychē* was corrupted: his mind was darkened, his emotions were degraded, and his will was defective. He became thoroughly depraved. This does not mean any particular man is as bad as he can be, but it does mean he is as bad *off* as he can be. What we mean by this is that there is nothing he can do on his own to restore immortality to his body, fellowship with his Creator, or nobility to his "soul."

But there is no general consensus on the above assertions among theologians. If there were, there might be more harmony in the world

---

[1] This is not the place for a full discussion of the image of God in man, but most also believe *capacity* is an important aspect of it. That is, animals have mind, emotion, and will. But only man has emotions that can love God, a mind that (when regenerated) can interact with the thoughts from God, and a will that can obey God.

[2] This involves the theological topic of the impeccability of Christ.

of soteriology. We must agree on that which was lost before we can agree on that which needs to be saved. As Robert Pyne observes:

> The difference between an "Arminian" and a "Calvinist" is in the degree to which God must intervene in our salvation—are we able to respond to the gospel, or are we so depraved that He must specifically enable the elect to respond? One's view of the atonement is related to this same issue—do we require only an example to follow, or is the entire race in need of outside deliverance?[3]

Some Hamartiology

There are some key passages that help us understand the consequences of sin for humanity. Clearly, things were not the same after the garden. The curse of Genesis 3:14-19 speaks of man's alienation from: 1) God; 2) Nature; 3) One's spouse; and 4) Satan. The spiritual death about which God had warned Adam became a reality. This does not mean that the spirit of man ceased to exist. This spirit, the inner man or holy of holies of the human being, is still there in the unregenerate person. We know this from Genesis 41:8 which says the *spirit of Pharaoh* was troubled when he awoke from a bad dream (בַּבֹּקֶר וַתִּפָּעֶם רוּחוֹ). This word for spirit (*ruaḥ*) is the same one used throughout the OT to refer to the human spirit. I cannot imagine anyone teaching that Pharaoh was regenerate. But he had a human spirit which was very active or alive. His human spirit was not dead.[4] But he was spiritually dead. By this we refer to the technical, theological meaning of death as separation. God was not resident

---

[3] Robert A. Pyne, *Humanity & Sin*, (Nashville, Tennessee, Word Publishing, 1999) 165-69. The way Pyne has framed his questions limits the options available for answers. Later in this discussion it will be argued that man is capable of some response to God's revelation, but he is not capable of coming to Christ on his own.

[4] "Dead" in the James sense of the word, that is, inactive or without vigor.

in his human spirit. God and Pharaoh were separated. Pharaoh was spiritually dead.

Eph 2:1 describes the state of the unbeliever as dead. Paul says before Christ we were "dead in trespasses and sins" (νεκροὺς τοῖς παραπτώμασιν καὶ ταῖς ἁμαρτίαιν). E. Best speaks of this kind of death as "a realized eschatological conception of death" in contrast to the believer's present realization of eternal life.[5] "He who has the Son has life; he who does not have the Son of God does not have life." The believer does not have to wait for physical death to receive eternal life. Nor does the unbeliever have to wait for physical death to experience spiritual death. Paul describes them as "without God in the world" (Eph 2:12) and "alienated from the life of God" (Eph 4:18). So this kind of spiritual death is one of separation and estrangement from God.[6] Paul says this death is related, in some way, to our trespasses and sins. The text literally says: νεκροὺς τοῖς παραπτώμασιν καὶ ταῖς ἁμαρτίαις ὑμῶν. The last word in this text is *humōn*, which means "your," "dead in *your* trespasses and sins." This raises the question as to the meaning of personal sin as it relates to spiritual death. Is it because of my personal sins that I am separated from God as an unbeliever? If so, then a baby would be born into this world one with God. He would not be alienated until his first personal sin. Or the text could be interpreted as speaking of a state. The unbelievers are dead *in* their trespasses and sins. This could imply that they were born into a state of sinfulness, and might open the door to the teaching of federal headship in Romans 5.

There is a little nursery rhyme known by every one of us. Although we do not know how it originated, it had its roots in our American heritage. It is admittedly silly in its sound and seems senseless in its content. We have read it to our children time and again as they grow up so that they know it by heart and, in turn, read it to their own children. Although nobody seems to understand the rhyme, it

---

[5] E. Best, "Dead in Trespasses and Sins (Eph. 2:1)," *Journal for the Study of the New Testament* 13 (1981): 17.
[6] H. W. Hoehner, "Ephesians," in *The Bible Knowledge Commentary*, vol. 2, ed. J. F. Walvoord and R. B. Zuck (Wheaton, IL: SP Publications, 1983), 622.

occurred to me recently that behind the scenes there is a profound truth it teaches:

> Humpty Dumpty sat on a wall;
> Humpty Dumpty had a great fall.
> All the king's horses and all the king's men,
> Couldn't put Humpty together again.

Now, I would venture to say that in your mind there is the image of an egg . . . right? Why? There is nothing in the nursery rhyme which mentions an egg. The one who wrote it probably did not have an egg in mind. Someone probably picked it up from the old New England Primer. Many of those in colonial days learned their grammar from that very familiar book. I also want to suggest that the child picked up his idea from the couplets used in that primer for the letters A and X. In the primer it reads, "In Adam's fall we sinned all; Xerxes the Great did fall and so must you and I." In a subtle fashion, that little couplet teaches not only the letters A and X, but also a very significant spiritual truth. That is, in the Fall we sinned all. You see, the one who wrote that little nursery rhyme was not talking about an egg which fell, but a man. And all the king's horses and all the king's men (the soldiers of all the kings throughout history) could not repair what had been lost when this man fell.

Of course, it was Adam who fell. He sat on a great wall of love and fellowship from which he had a great fall. And no one, from king to servant, could possibly put him together again. His name was not Humpty Dumpty, of course. It was Adam. And in Rom 5:12-21, we see the very serious ramifications, results, and consequences of Adam's fall. When we arrive at this key text we approach one of the most difficult and complex portions of the Word of God. Actually, these verses serve as a summary of all that has been presented so far in the Book of Romans. Verses 12-14 look back at the first great section of the book, which dealt with sin (Rom 1:18–3:20). Then verses 15-17 look back at the second great section on salvation from the penalty of sin (Rom 3:21–4:25). Finally, Romans 5:18-21 winds up the whole of Rom 1:16-5:21 and serves as a transition leading into the next great section beginning in Romans 6, which deals with sanctification. So, when Paul begins Romans 5:12 with "wherefore," he is going all the way back to the terrain covered from 1:16.

In Romans 5:12-14, we find the Origin of Sin, the Penalty for Sin, and the Imputation of Sin. "As by one man sin entered into the world" raises a couple of questions. We have already observed that, in one sense, sin entered into the world through Lucifer who fell (Rev 12:4 and Ezek 28:17) and was consigned to planet Earth. But even so, Eve sinned before Adam. So this makes us think that "world" must refer to something other than the globe. Satan brought sin to this globe. Hence, "world" must be a figure of speech for "human race." But still, did not Eve bring sin to the human race before Adam? Well, 1 Timothy 2:14 gives us an important distinction between the sin of Adam and the sin of Eve. Eve was deceived, but Adam was not. Adam knew just exactly what he was doing.

Here, then, we come to the first great principle we need to see concerning sin from this passage. There is a vast difference in God's eyes between sin that is deliberate and sin which is unknown (see Num 15:27-31). The fact that Adam knew exactly what he was doing is apparent just from the words used in this passage for his act: *hamartia* (missing the mark, Rom 5:12); *parabaseōs* (step over a line, 5:14); *paraptōma* (a fall, 5:15); *parakoēs* (disobedience, 5:19). The first two words tell us that Adam could see what he was doing. He missed the bullseye, which implied that he could see it. He stepped over the line, which again says he could see the line. The last two words speak of the personal offense taken by God when Adam sinned. It was God's word which had been defied. In one sense, Adam loved his wife more than God. And so he deliberately disobeyed the Lord. That was his downfall. Apparently, he was willing to face the consequences of his sin rather than be lonely again.

As a result, we are told that Adam brought sin into the world, that is, into the human race. "And death through sin." What does this mean? We remember that God told Adam in the day that he ate of the tree of the knowledge of good and evil, he would surely die. But Adam lived to be over 900 years old. Surely, then, God must have had another type of death in mind. Of course, He did. He meant spiritual death.

Adam's physical death was probably the result of his spiritual death. His separation from God had the effect of a death sentence on his body, just as union with God, after receiving Christ, is the guarantee of a glorified, eternal body (the Holy Spirit is the down payment or earnest money to prove this).[7]

Now we come to the very difficult clause, "and thus death spread to all men, because all sinned." We can see that death has spread to all men, but what does it mean when it says, "all sinned"? There are three popular views on the interpretation of this pregnant statement:

1. PERSONAL SIN. Some, like Pelagius, think it means every individual commits some sort of personal sin of his own deliberate will, and as a result of this personal sin, that person dies. We can dismiss this point or interpretation very quickly by pointing out that it does not explain infant mortality. Certainly, a three-month old infant has not committed any personal sin, yet some infants die. If personal sin causes death, then the death of these infants cannot be tied to personal sin. It must mean something else.

2. ORIGINAL SIN. This view tells us that when Adam sinned, a constitutional change took place in his person. His human spirit lost contact with God. His mind was *darkened*, his emotions *debased*, and his will *degraded*. And his body became *debilitated* and *decayed*. His entire person was changed for the worse because of his sin. From then on a corrupt nature, usually referred to as the sin nature, was resident within him. This corrupt nature was then passed down to all of his descendants. Hence, every individual born is born spiritually dead, separated from God, because of the sin nature within him. As the child grows, this nature will manifest itself soon enough. We do not need to teach a child how to lie

---

[7] Those seeing spiritual death here as well as physical (v. 14) include S. L. Johnson, "Romans 5:12—An Exercise in Exegesis and Theology," in *New Dimensions in New Testament Study*, ed. R. N. Longenecker and M. C. Tenney (Grand Rapids: Zondervan, 1974), 302; R. Y. K. Fung, "The Relationship between Righteousness and Faith in the Thought of Paul, as Expressed in the Letters to the Galatians and the Romans" (Ph.D. Dissertation, The University of Manchester, 1975), 381.

or disobey. Rebellion is bound up in the heart of the child. What we have to do is to teach the child to be truthful, to be obedient. That goes against his grain, against his nature. This, then, is original sin.

We might visualize it as camping on a mountain. Near the top of this mountain issues a beautiful spring of clear, cool, mountain water. We might drink of this water and feel that this is as pure as water can be. But unknown to us, a little further upstream is another camper. And unlike us, this camper is a rather gross guy. He dumps all of his garbage and refuse into the stream. So by the time the water gets to us, it is entirely polluted. And we drink polluted water into our bodies as the result of the action of this one man. And so does every other camper drinking from this stream. So do all the people in the valley. The action of one man polluted the water for the many. That is original sin, and many see this polluted nature in each of us resulting from Adam's sin as the cause of individual death.

3. IMPUTED SIN. This view is also known by the theologians as Federal Headship. Basically, it says that Adam acted as a representative for the whole human race. When he sinned, sin was charged to the account of all humans. We have a federal government in which state representatives in Congress vote on our behalf. In a presidential election you may have personally voted for a Democrat or a Republican. But if the electoral votes of your state go for someone other than the one you voted for, you are charged with having voted for the other person. Or when Mark McGwire hit his 62nd home run in St. Louis, every St. Louis fan in the park felt as though he had hit that home run. McGwire was their representative. So this view says we all sinned in Adam. Adam, as federal head of the human race, sinned; as our representative, sin was charged to the account of the entire human race and death came to the whole human race.

This Federal Headship or "representative" approach is rejected by many leading NT scholars: R. Bultmann, G. Friedrich, C. K. Barrett, H. J. Schoeps, W. G. Kümmel, G. Bornkamm, O. Michel, and E. Käsemann.[8] How can men be held responsible for the actions of another, especially someone who lived millennia before they were born?

So what *did Paul* mean by "all sinned" (5:12)? A closer look at the structure of Rom 5:12-21 shows that Paul interrupts the argument begun in 5:12 in order to clarify in 5:13-17 how *personal* sin is imputed and how "death spread to all" before he resumes the main argument in 5:18-21 to explain how "all sinned" *in Adam*. However, the word *katakrima in* 5:18—translated "condemnation" in most English versions—is not the *verdict*, but rather the *sentence* of incarceration by sin in Adam that leads to death. So the *reason that* "death spread to all" (5:12)—that all received "a death sentence, incarcerated by sin" (5:18a)—is that all were "made sinners" (5:19a): Through Adam's one act of disobedience all were *constituted* (*kathistēmi*) sinners—an *inherited condition* that spawns sin and thus incurs a death sentence, "even over those who had not *sinned according to the likeness of the transgression of Adam*" (= *personally imputed* sin) (5:12-13).[9]

Romans 5:12-13 and 19 thus exclude the forensic categories of personal imputation or federal headship as the *root* cause of "all sinned" in favor of the inherited condition *sinners by constitution*, that is, the "sin nature" or "original sin." The good news of Romans 5:15-21 is that what we have *lost* through our death in Adam is *gained* even more abundantly by life in Christ.

LOST IN ADAM	GAINED IN CHRIST
Physical Body	Spiritual Body
Fruit of the Garden	Fruit of the Spirit
Physical Life on Earth Forever	Spiritual Life on Earth
A Walk in the Garden	A Walk in New Jerusalem

---

[8] Fung, "Relationship between Righteousness and Faith," 382.
[9] See the more complete argument in David Anderson and James Reitman, *Portraits of Righteousness: Free Grace Sanctification in Romans 5-8*, (Lynchburg, Va: Liberty University Press, 2013).

So, each man or woman born into this world after Adam and Eve is born alienated and separated from his/her Creator. What can man do to overcome this problem?

The Nature of Depravity

Having concluded that sin and spiritual death are universal by virtue of Adam's fall, we must now explore the implications of that fact with regard to human ability. All of humanity is born into a state of incarceration by sin and death. Can we deliver ourselves?

What does our sinfulness mean, particularly as it affects our response to God? Are unbelievers capable of accomplishing their own salvation? Are they even able to do anything that can be considered "good"? Are they even naturally equipped to respond positively to the gospel? What is the extent of the unbeliever's ability?

These questions have been frequently discussed, but the classic debate took place in North Africa in the early part of the fifth century.

Pelagius versus Augustine

The groundwork for centuries of debate began with Augustine's response to Pelagius. But in order to understand their controversy, it helps to know a little about the men themselves. Few of us escape the wormhole that connects our experience to our theology. And these men were no exception.

Pelagius was born in approximately A.D. 354. Most trace his roots to the British Isles. A muscular man described by Jerome as having the body of a wrestler, he was also well-educated with fluency in both Greek and Latin. He was an accomplished lawyer and theologian. With so much human ability at his disposal it is not hard to see why Pelagius gravitated towards asceticism as the means of spirituality.

In fact, Pelagius believed a sinless life was possible after water baptism, if one wanted it badly enough. To that end, he denied traducianism, the teaching that Adam's guilt was passed on to his progeny. Little babies are born completely innocent without a trace of sin. The only grace absolutely necessary was in the case of an adult convert who needed the grace of water baptism to return him to his original state of innocence (birth). Once washed, he could lead a sinless life.[10]

Particularly disturbing to Pelagius was a statement he read while in Rome from the writings of Augustine: "Give me what you command, and command what you will." Pelagius thought this approach turned man into an automaton. In his Confessions (x.40), Augustine wrote:

> I have no hope at all, but in your great mercy. Grant what you command and command what you will [emphasis mine]. You enjoin on us continence, 'And when I knew,' said one, 'that none could be continent, except God gave it, this also was itself a part of wisdom, to know whose gift it was.' ... For he loves you too little who loves anything together with you, which he loves not for your sake. O love that ever burns and is never quenched! O Charity, my God, enkindle me! You command continence. Grant what you command and command what you will [emphasis mine].

Augustine was a contemporary of Pelagius but with a far different background. His roots were in North Africa and Italy. He was a man gripped by the headlock of passion. He took a concubine when he was just sixteen and kept her for fifteen years. She bore him a son, Adeodatus. He spent nine years in Manichaeism trying to overcome his addictions to the flesh before he gave up. When he finally agreed to send his concubine away and marry a woman approved by his mother, Monica, he immediately began an affair with another woman while waiting for his future wife to come of age.

So, it is not hard to recognize the impact of his "garden experience" on his life. As the story goes from his Confessions, the voice of an unseen child told him *tolle lege* ("take up and read"). The nearest literature he could find was a Bible. He opened to Romans 13:13-14 which reads, "Let us walk properly, as in the day, not in revelry and drunkenness, not in lewdness and lust, not in strife and envy. But

---

[10] G. Bonner, "Pelagianism," *The Dictionary of Historical Theology*, ed. T. A. Hart (Grand Rapids, MI: Eerdmans, 2000), 422.

put on the Lord Jesus Christ, and make no provision for the flesh, to fulfill its lusts." This led to his conversion to Christianity in 386. He was baptized by Ambrose of Milan in 387 and immediately returned to Africa in 388. Soon after, his mother and son died.

In his conversion Augustine turned completely against the flesh, coming very close to the dualism of Plato which regarded the flesh as evil. More on this later. But marching into the world as a new Christian, having given up his position as a teacher of rhetoric in Milan, and renouncing the ways of the flesh, he also sold all his goods and gave them to the poor. He retained only his family's home, which he converted into a monastery.

From all this it is not difficult to surmise that Augustine was not high on human ability. For him, it is all grace. His statement "grant what you command and command what you will" hinges on Philippians 2:12-13, which encourages believers to work out their salvation with fear and trembling, yet to remember that it is God who works in them both the desire to do His will and the power to accomplish the same. So, born the same year as Pelagius and living in the same arena, these twin towers of theology were bound to clash. One important note, however. Augustine was fluent in Latin, but not Greek, a fact which bit him on the heel more than once.

Pelagius reacted to this gloomy view of humanity and the God who would create such a passive being in such a helpless state. He resisted this apparent passivity by saying, "If I ought, I can." He writes in *Ep. ad Demetriadem* (xxxiii. 1110):

> Instead of regarding the commands of our illustrious King as privilege... we cry out to God, in the scornful sloth of our hearts, and say, 'This is too hard and difficult. We cannot do it. We are only human, and hindered by the weakness of the flesh.' Blind folly and presumptuous blasphemy! We ascribe to the God of knowledge the guilt of twofold ignorance: ignorance of his own creation and of his own commands. As if, forgetting the weakness of men, his own creation, he had laid upon men commands which they were unable to bear. And at the same time (God forgive us!) we ascribe to the

Just One unrighteousness and cruelty to the Holy One; the first by complaining that he has commanded the impossible, the second by imagining that a man will be condemned by him for what he could not help; so that (the blasphemy of it!) God is thought of as seeking our punishment rather than our salvation.... No one knows the extent of our strength better than he who gave us that strength.... He has not willed to command anything impossible, for he is righteous; and he will not condemn man for what he could not help, for he is holy.

Though it is somewhat controversial just who spread the theology based on the views of Pelagius, it is popular to condemn anyone who would mix works with their faith as some sort of Pelagian (Pelagian, semi-Pelagian). One who is considered the father of semi-Pelagianism was John Cassian (d. 435). He is usually described as one who did not think grace was necessary for salvation, but he did not agree with Pelagius that a sinless life was possible.

It would be easy to read his writings on the monastic ascent (*Purgatio*—to purge oneself of fleshly lusts; *Illuminatio*—to learn the paths of holiness; and *Unitio*—to bond together with the Spirit of God) and assume that he taught an ascetic/works approach to salvation. Not at all. Most of this criticism came from a misunderstanding by Prosper of Aquitaine. Prosper thought Cassian was teaching a step-ladder way of salvation. Quite the contrary, the step-ladder was for those who already had salvation from the penalty of sin. As Donald Fairbairn argues:

> Cassian did not believe that a person's good will was the beginning of salvation. Rather, he argues ... that salvation begins with God's gift of himself to people through Christ, a gift by which God draws a person into union with himself and makes him an adopted child. According to Cassian, a person's desire for virtue and moral purity is an attempt to deepen the union he already had with God, not an attempt to aspire to a union which is merely future. In the process of moral purification, God sometimes takes the initiative and sometimes waits for human

action, but this entire process is based on God's prior gift of grace to a person.[11]

Cassian's theology was approved by the Synod of Arles (AD 473), but condemned at the Council of Orange (AD 529). This council rejected the double predestination of Augustine and believed that God's grace could be resisted, but they could better be described as semi-Augustinian than semi-Pelagian. The same is probably true of John Cassian, although he seemed to seek a middle ground between Pelagius and Augustine. Over the following three centuries, the church leaned more toward Cassian and away from Augustine. In fact, Gottschalk was condemned, flogged, and imprisoned when he taught double predestination in 849.

And so even today, the debate still rages over the extent of human ability. Some brand the view of depravity of Five Point Calvinists as Total Inability instead of total depravity. Others say any seeking of light on the part of an unregenerate man is impossible since corpses are not capable of any motion at all, let alone movement toward God. But what does the Bible teach?

The Unregenerate Mind

There are several passages we need to examine to help us ascertain the state of the unregenerate mind:

Romans 1:28

Many would have us believe that the *adokimos (disapproved)* mind of this passage describes the mind of the unregenerate man. And there is no question that this passage does describe the mind of some unregenerate men, but not necessarily all unregenerate men. To say that it describes the mind of all unregenerate men is to overlook the obvious progression in the text when the phrase παρέδωκεν αὐτοὺς ὁ θεὸς is repeated in verses 24, 26, and 28. Such repetition usually indicates a progression in thought. Paul is explaining how

---

[11] D. Fairbairn, "John Cassian," ibid., 116.

the wrath of God *is revealed* from heaven against all the impiety and unrighteousness of men, who put the truth of God behind bars (*katechō*). If they continue to willfully shut their minds to the truth of God's existence, then He progressively turns them over to the control of their Sin Nature. That progression comes in three primary steps, the last of which is to turn them over to a mind which is "disapproved," that is, a mind which is no longer capable of discerning right from wrong. But this is the final stage of wrath against a persistently recalcitrant creation, a stubbornly rebellious creature. This is not the state of all unregenerate men. To say so is to contradict Paul's later teaching (Rom 2:14-16) when he says the unregenerate Gentiles have the law written on their hearts. This witness to God's will tells them right from wrong.

No, Romans 1:28 does not describe the state of all unregenerate minds. But Romans 1:18-20 does tell us that the unregenerate mind is capable of receiving divine revelation. Even the revelation of God in nature (cf. Ps 19:1-4) is light from above about a Supreme Being. Whether the unregenerate mind accepts or rejects this revelation is another matter. All Romans 1:18-20 says is that every thinking man has received this revelation, and those who willfully reject it are turned over to the tyranny of their own lusts.

First Corinthians 2:14

Here is another favorite passage to describe the inability of the unregenerate mind when it comes to interacting with the things of God. After all, it explicitly states that the natural man does not receive the things of the Spirit of God because they are foolishness to him, and he is not able to know them because they are spiritually discerned.

It is interesting that this passage (1 Cor 2:10-3:4) describes three types of men, each of which is characterized by a different aspect of the tripartite man: body, soul, and spirit. The man controlled by his flesh is described in 1 Corinthians 3:1-3. Such men are called σαρκικοι (*sarkikoi*), fleshly or carnal. They are said to be unable (οὐδε ἔτι νῦν δύναται) to receive the meat of the things of God. The term used here for their ability or lack thereof (οὐ δύναται) is the same word used of the ψυχικός (*psuchikos*) man in 2:14. It is said of this so-called "natural" man that he cannot know (γνῶναι is usually understood to be "experiential" knowledge as opposed to intuitive knowledge) the things of the Spirit of God because he is unregenerate, that is, because he does not have the Spirit. But if that argument holds up for the "natural" man, the same should be said of the "carnal" man in 3:1-3.

The "spiritual" man is singled out in 1 Corinthians 2:15 as the only one who can understand "all things," though he himself is understood by no one. The carnal Christian is not able to understand all things, as 3:1-2 indicates, because the carnal Christian is not "spiritual." However, whatever the "carnal" man does not "get," the "natural" man does not get either (see 2:9), not because he does not have the Spirit (which is true) but because he does not discern the things of the Spirit with his own spirit (2:10-11). So we cannot rely on this passage to support the Calvinistic notion of the "total inability" of the unbeliever, who at least in this respect, is comparable to the carnal believer.

Of course, there are those who argue that there is no such thing as a "carnal" Christian. For them, neither the "natural" man nor the "carnal" man is regenerate. However, there is good reason to believe that the "carnal" man is a believer. In 3:1 he is likened to the babe in Christ. Paul says he must speak to the "carnal" man as though he were speaking to a baby Christian. Since such dullness to the Spirit of God is comparable between the carnal Christian and the unbeliever, it raises the question of whether the unbeliever is sensitive to the Spirit of God in some *other* way. To address this question we turn to the Gospel of John.

John 16:7-11

A major proportion of the Upper Room Discourse is taken up by Jesus' teaching about the impending new role of the Holy Spirit, the third Person of the Trinity who is to be "sent" by the Father and the Son as soon as the Son is glorified. While most of this teaching refers to the Holy Spirit as the "Paraclete" who helps believers after Jesus returns to the Father, this help is afforded in the context of convicting the "world" of sin, righteousness, and judgment (Jn 16:7-11). As is evident in John 3:16, the "world" for John is comprised of people who do not yet believe in the Son. Yet those who do not believe are in some way receptive to the convicting ministry of the Spirit. If the "spirit" of these unbelievers cannot discern this conviction (1 Cor 2:10-11), then how can unbelievers come under conviction?[12]

The answer is *conscience*. Returning to our previous passage from Romans, the law came so that sin might be personally imputed, as all in Adam are brought under conviction by the law (5:13-14, 20a). Paul has already told us that this conviction occurs in the realm of conscience (2:14-15; 3:20). This conviction is graphically depicted in Paul's own life, both as an unbeliever "*in* the flesh" (7:5, 7-13) and as a "carnal" believer operating *according to* the flesh (7:14-25). It is apparent from John 16:8-11 that the Spirit speaks to unbelievers through conscience "from outside," as it were, and in a similar way through the "hearts" of believers (1 Jn 3:19-21). The "heart" here is very likely the Johannine equivalent of "conscience," as it "condemns" us. Hence, just like the law, the Spirit brings perceptible conviction through the conscience of even the unbeliever.

Second Corinthians 3–4

Second Corinthians 3:14 speaks of the minds of the unregenerate Jews as hardened because of the veil of the OT Law which lies over their hearts. And 2 Corinthians 4:3-6 says the god of this world has blinded the minds of the unbelievers, so they do not see the light of the gospel of the glory of Christ. So, a hardening and a blinding has taken place with regard to Christ himself, but these passages do not address the question of ability to respond to the light these unbelievers do see.

Ephesians 4:17-19

These verses say that unbelieving Gentiles walk in the futility of their minds, being darkened in their understanding, and are excluded from the life of God because of the ignorance which is in them, because of the hardness of their hearts. Having become callused, they have given themselves over to sensuality for the practice of every kind of impurity with greediness. This sounds very much like Romans 1:18-

---

[12] Many would respond that it is regeneration that answers this question. The nature and timing of regeneration will we be discussed later.

32, which speaks of the increasing control of the Sin Nature in the life of those who reject the revelation of God. It still does not answer the question of whether they *could* have responded to this revelation.

Conclusion

None of the passages dealing with the mind of the unbeliever addresses the questions we are asking about the ability of these unbelievers to respond to the revelation of God. The most that could be said is that some sort of ability to respond is implied by the fact that Romans 1:18-20 speaks of the accountability of those who reject the revelation of God given in nature. It makes little sense to hold people responsible for something which was impossible for them. Would we punish a Downs Syndrome child because he could not explicate a poem by Browning? Would we judge a man because he cannot bear children? No, to hold someone responsible for something he did not do, at the very least, implies some sort of capacity to do that for which he is being held accountable. These passages are really not much help.

The Unregenerate Will

Romans 3:9-12

Here, we read that no one is righteous, not even one; no one understands, and no one seeks for God; no one does good. But does this mean no one does righteous deeds, and no one does good things? Obviously not; Isaiah 59:6 acknowledges the righteous deeds of the unregenerate.[13] The point is that all our righteous deeds combined cannot accomplish our regeneration. This is an important passage on the inability of man to accomplish his own justification. But even this passage does not address the question concerning the ability of man

---

[13] C. C. Ryrie says, "Total depravity does not mean that everyone is as thoroughly depraved in his actions as he could possibly be, nor that everyone will indulge in every form of sin, nor that a person cannot appreciate and even do acts of goodness; but it does mean that the corruption of sin extends to all men and to all parts of men so that there is nothing within the natural man that can give him merit in God's sight" (*A Survey of Bible Doctrine* [Chicago: Moody, 1972], 111).

to respond or even to initiate a relationship with God. There is a big difference between saying, "No one seeks after God," and, "No one is *able* to seek after God."[14]

The Unregenerate Ability

This is truly the issue. Just what can an unregenerate man do? This goes to the very heart of the soteriological argument between Augustine and Pelagius. Can man respond on his own or initiate on his own, and if so, to what extent?

John 6:44

Here, the all-important term regarding man's ability is used: οὐδεὶς δύναται ἐλθεῖν πρός με. "No one *is able* (*dunatai*) to come to me." Left alone, this sounds as though no one can ever come to Christ. But if this were true, His invitation would be vapid when He beckons, "Come unto me all you who are heavy laden . . . I will give you rest." So the verse goes on to say, ἐὰν μὴ ὁ πατὴρ ὁ πέμψας με ἑλκύσῃ αὐτόν, "unless my Father who sent me *helkusēi* him." Again, the question involves just what the Father does for the unregenerate man. Hard Calvinists say this word *helkusēi* means "he drags."[15] In their view total depravity means not only that man is incapable of coming to God on his own, but also that God must drag the unbeliever kicking and screaming into the kingdom. God forces the unbeliever against his will. Support for this approach is taken from other uses of the verbs *helkuō* and its cousin *helkō* which occur in courtroom settings (Acts 16:19; Jas 2:6) or the context of a lynch mob (Acts 21:30). Since these are hostile settings, the one acted upon is acted upon against his will. Hence, he must be dragged.

Some even appeal to Kittel to try to prove that this verb means to

---

[14] Now, some of you may begin thinking the author is Arminian—that he believes in the ability of a human to come to God. No. I just said in this very paragraph that Romans 3 underscores the fact that a man cannot accomplish his own justification. But I am also saying that this passage does not address the question of man's ability to respond to the revelation God has given him.
[15] R.C. Sproul, *Chosen by God* (Tyndale, 1994), 69-72.

force or coerce.[16] On the contrary, Kittel[17] makes the exact opposite point as it pertains to John 6:44. Whenever a family context is in view, instead of a hostile context like a law court, there is usually the mention of love (cf. 4 Macc 14:13; 15:11; and Jer 31:3). The mother's cords of love draw her children to her. There is no hint of force here. Because of this, more moderate Calvinists correctly interpret John 6:44 to say that the Father *draws* the unbeliever to Christ. It is more the idea of wooing or persuading.

John 6:44 is very important to include with our other passages dealing with man's ability or lack thereof. Without the aid of the Father and the Holy Spirit in the wooing process, it would be accurate to say that man, on his own, cannot come to Christ. But it would also be inaccurate to say that the Father forces or drags a man kicking and screaming into His kingdom. It would be better to say that the Holy Spirit or the Father walk arm-in-arm with the elect into the Kingdom. We will spend more time on this in the discussion on election and predestination.[18]

But is there some definitive way to describe what the unbeliever can do in response to God's revelation? Yes, there is.

Acts 17:27

In this passage, Paul explains to the Athenians that God has arranged the seasons in accordance with His common grace, so that man might seek after God. The word here for "seek" (*zēteō*) is the same as we find in Rom 3:11 (although the attached preposition *ek* in Rom 3:21 usually intensifies the meaning of the verb, and in the LXX *ekzēteō* is invariably used of a very diligent searching, which involves the whole heart). The implication is that man does have the capacity to seek after God, but it does not say man has the ability to reach God on his own.

---

[16] Ibid. See also, Mathew Barrett, *Salvation By Grace, The Case for Effectual Calling and Regeneration*, (Phillipsburg, New Jersey, P & R Publishing, 2013).
[17] Ibid.
[18] See, Craig S. Keener, *The Gospel of John: A Commentary*, (Peabody Massachusetts, Hendrickson Publishers, 2003) Vol 1, 685 who affirms that this passage does not deny free will.

This passage also says if man seeks after God, there is the remote possibility that he will grope for Him and find Him. The verbs used here for groping (*psēlaphēsian*) and finding (*heuroien*) are aorist optatives, which are used in fourth class conditional clauses for remote possibility. As the Greek language shifted from the Attic to the Hellenistic, common Greek, the optative mood was disappearing and being absorbed by the subjunctive mood. There are less than seventy uses of the optative in the NT. But when a NT author went out of his way to use this mood, he did so very consciously and with specific meaning.[19] Here, the fact is that this mood indicates possibility, and since the optative mood is specifically a statement regarding the *will*, it suggests that man does have the capacity to grope after God and even to find Him.

However, there is nothing here to say that man is capable of finding God *on his own*. This passage must be combined with passages like John 6:44, John 6:65, and Romans 8:8. John 6:65 says no one can come to Christ unless (οὐδεὶς δύναται ἐλθεῖν πρός με ἐὰν μὴ—the exact wording as we had in 6:44) it is granted (δεδομένον—from *didōmi*, which speaks of a gift or giving) to him by/from the Father. So, it would appear that man does have the capacity to seek, to grope, and to find, but he cannot reach God on his own. It is a gift from God (Jn 6:65), and it involves the drawing, attractive power of God (Jn 6:44). And Romans 8:8 says that those who are "in the flesh" (οἱ δὲ ἐν σαρκὶ ὄντες) are not able (οὐ δύνανται) to please God.

Summary

There is no question that the Scriptures teach the total depravity of man. This depravity extends to all aspects of his being. He is thoroughly

---

[19] D. B. Wallace, *Greek Grammar Beyond the Basics* (Grand Rapids: Zondervan, 1996), 480, 699. See also Eckhard J. Schnabel, *Exegetical Commentary On The New Testament: Acts*, (Grand Rapids, MI: Zondervan Publishing, 2012) 735 for evidence of the possibility for people to desire and to respond to God. The significance of the optatives is also affirmed by Stanley Porter, *Paul in Acts* cited by Craig Keener, *Acts: An Exegetical Commentary*, (Grand Rapids, MI: Baker Academic, 2014) vol. 3, 2652.

depraved. But it does not mean that he is as bad as he can possibly be. The process of coming to God which involves a thoroughly depraved being appears to be one of cooperation between God and man. It is not true to say man has no capacity to respond to the revelation of God. God has revealed himself to all thinking people. He has revealed himself in the order of nature. But if a man takes this light he has received and locks it behind the bars of his hardened heart, he begins a slide down the banister of depravity, which allows his sinful passions to control more and more of his life. Ultimately, though he began as bad off as he could be (separated from God) he becomes as bad as he can be—consigned to a mind which cannot tell right from wrong. Somewhere along the way, God blinds his mind so as to limit the judgment upon him at the Great White Throne (just as Christ began teaching in parables to limit the judgment on the Pharisees who would ultimately reject Him).

But this does not mean man is incapable of responding to the light God has revealed about his existence in nature. Apparently, a man does have the capacity to seek, to grope, and to start down the path of finding God. But he cannot do this alone. He needs a guide and an encourager. When one responds to the light he has been given by God, he is given more light. He must decide what to do with this additional light. The Father is at his side to add whatever persuasion might be necessary for him to take the next step. Ultimately, the Father and the elect child come to Christ, and a new babe is ushered into the kingdom of God, arm-in-arm with his Divine Enabler. The entire salvation process is a gift of God that emanates from the grace of God (Eph 2:8-9).

This discussion is important in preserving the character of God, the essence of which is love. If we say that man is completely incapable of responding to God's light and persuasion, then we remove his capacity to choose. This reduces man to an automaton, precisely the view of a hard determinist or hard Calvinist. But more importantly, it turns God into a mad scientist, who is morally responsible for the evil in this world and whose hatred for mankind far exceeds his love. We would like to avoid this extreme.

Salvation in the Old Testament

Introduction

Salvation in the OT is a huge subject worthy of a course all to itself. In order to fit this topic into the overall subject of soteriology, we need to narrow our scope to the broad-brush strokes of salvation in the OT. But before we focus on these features separately, it will help us to get the "Big Picture."

We have already established that Satan came to this planet before man was created (see "The Sinfulness of Man"). He turned what should have been a garden into a garbage heap (Gen 1:2—*tohu wa bohu- formless and void*). And his rebellion challenged two aspects of God's character: His sovereignty and His love. Who has a right to rule the universe: Satan or God? And is God worthy of being loved? Man was created to answer these two questions (this is our metanarrative for the human race). By making a creature a little lower than the angels in terms of intelligence, mobility, power, and amount of revelation received, God attempted to demonstrate to Satan that these creatures would vote for Him instead of the Rebel. In so doing, not only would they answer the question regarding God's sovereignty, but they would also affirm God's character regarding love. "He who has my commandments and keeps them, he it is who loves me . . ." (Jn 14:21a).

As we know, Satan was clever enough to seduce man. Adam fell. His depravity or "sin nature" was passed on to all in the human race. But because God is love, He resolved to rescue His new creation from the effects of the fall, one of which was eternal separation from Himself. In this recovery plan God could demonstrate that He is loving and worthy of being loved, and He could also settle decisively the question concerning who has a right to rule the universe. But these questions would not be resolved in one generation. God wanted billions of His new creation to spend eternity with Him. Was He replacing the third of the host of heaven that followed Lucifer in his rebellion? We do not know. What we do know is that God wanted Adam to populate the whole earth, and God has not predetermined (*boulomai*) that any should perish (2 Pet 3:9).

From a human perspective, God gave man every chance to demonstrate his ability to love and obey God's standards. But the pattern of the garden repeated itself, time and time again. First came the test, then the failure, then the judgment. With each cycle God gave mankind a new opportunity, a new way of dealing with His creation. We call these cycles dispensations.[1] Following the "Age of Innocence" in the garden came the "Age of Conscience" outside the garden. God allowed man to govern himself internally with his conscience as his guide. But violence and homosexuality filled the land. Man failed the conscience test. Judgment came in the form of a universal flood. God started over with Noah and his family. Acknowledging that the internal guide of man's conscience was not sufficient to restrain the evil of man's depravity, God instituted external controls in the form of human government. Man was told once again to spread out over

---

[1] See Elliot Johnson, *A Dispensational Biblical Theology*, (Bold Grace Academic Publications, 2016) An older treatment of a biblical theology from a dispensational perspective is found in the works of Erich Sauer, *The Dawn of World Redemption: A Survey of Historical Revelation in the Old Testament*, (Grand Rapids, MI: Eerdmans Publishing, 1953) *The Triumph of the Crucified: A Survey of the Historical Revelation in the New Testament*, (Grand Rapids, MI: Eerdmans Publishing, 1951) and *From Eternity to Eternity: An Outline of Divine Purposes*, (Grand Rapids, MI: Eerdmans Publishing, 1954).

the earth and to institute capital punishment as a means of restraining evil in the world. But mankind failed again. They built not only cities, but also ziggurats to worship the stars. So once again, the cycle was completed as God judged mankind through diversity of languages to cause him to disperse.

God established a new order in His dealings with mankind (another dispensation). He realized (again from a human perspective) that the effects of the fall are such that man is incapable of "saving" himself. He embarked on a provocative scheme. He would create a Second Adam to recover that which was lost in the First Adam. This Second Adam would be able to "save" mankind from the fall because he would be more than man—he would be both God and man. And to verify his identity, his lineage would be traceable. Of course, that would require a unique nation set apart from the rest, so this lineage could not only be traced, but also predicted. To accomplish this daring plan, God selected one man and presented to him an overview of salvation for all mankind (Gen 12:1-3). If this man responded in faith, God would use him to bring forth the Second Adam. If he did not respond, God would find another. But Abraham responded, and the Jewish race was born. Through Abraham all the nations of the earth would be blessed, for through Abraham would come the Second Adam.

One of the conditions for God to bring forth the blessings promised[2] to and through Abraham was for his progeny to stay in the land. Due to their own lack of faith, the seed of Abraham failed to stay in the land. For their own survival, they went into Egypt. God disciplined them with centuries of captivity as slaves in Egypt. When the time of judgment was complete, another cycle was finished, and God established a new order in his dealings with mankind: The Law. Using Moses as a deliverer of His people from Egypt and of His standard of holiness through the written Torah, God brought His people back to the land of Israel, the locus for the blessings promised to Abraham and his seed to be fulfilled. Under the new administration (dispensation), the seed of Abraham needed to demonstrate their love

---

[2] This is often called the dispensation of Promise.

and loyalty (right to rule) to God through obedience to His revealed standard of holiness (The Law). If they would be faithful, blessings would flow in the land like milk and honey. If they were unfaithful, God's hand of discipline would remove them from the land in order to purge them of their idolatry. Once again, mankind proved unfaithful through the chosen nation (ah, the persistence of depravity), and the twelve tribes were deported through the hands of the Assyrians and Babylonians. Only a small remnant of the tribes returned from the captivity in Babylon. But they had learned their lesson. Idolatry had been purged from the nation.

The fullness of times had come. The world was ready for the God-man, the Second Adam through whom the effects of the fall could be reversed. But that is a NT story. In this brief overview leading up to the birth of Christ, we have traced the *Heilsgeschichte* (history of salvation) of God's dealings with man from Genesis to Malachi. What is important to observe from this overview is how God went from individuals, to nations, to a nation in His outworking of His plan for salvation. When we talk about "salvation in the OT," our minds seem to think in terms of how an individual could go to heaven during the OT era(s). But we must remember that the salvation history presented in the OT focuses more on the salvation of mankind collectively than it does on the salvation plan for individuals. For the most part, the salvation story of the OT is the story of the salvation of one nation. While narratives in the OT often center on the stories of individuals (Job, Ruth, Genesis 1-11), these narratives are prototypical object lessons nested within the overarching story of Israel's salvation and the ultimate salvation of a people separated (holy, sanctified) to bear His name with honor among the nations as a whole. The curtains of heaven are not pulled back to reveal the salvation drama in the lives of individuals. Thus, to try to ferret out the plan of salvation for individuals in the OT is somewhat at odds with the purpose of OT revelation.

Nevertheless, because dispensationalists have been unjustly accused of espousing two or more plans of salvation for individuals throughout the OT and NT, it is necessary to address certain OT *leitmotifs* in order to dispel this misconception. Therefore, we would like to discuss these subjects as they present themselves in the OT: the Gospel, Faith, Grace, Blood Sacrifice, Eternity, and the Messiah.

The Gospel

Since the word "gospel" means "good news," to find "the gospel" in the OT we must look for some good news. But this good news needs to be specific. "Gospel" is not an OT term. To even look for "the gospel" in the OT is to impose NT terminology on the OT. And in the NT, the term "gospel" is usually associated with the good news from God to mankind concerning His Son Jesus Christ. Probably the best we can do in the OT is to find some good news God promised man concerning a future deliverer for the human race.

Genesis 3:15

Keeping these constraints in mind, many believe Genesis 3:15 meets the qualifications of a promised deliverer. This statement to the serpent is an oblique promise to Adam and the woman. God says the serpent will bruise the heel of the woman's seed, but this same seed would crush the head of the serpent. This was "good news" to Adam and Eve and their progeny. They had already begun to experience the death God had promised (2:17) for heeding the serpent, and the promise that one of her own seed would crush the head of the serpent offered hope of life after death (3:20).

The trend in scholarship today is to remove most of the "messianic promises" from the text, something which we will discuss subsequently. And many dismiss Genesis 3:15 with regard to messianic import. But this is not universally true among OT scholars. Walter Kaiser, Jr. says:

> Genesis 3:15 has commonly been called the protoevangelium (the "first gospel") because it was the original proclamation of the promise of God's plan for the whole world.... it gave our first parents a glimpse, even if only an obscure one, of the person and mission of the one who was going to be the central figure in the unfolding drama of the redemption of the world. The "seed/offspring" mentioned in this verse became the root from which the tree of the OT promise of a

Messiah grew. This, then, was the "mother prophecy" that gave birth to all the rest of the promises.³

A most interesting feature of this promise is the use of pronouns. The pronominal suffix on the Hebrew verb "crush" actually goes with the word "heel" (תְּשׁוּפֶנּוּ עָקֵב). And this suffix is third person, singular, masculine, which translates, "You will bruise *his* heel," although "seed" is neuter. This pronoun cannot refer to the woman, as this would require a feminine referent ("her"). R. A. Martin observes that the Hebrew masculine personal pronoun occurs 103 times in Genesis, but only here did the LXX translators break the rules for agreement between gender and number for a pronoun and its antecedent. "The most likely explanation for the use of [masculine pronoun] *autos* rather than [the neuter pronoun for] *sperma* is that the translator has in this way indicated his messianic understanding of this verse."⁴

Apparently, Eve picked up on this promise. When she gave birth to Cain, she said, "I have given birth to a man, the Lord." Some translators reveal their prejudice here by translating this phrase: "I have given birth *with the help of* the Lord." But the words in italics do not have a Hebrew equivalent. A verb is usually supplied in translation when the given words do not make sense. But here the words are אֶת־יְהוָה אִישׁ, literally, "a man, the Lord." She thought her first son would be the one who would deliver them from the awful curse of life outside the garden. She expected Cain to crush the head of the serpent. How horrible it must have been for her when Cain crushed the head of his brother instead.

---

³ W. C. Kaiser, *The Messiah in the Old Testament*, Studies in Old Testament Biblical Theology (Grand Rapids, MI: Zondervan, 1995), 37-38. Also see, Herbert W. Bateman IV, Darrell L. Bock and Gordon H. Johnston, *Jesus The Messiah; Tracing the Promises, Expectations, and Coming of Israel's King*, (Grand Rapids, MI: Kregel Publishing, 2012).

⁴ R. A. Martin, "The Earliest Messianic Interpretation of Genesis 3:15," *Journal of Biblical Literature* 84 (1965): 425-27.

Genesis 12:1-3

Although this is usually referred to as the Abrahamic Covenant, most covenant scholars doubt that this gives us the full expression of this covenant, since it does not follow any known covenant form. There are only two covenant forms in the OT: the Suzerainty-Vassal Treaty (Deuteronomy) and the Covenants of Grant (Abrahamic, Davidic, New). The original covenant with Abraham was probably established while he was in Ur of the Chaldeans when God first appeared to him (Acts 7:2ff). Genesis 12:1-3 probably gives us a *précis* of this covenant, and we are told that all the families of the earth would be blessed in or by Abraham (the Hebrew can mean either "in" or "by"). This same promise was repeated three times to Abraham and once each to Isaac and Jacob (Gen 12:3; 18:18; 22:18; 26:4; and 28:14). In the NT, Paul referred to this promise as the heart of the gospel (Gal 3:8).

In a sense, this covenant issues a mission statement to Abraham and his descendants. Though they were a chosen people, they were to be a channel of blessing to all the nations, the Gentiles. The word "channel" is carefully selected because it is important to point out that the verb for "shall be blessed" has a niphal stem, which definitely makes the verb passive (וְנִבְרְכוּ). The point is that Abraham was not the active agent of blessing. He was only the channel. Genesis 12:7 mentions the "seed" of Abraham. Both here and in Genesis 3:15 the singular word "seed" can have a dual reference: single or collective ("descendants"). It can refer to one or to many. Again, Paul tells us in Galatians 3:16 that the Holy Spirit had a single referent in view (one seed) instead of the plural (seeds). But, of course, the OT readers did not have the advantage of Paul's explanation.[5] Yet, even in Abraham's day, they must have understood some sort of

---

[5] The issue of how the NT utilizes and informs our understanding of the OT has been a debated topic for scholars of both testaments. See the classic study, Richard N. Longenecker, *Biblical Exegesis in the Apostolic Period*, (Grand Rapids, MI: Eerdmans Publishing, 1999) and the more recent by Walter C. Kaiser, Darrell L. Bock and Peter Enns, *Three Views on the New Testament Use in the Old Testament*, (Grand Rapids, MI: Zondervan, 2007).

narrowing of the meaning of seed since the children of Abraham and Keturah were bypassed, as well as Ishmael, Esau, Ruben, Simeon, and Levi.

What did Abraham understand about his "seed"? Perhaps more than we might suspect. Again, the NT commentary helps us. Jesus tells the skeptics in John 8:56, "Your father Abraham rejoiced at the thought of seeing my day; he saw it and was glad." How, we might ask, did Abraham see Christ's day? We can only conjecture, but Hebrews 11:19 tells us that Abraham was able to march up Mt. Moriah with Isaac because he believed God could raise him from the dead. After seeing God supply a ram as a substitute for his son, he named the place "Yahweh Jireh," the Lord will provide. Perhaps this is the time Jesus referenced when Abraham saw His day, namely, that God would provide a blood sacrifice, and was glad.

This subject is large enough for a book of its own, so we must move on. But let us take note at this point that the OT was not without its gospel, its *good news*. From the outset, God gave good news to Adam and Eve about the future deliverance of the human race from their bondage to sin and its deleterious effects. But what, we might ask, did God require of man for salvation, whether as an individual or as a generation?

Faith

Genesis 15:6

Again, the NT explains the OT for us. Paul quotes Genesis 15:6 in Romans 4:3. It is his proof text that Abraham was justified by faith, not by works. At this point, and even before (see Heb 11:8), God could see into the heart of Abraham and know that a spiritual transformation had taken place by faith. And in Romans 4:16, Paul explains that for the descendants of Abraham to share his blessing they also had to share his faith: "That is why it depends on faith, in order that the promise may rest on grace and be guaranteed to all his descendants—not only to the adherents of the law, but also to those who share the faith of Abraham, for he is the father of us all."

Habakkuk 2:4

Here is another important text to establish the "faith" system in the OT for individuals. Habakkuk is concerned that God could use the dirty Gentiles, the Assyrians, to purge His people. He goes to the Lord to complain, but God's answer nullifies the complaint: "The just shall live by faith." Relax, Habakkuk. I may use a dirty vessel to clean my nation, but I am still fair. Those within the nation who put their faith in Me shall live. The just shall live by faith. Though the nation may be swept downstream, those individuals who swim upstream, by faith, will be saved.

Granted, there is no reference to heaven or eternal life here, but the NT picks up on this verse three times to emphasize the centrality of faith for those in right relationship to God. Paul uses it in his thematic statement for the entire book of Romans (1:17). He uses it again in Galatians 3:11 to contrast justification by the law with justification by faith. Finally, in Hebrews 10:38, it is used to exhort believers to endure in their faith in light of the imminent return of Christ.

It may well be asked why faith is not emphasized more in the OT, considering its emphasis in the NT. While that answer partly entails the notion of "progressive revelation," the major emphasis in the OT is on the national salvation of Israel and not individuals, as we have pointed out. And this salvation was understood as longevity and blessings "in the land." Yet even for the nation, ongoing faith for the living generation was required for blessing in the land. This is obvious after Kadesh-barnea. Those without faith perished in the wilderness. The following generation needed faith to follow Joshua into the land. When they followed the Lord by faith, they won the victory. When their faith faltered, they were defeated.

So, if faith is the *requirement* for blessing, what is the *means*?

Grace

A major misconception over the years concerning the OT versus the NT has been the doctrine that the OT teaches law for eternal salvation, and the NT teaches grace. Over the past thirty years E. P. Sanders has become well-known in NT scholarship for dispelling this notion.⁶ But long before Sanders came along, the work done by M. Kline on Suzerainty-Vassal treaties should have cleared up any misunderstanding.

The Suzerainty-Vassal Treaty

In his analysis of Deuteronomy, Kline explains most of the first four chapters as a historical prologue listing the gracious deeds and blessings of the sovereign or Suzerain, the Lord. In these chapters God reviews what He has sovereignly done to bless the Israelites in bringing them out of Egypt and keeping them fed, clothed, and watered during their forty years in the wilderness. This is all His sovereign grace on their behalf. And because of this grace, He appeals to their sense of gratitude in asking them to obey Him. "Benefits allegedly conferred by the lord upon the vassal were cited with a view to grounding the vassal's allegiance in a sense of gratitude. . . ."⁷ To be sure, He provides additional incentive to obedience by listing the curses and blessings which will accrue to them, depending on whether they are obedient or not. But He grounds His appeal in His initial acts of grace.

The Mercy Seat

The very provision of the mercy seat in the Holy of Holies should be an obvious declaration of God's grace in dealing with His people. Certainly, it is not insignificant that this mercy seat sat as the *foot stool* for the presence of God Himself rather than the table of showbread

---

⁶ E. P. Sanders says, "But surely non-Christian Jews saw themselves as remaining in the grace of God by remaining loyal to the covenant. Only if one simply equates 'the word of Christ' ([Rom] 10:17) with grace can one say that they rejected grace." He goes on to make the point that historical Judaism is very much founded on grace, but when the Jews rejected Christ and the gospel concerning Him, it is at that point that Paul could conclude that they had rejected God's highest revelation of Himself and, therefore, grace (*Paul the Law and the Jewish People* [Minneapolis: Fortress Press, 1983], 157).

⁷ M. G. Kline, *Treaty of the Great King* (Grand Rapids: William B. Eerdmans Publishing Company, 1963), 52. After this accounting of blessings in Deuteronomy 1:6-18, Moses reminds the Israelites of their infidelity and disobedience.

or the menorah. Though Yahweh certainly displayed and expressed His anger at the sin of His people, such anger reflected not only His righteousness but also His personal pain, His hurt because of the feelings of rejection He felt when His people sinned against Him and chose other gods. But His anger soon abated, and the love of a parent for his wayward child returned, attended by deep compassion, then mercy and forgiveness.

Even the sacrificial system has often been misunderstood by post-temple historians as some sort of appeasement for misdeeds. But listen to these words from a modern orthodox rabbi:

> The Hebrew word for "sacrifice" (korban, lehakriv) is from the same root as "to come near, to approach . . . to become closely involved in a relationship with someone." For this is meant to be the essence of the experience. Unfortunately, no word in the English language can adequately render the idea behind the Hebrew word korban. We use the word "sacrifice" for lack of a better word. The idea of a sacrifice or offering seems to indicate a gift or present; giving up something of value for another's benefit, or going without something of value yourself, for the benefit of another. None of this gift-giving idea, however, is present in the idea of the korban . . . . Thus, its true meaning can only be grasped through its root . . . the concept of coming close . . . . The Temple sacrifice is not an idea of giving something up or losing something of value; it strives for nearness to God . . . . When a sinner brought a korban, the offering showed him what he himself deserved were God to judge him severely. The sages taught that we are able to have some knowledge of God and His identity through His names, or attributes. Throughout the Book of Leviticus, God never refers to Himself with the Name Elohim in reference to the korbannot-offerings which denotes the Divine attribute of strict justice. This could be misconstrued to indicate that God is a vengeful, bloodthirsty deity who demands a sacrifice as reparation. But nothing could be further from the truth; such imagery is a heathen vision of God, an unforgiving God who accepts the death throes of an animal as a substitute for the forfeited life of a human being. But the only Name which the Bible associates with the offerings to God is HaShem,

YHWH—the attribute of Divine love and mercy. Precisely because He is the God of love, not the God of punishment and death, He has prepared the sacrificial system as a method of restoring and purifying man's moral and spiritual life.[8]

Of course, we should hasten to note that the sacrificial system was something God gave to people that were already in covenant relationship with Him. The sacrifices were for the purpose of maintaining fellowship, not for establishing a relationship. Nevertheless, in the full scope of "salvation," which includes salvation from the power of sin, as well as from the penalty of sin, it is important to emphasize the mercy of God. And mercy is just grace plus compassion. Hear, then, the prayer of the High Priest on the Day of Atonement:

> I beseech You, O Lord;
> I have sinned, rebelled, and transgressed against You, I, and my household;
> I beseech You, O Lord,
> Grant atonement for the sins,
> and for the iniquities and transgressions which I have committed against You,
> I, and my household.
> As it is written in the Torah of Your servant, Moses:
> For on this day atonement shall be made for you, to purify you from all your sins
> —before the Lord you shall be purified.[9]

As we can see from the above confession, the people were very much aware of their own sinfulness. In describing the legalism against which Paul reacted, Hubner has suggested that the School of Shammai taught absolute perfectionism, while the School of Hillel

---

[8] C. Richman, *The Holy Temple of Jerusalem* (Jerusalem: The Temple Institute, 1997), 13, 16.
[9] Ibid., 49.

said if the good outweighs the bad, you will be all right with God. But there is no evidence for this distinction. The very sacrificial system assumes that neither the people nor the priest could keep the Law perfectly. The sacrifices were their way of restoring fellowship after committing transgressions. But this raises the question of basis. If grace is the *means* of salvation in the OT, what is the *basis*?

Blood

From Adam on, blood has been the basis for salvation. We do not know all that transpired between God and Adam after the fall, but through the slaying of animals to make clothes for Adam and Eve, it is thought that God was teaching them that life will come through the death of another, and without the shedding of blood there would be no remission of sins.

In the regions of Sumer (modern-day Kuwait) and Babylon (modern-day Iraq), the offering of the first-born son to Molech was common.[10] Thus Abraham, who came from the area of Sumer, would have been familiar with child sacrifice and not shocked at the practice itself. However, he must have been confused initially when Yahweh asked him to sacrifice Isaac. As revelation progressed during the OT period, God prescribed a plethora of different sacrifices to suit every occasion. Yet as Hebrews points out, these sacrifices could never permanently take away sin but were simply a foreshadowing of the ultimate sacrifice which would completely erase the debt of sin for all those who would come to the cross.

It is mistakenly suggested that dispensationalists believe salvation came to OT saints through the blood of bulls and goats, while NT saints enter the gates through the blood of Christ.[11] We believe the blood of Christ is the *only* efficacious sacrifice for sins for all time. Just

---

[10] See Helmer Ringgren, *Religion of the Ancient Near East*, (Philadelphia, Pennsylvania, The Westminster Press, 1973) 162.

[11] See Clarence B. Bass, *Backgrounds of Dispensationalism*, (Grand Rapids, MI, Eerdmans, 1960), 34 and John Gerstner, *Wrongly Dividing the Word of Truth*, (Brentwood, Tennessee: Wolgemuth & Hayatt, 1991) 151-67.

as it applies proactively for sinners born after the cross, so it applies retroactively for sinners who lived and died before the cross.

So, at this point in our discussion we can say this: 1) The Requirement for Salvation in any age is the same—Faith; 2) The Object of our saving faith in any age is the same—God; 3) The Means of Salvation in any age is the same—Grace; 4) The Basis for our Salvation in any age is the same—the Blood of Christ; but 5) The Content of our Faith from age to age is *variable*.[12] This last point is an outgrowth of our concept of progressive revelation. We believe there is evidence that Adam and Eve will spend eternity with the Lord. But it is unlikely that they ever heard of "The Four Spiritual Laws."[13] There is much about the unfolding drama of God's redemption that was revealed in progressive steps. Obviously, we would expect people to have a much clearer understanding and picture of the Deliverer when and after He lived on earth. Before that time the people had promises about Him, but the picture was not clear—just shadows and types.

Speaking of progressive revelation leads us to two more subjects we need to cover in regard to OT salvation: Eternal life and the Messiah.

Eternal Life

If we were to ask certain OT saints what they thought heaven was like or what we would do for eternity in heaven, they might reply, "Say what?" Of the over two hundred uses of "heaven" in the OT, how many refer to the third heaven (where God dwells) as opposed to the second heaven (the universe)? Can you name any? And what about eternity?

Most of the references to eternity, eternal, and everlasting are connected to God's everlasting covenant or His loving kindness. Can you name any which refer to eternal life? And what about life after

---

[12] See Allen Ross, "A Biblical Method for Salvation; A Case for Discontinuity" in *Continuity and Discontinuity: Perspectives on the Relationship Between the Old and New Testament*, ed. John S. Feinberg (Wheaton, Illinois, Crossway Publishing 1988).

[13] A gospel tract originally produced by Campus Crusade for Christ.

death in terms of resurrection? Where are the resurrection passages in the OT? Can you name any?

There are specific passages which deal with the third heaven, eternal life, and resurrection, but the very fact that the references do not jump out of our memory bank quickly tells us how little these subjects are emphasized in the OT. Again, the emphasis is longevity and blessing in the physical land of Israel (Ex 20:12).

Nevertheless, there are some important concepts included in the OT, even though they are not displayed on the front cover.

Immortal Spirit

Ecclesiastes 12:1-8 says:

> Remember also your Creator in the days of your youth, before the evil days come and the years draw near when you will say, "I have no delight in them"... For man goes to his eternal home while mourners go about in the street.... Remember Him before the silver cord is broken and the golden bowl is crushed, the pitcher by the well is shattered and the wheel at the cistern is crushed; then the dust will return to the earth as it was, and the spirit will return to God who gave it. "Vanity of vanities," says the Preacher, "all is vanity!"

It is important to realize that this passage says nothing about resurrection. At physical death, there is the separation between the body and the spirit. This passage says the body (dust) returns to the earth as it was, and the spirit returns to God who gave it. However, it does not say that the body and spirit are reunited. Well, then, does the OT teach a bodily resurrection?

Resurrection

The concept of a resurrection in the OT is challenged by many scholars. They claim this is an intertestamental concept found abundantly in the apocryphal and pseudepigraphal literature written between the OT and the NT, but not found in the OT. The references to the widow's son at Zarephath (1 Kings 17:17ff), the son of the Shunammite (2 Kings 4:32ff), and the man whose dead body was thrown into Elisha's grave were all accounts of resuscitation of a mortal body. What about an immortal, glorified body?

As already mentioned, Hebrews 11:19 tells us that Abraham believed that God would or could raise Isaac from the dead were the sacrifice to have taken place. But even this could have been a resuscitation back to his mortal body, since Abraham told his servant, "We will worship and return to you." But the translations of Enoch and Elijah had to be to immortal bodies, even though these men did not go through physical death and, hence, resurrection of their bodies. In Hannah's song (1 Sam 2:6), we probably get an explicit statement about resurrection, especially if Sheol is understood as the physical grave instead of hell: "The Lord kills and brings to life; he brings down to Sheol and raises up."

Another passage which speaks of resurrection of the mortal body is Job 19:25-27: "For I know that *my Redeemer lives*, and at last He will stand upon the earth; and after my skin has been thus destroyed, then *from my flesh I shall see God*, whom I shall see on my side, and my eyes shall behold, and not another. My heart faints within me." Apparently, Job was secure in that hope that after his death, his *gōēl* (redeemer) would raise his body up and vindicate him. The Hebrew expression וּמִבְּשָׂרִי (*ûmibbᵉśāriy*) is properly translated "from my flesh" by the NASB. After his skin has been destroyed, from his own eyes, Job shall see God standing on his behalf as his Redeemer.

Though David may have been referring to his own temporal security in Psalm 16:9-11 ("Therefore my heart is glad, and my soul rejoices; my body also dwells secure. For you will not give me up to Sheol, or let your godly one see the Pit. You will show me the path of life; in your presence there is fullness of joy, in your right hand are pleasures for evermore"), Acts 2:26-35 speaks of the ultimate fulfillment of this passage as the resurrection of Jesus Himself. Of course, it is not fair to read the NT "answers" back into the OT era.

The first question is to try to understand what the OT readers thought when reading the psalm. But we cannot completely rule out what David may have seen through the eyes of the Holy Spirit in writing this psalm. We know David functioned as a prophet (Ps 110:1) when it came to messianic visions.

For an explicit statement of the resurrection in the OT, there is no better passage than Isaiah 26:19: "Our dead shall live, *my dead bodies shall rise*. O dwellers in the dust, awake and sing for joy!" Here is a definite promise that the righteous will be raised from the dead. And this is also affirmed by Daniel 12:2-3, though it also includes the general resurrection of the unrighteous: "And many of *those who sleep in the dust of the earth shall awake*, some to everlasting life, and some to shame and everlasting contempt."

Though this discussion on resurrection does not tell us anything about how some will be raised unto everlasting life while others go into everlasting contempt, it does expand the concept of what OT salvation includes. That is, it does extend beyond this physical life on earth, even though that is not the primary emphasis we find in the OT. But this brings us back to the Big Picture. The Second Adam is to restore what the First Adam lost. Eve was promised Someone to crush the head of the serpent. Mankind awaited a Messiah. The salvation of all mankind depended on the coming of the Second Adam. How much does the OT reveal about the Messiah?

The Messiah

For centuries scholars viewed many of the psalms as "Messianic Psalms" which pointed directly to Jesus. With the advent of critical scholarship, men like H. Gunkel and S. Mowinckel used form criticism and comparative religion to remove the Messiah from these psalms. They were interpreted as "enthronement" psalms celebrating an annual festival in which the king reenacted the rites of fertility cults from which the Israelites developed their Yahweh cult.

According to this approach, the Israelites were looking to an ideal king who could deliver them from their problems, but when the monarchy proved to be such a colossal failure, the post-exilic remnant gave up any hope of an ideal king from the line of David. The High Priest supplanted the king. It was not until the intertestamental period that messianic expectation and fervor developed.

But this line of thinking was more prevalent at the end of the nineteenth century. During the first quarter of the twentieth century, renewed interest in the origins of messianic expectation was stirred up by W. O. E. Oesterley[14] and H. Gressmann[15] and the pre-exilic concept of a Messiah spread again among scholars. Even in the early monarchy, royal psalms such as Psalms 2, 72, and 110 were understood to be explicit descriptions of that ideal king who would rule forever, that is, the Messiah. As one king after another in the monarchy fell short of the ideal, and as the foreign oppression increased, so did the desire for a Messiah.

R. E. Clements traces the development of the messianic debate. He sees a messianic expectation in Psalm 110, but agrees that "the disappointments and frustrations with the present political order led to a strongly focused projection of this picture of the ideal king into the future."[16] He agrees that the messianic hope definitely picked up steam during and after the exile. Nevertheless, four passages form a solid foundation of OT messianic expectation: 2 Samuel 7, Psalms 2 and 110, and Daniel 9:26. Each of these plays a central role in OT soteriology, but a full explication of them is beyond the scope of our present survey.

Before we leave the subject of messianic expectation in the OT, there is a NT passage which is often overlooked which I believe adds significantly to our understanding. In Hebrews 11:26, Moses was said to be "esteeming the reproach of Christ greater riches than the treasures in Egypt; for he looked to the reward." Of course, the Greek word Χριστοῦ came from the Hebrew word "Messiah." However, it is important to recognize this expectation as pre-Davidic. Apparently, the Egyptians mocked their Jewish slaves because of their messianic

---

[14] W. O. E. Oesterley, The Evolution of the Messianic Idea. A Study in Comparative Religion (London: Pitman, 1908).

[15] H. Gressmann, *Der Messias*, Forschungen zur Religion und Literatur des Alten und Neuen Testaments, vol. 43 (Göttingen: Vandenhoeck & Ruprecht, 1929). See also S. Mowinckel, *He That Cometh*, G. W. Anderson trans. (New York: Abingdon, 1956), for his monumental work during the middle of the century and G. Van Groningen, *Messianic Revelation in the Old Testament* (Grand Rapids: Baker, 1990), toward the end of this century.

[16] R. E. Clements, "The Messianic Hope in the Old Testament," *Journal for the Study of the Old Testament* 43 (June-September 1989): 3-19. See also *Jesus the Messiah*, Bateman, Bock, Johnston.

expectation. It could only have come from the Jewish fathers (Abraham, Isaac, and Jacob) who had passed the messianic promise down to their children, who then brought it to Egypt (Joseph and his brothers).[17] To deny this is to deny the inspiration of the NT.

---

[17] See J. H. Sailhamer, "Is There a 'Biblical Jesus' of the Pentateuch" and "The Theme of Salvation in the Pentateuch," in *The Meaning of the Pentateuch* (Downers Grove, IL: InverVarsity, 2009), 460-536; 562-601.

The Cross of Jesus Christ

It was P. T. Forsyth who said, "Christ is to us just what his cross is. All that Christ was in heaven or on earth was put into what he did there... Christ, I repeat, is to us just what his cross is. You do not understand Christ till you understand his cross."[1] The cross involves much more than just soteriology, but since that is our subject, we will limit our discussion of the cross to its soteriological impact.

The Biblical Doctrine of Atonement

Christ's death on the cross is described in many ways in the NT. To get a better appreciation for it, we must consider it from several different angles.

Christ Our Substitute

In 1 Corinthians 15:3 we read, "Christ died for our sins," and in John 1:29 the Baptist tells us that Jesus is "the Lamb of God who takes away the sin of the world." In Isaiah 53:6-7 we find that the Suffering Servant was led "like a lamb to slaughter" on behalf of Israel, of whom the prophet said, "All of us like sheep have gone astray, each of us has turned to his own way; but the Lord has caused the iniquity of us all to fall on Him."

---

[1] P. T. Forsyth, *The Cruciality of the Cross* (1909), 44-45, cited in J. R. W. Stott, *The Cross of Christ* (Downers Grove, IL: InterVarsity, 1986), 43.

The Lamb of God

Although some have suggested that "Lamb of God" does not refer to the Passover lamb since that lamb is not described as a sin offering in Exodus 12, it is still necessary to recognize that the Passover lamb was viewed as a sacrifice to appease the wrath of God because of man's sin (Ex 12:27).

Peter understands Jesus to be this Passover lamb (1 Pet 1:18-19), and Paul openly says, "Christ our Passover also has been sacrificed" for us (1 Cor 5:7). H. D. McDonald comments on the connection between the Lamb of God and the atonement:

> There is a whole theology of the atonement in the title the Lamb of God. And it cannot be successfully denied that the words which refer the title to Christ, and at the same time ally it with his work of bearing away the sin of the world, give to both title and work a vicarious and sacrificial capacity. Only in a vicarious and sacrificial way can sin be taken away by the lamb.[2]

But just what is the purpose of this substitution? There are a number of biblical terms which help expand our horizons of understanding. One of these is propitiation.

Propitiation

Because of the liberalizing trend away from the view of God as angry and toward an all-loving and accepting God, some theologians have argued that the concept of propitiation has nothing to do with satisfying God's anger. Rather, they argue that the meaning of *hilastērion* is rooted in the expiation of sin. C. H. Dodd has pioneered this approach in his *The Bible and the Greeks* in which he analyzes atonement concepts in the OT Hebrew and the Greek of the LXX. His conclusion is that the terminology derived from the verb *hilaskomai* does not look toward God and the need to appease His anger as much as toward guilt and the need to atone for sin. He concludes that the

---

[2] H. D. McDonald, *The Atonement of the Death of Christ: In Faith, Revelation, and History* (Grand Rapids: Baker, 1985), 73.

words involved are not to be regarded "as conveying the sense of propitiating the Deity, but the sense of performing an act whereby guilt or defilement is removed."[3]

The problem here seems to be the offensive parallel with pagan religions wherein the practitioners seem to be involved in "celestial bribery or appeasement of capricious, vindictive wrath."[4] But, as G. E. Ladd points out in his *Theology*, the words involved uniformly mean "to propitiate" in Josephus and Philo as well as the Apostolic Fathers.[5] And L. Morris writes, "If the LXX translators and the New Testament writers evolved an entirely new meaning of the word group, it perished with them, and was not resurrected until our own day."[6]

In Hebrews 2:17 we read, "Therefore, in all things He had to be made like His brethren, that He might be a merciful and faithful high priest in things pertaining to God, to make propitiation for the sins of the people." W. H. Griffith Thomas aptly notes two sides to propitiation that "His justice could not overlook sin and His love could not be indifferent to the sinner, and so what His righteousness demanded, His love provided, and Christ, God's gift to the world, is 'the propitiation for our sins.'"[7] J. Stott agrees, "For in order to save us in such a way as to satisfy himself, God through Christ substituted himself for us. Divine love triumphed over divine wrath by divine self-sacrifice."[8]

And in 1 John 2:2 we read, "And He Himself is the propitiation for our sins, and not for ours only but also for the whole world." This is the classic verse which argues against limited atonement; unless one takes the non-Johannine view that this means "the world of the

---

[3] C. H. Dodd, *The Bible and the Greeks* (London: Hodder & Stoughton, 1935), 94.
[4] J. Gundry-Volf, "Expiation, Propitiation, Mercy Seat," in *The Dictionary of Paul and His Letters* (InterVarsity, 1993), 279.
[5] G. E. Ladd, *A Theology of the New Testament* (Grand Rapids, MI: Eerdmans Publishing, 1974), 471.
[6] L. Morris, "The Use of *Hilaskesthai* in Biblical Greek," *Evangelical Theological Quarterly* 62 (1950-51): 233. See also, L. Morris, *The Apostolic Preaching of the Cross*, (Grand Rapids, MI: Eerdmans Publishing, 1965).
[7] W. H. G. Thomas, *Hebrews*, 37.
[8] Stott, *Cross*, 159.

elect." The passage is designed to encourage those who have sinned not to hide it but to confess it, knowing that the wrath of God has been satisfied through the blood of His own Son, Jesus Christ. There is no need to pull away into darkness. Come back to the light. We have an Advocate with the Father. Just imagine a lawyer who not only works *pro bono* but also pays the fines and debts for his clients.

But John further elaborates on this incredible love of God in 1 John 4:10, "In this is love, not that *we* loved God, but that *He* loved us and sent His son to be the propitiation for our sins." The position of *we* and *He* is highly emphatic in the original. He is not only the propitiator, He is the initiator.[9] He scaled the wall of our sins to come to us. He faced the stubborn rejection of our rebellion but kept coming, though through a veil of tears. Oh, how we fear rejection! And because our love is not perfect, rejection (especially from those we love the most—wives, parents, children, friends) causes us to withdraw like turtles, protected by a hard outer shell of impassiveness. But later in this same chapter John writes, " . . . perfect love casts out fear, because fear involves torment. But he who fears has not been made perfect [mature] in love."[10] And the very next verse says, "We love Him because He first loved us."

The classic verse on propitiation is Romans 3:24-25a, "They are justified by His grace as a gift, through the redemption which is in Christ Jesus, whom God put forward as a *hilastērion* by His blood, to be received by faith" (my translation). It is not really clear whether the Greek word here is a noun or adjective. As a noun it is used in the Greek Bible (Heb 9:5 and Ex 25:17-20) for the "mercy seat," the place where the atoning blood was sprinkled in the Holy of Holies. But Paul does not use Hebrew imagery in Romans to any great extent, and the place of atoning for the Christian was the cross, a very public display

---

[9] See, Zane C. Hodges, *Romans: Deliverance From Wrath*, (Corinth, Texas, Grace Evangelical Society, 2013), 99-105.
[10] The Greek word for "restraint" (*kolasin*) is usually translated "torment," but Moulton and Milligan have demonstrated from the papyri that it means "restraint" as witnessed by its usage in horticulture for pruning trees and thus stunting their growth.

as opposed to the work of the high priest on the Day of Atonement. Therefore, Ladd's understanding of an adjectival translation may be best: " . . . whom God put forward as a propitiatory *sacrifice*."[11]

Summary and Conclusion

What the liberal theologians overlook is the personhood of God. It is precisely because He is the epitome of both righteousness and love that He can become so angry. His righteousness has been failed and His love deeply hurt by the sin of mankind to whom He graciously gave the gift of life, especially those He adopted into His forever family. But since God gave His own Son to satisfy His righteousness, His love endures and His anger passes. We read of this conflict within the character of God in Hosea 11:1-8 where God as a Father wrestles with His anger toward the sin of His son Israel and His overwhelming love. He says:

> "How can I give you up, Ephraim?
>> How can I hand you over, Israel?
> How can I treat you like Admah?
>> How can I make you like Zeboiim?
> My heart is changed within me; all my compassion is aroused.
>> I will not carry out my fierce anger, nor devastate Ephraim again.
> For I am God, and not man— the Holy One among you.
>> I will not come in wrath." (Hos 11:8-9)

Jeremiah 5:7-9 describes God's feelings toward His wayward children:

> "Why should I forgive you?
> Your children have forsaken me
> and sworn by gods that are not gods.
> I supplied all their needs,
>> yet they committed adultery
>> and thronged to the houses of prostitutes.

---

[11] Ladd, *Theology*, 472.

They are well-fed, lusty stallions,
    each neighing for another man's wife.
Should I not punish them for this?" declares the LORD.
    "Should I not avenge myself on such a nation as this?"

In commenting on this passage P. Yancey writes:

In reading the prophets, I cannot help envisioning a counselor with God as a client. The counselor gets out one stock sentence, "Tell me how you really feel," and then God takes over.

"I'll tell you how I feel! I feel like a rejected parent. I find a baby girl lying in a ditch, near death. I take her home and make her my daughter. I clean her, pay for her schooling, feed her. I dote on her, clothe her, hang jewelry on her. Then, one day she runs away. I hear reports of her debased life. When my name comes up, she curses me. "I'll tell you how I feel! I feel like a jilted lover. I found my lover thin and wasted, abused, but I brought her home and made her beauty shine. She is my precious one, the most beautiful woman in the world to me, and I lavish on her gifts and love. And yet she forsakes me. She pants after my best friends, my enemies—anyone. She stands by a highway and under every spreading tree and, worse than a prostitute, she pays people to have sex with her. I feel betrayed, abandoned, cuckolded."[12]

Yancey concludes by saying:

The powerful image of a jilted lover explains why in His speeches to the prophets, God seems to "change His mind" every few seconds. He is preparing to obliterate Israel—wait, now He is weeping, holding out open arms—no, He is sternly pronouncing judgment again. Those shifting moods seem hopelessly irrational, except to anyone who has been jilted by a lover.[13]

---

[12] P. Yancey, *Disappointment with God* (Grand Rapids: Zondervan, 1991), 96-97.
[13] Ibid., 98.

Perhaps Stott's observations are the best conclusion to this discussion on propitiation:

> So then, God himself is at the heart of our answer to all three questions about divine propitiation. It is God himself who in holy wrath needs to be propitiated, God himself who in holy love undertook to do the propitiating, and God himself who in the person of his Son died for the propitiation of our sins. Thus, God took his own loving initiative to appease his own righteous anger by bearing it his own self in his own Son when he took our place and died for us. There is no crudity here to evoke our ridicule, only the profundity of holy love to evoke our worship.[14]

Christ Our Redeemer

Another important way of looking at the atonement is through the analogy of purchasing a slave and setting him free. This imagery involves two word groups: *agorazō, exagorazō, lutroō,* and *apolutrōsis*.

Redemption

The idea behind the words *agorazō* and *exagorazō* is a change of ownership. In 1 Corinthians 6:19-20 we read, "You are not your own; you were *bought* with a price"; and in 1 Corinthians 7:22-23, "He who was free when called is a slave of Christ. You were *bought* with a price; do not become the slaves of men." Though Paul does not come right out and state the price which was paid, it can be none other than the death of Christ. The purchaser was God the Father. As such, those purchased now belong to Him.

In Galatians 3:13 the preposition *ex-* is prefixed to the main verb form: "Christ redeemed us from the curse of the law, having become a curse for us." This time the price paid is clearly mentioned. Christ died, and the substitutionary character of His death in our place is stated as well. To try to please God through the law system was a

---

[14] Stott, *Cross*, 175.

curse. We were not redeemed by His perfect fulfillment of the Law but by His becoming a curse for us, which He did by hanging on a tree. If ever there was a place to connect the active obedience (His life) of Christ to His passive obedience (His death) to accomplish our redemption, this is it. But Paul does not do that. The price paid was His hanging on the tree for us. In Galatians 4:4-5 Paul uses this compound word again to say, "God sent forth His Son . . . to redeem those who were under the law, in order that we might be adopted as sons." Here the freedom from the Law was for the stated purpose of adoption into God's forever-family.

R. Pyne observes that in Greek culture slaves were able to purchase their own freedom by depositing an appropriate amount of money with the cultic priests. Apollo was then thought to be the buyer or redeemer, but in name only. By contrast, in Christianity Jesus is truly the Redeemer in that He is the one and only one paying the price in this transaction.[15]

Ransom

The noun *lutron* is not found in Paul, but it does occur in Mark 10:45 where we read that the Son of Man came to give His life as a ransom in the place of many. G. E. Ladd observes, "In both classical and Hellenistic Greek this word group [*lutroō, apolutrōsis*] is used of the price paid to redeem something that is in pawn, of the money paid to ransom prisoners of war, and of money paid to purchase the freedom of a slave."[16] And the same is true in the LXX.

Paul does, however, use the verb (*lutroō*) in Titus 2:14 where he says that "Christ gave Himself to redeem us from all iniquity." The ransom price is clear: It is Himself. Peter uses the same verb in 1 Peter 1:18-19 where the ransom price is clearly the precious blood of Christ. But Paul's favorite word is *apolutrōsis*, a rare word outside the NT that emphasizes the *cost* of redemption (Rom 3:24; 1 Cor 1:30;

---

[15] R. Pyne, "Notes," 53-54. Also see Morris, *Apostolic Preaching of the Cross*, 11-18.
[16] Ladd, *Theology*, 474. He also references F. Büchsel, *TDNT* 4:340 and A. Deissmann, *Light from the Ancient East*, 331f.

Eph 1:7; Col 1:14). And in 1 Timothy 2:6, we have the very significant compound noun *antilutron* where Christ "gave Himself as a *ransom* for all." The prefix *anti-* strongly supports substitutionary atonement.

The complementarity of these word groups is this: the "ransom" words emphasize that from which we were bought, that is sin and death, while the "redemption" words emphasize the change of ownership. L. Morris well summarizes the combined significance of both word groups:

1. The state of sin out of which humanity is to be redeemed. This is likened to a slavery that humankind cannot break, so redemption involves intervention from an outside person who pays the price human beings cannot pay.
2. The price that is paid. The payment of a price is a necessary element in the redemption idea, and Christ has paid the price of our redemption.
3. The resultant state of the believer. This is expressed in a paradox. We are redeemed to freedom, as children of God; but this freedom means slavery to God. The whole point of this redemption is that sin no longer has dominion. The redeemed are those saved to do the will of their Master.[17]

Christ Our Peace

Reconciliation

Reconciliation and peace go hand in hand. Both of these issue or result from our justification. Our forensic justification before God is His declaration of our righteousness or, put negatively, our acquittal of guilt. But reconciliation and peace deal with fellowship. Justification establishes our relationship, while reconciliation establishes our fellowship.

Perhaps the best passage that puts all three concepts together is

---

[17] L. Morris, *Apostolic Preaching of the Cross* (London: Tyndale, 2000), 58-59.

Romans 5:1-11. As a result of our justification, Paul says, we have *peace* with God through our Lord Jesus Christ. And because of this peace we have open access to God and His grace. And this peace also brings with it a present experience of His love which is poured out in our hearts through the Holy Spirit.

In order to underscore how great this love of God for us is, Paul uses three words to describe our state of alienation from God before we became His children. In v. 6 Paul describes us as "ungodly." Then in v. 8, he calls us "sinners." Then in v. 10, he claims we were God's "enemies." There is a progression here. To be ungodly is to lack God's character. To be a sinner is to miss the mark. But to be His enemy is to be in active rebellion against Him.

But as justified people, our past alienation has been taken away. Now we are reconciled (vv. 10-11). And Paul's emphasis here is on our present blessings in this life. If God justified us and reconciled us to Himself when we were His enemies, how much more will He do for us now that we are His children?

And because we have been reconciled to God, He has given to us the ministry of reconciliation: 2 Corinthians 5:18-20. We actually preach reconciliation to the world. And not only is reconciliation to God available to the world, but peace with each other is available through Him as well.

Peace

In Ephesians 2:13-18 Christ Himself is called our peace, but the peace Paul refers to here is the reconciliation of Jews and Gentiles. The enmity between them existed because of the Law, which he describes as a barrier, a dividing wall. "And He came and preached peace to you who were afar off and to those who were near. For through Him we both have access by one Spirit to the Father" (2:17-18).

Christ Our Sanctifier

Another aspect of the finished work of Christ is our sanctification. In Hebrews 10:10 we read, "By that will we have been sanctified through the offering of the body of Jesus Christ *once for all.*" The word of interest here is "sanctified" (ἡγιασμένοι, *hēgiasmenoi*), which is a perfect passive participle used in a periphrastic construction. The upshot of all this is that our sanctification here is spoken of as a finished product. The perfect tense speaks of action completed in the past with results lasting up to the present. And when it is used in the periphrastic construction, the point at issue is made emphatic; that is, the writer to the Hebrews is emphasizing the fact that at the cross *we were made perfectly holy*. The use of "once" (*ephapax*) also underscores the time and place when this work of sanctification was completed, that is, at the cross.

Just a few verses later the writer to the Hebrews uses this word for sanctification in the present tense. He says, "For by one offering He has perfected forever those who are being sanctified." This time the word for "sanctified" is the same Greek word, but in a different tense: ἁγιαζομένους (*hagiazomenous*), a present passive participle. In this verse (Heb 10:14), the author uses the perfect tense for "perfected" τετελείωκεν (*teteleiōken*), a verb we have seen before in reference to Christian maturity (Jas 2:22, where Abraham's faith was made complete or mature by his works, namely, the preparation to sacrifice Isaac). The meaning of this verb in the perfect is similar to that of the perfect tense of "sanctified." It is viewed as a completed action in the past, accomplished at the cross, once for all eternity: μιᾷ γὰρ προσφορᾷ τετελείωκεν εἰς τὸ διηνεκὲς τοὺς ἁγιαζομένους (*mia gar prosphora teteleiōken eis to diēnekes tous hagiazomenous*), "by one sacrifice . . . forever. . . ."

There is a noteworthy contrast between verses ten and fourteen of two different tenses for the same verb. In v. 10 our sanctification is completed at the cross, but in v. 14 it appears to be an ongoing process. So, here in one passage we find a beautiful statement of two incontrovertible truths: our *position* and our *condition* "in Christ." In our position we are seen as already perfectly holy; but in our present condition our holiness is still an action in process. Both are true, but how can they be true at the same time?

This is what Albert Schweitzer called the "mysticism of Paul." Of course, we are looking at Hebrews, but the same truth is taught in Paul. This same perfect passive participle ἡγιασμένοις is used in 1 Corinthians 1:2 of the saints at Corinth. The apostle says they are completely sanctified, even though we know from later in the letter that many of them are far from holy in their walk. Paul resolves the apparent contradiction when he says in v. 2 that their completed sanctification is "in Christ Jesus." That is a statement of their *position* (see Eph 1:3ff and Rom 6:1-10). They have been baptized into Christ and His crucifixion on the cross. That is their new position after believing in Him. Just that. They are *in Him*. And since they are "in Him," everywhere He went from the cross forward, they went also. That is why the apostle can say we believers are seated with Him in heavenly places at the right hand of the Father (Eph 2:6; Col 3: 1).

So right now, in Him, we are completely holy. But as the sanctifying process continues in our present walk, we realize that we are not yet perfectly holy in our *condition*. This is what theologians call the *nun noch nicht* or the "already, not yet" of eschatology. We saw this in Hebrews 1:13-2:14. Right now as He is seated at the right hand of the Father, Christ has defeated His enemies. But they are not completely put out of business. The devil and death still do their nasty work, not to be put out of commission until the end of the Millennium. They are defeated "now" but also "not yet." And so we are sanctified "now" but also "not yet." See Hebrews 2:8 where you actually read the words "now . . . not yet."

Truly, this must seem pretty mystical, as Schweitzer observed. Nevertheless, understanding this mysticism is crucial to the victorious Christian life. Paul argues for our victory based on our position. For us to have victory over even the discouragement of our defeats in our wrestling with sin, we must come back to the basic truths of who we really are in Christ. As we focus on our position, slowly but surely our condition conforms to our position. But as we focus on our miserable condition, it only gets worse. "As a man thinks in his heart, so is he." As I think about my sinfulness I become more sinful. As I think about my Savior and who I am in Him, I become more like Him. Holding these two truths simultaneously in tension brings the abundant life.

As Paul turns away from his deep theology in Colossians 1-2 to the application of this theology in Colossians 3—4, he appeals to his readers to *set their affections on things above, not on things on the earth* (τὰ ἄνω φρονεῖτε μὴ τὰ ἐπὶ τῆς γῆς). In the words of the hymn writer:

Turn your eyes upon Jesus;
Look full in His wonderful face.
And the things of earth will grow strangely dim,
In the light of His glory and grace.

Summary

And so, we can agree with Peter when he says we "have been given all things which pertain to life and godliness" (2 Pet 1:3). At the cross we have been given everything we need for life eternal and life abundant.

The Extent of the Atonement

The discussion on the extent of the atonement usually centers on whether Christ died for the entire human race or just the elect.[18] The origin of the debate is often credited to Theodore Beza, successor to John Calvin at the Geneva Academy, who taught that Christ died only for the elect. Moïse Amyraut[19] studied under Beza at the Geneva Academy and took exception to this teaching (which has become known as "Limited Atonement" or "Particular Redemption"). He was a champion of "Unlimited Atonement," and his teaching has become known as Amyraldianism. His followers accepted all points of the Synod of Dort except Limited Atonement. Thus, they were Four Point Calvinists. Lewis Sperry Chafer has been labeled an Amyraldian since it has been said that he was a "Four Point Calvinist," as have been many professors at Dallas Theological Seminary. They reject the teaching of Limited Atonement while accepting the other four points: Total Depravity, Unconditional Election, Irresistible Grace, and Perseverance of the Saints, although they do not define a couple of these points as do the Dortian Calvinists.

---

[18] The most thorough treatment to this topic to date is found in, David L. Allen, *The Extent of the Atonement: A Historical and Critical Review*, (Nashville, Tennessee: B&H Academic, 2016).

[19] B. G. Armstrong, *Calvinism and the Amyraut Heresy* (Madison, WI: University of Wisconsin Press, 1969).

The first to champion limited atonement, however, was Augustine. The teaching is a direct overflow of his fatalistic view of predestination. Though Augustine is often presented as asymmetrical on predestination (God chose some to go to heaven and passed over others to go to hell before the foundation of the world), his writings reveal otherwise. There are many places where Augustine sets forth his fatalistic understanding of "Double Predestination" (God chose some to go the heaven and chose the rest to go to hell before anyone was created). In *Enchiridion* 100, Augustine wrote:

> These are the great works of the Lord, sought out according to all His pleasure, and so wisely sought out, that when the intelligent creation, both angelic and human, sinned, doing not His will but their own, He used the very will of the creature which was working in opposition to the Creator's will as an instrument for carrying out His will, the supremely Good thus turning to good account even what is evil, to the condemnation of those whom in His justice He has predestined to punishment, and to the salvation of those whom in His mercy He has predestined to grace [emphasis mine].

Again, he echoes his view of Christian fatalism in his writings *On the Soul* (IV.16):

> That owing to one man all pass into condemnation who are born of Adam, unless they are born again in Christ, even as he has appointed them to be regenerated, before they die in the body, whom He predestinated to everlasting life, as the most merciful bestower of grace; while to those whom He has predestinated to eternal death, He is also the most righteous awarder of punishment not only on account of the sins which they add in the indulgence of their own will, but also because of their original sin, even if, as in the case of infants, they add nothing thereto. Now this is my definite view on that question, so that the hidden things of God may keep their secret, without impairing my own faith.

This view of fatalism was birthed by Augustine's novel understanding of original sin and baptismal regeneration of infants. He went against three hundred plus years of orthodoxy when he taught that Rom 5:12 meant that infants not only inherited the sin nature (*vitium*) of Adam but also the guilt (*reatus*) of Adam's sin, thus making every infant worthy of condemnation to hell. The addition of *reatus* to *vitium* was new. In the mind of Augustine it was necessary to combat the Pelagians, who taught the innocence of new-born babes. They allowed water baptism of infants but had no logical reason for doing so, since they did not believe an infant came into the world with the guilt of sin. Augustine justified infant baptism with *reatus*. He argued the *total inability* of infants since they resist water baptism and cannot possibly exercise their human will. God overcomes these problems (the guilt of sin and the total inability of the infant) with water baptism. The baptism is the "laver of regeneration" which washes away the guilt of sin and at the same time rebirths the infant so it is no longer incapable of faith or exercise of its human will.[20] But it was the total inability of the infant which necessitated double predestination. After all, if the child cannot will, then God must do it for him. And all of this is inextricably linked to their practice of baptizing infants.

So, back to Limited Atonement. If God predetermined who would go to heaven and who would go to hell before the creation of mankind, then it only stands to reason that Christ died only for those who would go to heaven—or so goes the argument. This came straight from Augustine's teaching on double predestination. In his words (*Homily* 1, 8 [on 1 Jn 1:1-2:11] in Vol VIII, 265-66),

> but he [the Apostle] knew that there would be some [the Donatists] who would set themselves apart, saying, "Lo, here is Christ, or, lo, there!" trying to show that he who purchased the whole is only in

---

[20] See K. Wilson's work on Augustine and *reatus* in "The Mortal Wound to the Anthropological *Regula Fidei*: Formation, Fall, and Free Will of Mankind from Clement of Rome through Augustine" (unpublished masters thesis, Golden Gate Seminary, 2006).

part. Therefore, he adds at once; "not only of our sins, but of the sins of the whole world." ... Think, brethren, what that means. Surely we are pointed to the Church in all nations, the Church throughout the whole World.

Hence, we get the Reformed teaching that references in John to "the world" really refer to the "world of the elect."[21] A contemporary of Augustine, Prosper of Aquitaine, repeated this teaching in his opposition to the Pelagians: "The Savior was not crucified for the redemption of the entire world."[22]

These men were followed by Peter Lombard (*The Four Sentences*). He argued for the sufficiency of Christ's death for the whole of mankind, but the efficiency for the elect only.[23] No one wrote again about the subject until Calvin, and there is some debate about his position. Writers like Brian Armstrong see a wide gulf between John Calvin and the Calvinism represented at the Synod of Dort; Roger Nicole sees more of a continuum between Calvin and Dort.[24]

Though we may not be able to ascertain Calvin's exact position on the subject, since he never really discussed it directly, there is no doubt where his successor at Geneva stood. As we will document later, Theodore Beza combined the Neo-Platonism of Augustine with Aristotelian logic to do his best to acquit God of being the morally efficient cause of evil. He was driven to such a defense by the double predestination taught to him by John Calvin. Beza also advocated double predestination and championed what we call supralapsarianism (also taught to him by Calvin),[25] the view that God predestined some to heaven and the rest to hell before his decision to create mankind or

---

[21] W. R. Godfrey, "Reformed Thought on the Extent of the Atonement to 1618," *Westminster Theological Journal* 37:2 (Winter): 134.
[22] Prosper of Aquitaine, Pro Augustino calumniantium, Article 9. See also Pro Augustino responsiones ad capitula obiectionum Vincentianarum, Article 1.
[23] P. Lombard, *Libri quatuor seutentiarum*, Vol. 192, column 799.
[24] R. Nicole, *Moyse Amyraut* (1596-1664) and the *Controversy on Universal Grace, First Phase* (1634-1637), Oh. D. Dissertation, Harvard University, 1966.
[25] Calvin, *Institutes*, III, 21.5.

for Christ to die for fallen man. Supra = *above*, or in this case *before*; lapse = *fall*. So, before the Fall of mankind, God decreed who would go to heaven and who would go to hell. Again, it is important to see the linkage between double predestination and limited atonement. After all, if God decided who would go to heaven and who would go to hell before He created mankind and before anyone fell and before the decree was made for Christ to die, then His death was only for the benefit of those elected to go to heaven.

Though Beza rejected the distinction of *sufficient* from *efficient*, the majority of Reformed theologians did not.[26] Especially significant was William Perkins who wrote:

> The potential efficacy is, whereby the price is in itself sufficient to redeem every one without exception from his sin, albeit there were a thousand worlds of men. But if we consider that actual efficacy, the price is payd in the counsel of God, . . . only for those which are elected and predestinated.[27]

By the time of Dort (1619) the vast majority of Reformed theologians held to the distinction between the sufficiency of Christ's death and its efficiency only for the elect. All of which really begs the question: why even have such a discussion on the extent of the atonement to begin with, if double predestination is an erroneous doctrine? To solve this dilemma, the discussion evolved into the order of God's decrees. Supralapsarianism claims that God decreed whom He would send to heaven and whom He would send to hell before His decree to create both groups of people. Then came His decree to permit the Fall and finally His decree to provide salvation only for the elect.

Finding this approach somewhat repugnant (to say the least), some tried to soften this harsh portrait of God by making His decree to create humans first; then came the decree to permit the Fall, the

---

[26] Godfrey, "Reformed Thought," 144.
[27] W. Perkins, *The Works of that Famous and Worthy Minister of Christ in the University of Cambridge*, M. William Perkins, vol. 2 (London, 1631), 609.

decree to predestine some for heaven and predestine others for hell,[28] and finally to provide salvation only for the elect. We call this *infralapsarianism*, the "infra" part meaning "below" or "after." In other words, the predestination decree came *after* the Fall, not before it (as in supralapsarianism). A contrasting chart would look something like this:

SUPRALAPSARIANISM	INFRALAPSARIANISM
1. God's decree to predetermine who goes to heaven and who goes to hell.	1. God's decree to create human beings.
2. God's decree to create both groups.	2. God's decree to permit the Fall.
3. God's decree to permit the Fall.	3. God's decree to predetermine who goes to heaven and who goes to hell.
4. God's decree to provide salvation only for those He sends to heaven.	4. God's decree to provide salvation only for those He sends to heaven.

It will be observed that both of these systems teach limited atonement, a teaching rejected by a large proportion of Western Christianity. Arminius reacted to the predestinarian teaching of orthodox Calvinism. When he died in 1609, his followers met and constructed their Remonstrance in five propositions. The second proposition dealt with the extent of the atonement, affirming

> That in agreement with this Jesus Christ the Savior of the world died for all men and for every man, so that he merited reconciliation and

---

[28] Most who are familiar with the literature on the decrees will argue against double predestination as a necessary part of either supralapsarianism or infralapsarianism. They are correct. However, double predestination was an integral part of Augustine's theology, and limited atonement was a resulting corollary. Though we realize that most have steered away from double predestination for obvious reasons, we are trying to be straightforward with the writings of Augustine, Gottschalk, Calvin, Beza, and Perkins, all of whom were supralapsarian and double predestinarian.

forgiveness of sins for all through the death of the cross; yet so that no one actually enjoys this forgiveness of sins except the believer— also, according to the word of the gospel of John 3:16, "God so loved the world that he gave his only begotten Son that whosoever believes in him shall not perish but have eternal life." And in the first epistle of John 2:2, "He is the propitiation for our sins; and not only for ours, but also for the sins of the whole world."

So here are the primary pillars of Arminianism: 1) Christ died with saving intention for all; 2) There is a sharp distinction between the reconciliation accomplished at the cross and the application of that reconciliation, the condition of which is a response of faith. The atonement here is unlimited. First came God's decree to create mankind. God had foreknowledge that man would fall, but He did not decree the Fall. He did decree to provide salvation for all, and He did decree to save all who would believe. Their table would look like this:

ARMINIANISM
1. God decrees to create man with free will.
2. God knows that man will fall.
3, God decrees to provide salvation for all.
4. God decrees to save all who will believe.

Observe that there is no predestination involved in any of these decrees. A Contra-Remonstrant position soon developed which contained eighty-five pages on the extent of the atonement, mostly upholding the *sufficient* versus *efficient* point of view. Crucial to the Remonstrant position was the decree of Christ to die before the decree of God to elect. This order ensured the death of Christ for all men. They claimed that their doctrine was not novel at all, but a position supported by Luther, Calvin, and Bullinger.[29]

This, then, is the background leading up to the Synod of Dort, out

---

[29] Godfrey, "Reformed Thought," 159.

of which developed the Five Points of Calvinism. The Synod (1618-19) took a more strict approach to the extent of the atonement than the Contra-Remonstrants and wished to reaffirm that Christ died only for believers. The Synod insisted that He died for the elect, making sure that the connection between predestination and the extent of the atonement remained intact.

After the Synod of Dort came the position of Moïse Amyraut (d. 1664), who wanted to maintain orthodox Calvinism with an adjustment to the extent of the atonement. His teachings might be summarized as follows:

AMARYLDINISM
1. God's decree to create man human beings.
2. God's decree to permit the fall.
3. God's decree to provide salvation sufficient for all.
4. God's decree to elect some for heaven and pass by others.

Amyraut was a strange mix of contradictions. He was as intent on defending John Calvin and his teachings as he was on contending against orthodox Calvinism (Beza and his followers). He was convinced that Beza went awry with his overemphasis on predestination as a foundation for theology, whereas Calvin thought the doctrine was a great mystery we should studiously avoid tackling.

Amyraut was convinced the sacrifice of Christ was universal in scope and intent and that God willed the salvation of all men. But at the same time he believed God predestined only a few to enjoy this salvation. And he refused to subject these two doctrines to the judgment of reason. Like his champion, whenever something in the Bible smacked of contradiction, Amyraut appealed to mystery as his out. Man's reason is not capable of understanding the ways of God; reason must bow to revelation. For him, faith is a condition for election, but election is the cause of faith. If this does not make much sense, no matter—it is just a mystery.[30]

---

[30] Armstrong, *Calvinism*, 215-18.

Truly, Amyraut sounds like he is lip-synching Calvin. What does not appear in Amyraut's writings is any realization that Calvin was supralapsarian. If Amyraut were truly returning to Calvin, he would also have been a proponent of limited atonement, a direct outgrowth of supralapsarianism. But enough background on the debate. What are the primary arguments in favor of limited atonement?

Arguments for Limited Atonement

God's Intent

The argument here is that the purpose of Christ's mission was to save the elect. His mission could not fail. He did not come to make salvation *possible* for all men. He came to make it *actual* for the elect. Arthur Pink tells us what he thinks about the *possible* approach when he writes:

> The story of the vast majority is that Christ came here to make salvation possible for sinners: he has done His part, now they must do theirs. To reduce the wondrous, finished, and glorious work of Christ to a merely making salvation possible is most dishonoring and insulting to Him.[31]

The problem with arguing over whether Christ came to die for all men or just those elected to go to heaven narrows the focus of the atonement to men. It is an anthropocentric view of the atonement, whether one argues for limited or unlimited atonement. We would argue that the intent or purpose for the atonement goes far beyond the anthropocentric to the theocentric. In fact, His entire plan for human history is theocentric. Satan's rebellion was scandalous. He called God's character into question, namely, is God sovereign, and is God worthy of being loved? God's plan for man (which includes the atonement) answers these questions.

---

[31] A. W. Pink, *The Satisfaction of Christ* (Grand Rapids: Zondervan, 1955), 110.

The sins of mankind open a new wound to God's character. Is He just? Rom 3:25-26 says (emphasis added),

> whom [Jesus Christ] God set forth as a propitiation by His blood . . . to demonstrate His righteousness, because in His forbearance God had passed over the sins that were previously committed, to demonstrate at the present time His righteousness, that He might be just and the justifier of the one who has faith in Jesus.

If we understand this passage correctly, the salvation of the elect was a secondary purpose or intent. In fact, we will be so bold as to claim that if no human being ever exercised saving faith, God would still have become man and died on the cross. Why? To silence the scandal that impugned God's character. Christ would have come and died, if for no other reason than to prove that God is just. That was His primary reason for dying—it was to defend His Father's character.

Trying to narrow God's purpose for the atonement, to the saving of the elect, falls far short of the biblical evidence. And if one bar on the cross proves to the angels and the world of mankind the justice of God, then the other proves His love as well. To limit His love to the "world of the elect" (Jn 3:16) is just as scandalous. As Dave Hunt has queried, *What Love is This?*[32]

The Efficacy of the Cross

Both sides of the debate believe that Christ's death was sufficient to pay for the sins of the entire world of mankind. Both sides also believe that His death was efficient only for the elect who will go to heaven. But "particular redemptionists" insist that passages like "By one offering He has perfected forever those who are being sanctified" (Heb 10:14) prove that the penalty for sin can only be paid once. In other words, if Christ paid the penalty for sin once, and God is satisfied (propitiation), why would condemned sinners have to pay the penalty again? That would be divine double jeopardy. Therefore, Christ's death did not pay the penalty for the non-elect; otherwise,

---

[32] D. Hunt, *What Love is This?* (Bend, OR: The Berean Call, 2004).

their penalty would be paid twice (once by Christ and once by the condemned sinner).

But is this not precisely the point? A condemned man on death row might have someone offer to and actually die in his place. But unless the man believes this outrageous act on his behalf has actually been accomplished, he will languish in jail until his own execution is at hand. So, the condemned sinner must believe what Christ has accomplished for him or he will never enjoy its benefits.

Arguments for Unlimited Atonement

The best arguments for Unlimited Atonement are based on two biblical passages. Anyone familiar with these should have all they need for a working understanding.

First John 2:1-2

Here we read that Jesus was the propitiation "for our sins, and not for ours only but also for the whole world." The obvious distinction between "ours" and "the whole world" makes it difficult to say that the death of Christ did not actually have an effect on the sins of the whole world. Some might have us believe that the first person plural in 1 John 1-2 refers only to John and the rest of the apostles. But in 1 John 2:1 the addressees are "my little children." This is immediately followed by the "we" of 1 John 2:2. To excise the little children of verse one from the "we" of verse two does violence to the grammar.

Others argue that "the whole world" designates only "the world of the elect." This is the same argument that is used for "the world" in John 3:16 by those who hold to Limited Atonement. However, to import "the elect" into the world in this passage or other Johannine passages is one of the more clear examples of eisegesis, or reading one's theology into the text. Again, "the whole world" of unbelievers is clearly distinguished from "the little children" (denoted by the pronoun "ours") whose sins are forgiven (1 Jn 2:1-2). Moreover, in John 17:6 we find Jesus praying for the "men You have given Me *out of* the world." Surely there is a distinction here between the men given to Christ and the world. We find the same distinction again in v. 9. Yet, this is the same author who penned John 3:16. You cannot have it both ways: "world of the elect" (in Jn 3:16) and "world of the non-elect" (Jn 17:6, 9).

Why would Dortian Calvinists go to such lengths to support Limited Atonement? Because many, if not most, of them realize that Five Point Calvinism is an air-tight system with each point evolving out of the point before it. If just one of the points fails, the entire system fails. The points are mutually dependent, not isolated and standing on their individual merits like the attributes of God.

Second Peter 2:1

Here we have a passage that speaks of false teachers who are "bought." The word for "bought" (*agōrazō*) is the same as in 1 Corinthians 6:19-20; 7:22-23 and is translated "redeemed" in Revelation 5:9; 14:3, 4. Now certainly, some of the elect can drift into false teaching. That is one of the warnings in near context (2 Pet 2:18-22).[33] And once one has been seduced by false teaching, he can become a false teacher. If the doctrine of eternal security is true, and we believe it is, then this false teacher is one of the elect. But is that the case with the false teachers of 2 Peter 2:1?

One could argue that the false teachers of 2 Peter 2:1 are elect people who were led astray and became false teachers were it not for 2 Peter 2:4ff. Here, he uses three analogies to describe the future fate of these false teachers: the fallen angels, the impious men of Noah's day, and Sodom and Gomorrah. The language and the parallels are too gruesome to describe a fate any less than eternal condemnation. So, if Peter is comparing these false teachers of verse one to the angels and people judged in verses four and following, then these false teachers are certainly not elect for heaven. Nevertheless, these false teachers were "bought" (the verb is an aorist participle, the action of which

---

[33] The plain reading of the text seems to indicate that these are genuine believers. See Jerome H. Neyrey, *The Anchor Bible: 2 Peter, Jude*, (New York, Doubleday Books, 2004) 221. Also see Thomas Schreiner, *The New American Commentary; 1,2 Peter, Jude*, (Nashville, Tennessee, Broadman & Holman Publishers, 2003) 360-364 for a good defense of this view although in the end he opts for the "phenomenological" believer view on page 364.

precedes the action of the verb on which it depends, "denying") at the cross.

This passage is such an embarrassment to Limited Atonement that many authors trying to defend Limited Atonement simply skip it in their defense.[34] Even if we were to argue that 2 Peter 2:1 speaks of false teachers who are elect, it would still contradict the fifth point of Calvin—the perseverance of the saints. Far easier just to opt for Unlimited Atonement.

Summary

This brief discussion is not intended to solve the atonement debate but is designed as an introduction to the issues. Is it a worthwhile debate? One wonders. It would certainly seem worthwhile to those who want to preserve the Five Points of Dortian Calvinism. However, as we have already mentioned, if one link in that chain is broken, the whole chain is broken.

But for those whose theology is not inextricably linked to Dortian Calvinism, it should be enough to say that Christ's death is *sufficient* to pay for the sins of the whole world of mankind, but *efficient* only for those who believe.

---

[34] D. N. Steele and C. C. Thomas, *The Five Points of Calvinism: Defined, Defended, Documented* (Philadelphia: Presbyterian & Reformed, 1963), 38-47; E. H. Palmer, *The Five Points of Calvinism* (Grand Rapids: Baker, 1972), 41-55.

Justification

There may be no doctrine more pivotal for church history than justification. The divergence of the Reformers from the RCC over this doctrine sealed the rift in the church for nearly five centuries. J. Pelikan calls justification "the chief doctrine of Christianity and the chief point of difference separating Protestantism and Roman Catholicism."[1] In our overview of this doctrine, we want to account for the primary schools of thought on the subject and what we understand to be the biblical teaching. Along the way, we want to address a number of thorny issues surrounding this doctrine.[2] For example, is justification something that occurs instantaneously, or is it a process occurring over a period of time? Is this a divine act by which God "declares" a person righteous or a process by which He "makes" them righteous? These questions and many more need addressing. But first of all, let us examine the various major schools of thought.

---

[1] J. Pelikan, *The Christian Tradition: A History of the Development of Doctrine*, 5 vols. (Chicago: University of Chicago Press, 1971-89), 4:139.

[2] For a complete summary of the various positions see, *Justification: Five Views*, eds. James Beilby & Paul Rhodes Eddy (Downers Grove, IL: InterVarsity Press, 2011). Also see N.T. Wright, *Justification: God's Plan and Paul's Vision* (Downers Grove, IL: InterVarsity Press., 2009) and John Piper, *The Future of Justification: A Response to N.T. Wright* (Wheaton, IL: Crossway Books, 2007).

Approaches

The Roman Catholic Church

Within sixty years of the death of Christ the church had been thoroughly Galatianized. Salvation by works was the prevailing doctrine of the day and remained so until Augustine. As we shall see, though he retained many of the doctrines of the traditional church of his era (like infant baptism), he was unique in his battle for grace. And though he may have espoused teachings which might prove to be the enemy of grace, in his own mind he battled against any slight flavor of Pelagian doctrine.

Unfortunately, Augustine spoke with great authority without having any facility in the original languages. His native tongue was Latin. The Koine Greek of the NT had been out of vogue for more than a century. When he tried to explain the meaning of the Greek verb *dikaioō*, he said it meant "to make righteous."[3] This understanding was incorporated into the doctrine of the RCC. The basic understanding was that justification was an act whereby God "infused" the character of Christ into the sinner at water baptism. However, the act was not completed at that point. "We are justified, but righteousness itself grows as we go forward."[4]

Through this life-long process, Augustine thought God could transform the inner man from one of lust to one of love. He believed the good works of a person were meritorious, but like so many who admit to such a view, he taught at the same time that all meritorious works of man were the product of the grace of God (Phil. 2:13—God gives believer the desire and the power to do his will).[5] He also

---

[3] Augustine, On the Spirit and the Letter, 45.
[4] Idem, *Sermon*, 158.5.
[5] Idem, *Letter*, 194.14. Modern theologians like Alan Stanley use Phil. 2:12-13 as their proof text to prove that works are a requirement for entrance to heaven, but they are not meritorious since God does these works through the believer. In fact, he separates between works done by the Spirit and works done by the flesh. The former are required for eternal life, but the latter are rejected. In Free Grace theology we would say works done by the Spirit will be rewarded, but those

believed that if the love of God were perfected in this life, a person would go directly to heaven without spending any time in purgatory. If such perfection were not reached, the sufferings of purgatory were necessary to prepare one for heaven.[6]

Under the umbrella of justification, Augustine also included the sub-doctrines of regeneration and sanctification.[7] To our way of thinking, this system contains obvious contradictions, but it all made sense to Augustine. Of course, since one was not justified instantaneously, he could not know that he was justified until he died. Augustine distinguished between the "saved" and the "elect." The saved are those who appear to have the fruits of the elect, but at some point before death, they fall away, thus proving they never were elect at all. And again, Augustine had the intellectual honesty to admit that such a system would not allow one to know he was elect until he died. The RCC adopted Augustine's doctrine wholesale and has perpetuated it to the present day. At the strategic Council of Trent (1545-63), the RCC responded to the doctrines of the Reformers. And because this council defined justification as the process of becoming righteous, justification must be augmented if one wanted to get to heaven.[8] A mortal sin could cancel out any accrued justification, but one could be restored through penance. And the RCC continued in Augustine's belief that it is not possible to know if one is going to heaven before death: "No one can know with the certitude of faith, which cannot admit of any error, that he has obtained God's grace."[9] The best one can attain to in this life is hope mixed with "fear and apprehension." God rewards the good works of His saints, even though He is the

---

done by the flesh will not be rewarded. What we treat as a reward issue Stanley treats as an entrance to the kingdom of God issue (Alan P. Stanley, *Salvation is More Complicated than You think: A Study on the Teachings of Jesus* (Authentic, 2007), Location 835 of 2705 (Kindle).

[6] Idem, *City of God*, XX.25; XXI.13, 16, 26.

[7] A. E. McGrath, *Iustitia Dei*, 2 vols. (Cambridge: Cambridge University Press, 1986-87), 1:60; L. Berkhof, *Christian Faith* (Grand Rapids: Eerdmans, 1979), 435.

[8] Council of Trent, X.

[9] Ibid., IX.

power source behind these works, and these rewards help pry open the gates of heaven.[10]

The Council of Trent put a curse on anyone who asserted that justification is not fostered by good works.[11] A further curse was put on anyone who believed good works were not meritorious for entrance to heaven.[12] The concept of "imputed" righteousness was believed to be a serious threat to moral effort. B. Demarest sums up the RCC approach when he says:

> Traditional Roman Catholics, in other words, trust in God's infusion of a new nature and plead the worth of their God-enabled works. Justification in Catholic theology is a comprehensive term that includes, among other things, what Protestants understand by regeneration and sanctification. For Rome, justification is not divine-wise an objective pronouncement of righteousness, but is human-wise a lifelong process of becoming righteous.[13]

Before leaving the views of the RCC, we would be remiss if we did not mention their claim that Mary the Blessed Virgin contributed "her share to the justification of the human race beginning with herself and extending to everyone ever justified."[14] Because she was the Mother of God, lived a holy life of good works, and also suffered at the cross, Mary accumulated a lot of extra merits with God which could be distributed to deserving saints to help them attain enough bonus points to enter heaven.

Pelagians (Liberals)

In our discussion of propitiation it was observed that many modern theologians object to an image of God as a wrathful, angry, jealous, vengeful God. The liberal theological view is that these OT

---

[10] Ibid., XVI.
[11] Ibid., Canon 24.
[12] Ibid., Canon 32.
[13] B. Demarest, *The Cross and Salvation* (Wheaton: Crossway, 1997), 350.
[14] J. A. Hardon, *The Catholic Catechism* (New York: Doubleday, 1975) 169.

concepts reflect a primitive, nomadic cult and that by NT times the concept of God had evolved to portray Him as merciful, forgiving, compassionate, and loving. God is, to them, not a stern law-giver and judge exacting the penal code, but a loving Father who awaits His prodigal children. They claim that the imputation of a righteousness totally foreign to a creature is absurd. Rather, righteousness is attained through moral improvement over time. All we need is to follow the example of Jesus and we too can fulfill the righteousness of the law. There is a little good in every man. All we have to do is fan the flame of this spark of good in order to build a fire of righteousness acceptable to God.

As explained earlier, Pelagius was the proponent of an anthropology that sees each person as Adam before the Fall. People can fulfill the law without God's grace, but the gift of grace makes it easier. Remission of sins comes through water baptism. With the help of God's grace post-baptismal people earn eternal life by being good.[15]

Albrecht Ritschl (d. 1889) is considered the father of modern liberalism. He saw God only in terms of love: "The conception of love is the only adequate conception of God."[16] The reason God became flesh was to overcome the fear and misconception mankind had of God as wrathful and vengeful. Imputed righteousness is "altogether false."[17] Forgiveness is something available to all men who will replicate the ethical life of Jesus.

This same song with some new verses (variations on a loving God) pops up in virtually all modern expressions of Pelagian doctrine.

Some Arminians

There are those among the Arminians who adhere to the governmental theory of atonement, which basically claims the death of Christ was a token payment by God for the sins of the world in order

---

[15] Demarest, *Cross and Salvation*, 348.
[16] A. Ritschl, *The Christian Doctrine of Justification and Reconciliation*, H. R. Mackintosh and A. B. Macaulay, eds. (Clifton, NJ: Reference Book Publishers, 1966), 274.
[17] Ibid., 70.

to uphold the moral order of the universe. They deny that justification imputes the righteousness of Christ to sinners. This understanding is "fictional."[18] To credit a person with righteousness which did not belong to him would encourage license.

John Wesley's view of justification included the forgiveness of sins and removal of guilt, but it also presumed the reshaping of their morals. He could not avoid the assimilation of sanctification into his understanding of justification.[19] He rejected the Lutheran concept of *"simul iustus et peccator,"* a sinner and a righteous person simultaneously:

> Least of all does justification imply that God is deceived in those whom He justifies; that He thinks them to be what, in fact, they are not; that He accounts them to be otherwise than they are. It does by no means imply that God . . . believes us righteous when we are unrighteous.[20]

And, according to most Arminians, justification is forfeited by willful sin. Therefore, assurance of ultimate justification is impossible in this life. This differs from Augustine in that he did not believe the elect could fall away, but rather that if one were to fall away, he was never elect from the beginning.[21]

---

[18] W. H. Taylor, "Justification," *Beacon Dictionary of Theology*, R. S Taylor, ed. (Kansas City: Beacon Hill, 1984), 298. J. Wesley says, "We do not find it expressly affirmed in Scripture that God imputes the righteousness of Christ to any" ("Minutes of Some Late Conversations," in *The Works of John Wesley*, 14 vols. [Grand Rapids: Zondervan, 1958], 8:277). Wesley did believe a sinner's faith was reckoned for righteousness, but for him this meant the removal of guilt and sin rather than the crediting of righteousness.
[19] Demarest, Cross and Salvation, 353.
[20] Wesley, "Justification by Faith," in *Works*, 5:57.
[21] See Roger E. Olson, *Arminian Theology: Myths and Realities* (Downer Grove, IL: InterVarsity Press, 2006).

Neoorthodox

Although there are many proponents of the neoorthodox point of view, we will look at it through the lenses of Karl Barth. He did not think justification was something we could experience. Rather it was a verdict on behalf of mankind in eternity past. God's decision to justify mankind thus opened the door for all men to be reconciled, since all of mankind has been justified. Christ came into the world to reveal this gracious decision on God's part to justify mankind and to remove the sin barrier blocking the covenant relationship between God and man.

So, according to Barth's understanding, a man is justified before he ever believes. He does not explain justification in terms of imputed righteousness. Rather it is the restoration of the covenant relationship between God and man, a covenant which was broken by sin. Instead of responding to the gospel to be justified, men who are justified respond to this "good news" as they hear about it. Justification for them becomes an existential reality.[22]

Reformers

The post-apostolic church did not wrestle with the doctrine of justification until Augustine. But after Augustine, no one really engaged a detailed study of the subject until Martin Luther. In his study which led to his conversion, Luther disagreed with Augustine. Having much more facility with the original languages, he concluded that *dikaioō* does not mean to "make" righteous, but rather to "declare" righteous. He found the word in a courtroom setting. Its usage, he determined, was primarily forensic. Justification, as opposed to sanctification, was a change in *standing*, not a change in *character*. And this change in standing occurred instantaneously, as opposed to the process approach of Augustine. The requirement for justification was faith alone. In this forensic decision, God not only freely pardoned man's sin, but He also imputed the righteousness of Christ to the believer's

---

[22] K. Barth, *Church Dogmatics*, G. W. Bromiley and T. F. Torrance, eds. (Edinburgh: T. & T. Clark, 1936-77), IV.1: 492.

account in heaven. This righteousness is "alien" because it comes from another and because no one could "earn" it.

Key to understanding Luther's concept of justification is the phrase *simul iustus et peccator*,[23] as previously mentioned. The believer is righteous in principle, but sinful in practice. This is what we call righteous in our *position* in Christ, but sinful in our *condition* on earth. He also taught that a believer could have assurance of his salvation,[24] but as we shall see, his logic fails at this point for two reasons: 1) He thought a believer could lose his salvation; 2) he believed good works are the litmus test for justification.[25]

Philipp Melanchthon, who taught Luther Greek, systematized the Lutheran wing of the Reformation. He flew right into the face of the Augustinian teaching that justification is "making" righteous rather than "declaring" righteous. "All our righteousness is a gracious imputation of God."[26] He also concurred with Luther in making a distinction between justification and sanctification.

John Calvin fell right in line with this approach. And like Luther, he believed in assurance of salvation for the believer. *Objective* assurance came through the promises of God's Word, while *subjective* assurance came through the work of the Holy Spirit in the life of the believer. He did think there were degrees of assurance:

> Surely, while we teach that faith ought to be certain and assured, we cannot imagine any certainty that is not tinged with doubt, or any assurance that is not assailed by some anxiety. On the other hand . . . we deny that, that in whatever way they are afflicted, believers fall away and depart from the certain assurance received from God's mercy.[27]

---

[23] Luther, *Works*, 26:232 and 25:260.
[24] Ibid., 26:377-78.
[25] Ibid., 34:183.
[26] P. Melanchthon, "Baccalaureate Theses," 10, in *Melanchthon: Selected Writings*, trans. C. H. Hill (Westport, Conn.: Greenwood 1978), 17.
[27] Calvin, *Institutes*, III.2.17 and III.4.27.

Calvin was so strong on assurance that he believed those who lack a significant degree of assurance are not believers at all.

Calvin was even stronger on the distinction between justification and sanctification than Luther: "To be justified means something different from being made righteous."[28] However, though he made a distinction between the two Calvin did not want to separate justification and sanctification. The RCC accused the Reformers of teaching license with their forensic justification. So Calvin was careful to link internal and external righteousness. External righteousness emanates from internal righteousness like rays of light from the sun: "You cannot possess Christ without being made partaker in his sanctification.... in our sharing in Christ, which justifies us, sanctification is just as much included as righteousness."[29]

The Heidelberg Catechism (1563), The Westminster Confession of Faith (1646), and The Westminster Shorter Catechism (1647) affirm the above approach to justification with similar wording.[30]

Neo-Reformed

In the late 20th Century a resurgence in Reformed theology began under the influence of men like John MacArthur, R. C. Sproul, John Piper, Tim Keller, and Wayne Grudem. These men have all the trappings of orthodox Reformed theology (excepting MacArthur, who is a Five Point Calvinist and a Dispensationalist, a hybrid position with a multiplicity of built-in contradictions) with an open door to the charismatic movement.[31]

Since all these men subscribe to the fifth point of Dortian Calvinism, they must somehow harmonize faith with perseverance/works. Writers like Alan Stanley use the standard Catholic formula

---

[28] Ibid., III.11.6.
[29] Ibid., III.16.1; 11.1.
[30] I am indebted to B. Demarest (*Cross and Salvation*, 345-62) for his basic outline of the historical review on the doctrine of justification.
[31] Collin Hanson, *Young, Restless, and Reformed: A Journalist's Journey with the New Calvinists* (Wheaton, IL: Crossway Books, 2008). Reformed theologians such as Wayne Grudem, John Piper and Sam Storms are also Charismatic.

when he says we will be justified by faith plus works. That is, he uses Philippians 2:12-13 to say we must work for our salvation, but the works we do are empowered and motivated by God. In other words, He gets the credit. So, Stanley differentiates between works done by the flesh, which will not adhere to faith any more than oil to water or clay to iron. Works done by the power of the Holy Spirit are those that couple with faith to yield eternal life.[32] Thomas Schreiner, who probably carries the flag of scholarship for the Neo-Reformed movement more than any other (especially since the passing of R. C. Sproul), combines faith and works in his salvation equation without apology:

> Paul clearly argues that good works are necessary for eternal life. Only those who sow to the Spirit will enjoy eternal life, and those who practice evil will not inherit the kingdom. James also teaches that justification is by works. No one will be justified if he or she fails to do good works.[33]

John Piper plays a tune on his pipe that tries to harmonize faith and works. According to him:

> Present justification is based on the substitutionary work of Christ alone, enjoyed in union with him through faith alone. Future justification is the open confirmation and declaration that in Christ Jesus we are perfectly blameless before God. This final judgment accords with our works. That is, the fruit of the Holy Spirit in our lives will be brought forward as the evidence and confirmation of true faith

---

[32] Alan Stanley, *Salvation is More Complicated than You Think: A Study on the Teachings of Jesus* (e-book, Location 830-46).

[33] Thomas R. Schreiner, "Justification Apart from and by Works: At the Final Judgment Works Will *Confirm* Justification," in *Four Views on the Role of Works at the Final Judgment* (Grand Rapids: Zondervan, 2013), 91.

and union with Christ. Without that validating transformation, there will be no future salvation.[34]

How many problems leap out at the reader from such a statement? Apparently, based on the substitutionary work of Christ alone, one can be united with Christ based on faith alone. But the declaration that we are blameless before God is yet future— "future justification." But this future justification only comes if our works portray a righteous transformation; without said works there is no salvation (justification).

In Piper's *vis à vis* with N. T. Wright, Wright's conclusion is not much different from Piper's, although Wright is not part of the Neo-Reformed movement:

> Present justification is the announcement issued on the basis of faith and faith alone of who is part of the covenant family of God. The present verdict gives the assurance that the verdict announced on the Last Day will match it; the Holy Spirit gives the power through which that future verdict, when given, will be seen to be in accordance with the life that the believer has then lived.[35]

How convoluted can we get? The "present verdict" (present justification) gives "assurance" that the "verdict announced on the Last Day" will be congruous with "present verdict," but only if one's life between the present verdict and the future verdict is righteous. But how is one to know today if one's life will be righteous tomorrow? Once again, the future verdict, my ultimate justification, depends on my present life of good works (righteousness).

In both of these approaches, which are sisters in the same family of faith/works righteousness, our salvation is a question mark until the Final Day when our works will be put on display to determine if our

---

[34] John Piper, "The Justification Debate: A Primer," *Christianity Today*, http://www.christianitytoday.com/ct/content/pdf/justification_june09.pdf, accessed January, 24, 2018.
[35] N. T. Wright, Ibid.

lives have been a true reflection of Christ-like living. And how does this differ from Catholicism?

On a positive note, it must be observed that the Neo-Reformed do not go as far as Chris VanLandingham, who for all practical purposes eliminates grace from the salvation equation. He reacts to E. P. Sanders's conclusion that we "are saved" by grace but maintain that salvation status through works.[36] VanLandingham simply claims we are justified by our works.[37] He arrives at this conclusion largely because he fails to see that "eternal life" includes a quality of life in the present at well as the future—"he who has the Son has life"—right now.

Summary

The approaches outlined above do not exhaust the various angles on understanding justification we find in the world today but are representative of the major groupings. The primary distinctions the student must keep in mind are: 1) "Made" righteous (infused) versus "declared" righteous (imputed); 2) Instantaneous versus a process; 3) Faith alone or faith plus meritorious works; and 4) Forensic versus existential. But after this brief overview of justification in history, it is time to look more closely at the Scriptures themselves.

Justification in the Scriptures

It must be acknowledged at the outset that the importance of justification in Paul's theological thinking has been a matter of some debate. He used the verb *dikaioō* fourteen times and the noun *dikaiōsunē* fifty-two times. But the verb is found outside Romans and Galatians only in 1 Corinthians 6:11 and Titus 3:7. Many fine scholars

---

[36] E. P. Sanders, *Paul and Palestinian Judaism: A Comparison of Patterns of Religion* (Philadelphia: Fortress, 1977), 517-18.

[37] Chris VanLandingham, *Judgment & Justification in Early Judaism and the Apostle Paul* (Peabody, MA: Hendrickson Publishers, 2006). Also see Paul A. Rainbow, *The Way of Salvation: The Role of Christian Obedience in Justification* (UK: Paternoster Press, 2005).

see justification as Paul's polemic against the Judaizers he confronts in Romans and Galatians but they think it was a rather peripheral doctrine, not central to his teaching such as our union with Christ.[38] George Ladd claims it is a false antithesis which contrasts justification with our union in Christ or the "already, not yet" of Schweitzer's form of "realized eschatology."[39] He understands justification as an eschatological blessing already enjoyed by believers in this life. He also sees our life "in Christ" as an eschatological blessing to be enjoyed today, but also a blessing which is a corollary of justification. To understand this, let us look first at the concept in the OT.

In the OT

The verb translated "to justify" is ṣadaq, which has the basic idea of conformity to a norm. Righteousness (ṣedeq, ṣᵉdāqâ) in the OT is not essentially an ethical quality. It is "that norm in the affairs of the world to which men and things should conform, and by which they can be measured."[40] The verb means to conform to the given norm, and in some forms such as the hiphil, it does mean "to declare righteous" or "to justify." In 2 Samuel 15:4 the forensic setting of the word can be seen from Absalom's appeal, "Oh that one would appoint me judge in the land, then every man who has any suit or cause could come to me, and I would *give* him *justice*," where the hiphil stem is used (הִצְדַּקְתִּיו). This can be seen again in Deuteronomy 25:1 where it says, "If there is a dispute between men and they go to court, and the judges decide their case, and they justify the righteous and condemn the wicked. . . ." Both Schrenk and Stigers argue for the forensic usage,

---

[38] See W. D. Davies, *Paul and Rabbinic Judaism* (1955), 222; W. Wrede, *Paul* (1907), 123; A. Schweitzer, *The Mysticism of Paul*, trans. by W. Montgomery (New York: Macmillan, 1931), 225.
[39] Ladd, *Theology*, 480. Schweitzer's realized eschatology does not exclude the "not yet" as does that of C. H. Dodd.
[40] N. Snaith, *Distinctive Ideas of the OT* (1944), 73.

but disagree as to the basic meaning of "being in right relationship" with someone.[41]

Ladd argues for the relationship concept and summarizes:

> As such, righteousness becomes a word of great theological significance. Righteousness is the standard God has decreed for human conduct. The righteous person is the one who, in God's judgment, meets the divine standard and thus stands in a right relationship with God.[42]

Eichrodt adds, "When applied to the conduct of God the concept is narrowed and almost exclusively employed in a forensic sense."[43]

For the Jews of Jesus' day, their oral interpretation of the law became the norm created by them. They developed a system of merits and demerits. In their eyes, God kept an account in heaven.

If the merits outweighed the demerits, the individual in question was in good standing with God. Strack and Billerbeck described this system in detail.[44] The study of the Torah, almsgiving, and deeds of mercy were especially credit-worthy. We can understand, then, how shocking Paul's theology would have been to the Pharisees, the upholders of the oral tradition. In Romans 3:26 God proves Himself just by justifying the ungodly. And this justification was without any works of the law (Gal 2:16; 3:11), a justification completely outside the scope of rabbinic teachings.

---

[41] See G. Schrenk, "δικαιοσυνη," in TDNT, 1964 ed., 2:195-96, and H. G. Stigers, "צָדֵק," in TWOT, 1980 ed., 2:752-55.

[42] Ladd, Theology, 481.

[43] W. Eichrodt, *Theology of the OT*, Old Testament Library, trans. by J. A. Baker (Philadelphia: Westminster, 1961), 1:240.

[44] H. L. Strack and P. Billerbeck, *Kommentar zum Neuen Testament aus Talmud und Midrasch* (Munich: C. H. Deutsche Verlagsbuchhandlung, 1961), IV: 6-11.

In the NT

Several aspects of the meaning of justification are important for a full understanding of the doctrine. One of the salient features of justification is that it is:

Eschatological

According to Jewish understanding, people will be judged in the afterlife for their deeds. Those who measure up will be justified or acquitted, not guilty. Those who fail will be condemned. At this final judgment God alone determines if a person is in right relation to Him, to be decided according to the norm set by God. The acquitted will be declared righteous and the guilty condemned. Hence, as Ladd points out, justification is an eschatological event.[45] Paul says as much when he uses δικαιωθήσονται in connection with eschatological judgment at the Lord's return (e.g., Rom 2:13; 8:33).[46] Christ Himself reveals such an eschatological understanding when He says, "And I say to you, that every careless word that men shall speak, they shall render account for it in the day of judgment. 'For by your words you shall be justified [δικαιωθήσῃ], and by your words you shall be condemned'" (Matt 12:36-37). For believers, this eschatological judgment occurs at the Judgment Seat of Christ; for the rest, at the Great White Throne (2 Cor 5:10; Rev 20:4-6).

But this is where Pauline eschatology reveals itself as unique, as Schweitzer noted. Though the ultimate verdict of justification is future, Paul also presents our justification as already past. That is precisely the point of the aorist participles in Romans 5:1 and 9. Believers "have been justified." Paul repeats this truth in 1 Corinthians 6:11 where he says, "You were justified in the name of the Lord Jesus Christ." It is another example of the "already, not yet" eschatology of the NT, seen especially in Hebrews. We do not have to wait until death for eschatological blessings. "He who has the Son *has* life." We do not wait until death to receive the gift of eternal life; nor do we have to

---

[45] Ladd, *Theology*, 482-83.
[46] See Schrenk, "δικαιοω," in *TDNT*, 1964 ed., 2:217-18.

wait until the next life to *enjoy* eternal life. The pouring out of His Spirit on all flesh is an eschatological blessing (see Joel 2:38ff), but we can receive the Holy Spirit now. The kingdom of God is a future dispensation but has also already begun.[47] And so, justification is the ultimate acquittal, but it has already taken place for believers. But justification is more than just eschatological; it is also . . .

Forensic

From both the OT and NT contexts which support a courtroom setting for the use of "to justify," it would seem to go without saying that the meaning of this word is forensic. Even some modern day Catholic scholars concede that its meaning is such. But because of the influence of the classic commentary by Sanday and Headlam on Romans, in which they suggested that the forensic righteousness imputed to a believer is "a fiction," we need to explain what we mean by imputed righteousness.[48] Here is the statement from Sanday and Headlam:

> The full phrase is δικαίουσθαὶ εκ πίστεω which means that the believer, by virtue of his faith, is 'accounted or treated as if he were righteous' in the sight of God. More even than this: the person so 'accounted righteous' may be, and indeed is assumed to be, not actually righteous, but ασεβη (Rom. iv.5), an offender against God . . . . There is something sufficiently startling in this. The Christian life is made to

---

[47] See *Dispensationalism, Israel, and the Church: The Search for Definition* eds. Craig A. Blaising and Darrell L. Bock (Grand Rapids, Michigan: Zondervan Publishing, 1992), *Three Central Issues in Contemporary Dispensationalism: A Comparison of Traditional and Progressive Views*, ed. Herbert W. Bateman (Grand Rapids, Michigan: Kregel Publications, 1999) and *Dispensationalism and the History of Redemption: A Developing and Diverse Tradition*, eds. D. Jeffery Bingham and Glenn R. Kreider (Chicago, IL: Moody Publishers, 2015).
[48] W. Sanday and A. C. Headlam, *Romans* (Edinburgh: T. & T. Clark, 1896), 36. The new edition of the *International Critical Commentary of the New Testament on Romans* takes the forensic view of the term while holding onto a theological connection of justification and sanctification, similar to Calvin. See C.E.B. Cranfield, *Romans*, vol.1 (Edinburgh: T. & T. Clark, 1975), 95.

have its beginning in a fiction. No wonder that the fact is questioned, and that another sense is given to the words—that δικαιοῦσθαι is taken to imply not the attribution of righteousness in idea, but an imparting of actual righteousness.[49]

From the above, it is clear that these authors struggle with Luther's concept that a person can be "at once righteous and a sinner." But it is important to understand this paradox lest we open the door for the "infusion" approach to righteousness simply because we are teaching that this righteousness is a "fiction."

Sanday and Headlam are saying that the believer is treated "as though" he is righteous, when in fact he is not. Vincent Taylor tried to get rid of the "fiction" idea by saying the righteousness is real, but it refers to a righteous mind rather than a righteousness in character: "He is righteous because, through faith in Christ the Redeemer, he gains a righteous mind," and "he really is righteous in mind and in purpose, although not yet in achievement."[50]

In solving this dilemma, let us remember that the basic meaning of "righteousness" in the OT was that of *relationship*. It was his "right standing" which gave the person a new relationship with the King, Judge, or other. When the Holy Spirit baptizes a believer into the body of Christ, that person has a *new identity*—he is among the "righteous ones" (δίκαιοι) in *Christ*, though still a "sinner" in *Adam* (Rom 5:19). It is a genuine *union*. And it is because the new identity "in Christ" gives the believer a *real* righteousness—the very righteousness of Christ—that the believer receives this "right standing" with God. This new relationship, as Ladd points out,[51] is not fictional; it is real. Romans 8:33-34 contrasts the act of justification with the act of condemnation: "It is God who justifies; who is to condemn?" This condemnation is not speaking of ethical character, but rather of a *judicial verdict* in response to a legal charge, hence the parallel: neither is the act of

---

[49] Ibid.
[50] V. Taylor, *Forgiveness and Reconciliation: a Study in New Testament Theology*, 2d Ed. (New York: Macmillan, 1956), 57.
[51] Ladd, *Theology*, 486.

justification a reference to ethical character, but rather to a *judicial acquittal/release* from a legal charge. The distinction necessary to understand this seeming paradox of being just and sinful at the same time is between *position* and *condition*. It is in our position (our standing) in Christ that we are truly righteous. Our account in heaven has already been credited (λογίζομαι, "imputed," is an accounting term) to our account in heaven. This is not fictional, and it is not an infusion of character into the believer. It is the very righteousness of Christ *in us* credited to our account in heaven by virtue of our position in Him. Our character revealed on earth is our condition.

This distinction between position and condition is not a peripheral truth in the Christian life. It is central and crucial because it is only as we focus on our position in Him that our condition begins to conform to His character (see 2 Cor 3:18). We *become* what we *think about* and *appropriate* for ourselves. When we focus on our miserable condition, it gets worse; when we focus on Christ and His righteousness already credited to us, we get better. That is precisely why, after an explanation of our new position in Christ in Romans 6:1-10, we are told: "So also you reckon [λογίζεσθε, the same word which is used for "imputed" in Rom 4:3] yourselves to be, on the one hand, dead to sin, but, on the other hand, alive to God in Christ Jesus."

Perhaps a reverse situation would be helpful. In 2 Corinthians 5:21 we read, "For He made Him who knew no sin *to be* sin for us, that we might become the righteousness of God in Him." Surely no one wants to suggest that Christ became sinful in His character. The verse says Christ knew no sin. His divine nature would not allow Him to sin. But the Father made Him sin by clothing Him with our sin as He bore our iniquities on the cross. These sins were imputed to Him. And so, His righteousness was imputed to us. But the *purpose* of that implicit imputation is that *we might become* (*genōmetha*) righteous in our condition.

Summary

As we look back over the ground covered concerning the doctrine of justification, is it fair to give the doctrine such a prominent place on the town square of Systematic Theology? After all, this doctrine is the primary point of contention between the RCC and the Protestants. It has caused division. And if it is so important for eternal life, why is the concept virtually absent from John's writings in general and the Gospel in particular?

We must conclude, with the Reformers, that justification is the very heart of the gospel. And the gospel is worth splitting over. There are only a handful of doctrines worth fighting for, and the gospel is one of them. Different biblical writers do couch concepts with different vocabulary, writing style, and figures of speech. In verbal plenary inspiration, it is understood that the Holy Spirit does not dictate. He superintends the human authors so that using their own personalities and vocabularies the autographs were communicated from God to man without error. We should not expect different authors to use identical phraseology for the same concepts; hence the difference between John and Paul. And we also find the concept of justification by faith in James 2 and Hebrews 11:7, so it is not as though the concept is completely unique to Paul.

Nevertheless, there is no NT author engaged in the defense of the gospel as much as Paul. He is the one whom we would expect to use legal terminology, since he acts as a lawyer in defense of gospel truth.

The Order of Salvation ("Ordo Salutis")

Franz Buddeus and Jacob Carpov were the first theologians to coin the phrase "*ordo salutis*."[1] This refers to either the temporal or logical sequence in which the various elements of salvation are imparted to the believer, from his calling to his glorification. Some groups have elements unique to their system, but in every system the believers get to glory; they just take different routes.

The Roman Catholic Church

By the time of Augustine (d. 430) infant baptism was in full swing. For centuries baptism had been viewed as one of the works which effected salvation. Augustine did not view water baptism as a meritorious work, but he did understand it to be the beginning of the various sacraments which would result in the ultimate glorification of the saints. From his time until today, the *ordo salutis* for the RCC is:

1. BAPTISM. At water baptism the individual is "born again" (Titus 3:5). Thus, the regenerating work by which the irresistible grace of God leads the sinner to salvation begins at the "laver of regeneration." Here, the guilt and penalty of original sin are removed, and, "Man

---

[1] I am indebted to B. Demarest (*Cross and Salvation*, 36) for the outline of this material.

is made white as a sheet, brighter than snow."[2] But water baptism was only good for past sins. Sins committed afterwards needed a further sacrament.

2. CONFIRMATION. Through this outpouring of the Holy Spirit those who have been baptized are able to become powerful witnesses for the Christ (Acts 8:15-17).

3. THE EUCHARIST. The transubstantiated wafer becomes the nourishment needed by the believer to remain in a state of grace. To be cut off from it is certain spiritual death.

4. PENANCE. This is how the post-baptismal sins are taken care of, especially the mortal sins of adultery, apostasy, and murder. The penance includes contrition, confession, and acts necessary to satisfy the local rector.

5. EXTREME UNCTION. This act just before death takes care of any unconfessed sins up to that point. Absolution from these sins takes place, and the believer is prepared for his beatific vision of God.

Because the theology of the RCC is so linked to the sacraments, which for them are means of receiving grace, they need to be listed as above. But within these sacraments are other elements in this order: *regeneration, repentance, faith, conversion, sanctification,* and *glorification*. All but the last of these are subsumed under their understanding of *justification*.

The Lutherans

Of course, since the Lutherans began with Martin Luther, their theology will reflect his. Luther, it must be remembered, believed in linear conversion (a succession of many steps) and that believers who had been regenerated could lose their salvation. Of course, like all who think salvation can be lost, he also thought it could be regained.

---

[2] F. G. L. Van Der Meer, *The Faith of the Church* (London: Darton, Longman & Todd, 1966), 367.

1. CALLING. God invites all to believe in Christ and provides sufficient grace for the unconverted to respond to the message.
2. ILLUMINATION. With the call comes the light. All who hear the call also are illumined to the benefits of receiving Christ and the consequences of not doing so.
3. REPENTANCE. This includes remorse for sins and the realization that salvation is offered through the work of Christ.
4. FAITH. After realizing that Christ can save, a person may choose to believe in Him.
5. REGENERATION. The transformation of being born again comes as a result of faith.
6. JUSTIFICATION. Forgiveness of sins and right standing with God result from being born again.
7. SANCTIFICATION. The justified now grow in holiness as they produce the fruits of faith.
8. PRESERVATION. If believers keep on believing, God will preserve them until the end. However, they can choose to stop believing, in which case they lose their salvation.

This order changes for infants, since Luther believed in baptismal regeneration. So, if an infant is baptized, regeneration moves to the head of the list, and all the other steps inevitably follow.

Reformed (Covenant)

For these, everything in the salvation process issues out of the covenant of grace God made with man.

1. CALLING. There is both a general call to all men and a special call to the elect. It is the Holy Spirit who illumines the mind, turns the heart toward God, and inclines the will to receive Christ.
2. REGENERATION. Since a thoroughly depraved person could not possibly make a decision for God, the Holy Spirit must give the

The Order of Salvation ("Ordo Salutis")

gift of new birth to enable a person to believe. So, one is clearly born again before he believes.

3. FAITH. The inevitable consequence of regeneration is faith. Faith is placed in Christ as Savior, a further gift of God.
4. REPENTANCE. God enables the new saint to grieve over his sins and to turn from all ungodliness.
5. JUSTIFICATION. Here, then, is the legal declaration of the righteousness credited to the account of the former sinner.
6. SANCTIFICATION. Though not separated from justification, the former is instantaneous, whereas sanctification is a process. Through this process the believer is progressively conformed to the likeness of Christ.
7. PRESERVATION. Believers do not so much persevere as God preserves. He keeps true believers from falling. If time allows, they will go on to maturity in Christ or they were not believers at all.
8. GLORIFICATION. Believers are changed into the likeness of Christ when He appears, their sin natures are removed, and they receive glorified bodies.

Reformed (Non-Covenant)

There are many in the Reformed tradition that do not hold to covenant theology. They often refine the *ordo salutis* even further:

1. ELECTION. God chose some to receive eternal life from eternity past irrespective of His prior knowledge that they would choose to receive Christ.
2. CALLING. Among the Reformed, this calling is irresistible, which is why it is called irresistible grace in the Five Point schema. This calling illumines the minds and softens the heart so the unbeliever can respond to the gospel.
3. REGENERATION. Again, the totally depraved person cannot exercise faith until the Holy Spirit has given him the capacity to do so

through the new birth. "The Spirit creates within him a new heart or new nature. This is accomplished through regeneration or the new birth by which the sinner is made a child of God and is given spiritual life. His will is renewed through this process so that the sinner spontaneously comes to Christ of his own free choice."[3]

4. REPENTANCE. Through the power of the Holy Spirit within them, the regenerate turns away from all sin.

5. FAITH. The regenerate now makes a personal decision to receive Christ as Savior and Lord of their lives.

6. JUSTIFICATION. The new believer is now declared righteous in the courtroom of heaven.

7. SANCTIFICATION. The justified person now begins the process of being made holy by the Holy Spirit. Though there are ups and downs, the "trend line" is always up.

8. PRESERVATION. Because it is God's power which preserves the elect, they cannot fall away from the faith. Therefore, the saints persevere until the end of their lives.

9. GLORIFICATION. When Christ returns, the elect are permanently rid of all aspects of the Fall; that is, they are glorified.

A very important aspect of all Reformed theology is the defense of the sovereignty of God. It is considered an affront to His sovereignty for man to have any part in the salvation process whatsoever. This would make God dependent on man, thus undermining His sovereignty. This is one of the reasons, if not the main reason, regeneration must precede faith in their system. For unregenerate man to be able to make a decision for Christ supposes that man can add something on his own to the salvation process, thus threatening the doctrine of total depravity while at the same time rendering an independent, sovereign God dependent on man to determine the final count in the New Jerusalem.

---

[3] D. N. Steele and C. C. Thomas, *Five Points of Calvinism*, 48.

Arminians

Those who consider themselves to be Arminians generally see it this way:

1. CALLING. For the Arminians, this call is universal. From the cross itself grace flows to all men and reverses the effects of the Fall, so they are capable of making a decision for Christ.
2. CONVERSION. This consists of repentance and faith. Since all men have been freed to make moral choices, whether good or evil, they are to work out their own salvation with fear and trembling. The emphasis is on "work out." Conversion is a synergistic activity.
3. JUSTIFICATION. This is not viewed as a judicial decision in the courtroom of heaven whereby the sinner receives the righteousness of Christ imputed to his account. Rather, it accomplishes the forgiveness of sins necessary for the proper moral government of the universe.
4. SANCTIFICATION. At some moment in time a "second blessing" experience occurs, which destroys the Sin Nature and gives believers perfect love for God and mankind.
5. PERSEVERANCE. Believers can fall from the faith and lose their salvation. They can be genuine believers, yet still fall away.

It is important to point out the place of *regeneration* in the Arminian system. They believe it is the umbrella over the entire process from conversion to sanctification.

Summary

It is tempting, at this point, to try to present an *ordo salutis* which would best represent the doctrine reflected in a Free Grace soteriology, but that would be premature. It is necessary to take a closer look at some of the elements not examined in the salvation process before an informed position can be posted concerning their place in the order of salvation. Some of these have already been examined, such as justification and sanctification. There is no dispute with regard to the place of glorification—last. And perseverance will be discussed in our study of eternal security. But election, calling, regeneration, and repentance need some more explanation.

It also must be observed that some like to have their cake and eat it too when it comes to the *ordo salutis*. They speak of temporal order and logical order. For example, Demarest makes this claim: "Conversion, regeneration, union with Christ, and justification occur simultaneously in the moment of decision for Christ, and not successively."[4] But in the same breath, it is argued that an unregenerate man cannot make a decision to receive Christ and must, therefore, be regenerated *before* (a temporal preposition) he can believe. It cannot be cogently argued that an element in the order of salvation has one position logically and another temporally.

"So what?" is a fair question. What difference does this order make? It is primarily an issue of divine sovereignty and human responsibility. Those heavy on sovereignty want to take man right out of the picture. So, God does everything to shape the pitiful lump of clay into the image of His Son to the point that the clay has no mind, emotion, or will in the matter whatsoever. To say he does would be to undermine the doctrine of divine sovereignty. Others who lean toward the ability of man want to minimize the effects of the Fall to the extent that God was active in creation and at the cross, but passive with regard to the salvation process within the individual; each person is capable of working out his own salvation. Hopefully, there is a mediating position found in the Scriptures.

---

[4] Demarest, *Cross and Salvation*, 43.

Repentance[1]

In his book *I Call It Heresy!* A. W. Tozer makes his position of lordship salvation clear when he says, " . . . true obedience is one of the toughest requirements of the Christian life. Apart from obedience, there can be no salvation, for salvation without obedience is a self-contradictory impossibility . . . . we need to preach again . . . a Christ who will either be Lord of all or he will not be Lord at all!"[2] In the same chapter, he reveals his understanding of the repentance in the Luke 15 parable of the "Prodigal Son" when he writes:

> [T]he first thing the returning sinner does is to confess: "Father, I have sinned against heaven and in Thy sight, and I am no more worthy to be called Thy son. Make me as one of Thy hired servants." . . .
>
> Thus, in repentance, we . . . fully submit to the Word of God and the will of God, as obedient children . . . . and if we do not give Him that obedience, I have reason to wonder if we are really converted![3]

Tozer is not alone in his convictions concerning repentance and its role in the salvation process.[4] In John MacArthur's classic "line in the

---

[1] This material originally appeared as an article in a Grace Evangelical Society journal.
[2] A. W. Tozer, *I Call It Heresy!* (Harrisburg, PA: Christian Publications, 1974), 11, 15.
[3] Ibid., 17, 19, emphasis added.
[4] By "salvation process" we refer to the *ordo salutis*, a term first suggested by the Lutheran theologians Franz Buddeus and Jacob Carpov in the first half of

sand" treatment of the salvation message in *The Gospel According to Jesus*, he states in no uncertain terms: "From His first message to His last, the Savior's theme was calling sinners to repentance—and this meant not only that they gained a new perspective on who He was, but also that they turned from sin and self to follow Him."[5] Another who sees repentance as an essential part of the salvation process is D.L. Bock, who says that "repentance ... is an appropriate summary for the offer of the gospel today."[6] He comes to this conclusion largely

---

the eighteenth century. The components usually discussed in Protestant circles include: calling, regeneration, faith, repentance, justification, sanctification, perseverance, glorification, and election. The order of these has been debated for centuries. See the previous chapter and Demarest, *Cross and Salvation*, 36-44.

[5] J. F. MacArthur, *The Gospel According to Jesus* (Grand Rapids: Academie, 1988), 161-62. He tries to show that L. S. Chafer, T. Constable, M. Cocoris, and C. C. Ryrie have all strayed from the true meaning of repentance by making it more or less synonymous with believing or simply changing one's mind about Jesus. He takes note of Chafer's arguments that the Gospel of John never mentions repentance, Romans uses the word only once, and Paul does not include it in his witness to the Philippian jailer (Acts 16:31). But, according to MacArthur, these are all worthless arguments from silence.

[6] D. L. Bock, "A Theology of Luke–Acts," in *A Biblical Theology of the New Testament*, eds. R. B. Zuck and D. L. Bock (Chicago: Moody, 1994), 131. He understands the terms *repentance, turning,* and *faith* as different ways to say the same thing (ibid., 129, n. 33). He does acknowledge that turning differs from repentance in that the latter is a "change of perspective," while the former is the "change of direction" which follows the change in perspective (ibid., 132). But for Bock faith and repentance are interchangeable, since a comparison of Acts 3:19 and Acts 11:21 shows that Luke substituted one term for the other in these parallel verses. In both instances the *turning* followed the *believing* or the *repenting*. But he goes on to make the *turning* a necessary part of the "single act" that saves. In Acts 14:15 he claims that we see the "reversal of direction necessary for salvation of unbelievers estranged from God . . . . Gentiles are said to be 'turning to God' in Acts 15:19, where the term alone is sufficient to describe the response that saves." Bock develops his understanding of repentance from Luke–Acts and calls Luke the "theologian of repentance," since he uses the noun eleven times in Luke– Acts out of the twenty-two uses in the NT and uses the verb fourteen times out of the thirty-four uses in the NT. At first Bock appears to distinguish between repentance and the deeds which should follow it (ibid., 130-31). He claims the NT meaning only gets *close* to the meaning of בוש (shub)

from Jesus' use of the term in Luke 24:47, which is Luke's version of the Great Commission.

Clearly, these men understand repentance to be a requirement for justification. In other words, in their discussions, repentance is for unbelievers. But others think repentance is for believers. John Calvin wrote: "Now it ought to be a fact beyond controversy that repentance not only constantly follows faith, but is also born of faith."[7] And C. H. Spurgeon said, "All the fruits meet for repentance are contained in faith itself. You shall never find that a man who trusts Christ remains an enemy to God, or a lover of sin."[8]

And so, it is fair to say that some Christian teachers believe that repentance is for unbelievers, while others think repentance is for believers. Which view is correct? In this study it is suggested that both

---

from the OT ("to turn or turn around") in some contexts (Lk 24:44-47). He describes repentance as a "change of perspective involving the total person's point of view." And "part of the change of perspective in repentance is to see sin differently and to recognize it is deadly when left untreated."

But as Bock's discussion proceeds, terms become muddled quickly. He claims that repentance is the change of *perspective* and turning is the change of *direction* which follows repentance. He then distinguishes between the root and fruit of a tree. But when he speaks of the root, it can be "planted by faith, repentance, or *turning* [emphasis mine]. Each of these three terms points to approaching God and resting in His provision and mercy." But the repenting is first in the *ordo salutis* (as one looks at life, sin, and God in a new way); then comes the turning (which alludes to a person's *taking up a new direction*); finally, faith arrives on the scene (the focus on God where one's attention ends up after his new orientation). And *all three* of these are described as the *root* of the tree which surely must grow before the *fruit* of the tree can be realized.

But in Bock's discussion it appears as though there is *fruit within the root*. One's direction in life (turning) is produced by the repentance (change of perspective). And both of these (repentance and turning) occur before one believes (an act which is still part of the root as defined by Bock). Hence, when the dust of these definitions has settled, one must both repent (get a new perspective) and turn (get a new life direction) before one can believe (get a new focus). Therefore, salvation = repentance + turning + faith, according to Bock.

[7] Calvin, *Institutes*, III.3.1.
[8] C. H. Spurgeon, "Faith and Regeneration," *Spurgeon's Expository Encyclopedia* (Grand Rapids: Baker, 1978), 7:141.

are right; in other words, repentance is for all men, unbelievers and believers alike. However, we will try to demonstrate that repentance is not a prior condition for unbelievers to come to a saving knowledge of Jesus Christ. The procedure for this study will be to review in more detail the positions taken on repentance throughout church history while categorizing those who thought repentance was for unbelievers and those who thought it was for believers. Then we will try to show from Scriptural examples that repentance is for all men.

Historical Positions on Repentance

Post-Apostolic Fathers through Augustine

A completely heretical but very influential document in the early church was *The Shepherd of Hermas*. The writer claims to have been a contemporary of Clement, presbyter-bishop of Rome (A.D. 92-101). Hermas is instructed by the "angel of repentance" dressed up as a shepherd. The call is for a lackadaisical church to repent. The writing is thoroughly legalistic and never mentions the gospel or grace. He speaks of the meritorious system of good works and the atonement of sin through martyrdom. There is no mention of justification by faith, but water baptism is indispensable for salvation.[9] And water baptism is the seal of repentance which "makes Christians into Christians.... Asceticism and penal suffering are the school of conversion."[10] Faith is the fruit of repentance and baptism seals it.[11]

Justin Martyr followed on the heels of Hermas and also saw water baptism as the work of regeneration. He said: "Those who are convinced of the truth of our doctrine... are exhorted to prayer, fasting, and repentance for past sins.... Then they are led by us to a place where there is water, and in this way they are regenerated,

---

[9] P. Schaff, *History of the Christian Church*, 5th ed. (n.p.: Charles Scribner's Sons, 1910; reprint, Grand Rapids: Eerdmans, 1967), vol. 2, *Ante-Nicene Christianity*, 684-87.
[10] J. Behm, "μετανοέω," in *TDNT*, 1967 ed., 4:1008.
[11] Ibid., 4:1007.

as we also have been regenerated.... For Christ says: Except you are born again, you cannot enter into the kingdom of heaven."[12] The importance of water baptism for Justin Martyr is underscored when he says, "The laver of repentance ... is baptism, the only thing which is able to cleanse those who have repented."[13]

In the post-apostolic period repentance almost immediately reflected the Judaizing influence against which Paul labored long and hard. Like almsgiving, repentance was considered a good work (*2 Cl.*, 16.4). Repentance is the achievement by which one secures salvation and life (*2 Cl.*, 9.8). Penitence with weeping and wailing could win God's forgiveness (Just. *Dial.*, 141.3). And so, even in the early second century repentance becomes connected with winning God's acceptance,[14] and repentance was linked to water baptism.[15]

By the time of Augustine (d. 430), infant baptism was in full vogue. And at the baptismal font "We are justified, but righteousness itself grows as we go forward" (Augustine, *Sermon*, 158.5). In the *ordo salutis* Augustine saw predestination, calling, justification, and glorification. But justification was the umbrella over everything from regeneration through sanctification.[16] And regeneration began at baptism. He actually called it "the saving laver of regeneration" (Augustine, *Sermon*, 213.8). Here the elect receive the external sign (the water of baptism) and the spiritual reality (regeneration and union with Christ). For Augustine "the sacrament of baptism is undoubtedly the sacrament of regeneration" (Augustine, *On Forgiveness of Sins, and Baptism*, II.43).

But unlike Hermas and other predecessors, Augustine did not view repentance as a work of man. It was the unmerited gift of grace

---

[12] J. Martyr, *Apol.* I., c. 61.

[13] J. Martyr, *Dial.*, 14.1.

[14] Behm, "μετανοέω," 4:1008.

[15] Baptismal regeneration was taught by not just Hermas (d. 140) and Justin Martyr (d. 165), but also Irenaeus (d. 200) and Cyril of Jerusalem (d. 386), which brings us to Augustine.

[16] Demarest, Cross and Salvation, 351.

which wrought regeneration, faith, and repentance in the sinner.[17] But even little children could be regenerated through baptism, which "cleanses even the tiny infant, although itself unable as yet with the heart to believe unto righteousness and to make confession with the mouth unto salvation" (Augustine, *On the Gospel of St. John*, 80.3). Nevertheless, elect children who had been baptized would inevitably go on to faith and repentance and growth in grace. All of these were elements of his understanding of justification. Since he was not familiar with Greek he misunderstood *dikaioō* to mean "to make righteous" instead of "to declare righteous" (Augustine, *On the Spirit and the Letter*, 45). This misunderstanding also led to the Catholic belief that justification is a life-long process. Of course, with this approach one could not know whether he was elect or not until he died.

Apparently, the church fathers and their successors believed in a "linear view of conversion."[18] Though conversion began at baptism, it was not considered complete until death. At baptism only the pre-baptismal sins were forgiven. The post-baptismal sins were a big problem. For this reason, many early Christians waited for baptism until their death beds. But surely there must be some way for those baptized as infants to have their personal sins forgiven. *Voilá!* Repentance or penance was the answer. Whereas the earlier church fathers were divided over how many times a person could repent after baptism, by the time of Augustine the number was unlimited (Augustine, *On the Creed*, 15-16).

The Latin Fathers made their understanding of repentance clear by their Latin translations of the Greek terms *metanoeō* (repent) and *metanoia* (repentance): *poenitentiam agite* ("to do [acts of] penance" and *poenitentia* ("[acts of] penance").[19] And this translation was preserved in Jerome's Vulgate.

---

[17] Ibid., 282.
[18] R. N. Wilkin, "Repentance as a Condition for Salvation" (Th.D. diss., Dallas Theological Seminary, 1985), 19.
[19] W. D. Chamberlain, *The Meaning of Repentance* (Grand Rapids: Wm. B. Eerdmans Publishing Co., 1943), 27-28.

So by the time of Augustine, penance for post-baptismal sins was the *modus operandi* for reinstatement to the Church. The acts of penance varied according to the nature of the sin and the temperament of the Father Confessor. The acts included fasting, prayers, weeping, begging, abstinence (for those married), shaving one's head, prostration, and the like. And penance could last a few days or many years.[20]

To summarize, repentance was primarily pre-baptismal in the post-apostolic fathers until infant baptism became the practice. As such, it was viewed as a work of man which helped him gain his salvation. Though not clearly defined, it certainly included some sort of contrition for sin and a renouncing of the same, specifically at the point of water baptism. By the time of Augustine, infant baptism was the norm. Post-baptismal repentance became the focus since regeneration took place and justification *began* at water baptism. This repentance became practically synonymous with not only contrition and confession, but also doing acts of penance. This understanding of repentance prevailed right through the Dark Ages and the Renaissance until the Reformers.

The Reformers and Repentance

Both Calvin and Luther rejected the notion that post-baptismal sins could be atoned for by contrition, confession, and acts of penance. It was their belief that all sins (past, present, and future) were covered by the blood of Christ when the sinner was baptized. Hence, acts of penance were unnecessary. For Calvin, repentance continued throughout the life of the Christian, but it is the *fruit* of faith, as noted previously. And faith cannot come in Calvin's thinking without regeneration. So, after the regenerating work of the Spirit, the gift of faith is implanted in the elect, and out of this faith comes repentance, which was defined as the mortification of the old nature (the flesh) and the quickening of the new nature (the spirit) unto

---

[20] Wilkin, "Repentance," 22.

holiness.[21] "Calvin understood by repentance what most later divines called sanctification."[22]

For Luther, repentance began at the point of faith. It involved genuine sorrow for sins committed and renunciation of all vice. He wrote, "Repentance is not penitence alone but also faith, which apprehends the promise of forgiveness, lest the penitent sinners perish."[23] Like Calvin, he connected repentance with faith and saw it as a lifelong process in Christians: "When our Lord and Master, Jesus Christ, said 'Repent,' He called for the entire life of *believers* to be one of penitence."[24] Unlike Calvin, he did think conversion was linear and incomplete until the end of one's life. One could fall away from the faith and lose his salvation. He could also return to the faith, but this return was not through acts of penance.

Post-Reformation Repentance

After the Reformation, the understanding of repentance went off in four directions, according to R. Wilkin:[25] 1) a willingness or resolution to stop sinning and a concomitant commitment to the Lordship of Christ;[26] 2) a change of thinking;[27] 3) contrition, confession, and doing acts of penance;[28] and 4) turning away from sin.[29]

---

[21] Calvin, *Institutes*, III.3.2,9.
[22] Demarest, Cross and Salvation, 248.
[23] M. Luther, *What Luther Says* (St. Louis: Concordia, 1959), 1210.
[24] B. L. Woolf, *Reformation Writings of Martin Luther* (London: Lutterworth, 1952), 32, emphasis added.
[25] Wilkin, "Repentance," 7-10.
[26] According to Wilkin, ibid., 7, the adherents include: J. Anderson, W. Barclay, H. Conzelmann, J. D. G. Dunn, D. Fuller, K. Gentry, J. Gerstner, L. Goppelt, W. Graham, G. Ladd, I. H. Marshall, J. I. Packer, J. R. W. Stott, and L. Strauss.
[27] Adherents include L. S. Chafer, G. M. Cocoris, H. A. Ironside, and C. C. Ryrie (ibid., 8).
[28] The view of the RCC. Rather than a condition for obtaining salvation, repentance is viewed as a requirement for maintaining it.
[29] Among those holding this view are J. Graham, G. Peters, A. H. Strong, and the *Westminster Confession of Faith Shorter Catechism* (ibid., 10).

Among reformed thinkers the bedrock position is that regeneration must precede both faith and repentance. This follows both Augustine and Calvin. Faith and repentance are understood to be "conversion." But an unregenerate person cannot believe, and repentance is the fruit of faith. C. H. Spurgeon (d. 1892) said, "Faith in the living God and his Son Jesus Christ is always the result of the new birth, and can never exist except in the regenerate."[30] So out of regeneration comes faith, and faith is the mother of repentance, which includes sorrow for sins and a forsaking of the same.[31] And, in all Reformed theology of the last two centuries surveyed by this author, justification follows repentance.

A. H. Strong (d. 1921) saw three simultaneous events: regeneration, repentance, and faith (in that order logically, if not simultaneously). The latter two had three elements, which corresponded to the mind, emotions, and will of man. For repentance there was: 1) mind—recognition of sin; 2) emotions—sorrow for sin; 3) will—abandonment of sin. Faith, too, had three elements: 1) mind—knowledge of the Gospel; 2) emotions—feeling the sufficiency of Christ's grace; 3) will—trusting Christ as Savior and Lord. So repentance was a determination to turn from all known sin, and faith was a determination to turn to Christ.[32] Thus, for both Spurgeon and Strong repentance is not a requirement for regeneration because regeneration precedes repentance and faith.

M. J. Erickson and B. Demarest reverse the order. That is, regeneration follows repentance and faith. Like Strong, they understand conversion to consist of repentance (the negative side) and faith (the positive side). For Erickson, repentance consists in sorrow for sin and the determination to turn from it. Faith equals the intellectual assent to the truth of the Gospel plus the emotional element of trust in the person of Christ. From a logical standpoint, regeneration is contingent on repentance and faith (the two of which

---

[30] Spurgeon, *Encyclopedia*, 7:139.
[31] Demarest, Cross and Salvation, 248.
[32] Ibid., 249.

equal conversion), but from a temporal standpoint these three occur simultaneously.[33] Demarest holds the same position.[34]

It seems apparent from the previous discussion that theologians cannot agree on whether repentance precedes regeneration or not. For some, repentance is a *condition for* regeneration, while others say it is the *fruit of* regeneration. So we are right back where we started. Some say repentance is for the unregenerate, and some say it is for the regenerate. Perhaps now is the time to look at the Scriptures themselves to see what they say. Are there examples of repentance for unbelievers? . . . For believers?

Scriptural Testimony on Repentance

Repentance is for Unbelievers

Can it be clearly demonstrated that repentance is for unbelievers? Of course it can. Much of John the Baptist's ministry was to unbelievers. We know this from John 1:7 where we are told that John came as a testimony concerning the Light (Jesus) that through Him all men might *believe*. It could be argued that many of the OT saints had already exercised faith in God's promises seen through the shadow of the Law, and now these "believers" needed to believe in God's highest revelation, His Son. Even so, they needed to believe after repentance. And most of these, more than likely, had not believed the first time, for John 5:35 implies that many Jews responded to the message of John and rejoiced in his light, but when the Messiah came on the scene, they did not believe in Him (Jn 5:36-47), nor were they saved (Jn 5:34). The point is that for most of John's listeners repentance came before regenerating faith. Hence, repentance was for unbelievers.

Jesus Himself had the same ministry. We see this in Mark 1:15 where He went into the regions of Galilee preaching the gospel of the kingdom and telling them to *repent* and to *believe* in the gospel. Of

---

[33] Ibid.
[34] Ibid.

course, this gospel is the good news of the King and His Kingdom, but the believing still comes after the repenting. The parallel passages in Matthew 9:13, Mark 2:17, and Luke 5:32 should also serve as clear examples of sinners who have yet to believe. It is not the just/righteous (*dikaious*) who need repentance, but tax collectors and sinners. Nevertheless, if one went way out on a limb and said these tax collectors and sinners were simply Jews in covenant relationship with Yahweh but out of fellowship with Him, that could not be said of Luke 24:47 where repentance and forgiveness of sins is preached to *all nations*. Surely, these nations were not in covenant relationship with Yahweh. Of course, the individuals in these nations needed to *believe* in order to be saved (Mk 16:16), but it is very likely that the call to repentance preceded the invitation to believe.

If the previous passages have not made it clear that repentance is for unbelievers, then Luke makes it obvious in Acts 17:30 where Paul speaks to Greek philosophers and other men of Athens. He says that God commands *all men everywhere to repent*. The reason for repentance is the impending judgment, which will take place through Christ whom He raised from the dead. After hearing this message concerning the resurrection of Christ, *some men . . . believed*. Is this not similar to the implications of 2 Peter 3:9 where God has not willed (*boulomai*, predetermined decision) that any men should perish, but that *all men* might have room (*chōrēsai*) for *repentance*? Surely, the "all men" refers to unbelievers.

Paul's testimony before the Ephesian elders should also be understood as an example of his preaching (Acts 20:21), which included *repentance* toward (*eis to*) God and *faith* toward (*eis to*) our Lord Jesus Christ. Again, it seems obvious the repentance preceded the faith. This is the same order of events implied by the listing in Hebrews 6:1ff. The writer starts with repentance and chronologically works his way through to judgment: repentance from dead works, faith toward God, baptisms, the laying on of hands, resurrection from the dead, and eternal judgment. Could an objective person not admit that the first step here is repentance?

In the passages referenced above, repentance is for unbelievers. But repentance is also for believers.

Repentance is for Believers

The call for Israel to repent as a nation is a unique example, which will be taken up in detail in our next study. But the Ninevites are an interesting case in point. Both Matthew 12:41 and Luke 11:32 tell us that the people of Ninevah *repented* at the preaching of Jonah. But when we read Jonah, it says "the people of Ninevah *believed* God, proclaimed a fast, and put on sackcloth, from the greatest to the least of them" (Jonah 3:5, emphasis added). The gospel accounts may be using the term *metanoēsan* (repented) as metonymy for the entire response of the Ninevites to Jonah's message (belief + repentance fruit),[35] but the first recorded response on the part of the Ninevites was their faith.

If the example of the Ninevites is not perfectly clear, then what about the call to repentance in Revelation 2 and 3? Five of the seven churches are challenged to repent (Smyrna and Philadelphia being the exceptions). Surely the majority of the people in these five churches would be regarded as believers. The church at Ephesus is not accused of apostasy. Rather the accusation is dead, cold orthodoxy. They had the right faith, but their devotion had waned; they had left their first love. Now they needed repentance. They needed to go back and do the first works, which would be a fruit of their repentance. Is this not a call to believers to repent? Of course it is. Even in the case of the church at Laodicea, many scholars agree that the issue here is not relationship; it is fellowship. Revelation 3:19 says, "As many as I love, I rebuke and chasten [*paideuō*].[36] Therefore, be zealous and repent." But the promise to those who repent is simply this: "I will come in to him and dine with him, and he with me." The promise is not relationship; it is fellowship. The picture is one of intimacy, of dining together, of enjoying one another's company.

Luke 15, with its three parables about repentance, issues out of the same setting. Jesus is eating and drinking with tax collectors and

---

[35] Since these people initially were unbelievers, the order here could be argued to be repentance + faith + fruit, but the first recorded response was their faith.

[36] A word consistently used in the NT for child-training.

Repentance

sinners. The Pharisees and scribes cannot understand how He can do this. The passage has long been a favorite passage of evangelists in their appeal to sinners to "come home." But what makes us so sure the lost sheep in Luke 15:4-7 is not a sheep? And what makes us so sure the coin of the next parable is not a coin which used to be on the necklace? And in the parable of the prodigal son, are we prepared to say he was not already a son with a father and part of the family before he took off? The call may well be to come home, but it is to people who already had a home, who were already part of the family, part of the flock.

As Z. C. Hodges writes,[37] the examples in Luke 15 could go either way. If an unbeliever is in view, the call is to repentance; if a believer is in view, the call is to repentance. The entire series of parables is in response to the Lord's practices regarding table fellowship. He is eating with tax collectors and sinners. What is necessary for a holy, righteous person to have table fellowship with sinful people? Those sinful people need to make a decision to repent, whether they are justified or unjustified. With this in mind, Jesus is more comfortable eating with tax collectors and sinners who have repented than with Pharisees and scribes who have not repented.

Perhaps this will make the issues more clear. We have *relationship* truth, which we will call "A" truth. Then we have *fellowship* truth, which we will call "B" truth. If someone asks a question about "B" truth, they get a "B" truth answer. If they ask a question about "A" truth, they get an "A" truth answer. Take the rich young ruler as a case in point. He asked how he could "inherit" eternal life. Jesus told him to go sell everything he had and give it to the poor. If we understand the question as one about "A" truth, then the answer about how to get into

---

[37] Z. C. Hodges, *Absolutely Free!* (Grand Rapids: Zondervan, 1989), 148-52. Hodges understands the call to repentance to be a call to a *harmonious relationship* with God, which he calls *fellowship*. To believe is the call to a permanent *saving relationship* with God. While belief for the permanent saving relationship is required only once, the need of repentance in order to establish fellowship with the Lord for the first time or to restore fellowship with Him will be repeated over and over again in the life of a believer.

heaven or how to establish a relationship with God is through works of self-denial. Most Protestant interpreters squirm at this point and are forced into explaining the passage from some sort of "evidence of faith" answer. But even if that is the correct interpretation, how many professing believers have gone out and sold all their possessions and given them to the poor as evidence of their faith? But what if the rich young ruler was asking a "B" question and Jesus gave him a "B" answer? What if *reception* of eternal life ("A" truth) is by faith, and *possession*[38] of eternal life ("B" truth) is by works (in the good sense, that is, empowered and motivated by the Holy Spirit—Eph 2:10; Gal 2:20). If the rich young ruler had asked an "A" question, Jesus would have given him an "A" answer. Instead, the man asked a "B" question and got a "B" answer. Of course, Jesus knew that to get "B" one must pass through "A." In order to *possess* eternal life, one must *have* eternal life. In order to *possess* the land, one must be *in* the land.

---

[38] The Matthean version (Matt 19:16) uses the verb εχω ("possess"), while the Lukan version (Lk 10:25) uses κληρονομέω "inherit"). In the OT *nḥl* and *yrsh* are used interchangeably, the one meaning "to inherit," the other meaning "to possess," respectively. A quick check of the concordance reveals that each word is translated both ways. Of course, the primary use of *yrsh* was in Deuteronomy. The people were to go in and possess the land. But there was a big difference between being in the land and possessing the land. In order to possess the land, very clear instructions were given to the people. When they failed to follow those instructions (such as with the Philistines), it was a failure in faith to possess the land. Now the Jews are in the land again, but they still have not possessed the land. They will not experience the full inheritance which belongs to them by virtue of the grant given to Abraham until Christ returns to win the land for them.

But it must be observed that this inheritance was a reward for faithfulness. So also in the Christian life every child of God is an heir (Gal 4:7) of many blessings which will be shared by all His children. But for the mature sons (Heb 2:10), there is a special inheritance/possession reserved in heaven ready to be revealed when Christ comes (1 Pet 1:4-5, 9). In fact, to drive this point home to the Hebrew Christians the author uses the word *peripoiēsin* (possession) in Heb 10:39. By faith these Christians can possess their life (*psuchēs*, their time on earth) for eternity. Romans 8:17 indicates a dual inheritance: heirs and joint heirs or co-heir for those who co-suffer and then who will be co-glorified.

So it is with repentance. It deals with "B" truth: fellowship. That is why Lk 17:3-4 is so illustrative. The discussion concerns a fractured fellowship between two brothers. In order for their fellowship to be restored, the offender must go to his brother and repent, while the offended brother must forgive the repenting brother. Then the two, who already have a permanent *relationship* (brother to brother), can once again begin to *enjoy* their relationship (=*fellowship*). Thus whenever we use the word relationship from this point forward we mean "A" truth, while fellowship refers to "B" truth. The offense had not ended their relationship; rather, it had broken their fellowship.

From the above passages, it should be clear that repentance is not simply a challenge to unbelievers. It's also an appeal to believers. Repentance is for all men? But just what is repentance? Does it mean "to change the mind," as many suggest? Or does it mean one must turn completely away from his sins, as others teach? The suggestion of this study is that repentance means more than simply a change of mind, but less than a complete turning away from one's sins, which can be externally observed. What, then, does repentance mean?

The Meaning of Repentance

We will not try to establish the meaning of this word from the comparisons of בּוּשׁ (*shub*, "to turn or turn around") and *niḥam* ("to be sorry or to comfort oneself ") in the OT, although these words will be discussed in our next study. The truth is that there is no term directly equivalent to *metanoeō* or *metanoia* in the OT. That is why the LXX never translates בּוּשׁ (*shub*) as *metanoeō*. In the LXX בּוּשׁ (*shub*) is translated as *epistrephō*, a fact which has led many to either equate *epistrephō* and *metanoeō* or to include *epistrephō* in the meaning of *metanoeō*.[39] Is this valid? Before discussing *epistrephō* in its relationship to *metanoeō* we need to examine the root meaning of *metanoeō* to see if that meaning is sufficient in its NT contexts.

It has already been pointed out that both Luther and Calvin wished to remove the concept of penance from the meaning of repentance.

---

[39] See Behm, "μετανοέω," 4:990-91.

An easy way to do that was to go to the root meaning of the word: *meta* = after; *noeō* = to think. When the two were put together, the effect of the *meta* was "after the fact" or "afterwards." It was to think about something later on and to have a reversal of opinion. So, repentance meant "to change the mind," a valid understanding in many non-religious contexts. But, is this meaning sufficient in its NT contexts, or are we guilty of the "root fallacy" when we assign this meaning to the word?[40]

Both John and Jesus preached, "Repent, for the kingdom of heaven is at hand" (Matt 3:2; 4:17). If we substitute the root meaning of *metanoeō* into this passage, does it make sense: "Change your mind because the kingdom of heaven is at hand"? Not really. Even if we start substituting items about which they were to change their mind (their own sinfulness, God's righteousness), something seems lacking. The exhortation would make more sense if we substituted "get right with God" as a meaning for repentance. "Get right with God because the kingdom of heaven is at hand." But "getting right with God" seems to involve more than just "changing one's mind."

If we look at Revelation 9:20-21, repent certainly carries more weight than "change your mind":

> But the rest of mankind, who were not killed by these plagues, did not repent of the works of their hands, that they should not worship demons, and idols of gold, silver, brass, stone, and wood, which can neither see nor hear, nor wool, and they did not repent of their murders or their sorceries or their sexual immorality or their thefts.

Surely, if there were a passage where "turning from one's sins" appears to be involved in the meaning of repentance, this one is it. To simply say that God continued to wipe these people out because they did not "change their minds" about their murders, et cetera, takes all punch out of the passage. But does it mean "to turn away from" as B.

---

[40] D. A. Carson, *Exegetical Fallacies*, 2d ed. (Grand Rapids: Baker, 1996), 28-33.

Demarest claims: "Repentance is a change of mind, ultimate loyalty, and behavior whereby pre-Christians turn from sin unto God?"[41]

Epistrephō is the NT term for "turning," just as it is in the LXX where it is used to translate בוש (*shub*) instead of *metanoeō*. But the use of *epistrephō* in the NT reveals that of its thirty-nine occurrences, in all but five, the turning can be externally observed by other people. James 5:19-20 is a case in point. In that passage a believer[42] has

---

[41] Demarest, Cross and Salvation, 252.

[42] There are two lines of argument offered to suggest the one who strays in this passage is not a believer. One is to say a brother is not a brother. Clearly the passage addresses brothers, and it hypothesizes that one of the brothers strays from the truth. It looks like James refers to a believer, unless, of course, a brother is not a brother.

The argument which says a brother is not a brother usually goes something like this. In every congregation we have professing Christians and possessing Christians. Only the latter are born again. Every church is a congregation mixed with sheep and goats, wheat and tares, believers and unbelievers, true brethren and false brethren. So just because James is addressing the brethren here does not mean all the brethren are believers.

Though that argument may work in certain contexts, it definitely falls short in James. In James 1:16-18 the "beloved brethren" are identified as the "us" and "we" of v. 18, which includes James, the author. And the passage says that "we" have been "brought forth" (*apekuēsen*—1 aorist active and a birthing term) by the word of truth that we might be a kind of first fruits of His creatures. Could there be a more clear statement of spiritual birth? These beloved brethren have been "born again."

But v. 19 immediately addresses these "beloved brethren" again. Surely it is the same group James just addressed in vv. 16-18. And will you notice that these beloved brethren are encouraged to receive the implanted Word with meekness, which is able to *sōsai* their *tas psuchas* (*save* their *lives*), the same Greek words we find in James 5:20 in reference to the straying believer whose life has been turned around. No, the brother-is-not-a-brother argument is specious indeed.

The only other way out of the obvious is to say the person who strays from the truth in James 5:19 is not identified as a brother, but as *tis* (anyone), meaning a member of the congregation but not one of the brethren. Again, the suggestion is completely out of context. All one has to do is to look in the immediate context at vv. 13-18 to see that *tis* has been used three other times to refer to believers in the congregation who have a certain need. Instructions are given as to how that need should be met. The sick person should call for the elders of the church,

strayed[43] from the straight and narrow ("the truth"), and another brother *turns* him *back*. This turnabout is clearly observable with the naked eye. It is not an *internal* turning or part of the root as suggested by D. L. Bock.[44]

And in the five instances where *epistrephō* might have been construed to mean something internal (Matt 13:15; Mk 4:12; Jn 12:40; Acts 28:27; 2 Cor 3:16), let it be observed that all five are a reference to the nation of Israel as a whole, a subject to be treated in the next study. Even so, the first four references refer to Isaiah 6:9-10, which has an interesting chiastic arrangement: "Make the heart of this people dull, and their ears heavy, and shut their eyes; lest they see with their eyes, and hear with their ears, and understand with their heart, and return and be healed." Notice the message goes full circle: heart, ears, eyes . . . eyes, ears, heart. Of course, the physical senses are used metaphorically, but the message has gone "around the horn," so to speak. If there were some sort of internal processing involved in their "turning," it would seem that the turning would have been in the chiasm. As it is not, and as the turning stands outside the chiasm, it appears that the turning is not part of the internalizing of the message, but rather deals with a subsequent external action.

Whether the above analysis of turning in Isaiah 6:10 bears any weight or not, the vast majority of the uses of the term *epistrephō* in the NT certainly deal with something externally observable. We conclude, therefore, that turning from one's sins in an observable manner may well be the *fruit* of repentance and/or believing (compare Acts 3:19 and 11:21), but the turning is not part of the *root*.

---

who will anoint him/her with oil and pray for that sick person. The prayer of faith will heal (*sōzō*) the sick. Surely no one will argue that this passage refers to an unbeliever. Neither should they argue based on the use of *tis* that Jas 5:19 refers to an unbeliever who strays from the truth.

[43] The Greek word *planeō* is certainly picturesque in that it portrays a believer in proper orbit around the Son of God, but he strays out of his appointed place in the heavens. Here is a believer who was reflecting the light of the Son for His glory, but some sort of black hole has sucked him out of orbit.

[44] See n. 5.

Yet, if repentance is more than a "change of mind," but less than an observable turning from sins, what is it? We suggest this meaning: *an internal resolve to turn from one's sins*. We think this meaning will make good sense in every NT use.

Conclusion

Once again, we ask the question, if repentance is the internal resolve to turn from one's sins, is repentance a condition for receiving eternal life? And once again, we conclude, no. Repentance is not a condition for *receiving* eternal life, but it is a condition for *possessing* eternal life. By possessing eternal life we refer to enjoying a quality of life that only the believer in fellowship with God can have. Repentance is not about relationship; it is about fellowship. In order to "get right with God," one must repent. If an unbeliever is in view, he must believe to receive the free gift of eternal life. He might repent before he believes or after he believes. It is his faith that saves him eternally, but it is his repentance which allows him to enjoy his faith. Repentance concerns fellowship.[45]

One might ask, "But how can God have fellowship with someone who has not actually turned away and forsaken all his known sins?" Perhaps an illustration will help. As a pastor I dealt week in and week out with men who are involved in addictive behaviors. I am comfortable eating lunch with these men, playing golf with them, and studying the Bible with them. But some of them are still caught up in their addictions. They have yet to turn away from them externally. But I can still feel comfortable with them and fellowship with them. How? Does not 1 Corinthians 5:11 tell me not to eat with them? Ah, the reason I can eat with them is that in each case these men have resolved within themselves that their behavior is wrong, and they want to be delivered from it. In other words, each of them has repented. They have not yet received the external victory. But they

---

[45] David Anderson, "The Role of Repentance in Salvation," in *A Defense of Free Grace Theology: With Respect to Saving Faith, Perseverance, and Assurance*, ed. Fred Chay (USA: Grace Theology Press, 2017), 89-119.

have internally resolved to turn away from their addictive behavior. Through the power of the Holy Spirit they will be delivered from the law of sin and death (Rom 8:2).

If any one of these men had not resolved within himself to turn from his sinful behavior, I could not enjoy fellowship with him. Is this not what Jesus was doing with winebibbers, tax collectors, gluttons, and sinners? He did not condone their sins. Nor did He indulge in the same. But He was having table fellowship with them. We can only conclude that they had repented, that is, they were convinced their wayward ways were wrong, and they wanted "to get right with God." In other words, they had resolved within themselves to turn from their sins. With that in mind, Jesus was willing to meet with them, to eat with them, and to explain the way of deliverance to them. The fruit of their repentance was their desire to meet with Him and would be their ultimate turning from their sins.

So, who is right? Is repentance for believers or for unbelievers? Both parties are right in that repentance is for both believers and unbelievers. Repentance is for all men. But repentance is not a condition for salvation; it is a condition for sanctification. It is not a condition for relationship; it is a condition for fellowship. To establish an eternal relationship with God, one must believe only once. But to enjoy ongoing fellowship with God, one needs to live a life punctuated by repentance.

There is one more Scriptural instance of repentance that has been a source of controversy among evangelicals: the call in the Gospels and Acts for a nation-wide repentance among the people of Israel. This is most explicit in the ministry of John the Baptist, followed by Peter's call for "men of Israel" to repent in the early chapters of Acts. The controversy concerns the nature and implications of John's "baptism of repentance" and Peter's call for repentance and baptism for "remission of sins."

National Repentance of Israel

John the Baptist had a clear, concise message to Israel: "Repent for the kingdom of heaven is at hand" (Matt 3:2). Jesus had exactly the same message: "Repent, for the kingdom of heaven is at hand" (Matt 4:17). And the people responded. They came in droves from Jerusalem, Judea, and the regions around the Jordan River. But when the Pharisees and Sadducees appeared on the scene (Matt 3:7), John was not impressed: "Brood of vipers, who has warned you to flee from the wrath to come? Therefore, start bearing fruit worthy of repentance" (my translation).

If we are going to understand the meaning of repentance for the nation of Israel, we must understand the setting for John's ministry, the meaning of the word "wrath," and the curse Jesus placed on the generation of Jews who put Him on the cross. And once we understand the national repentance of Israel, we can also unravel the relationship between water baptism and baptism of the Holy Spirit. After all, Augustine taught that the baptism of the Holy Spirit occurs during water baptism, and Calvin, Luther, Wesley, R. Shank,[46] and many others have hopped onto Augustine's baptismal bandwagon. Is that what the Scriptures teach, that a person receives the Holy Spirit while he is under the water or while the water is being sprinkled/ poured over him? If not, why not? Understanding the national repentance of Israel is significant for knowing when the baptism of the Holy Spirit occurs. This first requires us to study the setting for John's ministry.

The Setting for John's Ministry

Israel's Covenant with Yahweh

In order to understand the national call to repentance from John the Baptist, Jesus, and Peter to Israel, it is necessary to also understand

---

[46] Shank, *Elect in the Son* (Springfield, MO: Westcott, 1970) and *Life in the Son* (Springfield, MO: Westcott Publishers, 1961), admitted in a personal interview with this author in 1976 that the Holy Spirit is received while the new believer is under the water. When challenged with the example of Cornelius in Acts 10, he said Cornelius was an exception. When further challenged by the example of the thief on the cross (though baptism of the Holy Spirit was not an issue before Pentecost), he credited the thief with the baptism of "desire." The thief desired to get off the cross and get to the water, but since he could not, God credited him with righteousness because of his desire to be water baptized.

the covenant relationship between Yahweh and Israel. It began long before the Covenant of Moses with the Covenant of Abraham. This covenant was much different than the Mosaic Covenant. The latter was what M. Kline called the suzerainty-vassal treaty.[47] But the Abrahamic Covenant was identified by M. Weinfeld as a covenant of grant. In his words: "Two types of covenants occur in the Old Testament: the obligatory type reflected in the Covenant of God with Israel and the promissory type reflected in the Abrahamic and Davidic covenants."[48] In contrasting the two categories of covenants, Weinfeld comments:

> Both preserve the same elements: historical introduction, border delineations, stipulations, witnesses, blessings and curses. Functionally, however, there is a vast difference between the two types of documents. While the "treaty" constitutes an obligation of the vassal to his master, the suzerain, the "grant" constitutes an obligation of the master to his servant.... What is more, while the grant is a reward for loyalty and good deeds already performed, the treaty is an inducement for future loyalty.[49]

L. W. King was one of the first (1912) to publish the plates and translation of royal grants given to faithful servants in his work *Babylonian Boundary-Stones*.[50] These boundary-stones (*kudurrus*) are dated from 1450 B.C. to 550 B.C., or the entire period of the Babylonian history during which boundary-stones were employed for the protection of private property. Kings comments:

---

[47] M. Kline, *Treaty of the Great King* (Grand Rapids: Eerdmans, 1963), 9-10. More recent work has refined the outline offered by Kline with considerable benefit in the stipulations section (see S. A. Kaufman, "The Structure of Deuteronomic Law," *Maarav* 1 [April 1979]: 105-58), but the entire Book of Deuteronomy is generally recognized as one great suzerainty-vassal covenant.

[48] M. Weinfeld, "The Covenant of Grant in the Old Testament and the Ancient Near East," *Journal of the American Oriental Society* 90 (April-June 1970): 184.

[49] Ibid., 185.

[50] L. W. King, Babylonian Boundary-Stones and Memorial-Tablets in the British Museum (London: British Museum, 1912).

The Kudurru-texts had their origin under the Kassite kings of the Third Babylonian Dynasty, and, while at first recording, or confirming, royal grants of land to important officials and servants of the king, their aim was undoubtedly to place the newly acquired rights of the owner under the protection of the gods. The series of curses, regularly appended to the legal record, was directed against any interference with the owner's rights, which were also placed under the protection of the deities whose symbols were engraved on the blank spaces of the stone.[51]

These same royal grants were used in Israel from the time of Abraham right on through the time of David.[52] The land grants were, invariably, rewards for faithful service on the part of a vassal to his suzerain. It is worth commenting that a suzerainty-vassal relationship was the basis for a grant. In other words, kings did not give grants to strangers, that is, someone with whom there was no covenant relationship. The relationship preceded the reward.[53] It is the reward

---

[51] Ibid., x.

[52] The case for royal grants in the history of Israel is made by A. E. Hill, "The Ebal Ceremony as Hebrew Land Grant?" *Journal of the Evangelical Theological Society* 31 (December 1988): 399-406, but David's specific use of them is documented by Z. Ben-Barak, "Meribaal and the System of Land Grants in Ancient Israel," *Biblica* 62 (January 1981): 73-91. David may have become acquainted with the custom when he was given Ziklag by Achish, king of Gath, as a reward for his services as a military commander. But the story of Meribaal (2 Sam 9; 16:1-4; 19:17-31) shows that David practiced this custom of giving land as a reward for faithful service himself. There is also evidence from 1 Samuel 8:14 and 22:7 that the system of grants was in vogue during the time of David.

[53] The relationship with Abraham actually began in Ur of the Chaldeans, a fact often overlooked but made clear by Acts 7:2-3. When the text says, "The God of glory appeared to our father Abraham," the wording is technical jargon for establishing a covenant relationship. The Lord-Servant (Suzerain-Vassal) relationship was established in Ur. The stipulation was that Abraham leave Ur and go to a land this glorious God would reveal to him. Because Abraham was obedient to this stipulation, that is, because he was a faithful vassal, he was given the reward (Gen 15:1) of the covenant of grant, which was the land grant of Israel.

aspect of the grants along with the parallel terminology between the grants and the covenants with Abraham and David, which convince Weinfeld that these covenants are royal grants. Both Abraham and David loyally served their suzerain. Abraham is promised the land of Israel *because* he obeyed God (Gen 22:16, 18; 26:5), and David is promised dynasty *because* he served God with truth, loyalty, and righteousness (1 Kings 3:6; 9:4; 11:4, 6, 11, 35; 14:8; 15:3).[54]

---

[54] Here are some of the terminology parallels which point to faithful service: 1) "Kept the charge of my kingship" (Ashurbanipal to his servant Bulta) parallels "kept my charge, my commandments, my rules and my teachings" (Gen 26:5); 2) "Walked in perfection" (Aru 15:13-17) parallels "Walk before me and be perfect" (Gen 17:1); 3) "Stood before me in truth" and "walked with loyalty" parallels "who walked before you in truth, loyalty, and uprightness of heart" (1 Kgs 3:6); 4) "I am the King ... who returns kindness to the one who serves in obedience and to the one who guards the royal command" (Aru 15:6-7; 16:6-7; 18:9-12) parallels "the God ... who keeps His gracious promise to those who are loyal to Him and guard His commandments" (Deut 7:9-12) and "who keeps His gracious promise to your servants who serve you wholeheartedly" (1 Kgs 8:23); 5) "Land" and "house" seem to be the primary gifts given by kings, which parallel the gifts given to Abraham (land) and David (house = dynasty); 6) "Gives it to Adal-eni and his sons forever" (PRU III 16.132:27-38) parallels "for your descendants forever" (Gen 13:15) and "for your descendants after you throughout their generations" (Gen 17:7-8); 7) "On that day Abba-El gave the city" parallels "On that day Yahweh concluded a covenant with Abraham." According to Weinfeld, "on that day" has legal implications; 8) The delineation of borders for land grants is a clear parallel; 9) Marriage/adoption terminology used as a judicial basis for the gift of land or dynasty is quite prevalent among the secular and biblical grants.

By Abrahamic Covenant it should be pointed out that this author is referring to Genesis 15, not Genesis 12. In Gen 12:1-3 there is at least one stipulation regarding future obedience. Abraham had to go to the land. Any future reward for Abraham was contingent on his going to the land. This is what Acts 7:3 confirms. In fact, it is after he has gone to the land, built altars, and rescued his nephew (a parity obligation in the ancient treaties among co-vassals, according to D. J. McCarthy, *Treaty and Covenant: A Study in Form in the Ancient Oriental Documents and in the Old Testament*, Analecta Biblica, no. 21 [Rome: Pontifical Biblical Institute, 1963], 24-25), and shown his allegiance to the true Suzerain versus the false (the king of Sodom) by paying tribute (a normal vassal obligation [ibid., 32]) to the Suzerain's representative (Melchizekek) and having a covenant

The traditional premillennial distinction of "conditional" versus "unconditional" has muddied the waters.[55] As a matter of fact, the covenants of grant are conditioned upon obedience, but are unconditional after their inauguration (at least for the initial recipient).[56] The suzerainty-vassal covenants are unconditional in their initiation, but conditional after inauguration. The suzerain sovereignly initiated the covenant (as set forth in the historical prologues of these covenants), but any blessings accrued came only upon the condition of the vassal's loyalty to the stipulations. "Conditional" versus "unconditional" is both an over-simplification and an inadequate distinction. A better contrast between the two types is "motivation for future obedience" versus "reward for past obedience."

Here is the point. Once Abraham or David was given his grant, it could not be taken away. But since these grants included promises regarding future generations (seed), and since these grants were rewards based on the faithfulness of the initial recipient, how can the blessings (rewards) of the grant accrue to future generations if they are unfaithful? The answer is that they cannot. Isaac illustrates this principle in Genesis 26. Abraham has died. Now God appears to Isaac and challenges him to future obedience: do not go to Egypt. God promises Isaac that He will confirm or establish the oath He swore

---

meal with him (bread and wine [ibid., 172-73] that God says to Abraham, "... your *reward* shall be very great" (emphasis mine). The covenant of grant of Genesis is a reward for past faithfulness to the Suzerain.

[55] J. D. Pentecost, *Things to Come* (Grand Rapids: Zondervan, 1969), 65-69.

[56] In a private interview with this author in Jerusalem (February 24, 1998) Weinfeld did say that it is his opinion that after the Exile the Jews began to look at the Abrahamic and Davidic Covenants as conditioned upon their obedience to the Mosaic Covenant. It is too bad they did not understand it that way before the Assyrians and Babylonians were used to discipline them. In fact, it is hard to see how they could miss it after reading Deuteronomy 4:23-31.

However, though the fulfillment of the blessings of the grant covenants was conditioned on the obedience of a faithful generation, the promise to the line itself was unconditional after the grant had been given. The only question was which generation would be that faithful generation.

to his father, Abraham, if only Isaac will be obedient to stay in the land. Isaac was faithful, so the promises of the grant continued to flow through him.

Likewise, God appeared to Jacob in a dream. Jacob was going back to Haran to get a wife, the very place from which Abraham had come. God tells him that the promise given to his grandfather, Abraham, can only be fulfilled in Palestine. Thus, in Genesis 31:3, he tells Jacob to return. For the land blessings to flow through Jacob, he had to be obedient to God's voice. This same principle of obedience in order to possess the land can be traced right on through the Palestinian Covenant to the ultimate remnant that will possess the borders of the land grant originally promised to Abraham. No generation of Jews has yet had the faith necessary to fully possess the land promised in the Palestinian Covenant (Deut. 30:1-10). The promise to Abraham still holds, but God is waiting for a faithful generation to inherit the promise.

This same principle of faithfulness applies to the promise of seed. This aspect of the grant given to Abraham will come to pass. The Davidic grant in 2 Samuel 7 picks up on the seed aspect of Abraham's Covenant. For all David knew, Solomon would be the one to establish the Davidic throne forever. But Solomon was not capable of being the one to fulfill the everlasting nature of this grant. He was not found faithful (1 Kings 11:11, 35). The royal grant given to David would await a faithful seed worthy of everlasting rule. This principle of a "faithful generation" required for the fulfillment of the future aspects of the royal grants is a crucial link in connecting Jesus with the fulfillment of both the Abrahamic and Davidic Covenants. The rewards of the grants would not be realized by an unfaithful generation, or by an unfaithful ruler.

And so, just as Israel was looking for an ideal king to be their Messiah, Yahweh was looking for an ideal generation which would be faithful to the stipulations of the Mosaic Covenant (the suzerainty-vassal covenant). Through such a generation, He could fulfill the promises to Abraham, Isaac, and Jacob. He could fulfill the Abrahamic Covenant (the covenant of grant). But what happened to unfaithful generations?

An understanding of the grants may be helpful here, as well. Unfaithfulness on the part of a vassal did not nullify the covenant relationship in a suzerainty-vassal covenant. The suzerain sovereignly initiated the relationship and he maintained it as well. This is the argument of God throughout Hosea as well as Romans 9-11 and many other passages. The fidelity of the vassal did not determine the duration of the covenant. What, then, did a suzerain do with an unfaithful vassal? Customarily, he chose from among three different options: (1) he could invoke the curses of the covenant;[57] (2) he could declare holy war on the vassal;[58] and (3) he could draw up a new covenant.[59] Implicit in all three disciplinary options was the loss of any royal grants which may have been incorporated into the suzerainty-vassal treaty like incentive clauses. If a grant (by definition) only went to faithful vassals, it is intuitively obvious that the unfaithful vassal was not a candidate for a grant. In other words, he lost his reward. The suzerainty-vassal treaty (or a new one) was still in effect, but the bonuses contained in the incentive clauses (covenants of grant) would not be given. Thus, the danger facing an unfaithful vassal was both temporal discipline (heavier taxes, stipulations, or even death) and loss of reward (royal grant).

Hopefully, it can be seen from this discussion of covenants that when John the Baptist and Jesus began their ministries, God was looking for a faithful generation. But if the Jewish generation living during the first century A.D. was going to be faithful, it had to repent. This call to repentance for them as a nation or generation of Jews was really no different than God's call to them in prior centuries. And this leads us to a discussion of repentance in the OT.

---

[57] F. C. Fensham, "Common Trends in Curses of Near Eastern Treaties and *kudurru*-Inscriptions Compared with Maledictions of Amos and Isaiah," *Zeitschrift für die alttestamentliche Wissenschaft* 75 (January 1963): 172.
[58] Ibid., 172-74.
[59] Exodus 34, for example.

Israel's Repentance in the OT

According to E. Würthwein, there is no OT equivalent for *metanoeō* or *metanoia*.[60] That is why the term is so seldom found in the LXX (only fourteen times for the verb and always as a translation for *niḥam*[61] rather than *shub*). The LXX translation for *shub* is *epistrephō*, which as we have already seen is a term to be distinguished from *metanoeō*. Of the 1056 occurrences of *sh|b* in the OT, Würthwein thinks 118 have a religious context.[62] R. Wilkin counts 203 covenantal uses when the verb, noun, and adjective are combined.[63] In only one passage (the Ninevites of Jonah 3:5-10), is the word used for anyone other than Israel. The vast majority of the uses are a call from the prophets for Israel to return to covenant loyalty. Yahweh and Israel have an intimate relationship. As Würthwein comments:

> Hence Hos. can depict the relation between Yahweh and Israel in terms of a marriage in which the wife is unfaithful to her husband. Again, Is. can speak of sons who rebel, and Jer. can describe sin as forsaking Yahweh. All these expressions show that sin is simply turning away or apostasy from God. It is the more serious because Israel stands in a special relation to Yahweh.[64]

---

[60] E. Würthwein, "*metanoeō*," in *TDNT*, 1967 ed., 4:980.

[61] This verb, which meant "to be sorry" or "to comfort oneself," occurs 108 times in the OT, but only three of these deal with the repentance of men over sins (Jer 8:6; 31:19; and Job 42:6). In its theological context it usually refers to the repentance of God (see H. V. Parunak, "A Semantic Survey of *niḥam*," [*Biblica* 56, 1975]: 512-32). Jeremiah 8:6 concerns temporal discipline of Israel for her idolatry. Jeremiah 31:19 speaks of Israel's sorrow after she had returned to Yahweh. And Job 42:6 refers to temporal blessings received by Job after his repentance. None of these refers to any repentance prior to a covenant relationship or personal relationship (see Wilkin, "Repentance," 17).

[62] Würthwein, "*metanoeō*," 4:984.

[63] Wilkin, "Repentance," 13.

[64] Würthwein, "*metanoeō*," 4:985.

Repentance

The point here should be obvious. The call to repentance in the OT, if there was such a call,[65] was to a nation already in covenant relationship with Yahweh. They were viewed as married or as the children of a loving Father (Jer 31:3, 9). The "turning" summoned by the prophets was a "return" to fellowship with a God with whom they already had a relationship. Failure to return to the Lord would bring temporal judgment. Deuteronomy 4:23-31 sets the stage:

> Take heed to yourselves, lest you forget the covenant of the Lord your God which He made with you, and make for yourselves a carved image in the form of anything which the Lord your God has forbidden you. For the Lord your God is a consuming fire, a jealous God . . . . [Y]ou will soon utterly perish from the land which you cross over the Jordan to possess; you will not prolong your days in it, but will be utterly destroyed . . . . But from there you will seek the Lord your God, and you will find Him if you seek Him with all your heart and with all your soul. When you are in distress, and all these things come upon you in the latter days, when you turn [*shub*] to the Lord your God and obey His voice (for the Lord your God is a merciful God), He will not forsake you nor destroy you, nor forget the covenant of your fathers which He swore to them.

Note the features of this passage: 1) God's faithfulness to the covenant of the fathers (the Abrahamic Covenant, the covenant of grant) despite the unfaithfulness of succeeding generations to the Mosaic Covenant, the Suzerainty-Vassal Covenant; 2) the wrath of God, which is described as a consuming fire; 3) the temporal nature of the judgment; 4) a judgment that would destroy physical lives and scatter the Jews among the nations; and 5) the compassion of the Lord in the latter days toward the generation, which returns to Him and seeks Him with their whole heart.

It is noteworthy that the only uses of *shub* in the Pentateuch that refer to Israel's (or anyone's) turning to the Lord are in the passage

---

[65] We must remember there is no Hebrew term which is the exact equivalent of *metanoeō*.

just cited and Deut 30:1-10 (the Palestinian Covenant),[66] where it is said that the Jews can return to Yahweh from their dispersion among the nations if they do so with all their heart and soul. Thus, it can be concluded that the appeal to Israel to return to the Lord in the OT is an appeal to turn away from her infidelity to the Mosaic Covenant and to seek the Lord with her heart and soul. It is a call for fellowship, not relationship. Infidelity to the covenant evokes God's temporal wrath, but not His eternal judgment. Though individuals in the nation may undergo eternal judgment for lack of faith, the nation as a whole will never face eternal judgment.

The Corruption in Judaism

Much has been made of the condition of Judaism during John's era. There had not been a legitimate High Priest over Israel since 143 B.C. Annas finished his role as High Priest in A.D. 15, but simony and/or nepotism prevailed, and five of his sons followed as high priests, in addition to his son-in-law, Caiaphas. The latter may have been High Priest during John's day, but his father-in-law Annas[67] was the power behind the office (as witnessed by the informal trial of Jesus by night before Annas as well as Acts 4:6). And "Annas' Bazaar" has been well documented. Through corruption and graft, the temple till was full of money taken from the temple tax (one shekel instead of the normal half shekel), the money changers with their 12% surcharge, and the

---

[66] See Pentecost, *Things to Come*, 95-99, for a more detailed analysis of this covenant. This passage reaffirms the ongoing nature of the grant covenant to the recipient and his offspring. The grant, whether it was a land grant as in the case of Abraham or a dynastic grant as in the case of David, was the permanent possession of the line. However, once again, in order to enjoy the full blessings of the grant, God was waiting for a faithful generation of Jews who would possess the land, and the Jews were waiting for a faithful king who would reign from Zion.

[67] He is even called High Priest after his tenure is over, perhaps in the same manner as we address a former President as President So-and-So, even though his tenure is past. In the Jewish mind the High Priest was in office for life, so Annas may have wielded the influence of the Torah over the nation in spite of any Roman appointment.

sale of animals and birds for sacrifice. Truly the temple had become a den of thieves. The Copper Scroll lists 4,630 talents of gold[68] hidden around Israel to keep the Romans from getting it when Titus' army came through in A.D. 70. Many think this money came from the temple.[69] Whether it did or not, the record is clear that Judaism had been turned into a money-making scheme run by con artists. God had had enough. Judgment was about to fall on that kind of corruption, just as it did in the past when the Assyrians and then the Babylonians were used by God to purge His people.

John was calling the people out of corrupted Judaism. He realized the system was too far gone to change it from the inside out. So rather than going into Jerusalem to call the people to repentance, he went out into the wilderness. In order to declare their separation and disassociation from corrupted Judaism, they needed to repent and be water baptized.

If a Greek wanted to become a Jew, he needed to do three things: bring a sacrifice to Jerusalem, be circumcised (in the case of a male), and be water baptized. Through water baptism, one gained a *new identity*. He disaffiliated from the old and affiliated with the new, which was really to return and faithfully adhere to the original stipulations of the covenant of grant. To become a Jew one needed water baptism to disaffiliate with the Gentile ways and to affiliate and identify with the practices of Judaism. Similarly, if one wished to renounce corrupted Judaism, he also needed to be water baptized. That is exactly what John was asking the people to do. Whether or not John had any exposure to Qumran he did seem to share their distaste for the temple system in vogue during his day. The Essenes of Qumran disassociated from the temple community. So did John and his followers. For John knew that the wrath of God was coming upon that generation of Jews. This leads us to a discussion of the meaning of "wrath" in the NT.

---

[68] Since a talent could be anywhere from 25-75 lbs., the weight of this gold would be anywhere from 58 to 174 tons.
[69] R. Price, *Secrets of the Dead Sea Scrolls* (Eugene, OR: Harvest House, 1966), 280-282.

"Wrath" in the NT

John queries the Pharisees and Sadducees: "Who has warned you to flee from the wrath to come?" The word for "wrath" is *orgē*, a word used most frequently in Romans and Revelation. In neither of those books is there a clear reference to wrath that is eternal. Rev 6:17 refers to the end of the Tribulation Period as the "great day of His wrath." Though the word is used six times, it only occurs in Revelation 6-19, which describes the last seven years of Daniel's program for Daniel's people and his holy city, Jerusalem (Dan 9:24, 27). If the term were meant to include or refer to eternity, we would expect to find it after Revelation 19 in connection with hell or the lake of fire or the Great White Throne judgment. Not so.

In Romans, the first occurrence of "wrath" is in Rom 1:18. There the wrath of God *is being revealed* (*apokaluptetai*, present tense) from heaven upon all ungodliness and unrighteousness of men who suppress the truth in unrighteousness. God's wrath is then revealed in His turning men over to the increasing control of their sinful nature (vv. 24, 26, 28) until they cannot tell right from wrong (an *adokimos* mind). The salvation of Romans (see 1:16) goes beyond justification to deliverance from the tyranny of the sin nature in one's life to actually *reveal* God's righteousness by faith (see 1:17). Just as He was our substitute in death so must He be our substitute in life (see 4:25) to save us from "wrath" (see 5:9-10). By His death we are justified; by His life we are progressively sanctified. So Romans, which uses wrath more than any other NT book, does not refer to the wrath of eternity, but to the outpouring of God's anger against man's sin *in time*, whether now or at the Judgment Seat of Christ.[70]

---

[70] The reference in Romans 2:5 may look like eternal judgment at first blush. But it may also be taken as in 1 Thessalonians 2:16 where the Jews who have rejected Christ and hindered the cause of the gospel are filling up the cup of sins until God judges. The certainty of this judgment is expressed by Paul through a proleptic aorist (*ephthasen*, "will certainly come upon them" to the uttermost). This wrath is most likely the same wrath mentioned in 1 Thessalonians 1:10 and 5:9, but it does not preclude the outpouring of God's wrath on that generation of Jews who rejected Christ. They are a foreshadowing of the wrath to come in the

Repentance

So it goes in the rest of the NT.[71] Just one more example from Paul's letters should suffice to establish this point. Many expositors recognize 1 Thessalonians 1:10 and 5:9 as among the strongest scriptural proofs for a Pre-Trib or pre-wrath rapture.[72] Both of these verses use "wrath" in reference to the Tribulation period. Because they say that members of the universal church will be delivered from this wrath and are not appointed to this time of wrath, the "rapture" referenced in 1 Thessalonians 4:13-18 is a promise to be removed sometime before the wrath of the Lamb (Rev 6:16-17). Thus, once again, "wrath" is not

---

Tribulation Period. Romans 2:5 may be a similar reference. The "treasuring up" in Romans 2:5 is similar in concept to the "fill up" in 1 Thessalonians 2:16. And the "day of wrath" may well refer to the same wrath as we find in 1 Thessalonians (see also Zephaniah 1:14-18 for the day of God's wrath and Revelation 6:16-17 where the great day of His wrath has come), not to preclude the temporal judgment on the Jewish generation which rejected Christ. Most expositors agree that this section in Romans deals with the sins of the Jews. One problem with relegating Rom 2:5-10 to the Great White Throne is the reference to eternal life in v. 7. No eternal life is given at the Great White Throne. It is unlikely that Paul is hop-scotching back and forth across the Millennium with judgments. It is more likely that the judgment is the temporal wrath of the Tribulation Period immediately followed by the Judgment Seat of Christ and the separation of sheep and goats (Matt 16:27 and 25:31ff).

[71] John 3:36 is another verse which could easily be misunderstood for eternal judgment. But careful attention to the tenses reveals that both the eternal life mentioned and the wrath of God are present time experiences. The believer has eternal life right now, the moment he believes. It is not a gift given at some future judgment. So is it also with the wrath. Like Romans 1:18 this wrath is in the present: "the wrath of God *abides* on him."

[72] Robert Thomas, "1 & 2 Thessalonians" in *The Expositors Bible Commentary*, vol. 11 (Grand Rapids, Michigan: Zondervan Publishing, 1978), 248, 285. Michael Vlach, "The Eschatology of the Pauline Epistles" in *The Return of Christ: A Premillennial Perspective* eds. David L. Allen & Steve W. Lemke (Nashville, Tennessee: Broadman & Holman Publishing, 2011), 249. The most exegetically complete defense is "The Rapture in 1 Thessalonians 5:1-11" by Zane Hodges in *Walvoord: A Tribute*, ed. Donald K. Campbell (Chicago, IL: Moody Press, 1982), 67-79. Also see Marvin Rosenthal, *The Pre-Wrath Rapture of the Church* (Nashville, Tennessee: Thomas Nelson Publishers,1990), 246.

a NT reference to eternity, but rather to something temporal, whether presently or at the end of this age.[73]

The Cursed Generation

In this study we are suggesting that John the Baptist's use of wrath was consistent with the rest of NT usage. The "wrath to come" was something in time. This is not to say that those who rejected Christ will not suffer eternal condemnation (see Matt 23:33). But there was also a severe judgment in time. Jesus Himself defined the curse upon the generation which rejected Him in Matthew 23. In that passage, He excoriated the scribes, Pharisees, and hypocrites over and over again. Like John the Baptist, He referred to them as a brood of vipers (v. 33). Because they rejected not only Him, but also other righteous prophets (v. 34), wrath was to be poured out upon the generation which rejected Him. That wrath was unfolded in Matt 23:35-36. All the righteous blood from righteous Abel unto the blood of Zechariah, son of Berechiah . . . came upon that generation. Jesus went on to leave some indication as to what that judgment would look like a few verses later when He told His disciples that not one stone of the temple area would be left standing upon another (Matt 24:2). That prophecy was fulfilled when Titus brought his Roman army through in A.D. 70.

This brings us to the matter of the length of a Jewish generation. If the wilderness wanderings are any indication, then a generation was considered to be forty years. Is it a coincidence that Jesus began His ministry in A.D. 30 and the judgment of Titus came upon them in

---

[73] In Christian literature the word "wrath" is usually used to depict God's anger and vengeance against unbelievers for all eternity. By showing that the biblical use of the word usually translated "wrath" (*orgē*) is tied to time instead of eternity is not a denial of the eternal punishment of unbelievers forever and ever. Revelation 14:10ff certainly bears witness to the eternal torment of those that worship the beast and receive his mark. But showing that the word *orgē* is tied to time instead of eternity helps explain passages like Romans 1:18, 5:9, 9:22 (wrath here is being turned over to the control of our Sin Nature), 1 Thessalonians 1:10 and 5:9 (wrath here is the Tribulation Period), and Matthew 3:7 (wrath here is Titus and AD 70).

A.D. 70? Forty years: a Jewish generation. God gave the Jews of that generation forty years to separate from the corruption of Judaism if they wished to avoid the curse. When Titus came through, he killed 1,100,000 Jews—all the vindicating blood from righteous Abel to the blood of Zechariah.[74]

John's Ministry

John the Baptist was calling people out of corrupted Judaism. If they would confess their sins, repent, and be water baptized, they would be "back in fellowship" with Yahweh—then they would be walking in the light, ready, willing, and able to recognize the Messiah when He came to baptize with the Holy Spirit (Jn 1:25-33). It is noteworthy that John refers to Jesus as "He who is coming" (1:27, 30). John very likely had more than Isaiah 40 on his mind (1:23) when he saw himself as the one who prepared the way for the Lord. Malachi spoke of the messenger who would prepare the way for the Lord (Mal 3:1). Here it says the Lord will come to His temple. Behold, "He is coming," and who can endure the day of "His coming" (v. 2)? He will sit as a refiner's fire; He will purge the sons of Levi (v. 3). Of course, these verses refer to His second coming and the great and terrible day of the Lord (4:5). But John the Baptist was preparing the way for what he must have thought would be the only coming. And from his perspective, the day was coming, burning like an oven; neither root nor branch would be left (4:1; see Matt 3:1-12).

From our perspective, it is both *already* and *not yet*. Thus, when John the Baptist said, "Even now the ax is laid to the root of the trees" (Matt 3:10), he envisioned the wrath of God already beginning in terms of the hardening of the hearts of the leaders of Israel. For forty years these people who were already in covenant relationship with Yahweh had an opportunity to spare themselves from wrath. When Titus came, the tree fell. And He will indeed come *again* to

---

[74] Josephus Flavius, *War Against the Jews*, Book VI, Chapter IX, Section 3, www.bible.ca/pre-flavius-josephus-70AD-Mt24-fulfilled.htm. Accessed January 10, 2018.

Israel with fire (Mal 4:1-5). But Jesus would also baptize with the Holy Spirit those who identified with Him through John's water baptism of repentance at His *first* coming, in partial ("already") fulfillment of Ezekiel 36:25-27.

Peter's Ministry

This same invitation is exactly what Peter was offering the "men of Israel" at Pentecost. The entire company listening to him in Acts 2 was comprised of Jews who had come from around the Mediterranean world for Passover and stayed on through Pentecost. When they were convicted of having crucified a man who was both Lord and Christ (Acts 2:36), they asked what they should do. The answer Peter gives is an answer to the nation of Israel. He is calling the entire nation to repent and be water baptized to identify with the named Messiah, and they would be saved from wrath and receive the gift of the Holy Spirit. It was the same call given by John the Baptist, and this time the Holy Spirit was sent by Jesus Christ, just as John had promised. But they needed to identify unambiguously with that named Messiah through repentance and water baptism.

The clear connection between the wrath predicted by both John and Jesus and the call of Peter to the nation is made by Acts 2:40: "And with many other words he testified and exhorted them, saying, 'Be saved from this perverse generation.'" He was not telling them how to be saved from hell or the lake of fire (though that would be included in the package for those coming to faith for the first time). He was specifically telling them how to avoid temporal wrath—the impending judgment on that crooked generation.

Had the entire nation heeded the words of Peter at that point, presumably Jesus would have returned from heaven and set up His kingdom on earth to reign for a thousand years. But the entire nation had yet to hear, so Peter speaks again to the "men of Israel" in Acts 3. He again tells the story of Jesus and speaks of the guilt of the people and their leaders. Again he asks them to *repent* and *turn* (*metanoeō* + *epistrephō*, 3:19). If they would do that, a number of things would happen: 1) their sins would be blotted out; 2) times of refreshing would come from the presence of the Lord; and 3) Jesus would be sent. The English text of Acts 3:19-20 (NKJV) says "that . . . so that . . . that," which makes it look as though there are three successive purpose/result clauses. Actually, there are two, the second one having two parts. So it could be argued that the times of refreshing would come from the Lord's return to the earth. In other words, the King and the Kingdom are once again being offered to the nation of Israel. If they would repent, the King would return to set up His Kingdom. Peter goes on in this passage to speak of the judgment that would come upon those who rejected the Messiah (v. 23). Then he refers back to the covenant relationship the people of Israel had through Abraham. This covenant was a guarantee of future blessing to the seed of Abraham. The relationship was firm. Fellowship was not. The men of Israel needed to do nothing to establish a relationship between the nation and God. Yahweh had done that through Abraham in Ur of the Chaldeans before he went to the land of Canaan. But the nation of Israel needed to repent in order to restore fellowship with God and to receive the blessing promised to the faithful generation that would receive the Messiah.[75]

Water Baptism and the Holy Spirit

It is noteworthy that reception of the Holy Spirit in Acts is mentioned in connection with five groups or individuals (Acts 2, 8, 9, 10, 19). Each case when there was a time interval between their belief in Jesus and their reception of the Spirit (Acts 2, 8, 9, 19) it involved believers of Jewish lineage. The Samaritans of Acts 8 were half-Jews. The believers of Acts 19 had received John's baptism, so they were Jews. For each of these new believers, the gift of the Holy Spirit was *preceded* by water baptism so they could identify with the now named Messiah.

Cornelius is the prototype of Gentile salvation in Acts. Remission

---

[75] See Barry E. Horner, *Future Israel: Why Christian Anti-Judaism Must Be Challenged* (Nashville, TN: B&H Academic, nd), 252, 340 and Robert L. Thomas, *Perspectives On Israel and the Church 4 Views,* ed. Chad O. Brand, (Nashville, TN: B&H Academic, 2015), 87-111.

of sins for Gentiles came from the point of their initial belief (Acts 10:43). But not only remission of sins, reception of the Holy Spirit was also part of God's gracious dealing with any Gentile who would believe the good news. But when Gentile salvation was in view, water baptism *followed* baptism by the Spirit. When Cornelius and company believed the words being spoken to them, the Holy Spirit fell upon all those listening. Only then were they water baptized to attest their equal inclusion with Jewish believers (10:45-48; 11:12-18). They did not require water baptism to receive the Holy Spirit, and repentance is not mentioned. The men of Israel in Acts 3:19 had to "repent and turn" for times of refreshing to come, but the blessing came for the Greeks when they "believed and turned" to the Lord (Acts 11:21). Why? They had no need to repent of corrupted Judaism of that generation in order to identify with the named Messiah. The curse of Matthew 23 was only on the Jews of that generation who crucified the Messiah, not the Gentiles.

Conclusion

How, then, does this understanding of wrath, generation, and water baptism impact the meaning of "repentance" in relation to the nation of Israel? We are suggesting that John the Baptist, Jesus, and Peter had dual ministries. One was to call the nation of Israel back into fellowship with Yahweh. The covenant relationship had long since been established. The nation of Israel did not need a new relationship with God but they were sorely lacking in fellowship. The sacrificial system of the Mosaic covenant had been so corrupted that without a complete resolve to turn from this corruption (repentance) and the fruit that would go along with this repentance (the actual turning), they faced a severe, impending temporal judgment.

This fiery, but temporal, indignation may well have been the warning of Hebrews 10:26-39 (remember the "fiery" warning of Deut 4:23-31). For those Hebrew Christians to have believed in Christ but then to revert back to the corrupt sacrificial system of Jerusalem would leave them exposed to God's wrath. They had disassociated once from corrupted Judaism, but to re-associate would bring upon them the plagues of the curse.

John the Baptist, Jesus, and Peter were all trying to persuade Israel into the repentance and turning that would restore them to refreshing fellowship with God. The Pharisees and Sadducees were right. They were the physical seed of Abraham (Matt 3:9). As such, they did have a covenant relationship. But until a faithful generation of Jews came along, the blessings of the grant covenants (Abrahamic and Davidic: land and kingdom) would not be realized. Instead, they would experience the curses of the Suzerainty-Vassal Treaty (the Mosaic Covenant). The only way to avoid it was a complete turnaround.

But the ministry of John, Jesus, and Peter was more than calling the nation of Israel to repentance. John was the forerunner, the messenger sent to prepare the way of the Lord. "This man came for a witness, to bear witness of the Light, that all through him might believe" (Jn 1:7). Jesus also wanted men to believe in Him and His gospel (Mk 1:15; Jn 6:29-47). So did Peter (Acts 2:44; 4:4, 32; 10:43). Though the *nation* was called to repentance, *individuals* in the nation were called to believe *and* repent.

Some of these Jews were probably OT believers in the sense that many Jews under the old covenant were people who had placed their faith in that which God had promised them, and their faith was reckoned unto them for righteousness, just as Abraham's was. The word used to describe the "devout" men who observed the filling of the Holy Spirit at Pentecost is *eulabēs*, an adjective used only three times in the NT, and all by Luke. In fact, the noun (*eulabeia*) and the verb (*eulabeomai*) are also used only by Luke and the writer to the Hebrews. In the other two uses of the adjective, believers are clearly in view. In Acts 8:2 "devout" men carry off the body of Stephen for burial and mourn him. These are believers. And in Luke 2:25 it is Simeon who is described as just and "devout," and the Holy Spirit was upon him. Surely, this is what we might call an OT believer. It is very likely that many of the three thousand, who heard Peter's sermon in Acts 2, fell into this same category. Nevertheless, all those who responded to his message needed to place their faith in Jesus (Acts 4:12).

It is highly unlikely that those who were looking for the Messiah and were already justified before God, like Simeon, would not recognize and believe in Him when He appeared on the scene. But both these people and those who had never exercised faith in that which God had revealed under the old covenant had to place their faith in God's highest revelation, His Son Jesus Christ.

Peter clearly lays the blame on the people and their leaders for the crucifixion of Jesus, even though it was an act of ignorance ("Yet now, brethren, I know that you did it in ignorance, as did also your rulers" [Acts 3:17]). Now, as a nation, they needed to repent and turn (Acts 3:19) in order to have fellowship with God. But the individuals within the nation needed to believe in order to have eternal life, for the Lord was adding to the church daily those who were to be saved (Acts 2:47). As Paul said to the Jews in Antioch of Pisidia, "by Him everyone who *believes is justified* from all things from which you could not be justified by the law of Moses" (Acts 13:39, emphasis added). Hence, the nation needed to repent for *fellowship*. But the individuals within the nation also needed to believe for *relationship*. And it can be inferred that all Jews who believed (whether their faith in Jesus was subsequent to earlier faith or their initial experience of faith) also repented, were water baptized, and received the gift of the Holy Spirit. Acts 2:41 identifies those who gladly received Peter's word as three thousand people who were baptized. Just three verses later (Acts 2:44) we are told that these are those "who believed." The point of their belief was most likely when their hearts had been "pricked" by Peter's message (Acts 2:37). It is at that point that they ask what they needed to do in order to right this wrong. If they had not believed the message, there would be no point in asking what they should do to rectify matters. Hence, a strong argument can be made that these listeners at Pentecost first believed and then repented.

The same argument can be made for those listening in Acts 3. As he was making his appeal, Peter tells them to "repent and turn" (Acts 3:19) in order to have their sins blotted out and the times of refreshing from the presence of the Lord. But the response of the people who heard this message is recorded in Acts 4:4 where it says, " . . . many of those who heard the word *believed*; and the number of men came to be about five thousand" (emphasis added). Again, the order was most likely: believe = repent ⇒ turn (by being baptized and joining the new assembly of believers).

Thus, it can be said that for the nation and the individuals within the nation of Israel, relationship preceded fellowship; faith preceded repentance. The nation already had a relationship and needed fellowship. This was also true for some of the individuals within the nation. But whether certain individuals within the nation were already justified or not, the examples of Jewish repentance found in Acts were the result of faith, not the producer of it. Hence, for the Jews of that accursed generation, faith was the condition for justification, while repentance was the condition for sanctification; faith is for relationship, while repentance is for fellowship.

Faith

Much of the discussion in soteriology over the centuries involves the nature of faith. Though many Protestant teachers and denominations add requirements to faith to be accepted by God, none of them leaves faith out of the equation. Faith is essential. We must believe. But just what does that mean? Can faith be compartmentalized? Are there different types of faith found in the NT, such as permanent faith, passing faith, genuine faith, and spurious faith? Each of these questions must be addressed if we are going to be able to zero in on the NT meaning of faith.

In the Gospels

A good place to begin our exploration of faith is in the Gospels. The verb is used sparingly in the Synoptics: 11x in Matthew, 10x in Mark, and 9x in Luke. By contrast, it is used 99x in John. Oddly enough, the noun is never found in John. Ladd suggests the reason for this is that John wanted to avoid the possibility that faith was understood merely as "correct theology."[1] Since John was expressly written for evangelistic purposes (Jn 20:31), the prominent role of faith should tell us something about God's requirement for salvation. Especially unique in John, and to the entire NT for that matter, is the construction πιστεύω εἰς (*pisteuō eis*), which occurs nowhere outside the NT, that is, not even in the LXX. It would appear that it has been put together

---

[1] Ladd, *Theology*, n. 3, 307.

uniquely to communicate something about the Christian message of belief. According to A. Oepke (Kittel, 2:431-33), the preposition is used to indicate a *personal relationship*. And, whereas it is found only twice in the Synoptics (Matt 18:6 and Mk 9:42), John uses it over 30x between John 2:11 and 17:20. These facts are significant for our understanding of the nature of faith, as we shall see.

One of the chief attacks by J. MacArthur against C. Ryrie and Z. Hodges is to say Ryrie and Hodges define faith as "mental assent." MacArthur charges that those who so believe "have been deceived by a corrupted gospel. They have been told that faith alone will save them, but they neither understand nor possess real faith. The 'faith' they are relying on is only intellectual acquiescence to a set of facts. It will not save."[2] J. I. Packer claims, "Bare assent to the gospel, divorced from a transforming commitment to the living Christ, is by biblical standards less than faith, and less than saving, and to elicit only assent of this kind would be to secure only false conversions."[3] And, according to J. M. Boice, this approach to faith "reduces the gospel to the mere fact of Christ's having died for sinners, requires of sinners only that they acknowledge this by the barest intellectual assent, and then assures them of their eternal security when they may very well not be born again."[4]

In the Reformers

Before we evaluate these charges by MacArthur and company, it might be interesting to hear from the Reformers again, since lordship salvationists claim to have church history, especially Reformation history, on their side in the gospel discussion. As we do this, it is good to remember that Calvin claimed that his theology was every

---

[2] MacArthur, *The Gospel According to Jesus*, 170.
[3] Ibid., ix.
[4] Ibid., xi.

bit Augustinian, and Augustine said, "Faith is nothing else than to think with assent."[5]

No wonder, then, that Calvin wrote, "For, as regards justification, faith is something merely passive, bringing nothing of ours to the recovering of God's favor, but *receiving* from Christ what we lack."[6] Lordship salvationists affirm an active faith, one that produces good works and walks hand in hand with obedience. Anything less is false faith, they claim. But Calvin said, "We compare faith to a kind of vessel; for unless we come empty and with the mouth of our soul open to seek Christ's grace, we are not capable of receiving Christ."[7]

R. T. Kendall evaluates Calvin this way: "What stands out in Calvin's descriptions is the given, intellectual, passive and assuring nature of faith."[8] M. C. Bell concurs with Kendall when he writes, "Calvin taught that faith is fundamentally passive in nature, is centered in the mind or understanding, is primarily to be viewed in terms of certain knowledge."[9]

Therefore, apparently Calvin did not view faith as something which was akin to obedience or all-out commitment to follow Christ wherever He might go. Rather, as T. Lewellen observes, in Calvin's view obedience flows from faith and is part of the nature of the Christian life, and faith itself is reliance on the divine promises of salvation in Christ and nothing more.[10]

It seems the Reformers were in complete agreement on this approach to faith, even if they had many other points of disagreement. P. Melanchthon, who wrote the *Augsburg Confession*, defined

---

[5] A. Augustine "*On the Predestination of the Saints*" chap. 5, in *The Nicene and Post-Nicene Fathers of the Church*, 28 vols, trans. and ed. Phillip Schaff (Grand Rapids: Eerdmans, 1956), vol. 5: St. Augustine: Anti-Pelagian Writings, 499.
[6] Calvin, *Institutes*, III. xiii. 5, emphasis added.
[7] Ibid., III. xi. 7.
[8] R. T. Kendall, *Calvin and English Calvinism to 1649* (Oxford: Oxford University Press, 1979), 19. See also Calvin, *Institutes*, III. 2. 36.
[9] M. C. Bell, Calvin and Scottish Theology: The Doctrine of Assurance (Edinburgh: Handsel, 1985), 8.
[10] T. G. Lewellen, "Has Lordship Salvation Been Taught throughout Church History?" *Bibliotheca Sacra* 147 (January–March 1990), 57.

faith simply as "receptivity."[11] F. Pieper, the author of the modern standard theology of confessional Lutheranism wrote, "Saving faith is essentially the reliance of the heart on the promises of God set forth in the gospel.... In the preceding characterization of faith, we have stated ... that justifying faith must be viewed merely as the instrument or receptive organ for apprehending the forgiveness of sins offered in the gospel."[12]

In B. B. Warfield

So much for the Reformers. What about the defenders of Reformed theology? One of the staunchest, B. B. Warfield, has an extensive discussion on faith in his works, but never does he link it to obedience. As a matter of fact, he says *pisteuō* plus the dative case (which we would normally translate "to believe in" or just "to believe" someone or something) "prevailingly expresses believing assent."[13] To quote him more extensively:

> The central movement in all faith is no doubt the element of assent; it is that which constitutes the mental movement so called a movement of conviction. But the movement of assent must depend, as it always does depend, on a movement, not specifically of the will, but of the intellect; the assensus issues from the notitia. The movement of the sensibilities, which we call "trust," is, on the contrary, the produce of

---

[11] *Apology of the Augsburg Confession*, IV. 56, 112, 257. Also see *The Formula of Concord, Solid Declaration*, III. 8-14. See also R. D. Preus, "Perennial Problems in the Doctrine of Justification," *Concordia Theological Quarterly* 45 (1981); 163-84, for a good summary of the approaches to faith taken by Melanchthon and Luther.

[12] F. Pieper, *Christian Dogmatics*, 3 vols. (St. Louis: Concordia, 1953), 2:426, 437.

[13] B. B. Warfield, "Faith," in *Biblical and Theological Studies* (Grand Rapids: Eerdmans, 1968), 444.

the assent. And it is in this movement of the sensibilities that faith fulfills itself, and it is by that, as specifically "faith," it is formed.[14]

In English Puritanism

Well then, if the Reformers understood faith to be passive and simply trust or confidence in the promises of God, where did this idea of an active faith, which includes obedience and works, come from? The answer is the English Puritans. R. T. Kendall's work, previously referenced, establishes this development beyond all reasonable doubt. And Lewellen emphasizes this when he says:

> In the Puritan era . . . there was a shift in the definition of saving faith. In the generations following the Reformation, some theologians subtly changed the Reformers' definition of faith from a passive receptivity to an active response on the part of the sinner, centered in the will and containing both commitment and obedience.[15]

This shift in the understanding of faith from the Reformers' understanding is reflected in the Westminster Standards,[16] which are relied upon so heavily by lordship salvationists to prove their position. For example, in MacArthur's appendix whereby he tried

---

[14] Ibid., 403. Wayne Grudem thinks I have misread Warfield here and accuses me of making faith just an intellectual exercise devoid of trust [Wayne Grudem, *"Free Grace" Theology, 5 Ways It Diminishes the Gospel* (Wheaton, IL: Crossway, 2016), 114ff]. Nothing could be further from the truth as I discuss below in the section labeled "Straw Man."

[15] Lewellen, "Lordship Salvation," 58.

[16] *The Westminster Confession of Faith*, III. viii; XIV. ii (Philadelphia: Orthodox Presbyterian Church, n.d.). The Westminster Standards are the documents produced by the Westminster Assembly convened by the English Parliament from 1643 to 1649. These documents are the *Westminster Confession of Faith*, the *Shorter Catechism*, and the *Larger Catechism*. They form the doctrinal foundation of much of modern Presbyterianism. A slightly modified *Confession* called the *London Baptist Confession of Faith of 1689* also forms the doctrinal basis from which many of the modern Baptist churches have grown.

to establish lordship salvation as the historic position of the church, ten of the seventeen pages in this appendix are drawn from the Westminster Standards and the writings of post-Reformation English Calvinists.[17] It would certainly be fair to say that lordship salvation has its roots in a branch of traditional Christianity (to mix our metaphors a bit), but to make a sweeping statement like, "the view of faith that Hodges decries as a modern heresy is exactly what the true church has always believed,"[18] is misleading to say the least. To quote Lewellen once again:

> What is true ... is that MacArthur's view is embodied in the Westminster Standards and does have a long and powerful history in the Christian church. The idea that faith is an active commitment, including obedience, is the view of one strand of church history— English Puritanism—which is, of course, a powerful strand. One should not confuse that strand, however, with the "true church." Calvin disagreed with it; Lutheran theology has always opposed it; even today, some Reformed theologians do not accept it.[19]

In more modern church history, none other than the very liberal R. Bultmann includes a very tiny section of his long article on faith in which he tries to equate faith and obedience.[20] It is interesting that he uses verses like Romans 15:18 and 16:19 to prove his point when these verses do not even have the verb for believing or the noun for faith in them. Do lordship salvationists really want to filter their understanding of saving faith through Bultmann's grid? By contrast, the apostle Paul said, "For we maintain that a man is justified by faith apart from works of the law" (Rom 3:28, NASB). This verse separates

---

[17] MacArthur, *Gospel*, 221-37.
[18] Ibid., 222.
[19] Lewellen, "Lordship Salvation," 59. See G. H. Clark, *Faith and Saving Faith* (Jefferson, MD: Trinity Foundation, 1983), 110-18; R. T. Kendall, *Once Saved Always Saved* (Chicago: Moody Press, 1985); and M. C. Bell, *Calvin and Scottish Theology: The Doctrine of Assurance* (Edinburgh: Handsel, 1985).
[20] R. Bultmann, "*pisteuō*," in *TDNT*, 6:205-06.

the faith that justifies from works of obedience as far as the East is from the West. As J. Dillow pointedly asks, "If faith is the opposite of works of obedience (law) and is the opposite of works, by what mental alchemy can men seriously argue that, while faith is apart from works of obedience, faith itself includes works of obedience?"[21]

Unfortunately, more and more 21st Century theologians promote precisely said legerdemain. None other than D. A. Carson includes perseverance in his definition of faith: "In short, genuine faith is tied to perseverance ... part of the definition of saving faith includes the criterion of perseverance."[22] When confronted with the obvious claim of Paul that we are saved by faith without works and Carson's claim that faith without works (perseverance) is "spurious," Carson retreats through the same escape hatch used by Augustine and all those following in his train: " ... we are locked into mystery."[23] Sorry, folks, there is a difference between a mystery and a contradiction. More on this in our chapter on justification.

The "Straw Man" Factor

Another disturbing element in this discussion is what I will call the "straw man" factor. By this, I refer to erecting a point of view which one's opponent does not really hold and then constructing an argument to dismiss the stated point of view. That kind of argumentation is persuasive, but hardly fair. What merit is there in destroying a point of view that the "other side" does not hold? As has been demonstrated, lordship salvationists consistently accuse Free Grace writers of defining faith as "mental assent." The effect is to say Free Grace people believe faith is a detached, cold, intellectual process—salvation by ratiocination, in effect. Just the verbal connotations

---

[21] C. Dillow, *The Reign of the Servant Kings* (Hayesville, NC: Schoettle, 2002), 273.
[22] D. A. Carson, "Reflections on Assurance" *Still Sovereign*, eds. Thomas Schreiner and Bruce Ware (Grand Rapids: Baker Books, 1995), 264, 267. See also, *Salvation by Allegiance Alone*, Bates.
[23] Ibid., 264, 272.

turn us off. And rightly so. But is this a fair assessment of the faith espoused by Chafer, Ryrie, Constable, Cocoris, Hodges, and so many others at Dallas Theological Seminary? Hardly. After grappling with the artificial segmentation of faith into the compartments of the mind, the emotions, and the will, Z. Hodges notes the obvious. "The one thing we cannot do . . . is to believe something we don't know about."[24] He goes on to quote Rom 10:14ff where Paul says, "And how shall they believe in Him of whom they have not heard? . . . So then faith comes by hearing, and hearing by the Word of God." The point is, until the mind perceives a subject, it cannot be believed. Of course, this involves the intellect. But is this simply an intellectual exercise? Far from it. "To describe faith that way is to demean it as a trivial, academic exercise, when in fact it is no such thing. What faith really is . . . is the *inward conviction* that what God says to us in the gospel is true."[25] Hodges further defines faith as "firm conviction,"[26] "childlike trust,"[27] an "act of appropriation" of the truth of the gospel,[28] an "act of trust."[29]

The Psychologizing of Faith

Compartmentalization

There has been an effort on the part of many theologians to compartmentalize faith into its intellectual, emotional, and volitional elements. L. Berkhof,[30] claims MacArthur,[31] relates faith to the three compartments of the psyche of man: 1) *notitia*, the intellectual element, which is the understanding of a proposition; 2) *assensus*, the emotional element, which is the conviction and affirmation of

---

[24] Hodges, *Absolutely Free*, 31.
[25] Ibid., emphasis original.
[26] Ibid., 28.
[27] Ibid., 38-39.
[28] Ibid., 40-41.
[29] Ibid., 32.
[30] L. Berkhof, *Systematic Theology* (Grand Rapids: Eerdmans, 1939) 503-05.
[31] MacArthur, *The Gospel According to Jesus,* 173.

a proposition; and 3) *fiducia*, the volitional element, *which is the determination of the will to obey.*

But if one looks directly at Berkhof's work, he is teaching just the opposite of that which MacArthur claims. What Berkhof actually meant by the "volitional element" was not obedience, but trust: "This third element consists in a personal trust in Christ as Savior and Lord including a surrender of the soul as guilty and defiled to Christ and reception and appropriation of Christ as the source of pardon and spiritual life."[32] But as stated above, Z. Hodges defines faith with these same terms used by Berkhof: "trust" and "appropriation." That Berkhof clearly meant "trust" in his third element instead of a "determination of the will to obey" is evidenced by his label for this third element: *fiducia*. That Latin term means "confidence, trust, reliance, assurance."[33]

It is interesting to see how other authors explain the three elements. Demarest, for example, understands three elements: "*Faith* . . . involves an intellectual element—knowledge of the Gospel, an emotional element—feeling the sufficiency of Christ's grace, and a voluntary element—trusting Christ as Savior and Lord."[34] Notice how Hodges' base definition of "trust" is explained by Demarest as the volitional element of faith, whereas MacArthur understands "trust" to be part of the emotional element. Though some of this discussion might be relegated to semantics, it is important to address this element of the will. What role does the will play in the act of faith?

Faith and the Human Will

Many consider Archibald Alexander to be the leading Reformed thinker of the nineteenth century. Charles Hodge said Alexander was the greatest man he had ever known. And Alexander defined faith as

---

[32] Berkhof, *Theology*, 505.
[33] D. P. Simpson, "fiducia," in *Cassell's New Latin Dictionary* (New York: Funk & Wagnalls, 1968), 247.
[34] Demarest, *Cross and Salvation*, 249.

"simply a belief in the truth."³⁵ And Hodge himself in his commentary on Romans clarifies his understanding of faith in the Reformed tradition when he remarks, "That faith, therefore, which is connected with salvation includes knowledge, that is, a perception of the truth and its quantities, assent or the persuasion of truth of the object and trust or reliance."³⁶ Nowhere does he suggest or even hint that faith means or includes obedience.

The Apostle John put it still another way: "But as many as received Him, to them He gave the right to become children of God, even to those who believe in His name: who were born, not of blood, nor of the will of the flesh, *nor of the will of man*, but of God" (Jn 1:12-13). Of course, this is best explained by saying that the corrupt will of man cannot *cause* the new birth, but if there ever was a time to connect believing and the will of man in some *active* rather than *strictly passive* or *receptive* sense, John missed a grand opportunity.

Yet, NT theologians associate the will and commitment to obedience as the essence of faith in the most subtle ways. Consider this statement: "Saving faith... must include wholehearted *trust* and *commitment* to Christ, evidenced by obedience and good works. This aspect of faith involves cleaving to Christ and appropriating his benefits."³⁷ Remember again that Hodges included the words "trust" and "appropriation" in his definition of faith, but not "commitment."

Demarest works especially hard to establish a volitional aspect of faith that equates to obedience:

> Paul also affirmed that saving faith involves trust in and commitment to Christ (Acts 16:31; Col 2:5) or God (Rom 4:24; 1 Thess 1:8). For the apostle, faith involves intellectual understanding and emotional assent to cardinal truths...; but it also means volitional surrender to Christ, evidenced by love (1 Cor 13:2; Gal 5:6), obedience (Rom

---

³⁵ A. Alexander, *Thoughts on Religious Experience* (1844; reprint ed., London: Banner of Truth, 1967), 64.
³⁶ C. Hodge, *St. Paul's Epistle to the Romans* (1860; reprint ed., Grand Rapids: Eerdmans, 1950), 29.
³⁷ Demarest, *Cross and Salvation*, 260.

1:5; 16:26), and good works (1 Thess 1:3; Tit. 2:14; 3:8). Biblically speaking, a great gulf exists between knowing about a person and knowing the person in a relationship of trust and commitment. The former is theoretical and formal, the latter is experiential and personal. One may be a brilliant philosopher or theologian, be able to discourse eloquently about God, but fail to know Christ the Lord in a trusting relationship. Such a person has a form of knowledge, but not the knowledge of faith.[38]

While there is much in this paragraph with which we agree (knowing *about* a person versus *knowing* the person), there are also a number of things which are very troubling. For one, the first four references tell us nothing about the *meaning* of faith; they only mention the object (Christ or God). Acts 16:31, for instance, just tells the Philippian jailer to *believe*. Paul does not stop to explain to him that believing means trust *and commitment*. Here Demarest is begging the question; that is, he assumes what he is trying to prove.

Another problem is the assertion that "faith involves intellectual understanding and emotional assent to cardinal truths...; but it also means volitional surrender to Christ, evidenced by...." Where is the scriptural proof that faith means volitional *surrender*? To say that faith is *evidenced by* the love, obedience, and good works in the passages mentioned is one thing, but to imply that volitional surrender *necessarily produces* these works at all is another.

A third problem with Demarest's statement is that none of the final seven scriptural references deals with saving faith, meaning the act of faith which issues in a new birth. Each of them is dealing with the love, obedience, and good works of people who are already believers. They deal with sanctification, not justification. The Titus references make this plain: "who gave Himself for us, that He might redeem us from every lawless deed and purify for Himself His own special people, zealous for good works" (Tit 2:14) and "that those *who have believed* in God should be careful to maintain good works" (Tit 3:8). There is

---

[38] Ibid., 260-61.

nothing in these verses at all to prove his point that regenerating faith necessarily included an act of the will that entails active commitment and surrender to a life of good works.

We must be very careful to avoid including the *evidence* of faith in our *definition* of faith. No one will argue that devotion to Christ and good works in His name cannot be *evidence* of faith. (We could argue that they are not *conclusive* evidence because the false teachers of Matthew 7 did many good works in Christ's name, but were rejected by Him as unbelievers.) And these good works could include works of obedience. *But it is the faith that produces the obedience, not the obedience the faith.* Nor can the obedience be part of the faith. Dillow points out the weakness in MacArthur's argumentation when he says:

> MacArthur ... carefully states, "The biblical concept of faith is inseparable from obedience." But possible, or even inevitable, consequences of faith are not to be equated with faith itself. Faith does NOT mean "to obey." It is NOT "the determination of the will to obey the truth." Faith is "reliant trust." ... to import notions of obedience into the word "faith" is contrary to the teaching of the apostle Paul.
>
> It seems somewhat evasive to argue that this apparent inconsistency is a "paradox".... To say that faith can equal obedience and not equal obedience is not a paradox; it is a contradiction.... When MacArthur speaks of works being worked in us, his doctrine of justification differs not a whit from Catholicism's idea of justification making us righteous.[39]

A "Decision" for Christ

What do we mean when we say, "So-and-so made a decision for Christ"? Isn't a decision an act of the will? If faith does not have a volitional element, is it bad terminology to speak of a "decision for Christ" when we are referring to a conversion experience? R. T. Kendall likes to speak of believing more as a "persuasion" than

---

[39] Dillow, *Reign*, 74-76, emphasis added.

a "decision."[40] But I am not convinced that the word "decision" is wrong; yet it is important to clarify just what this decision entails. I would suggest that a decision for Christ means that someone decided (chose) to *trust Christ as Savior*. Indeed, Revelation 22:17d says, "Whosoever *wills*, let him receive of the water of life freely" (KJV), and John 5:35-40 emphasizes to "be willing" as implicit in "believing." Faith is pictured in John 1:12 and Revelation 22:17d as "receiving" a gift.[41] Presumably, one can decide to receive the gift or reject it. But that is a lot different from deciding to *obey Christ as Master of his life*. Christ asked those who received the water of life to follow him with total surrender and commitment, but the issue is whether the latter is a *condition* for salvation as an *integral element* of faith or just a *desirable consequence* of faith which can occur *concomitantly, subsequently,* or *not at all*.

Summary

The charge of "mental assent" and "intellectual faith" as a less than adequate faith is an unfair and inaccurate assessment of the Free Grace position on the meaning of saving faith. Neither intellect, nor emotion, nor will can be cleanly isolated as *the* key determinant of saving faith. Free Grace adherents have repeatedly defined faith as "trust," "confidence," "reliance," and "appropriation." These are the same words used by the original Reformers and many leading Reformed theologians of the last couple of centuries. It was only the English Puritans and their adherents who have added the "obedience" element to the meaning of faith.

We have no problem with Berkhof's division of faith into an element of the mind (*notitia*), and element of the emotions (*assensus*), and an element of the will (*fiducia*). This chart, which expresses my own view, harmonizes well with Berkhof:

---

[40] R.T. Kendall, *Calvinism and English Calvinism to 1649* (Oxford: Oxford University Press, 1981), 28, 200.

[41] The Greek word for "freely" (δωρεὰν) is the same one used (in noun form) to emphasize the absolutely free nature of the gift of grace given in Rom 5:15 and 17.

THE NATURE OF FAITH

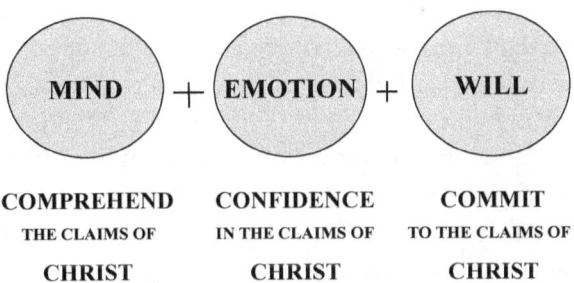

It should be obvious from this chart that we believe the volition of man plays a significant role in the essence of faith. However, that role is to commit to the claims of Christ as to his person and work, not a commitment to obey all of Christ's commandments. To claim that exponents of Free Grace view faith as an intellectual exercise is patently false.[42]

Types of Faith in the NT

Those who want to hold out for a distinction between "head" faith and "heart" faith usually appeal to experience. Many of us, including myself, can remember attending church in our early years and hearing about Jesus as the Son of God who took away the sins of the world. Many of us believed these facts, or at least never seriously doubted them, but we are convinced we became "true" believers at a later date in our lives when we trusted Christ as our personal Savior. What was that belief we had in the early years? Wasn't that "head" faith as opposed to "heart" faith? I would say, yes, but the Bible does not refer to it as "faith." There is a sense in which we can believe some facts about Christ, but they have no personal effect on our lives. It may be more helpful to refer to this as *conceding* or *recognizing* truth (as in

---

[42] Wayne Grudem, *"Free Grace" Theology—Five Ways It Diminishes the Gospel* (Wheaton, IL: Crossway, 2016), 112-18.

Jas 2:20, NASB) than as *faith*, which entails *appropriating* that truth to our own lives, *trusting* in it to *receive* life from God through Christ alone.

Many of us can relate to the popular illustration of faith where Blondin, the tight-rope walker, offered to roll someone across Niagara Falls in a wheelbarrow. If bets were taken, there were probably many standing around who believed Blondin could do it. But how many of them would be willing to get into the wheelbarrow? It is only when they decide to get into the wheelbarrow that their faith shifts gears from head faith to heart faith, from casual persuasion to personal trust. I relate to this illustration and believe it is valid. The question is whether or not the NT knows anything of this distinction between head faith and heart faith. We would suggest it does not.

False Faith in James 2:14-26

Those who like to find distinctions in faith in the NT have only a few passages on which to lean. The best known fortress for false faith is James 2:14-26, where "that faith" is explained as a spurious, inauthentic faith. We devote a great deal of space (see Appendix A where we use the hermeneutical circle to show that the faith referenced in James is not dealing with the salvation from the penalty of sin) to exposing this analysis of the passage as inconsistent with many details of the text, such as the meaning of the word "dead." It is not used to mean "fake, false, or spurious." It means "inactive, not vibrant, not 'on fire.'"

False Faith in John 2:23-25

Another NT passage used to show that people can believe in Christ without being "saved" is John 2:23-25. But a detailed look at this passage shows why it does *not* depict less-than-saving faith:

> Now when He was in Jerusalem at the Passover, during the feast, many believed in His name when they saw the signs which He did. But Jesus did not commit Himself to them, because He knew all *men*, and had no need that anyone should testify of man, for He knew what was in man.

Many, if not most, expositors explain the belief of the "many" in John 2:23 as "inferior" faith, inferior to the point that these people were not regenerated. S. Toussaint does not think faith based on signs is "trustworthy" faith.[43] Nor does E. Blum.[44] Ditto for W. H. Harris.[45] It seems that faith based on signs is shallow, insufficient faith. But where is the merit for this thinking? Apparently, it comes from the Lord's response to these believers in which He was not willing to commit Himself to them because of His supernatural knowledge of their hearts. He must have seen something in their hearts which caused Him not to trust them (*pisteuō* is the same verb used to denote both Jesus' *trust* in them and their *belief* in Him). There is nothing inherent in the statement about their faith which distinguishes it from the faith of many others in John. In fact, there is much more evidence to support genuine faith here than insufficient faith.

Pisteuō eis

Perhaps the strongest support is the exact terminology used: πολλοι επιστευσαν εις το όνομα αυτού (*polloi episteusan eis to onoma autou*). As previously observed, the combination of the verb *pisteuō* and the preposition *eis* is absolutely unique to Christianity. There are no examples of this combination in the LXX or extant extra-biblical Greek. And since *eis* is used in other ways to express "personal relationship," it is believed by almost all expositors that this construction was "coined" by NT authors to express the belief in Jesus which establishes a personal relationship with Him. Of particular interest is the fact that John uses the combination thirty out of the thirty-two occurrences in the NT, and John's express purpose for eliciting faith was *life in His name*.

A concordance search tells us that the first use of the combination

---

[43] S. Toussaint, "Acts," in *The Bible Knowledge Commentary* (Wheaton, IL: Victor, 1983), 373.
[44] E. Blum, "John," in *The Bible Knowledge Commentary* (Wheaton, IL: Victor, 1983), 280.
[45] W. H. Harris, "A Theology of John's Writings," in *A Biblical Theology of the New Testament*, ed. R. B. Zuck and D. L. Bock (Chicago: Moody, 1994), 224-26.

under scrutiny was in John 1:12: "But to as many as received Him, He gave the right to become the children of God, even to those who *believe in His name.*" This is one of the most common verses used in evangelism, even today. No one questions the meaning of believing in His name in Jn 1:12 or even hints that this belief is insufficient for entrance into the forever family. And things get even more interesting when we realize that the very next use of the phrase is in John 2:23, the passage in question. There is nothing at all between John 1:12 and John 2:23 to suggest to us that John is going to use this construction to mean something completely different than he did in his first use.

Especially troubling for anyone trying to say that believing in the name of Jesus is insufficient for regeneration, is the fourfold use of "believe in" found in John 3 where Jesus is explaining to Nicodemus what is necessary to be born again (or from above)—vv. 15, 16, 18, and 36. In 3:18, Jesus specifically says the reason a man will be condemned is "because he has not believed in the name of the only begotten Son of God." In the primary purpose statement for the Gospel (Jn 20:31), John clearly declares that life comes "through His name."

Z. Hodges comments:

> It seems truly incredible in the light of such crucial assertions as these that John should declare in 2:23 that "many believed in His name" and at the same time should hold the opinion that those who did so did not have life and still stood under God's condemnation. Absolutely nothing in John's usage of ἐπίστευσαν εἰς τὸ ὄνομα αὐτοῦ prepares his readers for such a conclusion.[46]

John uses the *pisteuō eis* construction many more times to indicate regenerate individuals (besides 3:15, 16, 18, 36, see 4:39; 6:29, 35, 40; 7:38, 39, to cite a few more). If he wanted to single out the group in Jn 2:23 as having an inferior faith to the others mentioned, why did he use exactly the same phrase to describe their faith, especially a

---

[46] Z. Hodges, "Problem Passages in the Gospel of John. Part II: Untrustworthy Believers—John 2:23-25," *Bibliotheca Sacra* 135 (April–June 1978), 139. I credit him for much of this helpful analysis of this passage.

phrase which has been coined to indicate those who had expressly established a personal relationship with Christ through faith in His name? It makes no sense.

Nevertheless, commentator after commentator concludes that these people had a shallow, insufficient faith. It was based on "signs," after all, as though this in itself vitiated their faith to the point that it was insufficient. W. Hendriksen writes:

> Many trusted in his name; i.e., because of the manner in which his power was displayed they accepted him as a great prophet and perhaps even as the Messiah. This, however, is not the same as saying that they surrendered their hearts to him. Not all faith is saving faith (cf. 6:26).[47]

Not only has Hendriksen imported his own understanding of faith into the passage (surrendering the heart), but his cross reference in John 6:26 says nothing about faith at all since faith is not even mentioned in the verse.

Two Categories?

W. Hall Harris is one who is convinced that John recognizes different qualities of faith in his gospel. He uses John 2:23-25 as a prime example and comments, "If these were genuine believers, Jesus' refusal to entrust Himself to them is extremely difficult to explain, especially since the gospel of John places people in only two categories: those who come to the light, and those who choose to remain in darkness (cf. 3:19-21)."[48] But is Harris' statement accurate? Are there only two categories? What about the categories of belief and unbelief? These two categories are used in John much more than light and darkness. And concerning these two categories John remarks, "He that believes on him is not condemned: but he that believes not is condemned already . . . " (3:18). As Hodges points out,

---

[47] W. Hendriksen, *A Commentary on the Gospel of John*, 3d ed. (London: Banner of Truth, 1964), 127.
[48] Harris, "John's Writings," 225.

For John, those who believe are in one class and those who do not are in another: "But you believe not, because you are not of my sheep, as I said to you" (10:26). The Evangelist never sets before his readers some kind of twilight zone where men have believed yet somehow are not the Savior's sheep.[49]

What about John 6:60-66?

Harris goes on to defend his position that there are believers without eternal life and believers with eternal life in John by his reference to John 6:60-66 where he observes:

> Inadequate faith is also the point of John 6:60-66 . . . . many of His disciples began to grumble (v. 60). In responding to them Jesus noted, "Yet there are some of you who do not believe" (v. 64). After this John added the comment that Jesus had known from the beginning which of them did not believe (probably an allusion to 2:24-25) . . . . Proof that Jesus' evaluation of these false disciples was correct is indicated by their actions. "From this time many of his disciples turned back and no longer followed him" (6:66). Perseverance with Jesus is an outward sign of genuine belief.[50]

This is amazing stuff. When one reads John 6:60-66 he searches in vain for any statement or indication that those addressed by Jesus had any kind of faith. It never says they believed in the first place. How can "inadequate faith" be the main point of seven verses which never discuss or even mention faith once? All the passage does say is that these people did not believe. Yes, absolutely, unbelief is one of the categories we find in John. Belief and unbelief. These people fell into the category of unbelief. And Harris' parenthetical connection with 2:24-25 is a huge leap. But that is about as close as anyone can come to saying this group believed.

The John 6 passage does have something to say about believers,

---

[49] Hodges, "Problem Passages," 144.
[50] Harris, "John's Writings," 225-26.

but not in 6:60-66 where those who do *not* believe are singled out. Note especially 6:40, "And this is the will of Him that sent Me, that everyone who sees the Son and believes in Him [πιστεύων εἰς αὐτὸν] may have eternal life; and I will raise him up at the last day." Notice the "everyone." In John's thinking, there is no one who has believed that will not be a partaker of the gift of eternal life and resurrection at the last day.

So, getting back to John 2:23-25, two more questions must be answered before we can satisfactorily leave the passage: 1) Is belief based on signs less than saving faith; 2) If these people, who believed, were regenerate, why was Jesus reluctant to entrust Himself to them?

Sign Faith

The first question is easy. Of course, faith in Christ based on signs is saving faith. The very reason He did miracles was to convince people that He was who He claimed to be. It was to get people to believe in Him. Even Harris observes that the verb πιστεύων εἰς is used only four times after John 12. The other thirty uses are in the first twelve chapters. Yet, all the miracles except the resurrection are in John 1–12. Harris appears to undermine his own argument against sign faith as being sufficient when he says, concerning the conjunction of πιστεύων εἰς and the miracles in John 1–12,

> This is perfectly understandable since chapters 1–12 deal primarily with the sign-miracles and discourses where the issue is who Jesus is and the necessity of believing in Him, whereas chapters 13–21 record Jesus' Farewell Discourse to His disciples (who have already believed in Him) and the events of the passion.[51]

Precisely! The signs were given to persuade people to believe in Jesus. You can't have your cake and eat it too. You can't say the signs were given to help people believe in Jesus and then say when they believe in Jesus because of the signs, their faith is inadequate.

Rather than disparaging faith that is based on seeing His works,

---

[51] Ibid., 224.

Jesus seems to hold those responsible who have seen His works and not believed: "If I do not do the works of my Father, do not believe Me. But if I do, though you do not believe Me, *believe the works, that you may know and believe* that the Father is in Me and I in Him" (Jn 10:37-38). The works were done to convince them to believe in Him. If they saw the works He did and did not believe in Him, they were without excuse.

Though there is a special blessing for believing *without* seeing special signs, as Jesus tells Thomas in John 20:29, John says in the very next verses (Jn 20:30-31), "And truly Jesus did many other signs in the presence of His disciples, which are not written in this book, but these are written that you might believe that Jesus is the Christ, and believing, you might have life in His name." The "these" refers to the signs John did record in his gospel. He specifically recorded them *so that you might believe*. Is "sign faith" *inadequate* faith? Not according to John.

Christ's Reluctance

This still leaves the question as to why Jesus was not willing to entrust Himself to genuine believers, if they were genuine. To understand this, we need to look more closely at a *leit motif* in John, that is, the theme of *intimacy*. In both his gospel and his first epistle, John is concerned with intimacy. Another word for intimacy is fellowship. And whereas fellowship is the main theme of his first letter with relationship being a sub-theme, it is just the opposite in his gospel. Relationship is the main theme, and fellowship is a sub-theme. But make no mistake about it, there is much about fellowship or intimacy contained in the gospel.

John can very much be outlined according to the design of the tabernacle or temple. We have, of course, the outer court where the Gentiles could enter, the holy place with the candelabra and table of showbread, and the holy of holies where only the high priest could enter. And in John 1–12, we have the evangelistic outreach to the world; then in John 13–16, we have special light and food being shared only with those who were His, the eleven disciples with the one unbeliever sent out into the night; and finally in John 17, the

High Priest Himself is praying for those who are His. The first twelve chapters are primarily evangelistic, and we only get hints as to the truths concerning fellowship and/or intimacy which are to come. The focus in these chapters is on relationship. But in John 13–16, the emphasis switches, as we would expect, because now He speaks to believers who already have a relationship. They have had a bath; now they need to have their feet washed. The focus here is not on relationship, but fellowship. So, it is in these chapters that the truths concerning intimacy with Him become central.

Thus, we find Jesus saying things like, "He who has My commandments and keeps them, it is he who loves Me. And he who loves Me will be loved by My Father, and I will love him and manifest Myself to him" (Jn 14:21). Notice the conversation does not revolve around "knowing" or "believing," but rather "loving." Now we get into truth about obedience. If we want to establish an equation for obedience, this is it: obedience = love; obedience ≠ faith. And love is the language of intimacy and fellowship. But notice especially the word ἐμφανίσω (*emphanisō*), which BAGD suggests means "to reveal" in this context. It is to those who love Jesus that He is willing to reveal Himself. He will open up in a love relationship. So will we. Are you comfortable entrusting the deepest passions of your heart to people who don't really love you? Unlikely. Neither was Jesus. It requires a lot of trust.

That is why Jesus was not ready to entrust Himself to the new believers in John 2:23. They believed in Him. But He knew their hearts at this point, and He knew they did not yet love Him. Is this so surprising? As we grow in Christ, we love Him more and more. And the more we love Him, the more willing we are to obey Him. And the more we obey Him, the more He opens up to us.

Jesus explains the same truth later in the Upper Room when He says, "You are my friends if you do whatever I command you" (Jn 15:14). He does not call them His children if they do whatever He commands. They are His friends—intimacy. And to His friends goes a special privilege: "No longer do I call you servants, for a servant does not know what his master is doing; but I have called you friends, for all things I have heard from my Father I have made known to you"

(Jn 15:15). He reveals more to His friends than to His servants. And His friends are those who obey. His children are those who believe.

To the new believers in John 2:23, He had revealed who He was: the Messiah and the Son of God. They believed and were born again. But He was not ready to reveal more of Himself than that because He knew they were not yet His friends, an intimacy defined by obedience.

"Secret Service" Christians

There are many places were John tells us about believers who were not yet the friends of Jesus. Note the contrast between the disciples who openly followed Him and the new believers in John 12:42: "Nevertheless even among the rulers many *believed in Him*, but because of the Pharisees *they did not confess Him,* lest they should be put in out of the synagogue." There is no indication that these rulers were false professors. Here we have the same Greek expression so key to John's indication of a personal relationship with Christ: ἐπίστευσαν εἰς αὐτόν. These rulers were born-again believers, but because of their fear (not of death, but loss of the favor of men) they were not willing to openly identify with Jesus (*confess Him*; remember Rom 10:9-10?).

And remember *Nicodemus*, who came to Jesus *by night*? We are told that he was a ruler (ἄρχων) of the Jews, the same term applied to those who believed in Jesus in John 12:42. Other expositors have noted the linkage between John 2:25 and 3:1: ἄνθρωπος ("man"). Could it be that Nicodemus was one of these *men* who believed in 2:23 because of the signs he had seen, but was still unwilling to openly identify with Him because he was a ruler of the Jews and would be expelled from the synagogue?

But even if Nicodemus trusted Christ later (in Jn 12:42 perhaps) he was clearly a believer by the time of the crucifixion and one who was ready to openly identify with Jesus (confess). He shows up with *Joseph of Arimathea* in John 19:38-39 as one who requested the body of Jesus for burial. The text says Joseph was a disciple, "but *secretly*, for fear of the Jews," just like Nicodemus, the one who first came to Jesus "by night." Now Nicodemus was ready to come out of the closet. These two men had apparently been believers for some time. But they did not become Jesus' *friends* until after He died. No wonder we do not hear much about them in the interim between "the first" and the end; they were in the closet. Credit them for coming out at the end, but Jesus knew the heart of man (2:25), and He was unwilling to disclose, manifest, or entrust Himself to those who were unwilling to openly identify with Him. Perhaps, that is why He chose humble fishermen like Peter, James, and John for his first disciples. They did not have as much to lose as the "rulers of the Jews." They were willing to identify with Him. They became His best friends and the great apostles who will rule over the twelve tribes of Israel when the King comes again. Just think about what Nicodemus and Joseph of Arimathea missed while they were in the closet as well as in the next life!

Summary and Conclusion

Suffice it to say, despite the consensus in the commentary tradition, we have no conclusive evidence in the NT for different categories of faith. Different levels, yes; different categories, no. Faith is faith, real faith, genuine faith, through and through. It is true that not all faith in the NT is saving faith. Faith as small as a grain of the mustard seed is enough to move a mountain (because it is *real* faith), but that is not *saving* faith. The faith that "makes you whole" is also real faith, but not necessarily saving faith. The faith of the demons in James 2 is *real* faith (that is why they trembled), but it is not *saving* faith. Saving faith obviously needs to be tethered to the person and work of Jesus Christ.

So, we are not taking issue with the assertion that some faith in the NT is not saving faith. We are taking issue with the notion that some faith in Jesus as Savior in the NT is not saving faith. The NT knows of no sub-level or insufficient faith in Christ as Savior that does not save. Even Simon Magus of Acts 8:13 had saving faith. There is nothing in the text to indicate that his belief and baptism were to be distinguished from the others in Samaria. And to use the "fruity" argument, His baptism (an open identification with Jesus), his spiritual hunger, and his quick post-baptismal repentance all bear witness to a genuine conversion.

Though saving faith *begins* as an assessment of revealed truth—most notably, God's promises—it is not *consummated* until one trusts those promises. One must appropriate those promises for himself and be fully persuaded and confident in those promises as his only hope for life eternal. Such faith is not a casual, detached, intellectual process and conclusion. It is an act of trust, whereby one puts the full weight and consequences of his sins on the cross of Christ to open the gates of heaven.

One final note: Recall our prior discussion ("The Sinfulness of Man") that Adam and Eve experienced *spiritual* death the moment they sinned, just as God had warned them (Gen 2:17), even though they did not *physically* die until hundreds of years later. Similarly for John (and for us!), God's promise of life—eternal life—is not simply a promise of a destiny *with* God forever rather than *apart from* God forever. God promises life now that will last forever, but our present *experience* of that life depends on daily faith in God's gift of Christ (Rom 6:23). This is the essence of *abiding*: When we abide *in Him* through faith, we have eternal life abiding *in us*, right now.

Eternal Security

Introduction

If you were to die today, do you know where you would be spending eternity? Or would you agree with one who claimed, "I don't think it's possible to know where we will spend eternity until we die"? We believe such knowledge is possible long before death shows up for its appointment. In fact, such knowledge is essential if you are to experience the "rest prepared for the people of God" while you yet live on earth. An ancient proverb offers this sage counsel:

> He who knows not and knows not that he knows not is a fool; shun him.
> He who knows not and knows that he knows not is simple; teach him.
> He who knows and knows not that he knows is asleep; awaken him.
> He who knows and knows that he knows is wise; follow him.

When it comes to knowing God in a personal way and knowing that we will be with Him when we die, all of us fall into one of the four categories outlined by the above proverb. Some don't know and don't know that they don't know. They are lost, but don't realize it. For those in this category, the message of Romans 3:10-18 is desperately needed: "There is none righteous, no, not one." All men without Christ stand sinful before God, condemned to an eternity separated from Him.

Some, however, don't know and know they don't know. The message of 2 Corinthians 5:21 meets their need: "For He has made Him [Christ] who knew no sin *to be* sin for us, that we might become the righteousness of God in Him." Jesus took the rap for us. He died that we might live—forever.

But the most tragic category includes those who know but don't know that they know. They are the believers who are saved and whose destiny is certain, but who do not know they are saved or are not sure of their salvation and ultimate destiny. They desperately need to understand the message of eternal security, so that they can enter into the fourth category of people who know and know that they know.

No one has more peace and rest in this life than the person who knows God the Father through God the Son and knows that he knows Him. But are people in this fourth category presumptuous and spiritually overconfident? Can one really know, and know that he knows in this life? That question is our subject in this study.

Let's examine this subject under five categories: a Simple Definition, the Theological Possibility, the Basic Support, the Primary Objections, and the Practical Benefits. First of all, let's lay out a definition.

Simple Definition

Perhaps the simplest, shortest definition of eternal security is: "Once saved, always saved." Of course, the all-inclusive word "always" causes immediate reactions. When we hear the words "always, never, every," etc., we start looking for exceptions. Nevertheless, this definition can stand the bombardment. It shines as one of the brightest doctrinal lights in the Bible: Once you believe, you can never be lost; you can never go to hell. Christ will always be your Savior. You can nail down your eternal destiny once and for all so you never have to worry about it.

Obviously, any doctrine so sprinkled with the qualifying terms like "never, always, and all" is going to be challenged. Can it meet the test?

Theological Possibility

Once saved, always saved. That's a big statement. Is this even possible? What are the factors involved in this doctrine of eternal security? Once we boil down the excess that has drowned this doctrine in obscurity, only two factors lie at the bottom of the pan: man's sin and God's provision.

Man's sin separates him from God. Man's sin sends him to hell. If man is to escape this horrible pit, God must make some sort of provision to pay the just penalty for man's sin. Clearly, Christ's death on the cross is the payment for man's sin provided by God. The question of eternal security hinges on whether this provision pays for *all* man's sin. Is atonement limited?

At this point, opponents of eternal security confuse the issue by dividing sin into six categories: past and future, bad and worse, confessed and unconfessed. This is like trying to divide a barrel of black oil into six compartments. Even if we do so, the oil in each compartment is still black, and it's still oil. Most of those who believe a Christian can lose his salvation do not believe God's provision covers future as well as past sins, the black sins as well as the gray ones, the unconfessed sins as well as the confessed ones. If eternal security is a theological possibility, then Christ's death must be powerful enough to burn up this entire barrel of sin, not just two or three compartments. God's provision must pay the debts accrued by *all* our sins irrespective of time, degree, or confession.

Fortunately, God has not remained silent on these matters. He clearly spoke to this very issue in Hebrews 10. In this passage the Holy Spirit compares the sacrifice of bulls and goats with the sacrifice of God's Son. The former simply cannot deal with *future* sins. Once a year, the people had to return to Jerusalem to offer another sacrifice for their sins of that past year. When they left Jerusalem they had a clean slate. But the marks against them accumulated throughout the year until the Day of Atonement rolled around again. Since their sacrifice did not deal with future sins, these people had to keep on sacrificing year by year.

But the sacrifice of Jesus ended the necessity for yearly sacrifice. What was "not possible through the sacrifice of bulls and goats" (Heb 10:4) was possible through the sacrifice of the Lamb of God. Three Greek words in Hebrews 10 emphasize this possibility.

First, the adverb *ephapax*. This word is found only five times in the NT. Four of the five times, it is used to refer to Christ's death as payment for our sins (Rom 6:10; Heb 7:27; 9:12; and 10:10). It means "once for all" (Heb 10:10). The meaning is clarified in Heb 10:12, "one sacrifice for sins forever." Christ's death is God's one and only provision for man's sin and it sufficiently pays for all his sins. No *time* distinction is made. When Christ ascended into heaven, He sat down at the right hand of His Father, signifying His finished work. No further provision would be made. *Ephapax*. Once for all. All sins—past, present, or future; black, gray, or white (of course, all sins are black in reality); confessed, unconfessed; known, and unknown—all sins have been paid for.

To cement our understanding, a second Greek word underscores the sufficiency of Christ's death as payment for future sins: *diēnekēs*. This word occurs only four times in the NT, all of them in Hebrews (7:3; 10:1, 12, 14). It means "forever, everlasting, continual succession, without ceasing." The point is that the sacrifice of Jesus was good "forever," whereas the sacrifice of bulls and goats was good only for a year. Hence, one sacrifice made nearly two thousand years ago has been sufficient for all of the sins committed since. Of course, these were all "future" sins. This same sacrifice, then, has removed the debt of all the sins we will commit in the future as well.

Someone might object by saying, "Yes, I believe the death of Christ is *sufficient* to pay the penalty for my future sins, but it is only *efficient* to do so when I confess these sins." Such an objection might hold up if it weren't for the third Greek word in Hebrews 10, which clinches the case for eternal security. This word is *perielein*, found in Heb 10:11. The translation is "take away." Literally, it means "to remove something from around someone or something." It's used for casting away the anchors holding a ship back, and for removing the noose from a man's neck. Man's sin had become a hangman's noose around his neck, but Christ's death has removed the noose once and for all. In other words, Christ's death is not like a slush fund which is sufficient to pay for all the debts we may pile up in the future, but only efficient to pay for those debts when we write a check on the account (confess). Not at all. Christ's death took away the noose of all sins irrespective of time, degree, or confession—it can never go around our necks again.

Not only do these three Greek words highlight our eternal security, but so does one Greek tense in Hebrews 10—the perfect tense, which emphasizes an act completed in the past with present effects. It is completed action in the past with ongoing results, which speaks of a *permanent* state. We find this tense in the word "sanctified" (10:10) and "perfected" (10:14). To sanctify (*hagiazō*) means "to make holy"; to perfect (*teleioō*) means "to make whole, complete." In Heb 10:10-14, God tells us that the offering of Jesus, His provision for our sins, has *permanently* made us holy and whole!

So, eternal security is not only a theological possibility, it's a theological *reality*. Hebrews 10 makes it clear that God's provision has completely blotted out and destroyed all our sins once and for all. Christ's death sufficiently and efficiently covered the sins of believers from Adam to Christ (past sins) and from Christ until today (sins future with respect to His death). God's provision more than adequately covers man's sin.

Having established the theological possibility of "once saved, always saved," let's expand on the basic support for this doctrine.

Basic Support

Some refer to the doctrine of eternal security as "the perseverance of the saints." Perhaps a better expression would be "the preservation of the saints." The former emphasizes man's efforts while the latter centers on God's efforts. In the final analysis the eternal security of the believer rests on the power of God to preserve the saints, not on the power of the saints to persevere.

It is like the father who was leading his little boy across a busy intersection hand-in-hand. They had nearly crossed the street when the little boy slipped and fell. But before he could hit the ground, his father's powerful right arm whisked him onto the curb with one great swing. Pleased, the little boy looked up at his father and exclaimed, "I helded on, didn't I, daddy?" His father smiled and replied knowingly, "Yes, you did, son, but I helded on first." So it is with God's preservation of His saints. It's His holding on to us, not our holding on to Him, which lies at the core of eternal security.

In light of the fact that eternal security rests on the person and work of God, the best evidence for this doctrine comes from the contribution each member of the Godhead makes toward the preservation of the saints. Therefore, let's look at two contributions made by each member of the Godhead that add up to eternal security.

God the Father

His Omnipotence

Numerous verses testify to the ability of God to preserve His children and the inability of anyone or anything else to overcome His power to do so. Consider, for example, the strength of this chain of verses:

1. My Father, who gave them to me, is greater than all; and no man is able to pluck them out of my Father's hand" (Jn 10:29). This includes the believer himself.

2. "And being fully persuaded that what He had promised, He was able also to perform" (Rom 4:21). God has promised eternal life to all who believe. He is able to perform what He has promised.

3. "If God be for us, who can be against us? . . . For I am persuaded that neither death, nor life, nor angels, nor principalities, nor powers, nor things present, nor things to come, nor height, nor depth, nor any other creature, shall be able to separate us from the love of God, which is in Christ Jesus our Lord" (Rom 8:31, 38-39). Some object that this verse speaks of the love of God, not God Himself. But can one be separated from God eternally without also being separated from His love? And note especially the words "nor things to come." That includes your future sins. They cannot separate you from the love of God.

4. "Now unto Him Who is able to keep you from falling, and to present you faultless before the presence of His glory with exceeding joy" (Jude 24). To say one can lose his salvation is to say God cannot keep him from losing it. Who is more powerful, God or us? Denial of eternal security is a slam on the omnipotence of God.

His Unconditional Love

The unconditional character of God's love lifts it several levels above man's love. "God proved His love toward us, in that while we were still sinners, Christ died for us" (Rom 5:8). We didn't deserve His love then because of our sins. Has God's love become less *since* we believed, so that our sins now cancel out the benefit of Christ's death for us? On the contrary, "much more then, being justified by His blood, we shall be saved from wrath through Him" (Rom 5:9). He loves us "much more" now that we are His children than when we were His enemies. If our sins didn't turn off the faucet of His love before salvation, they certainly won't after salvation.

Hence, the Father's great power and His great love under gird the doctrine of eternal security. What about Jesus?

God the Son

His Death

As we have already seen in Hebrews 10, the death of Christ removed the hangman's noose of sin from the believer's neck once and for all. To deny this truth is to say the blood of Christ wasn't good enough to cover all our sins irrespective of time, degree, or confession. That would mean that Christ's work wasn't enough and now we must add our own good works to His in order to maintain our salvation. What an insult to the person and work of our Lord and Savior!

His Prayers.

1. AS OUR ADVOCATE. In 1 John 2:1-2 we read: "And if anyone sins, we have an advocate with the Father, Jesus Christ the righteous: And He is the propitiation for our sins." Whenever we sin after salvation, Jesus Christ acts as our lawyer to defend us against the accusing finger of Satan. Our Lawyer (Advocate) rests His case on His own shed blood which fully satisfied (propitiated) God's demand for justice. He merely states that the debts accrued by our sins have been paid in full. Case dismissed.

2. AS OUR INTERCESSOR. In Hebrews 7:25 we read, "Therefore He is also able to save to the uttermost those who come to God through

Him, since He always lives to make intercession for them." An example of such intercessory prayer by Christ on our behalf can be found in John 17:11: "Holy Father, keep through your own name those whom you have given me, that they may be one, as we are." The rest of the chapter presents similar petitions to the Father. To say that a believer, once saved, can be lost doesn't say much for Christ's prayer life, does it?

Thus, Christ's past work on the cross and present work in prayer buttress the doctrine of eternal security. What can we say about the Holy Spirit?

God the Holy Spirit

His Indwelling

When one becomes a Christian, the Holy Spirit comes to live inside of him. According to Christ, this resident ministry is permanent, for He said, "I will pray to the Father, and He will give you another Comforter that He may abide with you forever; even the Spirit of truth ... He dwells with you and shall be in you" (Jn 14:16–17). As Lewis Sperry Chafer has so well expressed, "He may be grieved, but He will not be grieved away. He may be quenched ... but He cannot be extinguished. He never leaves the Christian, else the word of Christ is untrue and His prayer is unanswered."[1]

His Sealing

We are told in Eph 4:30 that the Holy Spirit has sealed us unto the day of redemption. This seal in NT times had three uses:

1. TO AUTHENTICATE. Paul said the Corinthians were the "seal" of his apostleship. They authenticated him as an apostle. Just so, the Holy Spirit marks us out as authentic Christians.

---

[1] Lewis Sperry Chafer, *Systematic Theology*, "Soteriology," III (Dallas: Dallas Seminary Press, 1948), 336.

2. TO PROTECT. The 144,000 in Revelation 14 are "sealed," that is, they are protected from death. So, the seal of the Holy Spirit protects us from the second death (eternal separation from God).

3. OWNERSHIP. The seal was like a brand on cattle, a mark of ownership. So the seal of the Spirit marks us out as belonging to God. We are His "purchased possession" (Eph 1:14). "Now I belong to Jesus, Jesus belongs to me; not for the days of time alone, but for eternity."[2]

Clearly, the indwelling and sealing ministries of the Holy Spirit point toward the permanent protection we have from God until the day of redemption. That's eternal security.

Conclusion

Our security depends not on us, but on God. It's not *our* persevering power that guarantees our salvation. It is the Father's infinite power and unconditional love, the Son's once-for-all sacrifice and present prayer ministry, the Spirit's permanent indwelling and protective sealing—all these contributions from the individual members of the Godhead add up to one conclusion: our eternal security. Thus, any denial of eternal security constitutes a frontal attack against the character and work of God. What are some of these objections to eternal security?

Primary Objections

Almost all the objections raised against the doctrine of eternal security can be traced to a failure to distinguish between relationship truth and fellowship truth, or between the requirements for salvation and the requirements for discipleship, or between God's eternal judgment and His temporal judgment, or between literal language and figurative language. When we understand these distinctions, the objections melt away. Let's examine them.

---

[2] Lyrics by Norman John Clayton (b. Jan. 22, 1903; d. June 1, 1992).

Relationship versus Fellowship

When a man adopts a little boy, a relationship has begun. It's a father-son relationship. That's permanent. No matter how disgraceful the boy may act, he's still his father's son. But whether the father-son relationship is an enjoyable one or not depends on their fellowship. If the boy runs away from home and even changes his name, the relationship still exists, but the fellowship doesn't. If fellowship is to be restored, the boy must come home and ask his father's forgiveness and submit to his father's authority.

This distinction between relationship and fellowship helps explain how a child of God can conceivably run far from his Father—even deny the faith and "family background" (= apostasy)—yet remain a Christian. The relationship he has with his heavenly Father will never change. It's a Father-son relationship. But that relationship can only be enjoyed through personal fellowship with his Father. The sinning son must seek his Father's forgiveness and submit to His authority. Then fellowship is restored.

When we understand the difference between relationship and fellowship we can also understand how someone can die in a car wreck with an unconfessed sin and still go to heaven. Very simple: confession of known sin is the condition required by God for fellowship (1 Jn 1:3, 9). Confession has nothing to do with relationship. The Christian who dies with an unconfessed sin still has the father-child relationship, but he dies out of fellowship with his Father.

Position versus Condition

Sometimes God describes us from the viewpoint of our *position in Christ* in the heavenlies (Eph 1:3ff), and sometimes from the viewpoint of our *condition in time* on earth (Romans 8). In our position we are already holy and blameless before God (Heb 10:10; 1 Cor 1:2); but in our condition we may be spiritual or carnal, controlled by the Spirit or by the flesh. As we focus on our position in Christ, our condition slowly conforms to our position (2 Cor 3:18). When God says, "Be holy, because I am holy" (1 Pet 1:16), He's appealing to our condition. But when He says we are "sanctified in Christ," He's affirming our complete holiness in position.

Thus, it is that a group of very unholy people such as the Corinthian Christians (full of lust, carnality, and jealousy) could be labeled "sanctified" (1 Cor 1:2). They were holy in their position, but unholy in their condition. Paul never threatened them with loss of position because of their condition. Rather, he appealed for improvement in their condition on the basis of their position (Col 3; Eph 4). And so it is that any Christian may be secure in his position yet ungodly in his condition. Mind you, this is not an *excuse* for his condition; rather, it's a *defense* of his position.

Salvation versus Discipleship

Passages on inheritance such as Ephesians 5:5 and Galatians 5:21 have caused confusion for some. These passages list gross moral sins and flatly state that no practitioner of such sins will inherit the kingdom of heaven. One answer to the obvious problem here would be to say that the one *continually* practicing such vices simply isn't a Christian. While this *may* be true, we all know of people who have all the evidence of rebirth except for certain habits which seems to persist year after year. Were they never Christians to begin with or will they lose their salvation? May we suggest ... neither?

Actually, the word "inheritance" is a tip-off that the passages concern discipleship. Luke 14 beautifully contrasts the free gift of salvation (parable of the great supper) and the high price of discipleship. Christ encourages and actually "strongly persuades" (Lk 14:23) men to accept the invitation to a free meal at salvation supper, but He sternly warns men of starting down the discipleship road without counting the costs (possibly friends, family, wealth, health, even one's life). He says, "There are too many half-built towers strewn across the countryside which are a negative testimony to my name. I would rather you not start down discipleship road if you don't intend to finish."

Nevertheless, the rewards of discipleship are many. Passages like Matthew 19:27-30; 25:34ff, Colossians 3:24-25, James 2:5, and Revelation 21:7 all bring out the rewards coming to those who serve the Lord faithfully. Each of these is an "inheritance passage." And in each case the inheritance or rewards received at the Judgment Seat of Christ—1 Corinthians 3:12-15, 2 Corinthians 5:9-10)—are given on the basis of our works *after* we become Christians. So, passages which warn of the loss of inheritance address not our salvation but our *rewards*.

John 15:6 also fits into this category, although we don't find the word "inheritance" or "reward." The word "abide" tells us we are dealing with fellowship truth. Here is a Christian not abiding in Christ. He has a relationship with Him but no fellowship. Obviously, he's not working for the Lord. He's saved, but not a disciple. Hence, the test of fire (1 Cor 3:13) will destroy his works like wood, hay, and stubble. There will be no rewards, no inheritance. First Corinthians 9:27 also falls into a context of discipleship and rewards.

Eternal versus Temporal

Many of the so-called problem passages in the area of eternal security are problems because of a failure to discern whether the warning will be realized *in time* (including the Judgment Seat of Christ) or *for eternity*. For example, many such warning passages in Hebrews (2:1-4; 3:7-4:16; 5:11-6:20; 10:26-39; 12:3-29) each speak of judgment for unfaithfulness that will be carried out in time. The peril of those Hebrew Christians who fell back into temple worship with the Christ-rejecting Jews would be death at the hands of the Roman army in AD 70. For a less severe falling away comes temporal chastening, as a father to his son (12:5-11). But in every case, the warning was of a temporal judgment to come while men were still on earth. Heaven never enters the picture.

Second Peter 2:20-22 also opens up when seen in its temporal context. That these are Christians is proven by the uses of *epiginōskō* in 2:20-21. This term signifies full experiential knowledge of Christ, not merely conceding facts *about* Christ. What then is the "latter end" of these Christians that "is worse than the beginning"? Their *condition* after turning from the way of righteousness is even worse than when they became Christians ("the beginning") and they will suffer loss at the Judgment Seat of Christ. "The dog has turned to his own vomit again, and the sow that *was washed* to her wallowing in the mire." The "latter end" here refers to time, not eternity. It's their latter moral state in this life when compared to their moral state before they escaped the pollutions of this world.

Although the above distinctions between relationship and fellowship, position and condition, salvation and discipleship, time and eternity dissolve the vast majority of objections to eternal security, there are a few minor objections which must be handled separately:

1. "If we deny Him, He also will deny us" (2 Tim 2:12b). While it sounds like we can forfeit salvation, 2 Timothy 2:13 says, "If we are faithless, He remains faithful; He cannot deny Himself." The word "faithless" is better translated "do not believe" (*apistoumen*). If we deny the faith and reject Him, Christ still lives within us and cannot deny Himself, but He *will* deny our reign with Him (2 Tim 2:12a; Rom 8:17b).

2. While admitting that salvation is a free gift (Rom 5:15-16), some claim that a person can always give the gift back. However, the clear testimony of Scripture is that "the gifts and calling of God are irrevocable" (Rom 11:29). God who chose to give us this gift will not take it back, so we couldn't return it if we wanted to.

3. "This makes grace cheap. All you have to do is believe and then you can live any way you please." Grace costs us nothing; yet it cost God everything—His Son's life. Moreover, while a Christian theoretically *can* live any way he pleases, we have seen that an unholy life forfeits both the "abundant life" Christ offers on earth and the future reward He offers at the Judgment Seat of Christ. It also brings a believer under the temporal judgment or discipline of God.

4. "The Bible says you can fall from grace (Gal 5:4; cf. Heb 4:1)." Here Paul compares two planes of life. Living under grace is life on the higher plane. To live the Christian life under the law, as the Galatians were trying to do (see Gal 3:3), is to sweat through life on the lower plane. In essence, such a Christian has fallen from

the higher plane to the lower. He has fallen from grace (and God's "rest").

5. "Hebrews 6:4-6 says it's impossible to be saved after you fall away." No, it says it's impossible to be saved twice ("renewed ... *again* to repentance"). Ironically, all those who say a Christian can lose his salvation due to some heinous sin also claim he can get it back through repentance of that sin. No way, says Hebrews 6. If it's true that a Christian can lose his salvation, it's also true he can never be saved again. On the other hand, this passage may be saying that when a Christian progresses far along the road of righteousness and then turns away from the faith, it is impossible for *man* to renew him to repentance. He may be too far gone to be persuaded by human reasoning. But this does not mean it would be impossible for *God* to turn him around. With God all things are possible. In either case, the passage does not categorically speak of loss of salvation.[3]

6. "Revelation 22:19 says anyone who takes away from the words of the Revelation will have his part taken away from the 'book of life.'" There is no manuscript support for translating "book of life." It should read "*tree* of life." Either it's another loss of rewards passage or it refers to non-Christians. The first option is supported by translating the word *meros* in 22:19 as in John 13:8, "part" or "portion," a clear allusion to *fellowship* not *relationship*. The allusion in Revelation 3:5 to blotting out a name from the book of life has three possible explanations. First, the statement that Christ would not blot out the name of the overcomer could be a figure of speech called "litotes," an understatement designed to emphasize what God *will do*; that is, *confess his name before God and His angels* (like saying "not bad" to mean "very good"). In this case it would not admit the possibility of "blotting out" in the first place. Secondly,

---

[3] For a concise argument that Hebrews 6 is neither addressing loss of a believer's salvation or an unbeliever's lack of same, see Anthony B. Badger, "Doesn't Hebrews 6 Say if We Fall Away We Cannot Be Saved?" in *21 Tough Questions about Grace*, Grant Hawley, ed., (Allen, TX: Bold Grace, 2015) 227-36.

it's quite possible that every man's name is in the book of life until he rejects Christ as Savior. At that time his name is blotted out. Only the names of believers are left. Thirdly, only half the residents of Rome were citizens. When a citizen committed an unusually barbarous crime, the city officials ceremoniously erased his name from the book of citizens. He remained as a *resident*, but he lost the rights and privileges of a citizen. Hence, the possibility of having one's name taken from the book of life would not threaten one's residence in the kingdom; it would threaten his rewards in the kingdom.

Now that we have defined, documented, and defended the doctrine of eternal security, we might ask, "So what: How does this affect my Christian life?" Here are some of the practical benefits.

Practical Benefits

No one on this earth enjoys as many blessings as the man who knows God and knows that he knows God. He is blessed *because* he enjoys a life of liberty, not legalism. He doesn't have to perform in order to gain or maintain God's favor. He can "stand fast, therefore, in the liberty with which Christ has made us free, and be not entangled again in the yoke of bondage" (Gal 5:1). The walk of the secure Christian is blessed *because* he enjoys a life of confidence, not condemnation. He can come boldly before the throne of grace that he may obtain mercy and find grace to help in time of need. That "grace to help in time of need" may be restoration to fellowship. Knowing he's already "accepted in the Beloved" (Eph 1:6) as far as his relationship with the Father is concerned, the believer can confidently expect restoration to fellowship. But the insecure believer lives a life of constant self-condemnation, never quite sure of his present standing with God.

Furthermore, the secure believer is blessed because he enjoys a life of *rest* (Matt 11:28-32), not *resolutions*. One who believes his standing with God depends on his own performance frequently finds himself crawling back to God, promising to do better, making new resolutions he can never keep. But the secure believer can enter the rest which remains for the people of God (Heb 4:9).

Have you visited San Francisco and seen one of the seven man-made wonders of the world, the Golden Gate Bridge? The major span of the bridge stretches 4200 feet, the longest single span in the world at the time of its completion in 1937. The construction of the bridge includes an interesting but little-known feature. You can imagine how difficult it would be to construct such a bridge. When completed, the tab came to 27 million depression dollars. And part of that great expense was due to the slowness of the work. For one thing, it was difficult to find men who were willing to work on the bridge. During construction of the first half of the bridge, twenty-three men fell to their deaths in the cool Bay waters below. So, who wanted to risk his life on this bridge? No safety devices were being used. Finally, however, in constructing the second half of the bridge, they decided to use the greatest safety net ever made. The net itself cost $100,000 but it paid for itself. For one thing, it saved the lives of ten men who fell from the bridge during construction of the last half. But the net also paid for itself in the time saved over the latter half of construction, for the work itself went 15-25% faster than before, since the men were relaxed after being relieved of the fear of falling. The knowledge that they were safe even should they slip and fall allowed the men to devote all their energies to the task at hand.

No one can do his best work when he's afraid of what might happen if he slips up. No doubt, God wants us to live a life of good works after we have been saved (Eph 2:8-10). But if we envision God holding a big hatchet over our heads, ready to cut us off when we slip up, then our good works will be motivated by fear. Serving God out of fear not only keeps one from doing his best work, it also robs the believer of his joy. He's performing because he *has* to, not because he *wants* to. The believer who knows God has a safety net stretched out underneath him can serve God freely, out of a grateful and loving heart!

May God lead you to become one of those who know God and know that they know Him. Is such knowledge possible? Not only is it possible, it is essential. Without such knowledge the believer walks on eggshells before God. He lives a life of paranoia, legalism, self-condemnation, and resolutions. With such knowledge we enjoy a life of peace, liberty, confidence and rest. How is it with you, my friend? If you were to die today, do you know where you would be spending eternity tomorrow?

Assurance of Salvation

Closely related to eternal security is the subject of assurance. That is why so much emphasis was placed on knowing and knowing that we know in our discussion of eternal security. Obviously, if eternal security is a correct doctrine, one's eternal destiny is not in jeopardy whether that person is aware of this truth or not. But the blessedness spoken of in our previous discussion is being aware that one's eternal destiny is not in question. To know without doubt that one will spend eternity with his Maker is what we call assurance of our salvation. This might seem like a logical corollary from eternal security, but it has become one of the greatest issues in conservative theology. Some of our discussion will be a review of material we have already covered, and some of it will be new. There are really two questions: 1) Is it possible before death to know one will go to heaven? 2) If such assurance is possible, what is the basis for this assurance? At stake in this discussion is no less than our motivation for Christian living, and some might even say that without assurance of salvation a person cannot be justified. Once again we begin with Augustine, since so much theology of our century is based on his system.

Augustine and Assurance

Augustine simply did not think one could have assurance of salvation in this life. We must remember that he translated *dikaioō* as "to make righteous." With this understanding of justification, he believed the process of becoming righteous was life-long. He also believed a person could appear to be one of the elect up until the very end of his life, but if he fell away from the faith at the end, he proved that he was one of the saved, but not one of the elect, so he made a curious distinction between the "saved" and the "elect."

In L.S. Chafer's discussion of eternal security he quotes from Principal Cunningham on this aspect of Augustine's theology:

> Augustine seems to have thought that men who were true believers, and who were regenerated, ... might fall away and finally perish; but then he did not think that those persons who might, or did, thus fall away and perish belonged to the number of those who had been predestinated, or elected, to life.... Augustine's error, then, lay in supposing that men might believe and be regenerated who had not been elected to life, and might consequently fail of ultimate salvation.[1]

Because of this distinction between the saved and the elect, Augustine did not think it was possible to know where one would spend eternity until he died. We must credit Augustine for being a consistent thinker on this particular point. It should be obvious that if a person could appear to be elect, could actually be a true believer, could be regenerated, but then could fall away at any time before the end of his life and thus prove he was not elect, then that person could never know for sure if he was elect until he died.

It is important to understand that this approach was the logical conclusion to Augustine's view of Matthew 24:13 and similar passages. Since he did not believe in a literal 1,000-year reign of Christ on earth, he understood passages like Matthew 24:13 to refer to spiritual salvation. Therefore, only those who persevere in their Christian walk until the end "of their lives" will be saved to go to heaven. But we will not know if a person is going to persevere to the end *until* the end. Hence, a person could never be sure of his salvation until he died. And this is the understanding of the RCC today. They got it from Augustine.

---

[1] P. Cunningham, Historical Theology, 3d ed., 2:490, quoted in L. S. Chafer, Systematic Theology, III (Dallas: Dallas Seminary Press, 1969), 270.

Luther and Assurance

According to Martin Luther, saving faith is

> the sort of faith that does not look at its own works nor at its own strength and worthiness, noting what sort of quality or new created or infused virtue it may be.... But faith goes out of itself, clings to Christ, and embraces Him as its own possession; and faith is certain that it is loved by God for His sake.[2]

What is the source of this certainty? According to Luther it comes from leaning on the promise of God's mercy in the gospel, and not from any sense of internal change. "For certainty does not come to me from any kind of reflection on myself and on my state. On the contrary, it comes solely through hearing the Word, solely because and in so far as I cling to the Word of God and its promise."[3] Apparently, for Luther the Word of God was the only source of assurance he needed.

S. Pfürtner writes, "Luther placed the certainty of salvation at the very heart of his Reformation message.... Faith, to Luther, is pure reception and seizure of the message of salvation with the act of which the sinner, falling into despair, yields to God and his forgiving grace."[4] To focus on one's fruits as a source of assurance would be to separate assurance from faith and lead to its destruction. The Lutheran *Formula of Concord* (1577) states in no uncertain terms:

> We believe, teach and confess also that notwithstanding the fact that many weaknesses and defects cling to the true believers and truly regenerate, even to the grave, still they must not, on that account, doubt either their righteousness, which has been imputed to them by faith, or the salvation of their souls, but must regard it as certain that,

---

[2] M. Luther, *What Luther Says: An Anthology*, comp. Ewald M. Plass, 3 vols. (St. Louis: Concordia, 1959), 1:496, emphasis added.
[3] Quoted by S. Pfürtner, *Luther and Aquinas on Salvation* (New York: Sheed and Ward, 1964), 125.
[4] Ibid., 29, 35.

for Christ's sake, according to the promise and immovable word of the holy Gospel, they have a gracious God.[5]

The strange inconsistency in Luther's thinking was that he could believe assurance was based on the promises of God and at the same time think a believer could lose his salvation if he did not persevere to the end.[6]

Calvin and Assurance

It should come as no surprise to us that Calvin held the same position as Augustine on assurance since Calvin credited Augustine for his whole system except for a revised view of justification, which Calvin adopted from Luther. But to hold to the same position as Augustine while changing the definition of justification from "to make righteous" to "declare righteous" forced Calvin into a number of inconsistencies in his theology.

It should be obvious that a belief in justification that would bring forgiveness of all sins (past, present, and future) should also bring with it assurance. If this justification comes by faith alone without works of the law, and if this justification can wipe away my future sins before I even commit them, then I should be able to have assurance of my salvation the moment I believe. Future sins cannot affect my eternal destiny because I am forgiven of them when I am declared righteous at the moment of my faith.

And in some of his statements, this is exactly what Calvin taught. We might remember that he thought assurance was a necessary corollary of faith. In fact, Calvin's definition of faith includes assurance: "We shall now have a full definition of faith if we say that it is a firm and sure knowledge of the divine favor toward us, founded on the truth of a free promise in Christ, and revealed to our minds, and

---

[5] *The Formula of Concord,* Epitome III (Affirmative Theses), 6.
[6] *Beggars All, Reformation & Apologetics,* "Did Luther Believe Salvation Can Be Lost?" (October 7, 2009).

sealed on our hearts, by the Holy Spirit."[7] He described faith as firm conviction,[8] assurance,[9] firm assurance,[10] and full assurance.[11] Bell says, "Without question, Calvin teaches that assurance of one's salvation is of the very essence of faith. Assurance is not an optional extra for the believer."[12] And A. N. S. Lane writes:

> For Calvin, it was not possible to partake of salvation without being sure of it. Assurance is not a second stage in the Christian life, subsequent to and distinct from faith. In the following century, some of his followers did separate them in this way and this, together with a departure from Calvin's ground of assurance, led to a widespread loss of assurance.[13]

This assurance came with faith and was a part of faith. It did not evolve at a later date from introspection of one's faith or inspection of one's fruit. If one truly believed in the finished work of Christ on the cross, he should have assurance of his eternal standing before God. He did think assurance was in varying degrees, but if a high percentage of assurance was lacking, Calvin did not think the person was a believer or elect. This would seem consistent with his view of justification at a moment in time.

But because of heavy criticism from the RCC that the Reformed approach to justification would encourage license among their followers, Calvin sought to fuse the connection between justification and sanctification. The result was the teaching that if one is truly justified he will go on to sanctification. If one is not progressively sanctified, he is not justified. Since Calvin also adopted Augustine's

---

[7] Calvin, *Institutes*, 3.2.7.
[8] Ibid., 3.2.2.
[9] Ibid.
[10] Ibid.
[11] Ibid., 3.2.22.
[12] Bell, *Scottish*, 22.
[13] A. N. S. Lane, "Calvin's Doctrine of Assurance," *Vox Evangelica* 11 (1979): 32- 33.

amillennialism, he interpreted Matthew 24:13 just as his predecessor, thus, concluding that the elect will keep growing in Christ until the end of their lives, since only those who persevere until the end of their lives will be saved.

In order to support this system, Calvin developed the insidious doctrine of "temporary faith." He came to this understanding from his interpretations of the parable of the sower, the warning of Hebrews 6, and the warning to the people saying, "Lord, Lord ... " in Matthew 7.[14] Here, for example, is what Calvin said concerning Hebrews 6:4-5:

> I know that to attribute faith to the reprobate seems hard to some when Paul declares it (faith) to be the result of election. This difficulty is easily solved. For ... experience shows that the reprobate are sometimes affected by almost the same feeling as the elect, so that even in their own judgment they do not in any way differ from the elect.[15]

Hence, the people in Hebrews 6 could have been enlightened, have tasted the Word of God, the heavenly gift and the power of the age to come, but still fall away and prove they were never elect.

Calvin seemed to think that allowing the reprobate such full experiences of Himself justified His rejection of them for eternity. Dillow explains:

> The central claim of this teaching is that God imparts supernatural influences to the reprobate which approximate, but do not equal, the influences of effectual calling. He is illuminated, he tastes, he grows, and he has similar feelings as the elect. However, it seems God is deceiving this man into believing he is elect so that God can be more than just in condemning him when he finally falls away. After all, the man had these "tastes."[16]

---

[14] Dillow, *Reign*, 254.
[15] Calvin, *Institutes*, 3.2.11.
[16] Dillow, *Reign*, 254.

Apparently, such deep experiences with God make the reprobate all that much more inexcusable when they do not really believe. This operation of the Spirit was an "ineffectual" calling, "an inferior operation of the Spirit."[17]

Now, imagine the implications of a statement like this for assurance: "Experience shows that the reprobate are sometimes affected in a way so similar to the elect, that even in their own judgment there is no difference between them." So, here we have two groups of people who look like the elect, and both groups "in their own judgment" are elect. However, according to Calvin some of those who look like the elect (meaning they have the same fruit as the elect) and think they are elect are not in fact elect and will prove this fact by falling away some time before they die. This poor class of people consists of the reprobate who think they are elect, but are self-deceived. Can it be more transparent? With such a teaching no one could know he was one of the elect until he died. Of course, that is precisely what Augustine taught, and Calvin would have admitted the same had he been consistent within his own system. Alas, he was not.

Because of the terrible possibility that one might actually be one of the reprobate when he thought he was one of the elect, Calvin says, "Meanwhile, believers are taught to examine themselves carefully and humbly, lest carnal security creep in and take the place of assurance of faith."[18] So, now we have a distinction between "carnal security" and "assurance of faith." Calvin is now stretching as far as he can to maintain the Reformed doctrine of instantaneous justification in an amillennial system of theology which says the just must persevere until the end or they were never just in the first place. "In the elect alone, He implants the living root of faith, so that they persevere even to the end."[19] Does this sound like Augustine, who believed God only gave the gift of perseverance to the elect?

Apparently, Calvin even thought some of the "soils" in the parable of the sower that produced fruit were not elect: "... just as a tree

---

[17] Calvin, *Commentary*, Lk 17:13; *Institutes*, 3.2.12; 3.2.11.
[18] Ibid.
[19] Ibid.

not planted deep enough may take root but will in the process of time wither away, though it may for several years not only put forth leaves and flowers, but produce fruit."[20] He must have realized the implications of some of his teachings because, much like J. MacArthur, he sprinkles his writings with answers to supposed objections which only confuse the issue more. Take this one, for example:

> Should it be objected that believers have no stronger testimony to assure them of their adoption, I answer that there is a great resemblance and affinity between the elect of God and those who are impressed for a time with fading faith, yet the elect alone have that full assurance which is extolled by Paul, and by which they are enabled to cry, Abba, Father.[21]

My, that really helped. How is the believer (whether real or imaginary) to know if he has *full* assurance? Maybe his assurance is only part assurance, but how is he to know? R. T. Kendall recognizes the problem here when he writes:

> And if the reprobate may experience "almost the same feeling as the elect," there is no way to know finally what the reprobate experiences. Furthermore, if the reprobate may believe that God is merciful towards them, how can we be sure our believing the same thing is any different from theirs? How can we be so sure that our "beginning of faith" is saving and is not the "beginning of faith" which the reprobate seems to have?[22]

Calvin digs an even deeper hole by speaking of an inner assurance given by the Spirit to the elect, and then says the reprobate can have a similar sensation. With this kind of teaching, one could never have assurance of his salvation. He could only know he is elect when he dies. The pressure from the RCC trapped Calvin into the very same

---

[20] Ibid.
[21] Ibid.
[22] Kendall, *Once Saved*, 24.

fear of the eternal future inherent in the Catholic system that he was trying to escape. Dillow hits the nail on the head when he observes:

> In the final analysis, Calvin has thrown away the possibility of assurance, at least until the final hour. When he grants that the only certain difference between the faith of the elect and the faith of the reprobate is that the faith of the former perseveres to the end, he makes assurance now virtually impossible.[23]

This approach to assurance differs little, if at all, from that of the churches of Christ,[24] as evidenced by one of their chief spokesmen, R. Shank: "Obviously, it can be known only as one finally perseveres (or fails to persevere) in faith. There is no valid assurance of election and final salvation for any man, apart from deliberate perseverance in faith."[25] But Shank is a pure Arminian who left the Southern Baptist Convention over the issue of eternal security. It is strange how similar aspects of these two systems (Calvinism and Arminianism) become when one studies their doctrines of perseverance. C. Hodge typifies this group:

> Election, calling, justification, and salvation are indissolubly united; and, therefore, he who has clear evidence of his being called has the same evidence of his election and final salvation . . . The only evidence of election is effectual calling, that is, the production of holiness. And the only evidence of the genuineness of this call and the certainty of our perseverance, is a patient continuance in well doing.[26]

Or, as J. Murray put it, "The perseverance of the saints reminds us very forcefully that only those who persevere to the end are truly saints."[27] We must realize that all of this on perseverance developed

---

[23] Dillow, *Reign*, 258.
[24] According to Robert Shank this is the preferred designation.
[25] R. Shank, *Life in the Son: A Study of the Doctrine of Perseverance* (Springfield, MO: Westcott, 1961), 293.
[26] C. Hodge, *St. Paul's Epistle to the Romans* (1860; reprint ed., Grand Rapids: Eerdmans, 1950), 212.
[27] Quoted by Dillow, *Reign*, 259.

out of Augustine's switch from premillennialism to amillennialism (see chapter one). So, from Augustine to Calvin, and from Calvin to the English Puritans, and from the English Puritans to their nineteenth and twentieth century followers, the poison of false doctrine has trickled down the mountain stream, into the river, and, finally, into the ocean of Catholic and Protestant theology. Oh, what a tangled web we weave when we change one aspect (eschatology: from premillennial to amillennial) of the theological spreadsheet of Scripture. Dillow concludes, "In other words, the only real evidence of election is perseverance, and our only assurance of the certainty of persevering is—to persevere! So, on this ground there is no assurance at all!"[28]

To their credit, some in the Reformed camp recognize the inconsistency in saying one can have assurance while also saying one must persevere to the end of his life to be saved. M. Roberts writes:

> We may cling tenaciously to the doctrine of Final Perseverance and yet at the same time we may legitimately view our own personal profession of faith with something akin to uncertainty. More positively, we may say that this fear of being adokimos or castaway [from 1 Cor 9:26-27] is one of the great hallmarks of those who are elect and who finally do persevere. All who lack it are possessed of a sickly presumption, which needs correcting from the pulpit or which—God forbid—they will have to unlearn by the sad experience of falling.[29]

So, there you have it. Words like "uncertainty" and "fear" expose the doctrine of perseverance as explained by Augustine and those influenced by him for what it is: a doctrine of uncertainty and fear.

By holding to that doctrine, no one can ever know he will go to heaven until he dies. Augustine admitted as much. So does Roberts. He says "fear . . . is one of the great hallmarks of those who are elect." He calls the doctrine of assurance a "sickly presumption." But if we

---

[28] Ibid., 258-59.
[29] M. Roberts, "Final Perseverance," *The Banner of Truth* 265 (October 1985): 10-11.

want to talk about what's healthy versus sickly, which is healthier, to raise children in an atmosphere of love where obedience is encouraged *because* they are unconditionally accepted by their parents or in an atmosphere of fear where the children really never know if they are performing up to the level necessary to win the love and acceptance of their parents? The answer is so obvious; the question is rhetorical.

Theodore Beza and Assurance

Theodore Beza (d. 1605) took a real turn in the road. He believed in limited atonement, a view he does not seemed to have gotten from Calvin.[30] His supralapsarianism, which taught that God elected some for heaven and selected the rest for hell before he even decreed to make these humans in the first place, could only conclude that Christ died for the elect only. The trick, then, was how to determine if you were elect or not.

Whereas Calvin said assurance came from looking to Christ,[31] Beza warned us not to look to Christ because,

> We could be putting our trust in One who did not die for us and therefore be damned. Thus we can no more trust Christ's death by a direct act of faith than we can infallibly project that we are among the number chosen from eternity: for the number of the elect and the number for whom Christ died are one and the same. The ground of assurance, then, must be sought elsewhere than in Christ.[32]

In evaluating this drastic fork in the road taken by Beza, Kendall observes:

---

[30] Kendall, *Once Saved*, 13-18. In his commentary on Mark 14:24 Calvin says, "The word 'many' does not mean a part of the world only, but the whole human race." In *Concerning the Eternal Predestination of God*, 148, he says, it is "incontestable that Christ came for the expiation of the sins of the whole world." In his commentary on John 1:29 he comments, "And when he says the sin of the world he extends this kindness indiscriminately to the whole human race."
[31] Calvin, *Institutes*, 3.24.5.
[32] Kendall, *Once Saved*, 32.

Beza directs us not to Christ, but to ourselves; we do not begin with Him, but with the effects, which points us back, as it were, to the decree of election. Thus, while Calvin thinks looking to ourselves leads to anxiety, or sure damnation, Beza thinks otherwise. Sanctification, or good works, is the infallible proof of saving faith.[33]

But Beza also ascribed to the "temporary faith" of Calvin. This contradiction in their theology undermined any possibility of valid assurance in their followers. For Beza, sanctification is the infallible proof of saving faith. Yet strangely, the reprobate can have all the fruits of the elect. Thus, the reprobate *appear* to be progressively sanctified. How, then, can one tell from sanctification whether or not he is elect? Obviously, he cannot. But he retreats to the "safe" haven of good works in 2 Peter 1:10 and concludes that only through persevering to the end of one's life can one know he is elect. But isn't that what Augustine taught, that is, you cannot really know until the very end of your life?

William Perkins and Assurance

J. Dillow calls Perkins the third member of the "Calvinist Trinity" (Calvin, Beza, and Perkins).[34] He adopted the temporary faith of Calvin and the supralapsarianism of Beza and built an entire system of assurance around 2 Peter 1:10. Fruit inspecting is the key. Here are the necessary fruits that prove one is elect:

1. Feelings of bitterness of heart when we have offended God by sin
2. Striving against the flesh
3. Desiring God's grace earnestly
4. Considering that God's grace is a most precious jewel
5. Loving the ministers of God's word

---

[33] Ibid., 33.
[34] Dillow, *Reign*, 263.

6. Calling upon God earnestly and with tears
7. Desiring Christ's second coming
8. Avoiding all occasions of sin
9. Persevering in the effects to the last gasp of life.[35]

Is this incredible or what? If the only way for me to have assurance is by having these nine fruits in my character, then the ninth fruit must be present. But the ninth requires me to persevere until my last gasp. How, then, can I be assured I am elect until my last gasp? Obviously, I cannot.

The direct result of W. Perkins and his list was English Puritanism and their lists of what it meant to be godly. Along with their legalism went the concomitant lack of joy so pervasive in all Christian groups where grace has been obscured by law.

Arminius and Assurance

R. T. Kendall is a particularly interesting read because he was a Reformed theologian and a British Rector. He has a unique perspective on English Puritanism that we in America will never have. He concludes that when it comes to assurance, the Calvinists of the Puritan persuasion and Arminians have the same position:[36]

> If Perkins holds that the recipient of the first grace must obtain the second (perseverance) or the first [initial faith] is rendered invalid, there is no practical difference whatever in the two positions. If the believer does not persevere (whether Arminius or Perkins says it), such a person proves to be non-elect.[37]

Arminius included active will and obedience as requisites of faith, exactly as J. MacArthur has done. He claimed that faith had three

---

[35] W. Perkins, *Works*, 1:115.
[36] Kendall, *Once Saved*, 143.
[37] Ibid., 144.

parts: repentance, trust in Christ, and obedience to God's commands. Does this not sound like J. MacArthur? And assurance comes from the fruits of faith.

The Westminster Standards and Assurance

When the Westminster divines gathered in the 1640s, there was no one there who represented Calvin's views. In fact, they completely turned the tables on Calvin's doctrines of faith and assurance. Faith and its volitional component became active instead of passive. They completely avoided Calvin's doctrine of temporary faith, and for good reason. Whereas Calvin wanted to base assurance on looking to Christ, these Puritans wanted to base assurance on looking to themselves and their fruit. But if the reprobate could have the same fruit as the elect, obviously there could not be any assurance in this life.

As for assurance, the Westminster Confession of Faith (18.3) says, "Assurance of grace and salvation, not being of the essence of faith, true believers may wait long before they obtain it." The Puritans dedicated entire volumes to the introspection necessary to ascertain whether one's faith was sufficient to save them. In commenting on his 650-page tome called *Discourse concerning the Holy Spirit*, J. Owen (d. 1683) stated that his main purpose was to help professors of Christ to determine whether or not they were possessors of Christ.[38]

Modern Fruit Inspectors

Many modern and popular expositors have hitch-hiked on the Puritan philosophy of assurance. J. M. Boice said, "It is necessary that we do these good works (as Christians in all ages have), for unless we

---

[38] J. Owen, *The Works of John Owen*, 16 vols., vol. 3: *A Discourse concerning the Holy Spirit* (1677; reprint, Edinburgh: Banner of Truth Trust, 1965), 45-47, 226- 28. Also see, Michael P. Winship, *Making Heretics; Militant Protestantism and Free Grace in Massachusetts, 1636-164*, (Princeton, New Jersey, Princeton University Press, 2002) for an extensive explanation of how Puritan theology evolved in colonial America and the opposing theology which was labeled, "The Free Grace Controversy".

do, we have no assurance that we are really Christ's followers."[39] W. Chantry writes, "Only when God is loved supremely and the spirit of the law kept has a man any reason to believe that he has been truly born of God."[40] And J. MacArthur reasons,

> The Bible teaches clearly that the evidence of God's work in a life is the inevitable fruit of transformed behavior. Faith that does not result in righteous living is dead and cannot save. Professing Christians utterly lacking the fruit of true righteousness will find no biblical basis for assurance they are saved.[41]

In another place, he states, "The fruit of one's life reveals whether that person is a believer or an unbeliever. There is no middle ground."[42] Once again, we must insist that some of these modern fruit inspectors are fighting a "straw man." They like to speak of the Free Grace position as promoting the belief that one can genuinely be born again without any demonstration of good fruit in the life of the believer. But is this a fair assessment? Definitely not! Listen to Z. Hodges:

> Of course, there is every reason to believe that there will be good works in the life of each believer in Christ. The idea that one may believe in Him and live for years totally unaffected by the amazing miracle of regeneration, or by the instruction and/or discipline of God, his heavenly Father, is a fantastic notion—even bizarre. We reject it categorically.... But this is not at all the point. The issue

---

[39] J. M. Boice, *Christ's Call to Discipleship* (Chicago: Moody, 1986), 166. This is his only reference to assurance in the book.
[40] W. Chantry, *Today's Gospel: Authentic or Synthetic?* (Edinburgh: Banner of Truth, 1970), 74.
[41] MacArthur, *The Gospel According to Jesus*, 23.
[42] Ibid., 178.

here is assurance. And with this, works can play no decisive role whatsoever.[43]

Some seminary professors who believe in Free Grace do not say that good works or fruit in the lives of believers have no value in assurance whatsoever. But these works are relegated to a secondary, corroborating role. The only essential ground for the assurance of the believer's salvation is the promises of God. They are sure and firm. The experience of the believer can offer confirming evidence, but it is only secondary to the promises of God's Word and is nowhere taught in Scripture as essential for assurance.

No passage makes the prominence of God's Word in the assurance of salvation more clear than 1 John 5:13 where it says, "These things have I *written* to you who believe in the name of the Son of God, that you may *know* that you have eternal life . . . " (emphasis added). Countless tracts have used this verse to give assurance to new believers of their destiny in Christ. Yet, even this verse has been twisted by some into a thematic statement for the epistle. Then they explain the epistle as one which has a list of ways to test your experience to see if you have the necessary proof to be assured of your salvation.[44] These tests include responsibilities of the believer such as "abiding" (2:6, 26) and "keeping His commandments" (2:3, 7-10).

Such tests only stir up doubt, confusion, or self-deception. If keeping His commandments is the test, then I must ask:

1. How many do I have to keep?

2. How long do I have to keep them?

3. Do I have to keep them perfectly?

---

[43] Z. Hodges, "We Believe In: Assurance of Salvation," *Journal of the Grace Evangelical Society* 3 (Autumn, 1990), 7, emphasis added.

[44] See Christopher D. Bass, *That You May Know; Assurance of Salvation in 1 John*, (Nashville, Tennessee, Broadman & Holman Academic, 2008) and I. Howard Marshall, *The Epistles of John*, The New International Commentary on the New Testament, (Grand Rapids, Michigan, Eerdmans Publishing co. 1978) 243.

4. Are some more important than others?
5. Will He grade on a curve?

The believer quickly becomes disoriented on a sea of subjectivity. If we answer 1) keep all of them; 2) keep them until you die; 3) be perfect as your Father in heaven is perfect; 4) all sin is sin so they are all equally important; and 5) there is no curve, then we are right back to the Law, which required perfect obedience for acceptance. Do we want to promote perfect obedience to the Law of Christ (this dispensation, not Mosaic) as the standard for assurance? Obviously not. There would be no assurance. So, the standard is reduced to one of relativity, and relativity is completely subjective. Again, no one would know. Someone might say, "But I am keeping them today, so I have assurance today that I am a child of God." But what about tomorrow? If it is possible to slip tomorrow, then there is no assurance tomorrow. But then that would mean that the good behavior today is possibly being produced by someone who is not elect. If we admit that, then present good behavior is no guarantee either. Z. Hodges addresses this:

> But if it is claimed that the true believer is eternally secure—yet must base his assurance on his obedience to God's commands—in that case, 1 Jn 5:13 becomes a highly misleading statement! For even if I am living obediently right now the possibility exists . . . that I may cease to do so in the future. But if I did cease to do so, that would prove that I am not now a Christian despite my obedient lifestyle. Thus, my present obedience does not prove my Christianity and thus, too, I cannot know at any time before the end of my earthly career that I possess eternal life. So, if John had meant we must test our Christianity by our current or ongoing obedience, he could not have honestly said that we can know we have eternal life. But that is precisely what he does say![45]

---

[45] Hodges, 5. See Gary W. Derickson, *1,2,3 John*, Evangelical Exegetical Commentary, (Bellingham, WA, Lexham Press, 2014) 23-28

The theme of the epistle is not found in 1 John 5:13. The stated purpose of the epistle is found right where you would expect to find it, in the introduction of 1 John 1:1-4. There we find the word "fellowship" twice. In both the Upper Room discourse of his gospel and his entire first epistle, John is primarily concerned with fellowship. The "things written" in 1 John 5:13 are not a reference to the entire epistle as so many assume. Instead they refer to what has been written in 5:1-12, as many technical scholars have observed.[46] This is exactly the way John has used *tauta + graphō/egrapsa + humin* (these things + I write/have written + to you) in other portions of the epistle (see 2:1 in reference to 1:5-10 and 2:26 in reference to 2:18-25). The key term in the text is μαρτυρία/*martyria*, which means "witness" or "testimony." Notice how many times it (or its verb form) occurs in 5:9-12:

⁹ει την μαρτυριαν των ανθρωπων λαμβανομεν η μαρτυρια του θεου μειζων εστιν οτι αυτη εστιν η μαρτυρια του θεου ην μεμαρτυρηκεν περι του υιου αυτη ¹⁰ο πιστευων εις τον υιον του θεου εχει την μαρτυριαν εν εαυτω ο μη πιστευων τω θεω ψευστην πεποιηκεν αυτον οτι ου πεπιστευκεν εις την μαρτυριαν ην μεμαρτυρηκεν ο θεος περι του υιου αυτου ¹¹και αυτη εστιν η μαρτυρια οτι ζωην αιωνιον εδωκεν ημιν ο θεος και αυτη η ζωη εν τω υιω αυτου εστιν ¹²ο εχων τον υιον εχει την ζωην ο μη εχων τον υιον του θεου την ζωην ουκ εχει ¹³Ταυτα εγραψα υμιν τοις πιοτευουσιν εις το ονομα του υιου του θεου ινα ειδητε οτι ζωην εχετε αιωνιον

⁹If we receive the **witness** of men, the **witness** of God is greater; for this is the **witness** of God which He **has testified** of His Son. ¹⁰He who believes in the Son of God has the **witness** in himself; he who does not believe God has made Him a liar, because he has not believed the **testimony** that God has given of His Son. ¹¹And this is the **testimony**: that God has given us eternal life, and this life is in His Son. ¹²He who has the Son has life; he who does not have the Son of God does not

---

[46] R. E. Brown (*The Epistles of John*, Anchor Bible [Garden City, NY: Doubleday, 1982], 608), lists them as Alexander, Brooke, Klöpper, Schnackendburg, and Schneider.

have life. ¹³ These things I have written to you who believe in the name of the Son of God, that you may know that you have eternal life.

What John is arguing for in this passage is the credibility of God's testimony (witness). It is greater than that of men. And this witness or testimony is that God has given us eternal life, and this life is in His Son. We can either accept or reject this testimony. If we believe it, we internalize the testimony so that it is in us, in our hearts. If we reject the testimony, we are calling God a liar (not a very good option, n'est ce pas?). But if we believe the testimony, we also believe in Jesus. And if we believe in Jesus, we can *know* that we have eternal life because this life is in His Son. If we have the Son, we have life. All we have to do is believe.

Notice that we are not called upon to search our faith to see if it is real. We do not have to have "faith in our faith." We are called upon to have faith in what God says about His Son. Our assurance is at stake here, yes, but more important than that is the credibility of God. It is His witness that is at stake. We either believe it or reject it. In fact, in 1 John 5:13 we find echoes of John 5:24 where it says, "Most assuredly, I say to you, he who hears My word and believes in Him who sent Me has everlasting life, and shall not come into judgment, but has passed from death into life."[47]

Conclusion

Often, in a discussion on assurance, I will ask a lordship salvationist if he thinks he will go to heaven when he dies. The answer is invariably yes. When asked why or on what ground, the answer is usually something related to the evidence of the Holy Spirit working in his life. But when asked if it is possible for him to have a serious fall, he will usually answer yes, because he knows 1 Corinthians 10:12 cautions him against presuming he could not fall. But what if he falls and produces rotten fruit for a long period of time? What

---

[47] See, Dave Anderson, *Maximum Joy: First John - Relationship or Fellowship?* (Grace Theology Press, 2016), 34.

would that prove? They usually squirm here and say it would prove they never were Christians in the beginning. Aha! Then, what would we be forced to say about your good works today? The only answer is that these good works are being produced by someone who is not elect. But if these good works are being produced by someone who is not elect, by what manner of casuistry can they be construed to be a present ground of assurance that one is elect? Obviously, the cannot.

And so it goes with the whole doctrine of perseverance until the end of one's life on earth. Those who hold to this must inherently believe that those who think they are elect might prove they are not by falling away and not coming back at some point before they die. If this is true, then it must also be admitted that any good fruit or good works being relied upon in the present are false grounds for assurance of one's salvation since a subsequent falling away from the faith might prove that these good works were being produced by someone who is not elect in the first place. Hence, *present* faithfulness is an unreliable basis for present assurance. Only *future* faithfulness can provide any grounds for assurance. But the future is always out there. Until one dies, one can always fall away. Present faithfulness is not firm footing for assurance of salvation.

Sometimes, Demas (Col 4:14; 2 Tim 4:10; Phile 24) is raised as a case in point. Second Timothy 4 tells us that Demas left Paul after serving with him off and on for fifteen years. He went "after this world." What does that tell us about Demas? It is asserted that if he never came back, it means he never was a believer. But what if he did come back? Well, that proves he was a believer since he repented and was persevering. But what if he wandered away after this world a second time? Well, that proves he never was a believer. But, what if he repented and came back a second time? So, on it goes, and this cycle could be repeated until the end of his life. So, when would Demas ever have known whether he was elect or not? Only when he dies, of course . . . with no assurance in this life.

What is being argued here is not whether a regenerate person should or should not have good fruit in his life. Obviously, he *should* have good fruit. But we are arguing that fruit is not the ground of his assurance, and if a person ever looks to his persevering fruit as the ultimate ground of assurance, he can never have assurance. We believe a person can have absolute assurance that he is born again the moment he believes. We can give him this assurance, not because of a change in his life which we can feel or see, but because we believe without doubt the promises of God which offer eternal life as a free gift to anyone who believes in Jesus Christ as the Son of God and Savior from our sins.

Regeneration[1]

Introduction

In every "system" of theology, there are certain doctrines so imbedded in that system that to uproot them would fell the entire tree. In his excellent work on epistemology, David Wolfe explains that good systematic theology requires four criteria to even qualify as a system.[2] He believes the adequacy, rationality, reliability, and suitability of a system of theology can be evaluated or validated on the basis of these four criteria. The failure of a system to meet these criteria indicates its weakness and the likelihood that theological reconstruction on a system-wide level is necessary or conversion to some other more suitable system is demanded for intellectual honesty. The four criteria are:

1. CONSISTENCY—the assertions, hypotheses, and opinions expressed by the system should be free from contradiction.
2. COHERENCE—the assertions and hypotheses should be related in a *unified* manner.

---

[1] This material originally appeared as an article in a Grace Evangelical Society journal.
[2] David Wolfe, *Epistemology: The Justification of Belief* (Downers Grove, IL: InterVarsity Press, 1982), 50-55.

3. COMPREHENSIVENESS—the system should be applicable to *all* evidence.

4. CONGRUITY—the system of assertions, hypotheses, etc. must *"fit"* all evidence. It must be accurate, adequate, and precise to *fit* all data. In other words, the whole must equal the sum of its parts. If one part of the whole is out of sync with the whole, then the whole must be revised to include this part without throwing the other parts out of sync. We are searching for the interpretation which best *"fits"* all the data.[3]

Another characteristic of any system of theology is what is called "ingression," which simply means that some claims or hypotheses might be more deeply embedded or more crucially interconnected within a system than other assertions. We call this "depth of ingression." Opinions that are not very deeply ingressed in a system may be relinquished or proven false without much change in the system. However, items that are more deeply ingressed are more dependent on the system, and the system is more dependent on them. The testing of these matters is thus more crucial to the system and must be conducted more carefully with a great deal of evidence before any changes in a system would be justified—or, at least, probably before they will be accepted by those committed to that system. For example, in Dispensationalism the doctrine of separation between Israel and the Church is deeply ingressive. Remove this separation and Dispensationalism dissolves faster than sugar in tea.

Likewise, in most Reformed theology the doctrines of Total Depravity and Regeneration are deeply ingressed. As R. C. Sproul points out in his analysis of Lewis Sperry Chafer's dispensationalism, "When we turn to Chafer's (and historic Dispensationalism's) view of regeneration, we focus on what I believe is the most crucial point of the debate between Dispensationalism and Reformed theology."[4]

---

[3] This is similar to the concept of "Intrinsic Genre" articulated by E.D. Hirsh Jr, *Validity in Interpretation* (New Haven, Yale University Press, 1979) 81-86.

[4] R. C. Sproul, *Willing to Believe* (Grand Rapids: Baker, 1997), 193.

If the Reformed view of regeneration is in error, then their view of Total Depravity is also off center. And if their view of Total Depravity misses the mark, then the most "ingressed" of all their doctrines is uprooted, and the tree falls.

In the typical Reformed presentation of the *ordo salutis* (order of salvation), regeneration precedes faith. This understanding arises out of the Reformed view of Total Depravity, which argues that man has no part at all in the salvation process because a completely fallen person is incapable of doing anything to help effect his own salvation. To assert otherwise would be tantamount to teaching salvation by works. Once again, we call upon R. C. Sproul to explain this point of view:

> The logical priority of regeneration in Reformed theology rests on the doctrine of total depravity or moral inability. Because fallen man is morally unable to incline himself by faith to Christ, regeneration is a logical necessity for faith to occur. If we were to posit that faith precedes regeneration, then we would be assuming that unregenerate people, while still in an unregenerate state, have the moral ability to exercise faith. If the unregenerate can exercise faith, then it follows clearly that they are not fallen to the degree of moral inability, as claimed by classical Augustinian and Reformed theology. This would involve an Arminian or semi-Pelagian view of the fall.[5]

And it would not be unfair to say that the other four points of Dortian Calvinism[6] (Unconditional Election, Limited Atonement, Irresistible Grace, and Perseverance of the Saints) are an outgrowth

---

[5] Ibid., 194.
[6] We refer here to the brand of Calvinism which developed at the Synod of Dort (the city of Dordrecht) over half a century after John Calvin's death in reaction to the tenets of James Arminius. There are many who believe the Calvinism which came from Dordrecht had moved a long way from that taught by John Calvin himself due to the influences of Theodore Beza's supralapsarianism and William Perkins' criteria for fruit-inspecting (see R. T. Kendall, *Calvinism and English Calvinism to 1649* [Oxford: Oxford University Press, 1979]).

of this doctrine of Total Depravity. We must remember that a "system" of theology must have not only consistency, it must also have coherence. Everything must hang together. Perhaps, in our high tech world, another way to describe "Systematic" Theology is "Spreadsheet" Theology. When one changes one item in a spread sheet, all the other items change as well. Coherence requires it. That is why when Augustine became amillennial (a change in the eschatological column), it changed his view of justification (a change in the soteriological column).[7]

Hence, we agree with R. C. Sproul: regeneration is one of the crux interpretations that distinguishes Reformed theology from Dispensational theology. Perhaps it would be helpful, then, to delve deeper into the background of the Reformed view of regeneration, especially in regard to the order of salvation. Where did their understanding of regeneration before faith actually originate? And what is their theological defense for such a view?

Regeneration in History

Augustine

His Background

Many of our studies begin with Augustine, the first of the Church Fathers to seriously delve into grace and doctrines other than Trinitarian issues. His teaching has affected the RCC, Lutherans, Calvinists, Arminians, and Anglo-Catholics right up until today. And Augustine taught baptismal regeneration, but he was not the first. This discussion thus duplicates some of the previous material on baptism, repentance, and justification. A completely heretical, but very influential document in the early church was *The Shepherd of Hermas*. The writer claims to have been a contemporary of Clement, presbyter-bishop of Rome (AD 92-101). Hermas is instructed by the

---

[7] Augustine repeatedly uses Matthew 24:13 as a proof text for his understanding of perseverance as a requirement for salvation and a proof of election (*Rebuke and Grace*, 10, 16; *To Vincentius*, 9).

"angel of repentance," who is dressed up as a shepherd. The call is for a lackadaisical church to repent. The writing is thoroughly legalistic and never mentions the gospel or grace. He speaks of the meritorious system of good works and the atonement of sin through martyrdom. There is no mention of justification by faith, but water baptism is indispensable for salvation.[8] And water baptism is the seal of repentance which "makes Christians into Christians. . . . Asceticism and penal suffering are the school of conversion."[9] Faith is the fruit of repentance and baptism seals it.[10]

Justin Martyr followed on the heels of Hermas and also saw water baptism as the work of regeneration. He said: "Those who are convinced of the truth of our doctrine . . . are exhorted to prayer, fasting and repentance for past sins. . . . Then they are led by us to a place where there is water, and in this way they are regenerated, as we also have been regenerated. . . . For Christ says: Except you are born again, you cannot enter into the kingdom of heaven."[11] The importance of water baptism for Justin Martyr is underscored when he says "the laver of repentance . . . is baptism, the only thing which is able to cleanse those who have repented."[12]

Irenaeus (d. 200) also linked water baptism with regeneration because of passages like John 3:5 and Titus 3:5. And Cyril of Jerusalem (d. 386) called water baptism the "chariot to heaven." He believed the only way to get to heaven without water baptism was through martyrdom. By the time of Augustine (d. 430), infant baptism was in full vogue. And at the baptismal font, "We are justified, but righteousness itself grows as we go forward."[13] In the *ordo salutis* Augustine saw predestination, calling, justification, and glorification. But justification was the umbrella over everything from regeneration

---

[8] Schaff, *History*, vol. 2, *Ante-Nicene Christianity*, 684-87.
[9] Behm, "μετανοέω," 4:1008.
[10] Ibid., 4:1007.
[11] J. Martyr, *Apol.* I., c. 61.
[12] J. Martyr, *Dial.*, 14.1.
[13] Augustine, *Sermon*, 158.5.

through sanctification;[14] and regeneration began at baptism. He actually called it "the saving laver of regeneration."[15] Here the elect receive the external sign (the water of baptism) and the spiritual reality (regeneration and union with Christ). For Augustine, "the sacrament of baptism is undoubtedly the sacrament of regeneration."[16]

But unlike Hermas and other predecessors, Augustine did not view regeneration as a work of man. It was the unmerited gift of grace which wrought regeneration, faith, and repentance in the sinner.[17] But little children could definitely be regenerated through baptism, which "cleanses even the tiny infant, although itself unable as yet with the heart to believe unto righteousness and to make confession with the mouth unto salvation."[18] Nevertheless, elect children who had been baptized would inevitably go on to faith and repentance and growth in grace. All of these were elements of his understanding of justification. Since he was not familiar with Greek, he misunderstood *dikaioō* to mean "to make righteous" instead of "to declare righteous."[19] This misunderstanding also led to the Catholic belief that justification is a life-long process. Of course, with this approach one could not know whether he was elect or not until he died, which is exactly what Augustine[20] and the RCC teach.

The non-elect may receive the external sign of water baptism, but there is no internal spiritual transaction. Augustine believed that infants are cleansed from original sin at water baptism. Unbaptized infants and baptized infants who are non-elect remain under the control of the devil. Baptized infants, who are elect, will inevitably go on to faith and repentance. So, although Augustine leaned on God's grace for salvation, water baptism was, without question, one means by which this grace was received.

---

[14] Demarest, *Cross and Salvation*, 351.
[15] Augustine, *Sermon*, 213.8.
[16] Idem, *On Forgiveness of Sins, and Baptism*, II.43.
[17] Demarest, *Cross and Salvation*, 282.
[18] Augustine, *On the Gospel of St. John*, 80.3.
[19] Idem, *On the Spirit and the Letter*, 45.
[20] Augustine, *On Rebuke and Grace*, 40.

Thus, we can see that the historical background of water baptism is very important for understanding Augustine's view of regeneration before faith. But so is his logic.

His Logic

As incredibly bright as Augustine must have been, his training was in rhetoric, not exegesis. His language was Latin, not Greek. We have already seen how his mishandling of the word *dikaioō* has had grave consequences in church history, at least from the Protestant perspective. Much of his theology comes from the sheer weight of his logic. He does little to defend his views of baptismal regeneration and infant baptism from the Scriptures. Like most of us, he filtered Scripture through his own experience. Realizing that he had been a slave of lusts before his conversion, he deduced from his experience that he was totally depraved, completely *unable* to extricate himself from his prison of passion.

Reasoning from his understanding of total depravity in opposition to Pelagius and his view of innocent until guilty, Augustine concluded that fallen man has no part at all in the salvation process, including faith. Fallen man cannot believe, he reasoned. Therefore, he must be born again (regenerated) in order to believe. Without a shred of biblical data, Augustine built his *ordo salutis* in the halls of logic, that is, human reason. With his understanding of total depravity (every area of man is affected,[21] including his reason), it is a wonder he put so much faith in his own logic. Nevertheless, it is important to see that his understanding of regeneration was born of a marriage between tradition and logic, not the Scriptures.

Roman Catholics

The RCC followed Augustine's lead. Thomas Aquinas said, "Baptism opens the gates of the heavenly kingdom to the baptized."[22] Aquinas was the first to write of the "baptism of desire" when he

---

[21] This is an understanding with which Dispensationalists generally agree.
[22] T. Aquinas, *ST*, III, q. 69, art. 7.

said of those who, for one reason or another, could not get to water for baptism, "Such a man can obtain salvation without actually being baptized, on account of his desire for baptism ... whereby God ... sanctifies man inwardly."[23] At the Council of Trent (1545-63), the waters became murky. Whereas Augustine saw regeneration as instantaneous and justification as a life-long process, this council decided that regeneration only *began* at water baptism. They sort of combined regeneration, justification, and sanctification together into one gathering pool of God's grace. Of course, this pool was only accessible through the channels of the sacraments (water baptism, eucharist, etc.).

The Second Vatican Council (1963-65) required faith and baptism for salvation. However, the Vatican tower has tilted in the direction of inclusivism in which all of mankind can be oriented to the life of God and all men can be saved by the "baptism of desire." This baptism of desire is equivalent to the *implicit faith* possessed by uneducated people. Thomas Aquinas taught that this implicit faith would suffice for salvation.[24] And post-conciliar Catholics equate this implicit faith with the baptism of desire, thus opening the door for all men to go to heaven:

> Those who, through no fault of their own, do not know the Gospel of Christ or his Church, but who nevertheless seek God with a sincere heart, and, moved by grace, try in their actions to do his will as they know it through the dictates of their conscience—those too may achieve eternal salvation. Nor shall divine providence deny the assistance necessary for salvation to those who, without any fault of theirs have not yet arrived at an explicit knowledge of God, and who, not without grace, strive to lead a good life.[25]

The same dogma has been confirmed by Catholic theologians like G. Baum who says, "One may seriously wonder whether baptism

---

[23] Ibid., III, q. 68, art. 2.
[24] Ibid. II, q. 2, arts., 6-7.
[25] Second Vatican Council, Dogmatic Constitution on the Church, II.16.

of desire is not the way of salvation for the great majority of men in this world chosen to be saved."[26] And from the Vatican we read, "Everyone does not strictly 'need' baptism to become a child of God and an heir of heaven. Every person, by reason of birth and God's universal offer of grace, is already called to be a child of God and an heir of heaven."[27]

Lutherans

It would appear to be a great contradiction, but Luther died still believing in baptismal regeneration for infants. He said God "himself calls it [baptism] a new birth by which we are... loosed from sin, death, and hell, and become children of life, heirs of all the gifts of God, God's own children, and brethren of Christ."[28] In *The Small Catechism* (1529), Luther wrote:

> Baptism is not merely water, but it is water used according to God's command and connected with God's Word.... How can water produce such great effects? It is not the water that produces these effects, but the Word of God connected with the water, and our faith which relies on the Word of God connected with the water.... When connected with the Word of God [the water] is a Baptism, that is, a gracious water of life and a washing of regeneration in the Holy Spirit. (IV)[29]

But not only does regeneration come with water baptism, so does faith and justification. This is the same justification which Luther so defended as occurring at the moment in time and which declared a person righteous before God so as to effect forgiveness for all sins, past—present—future.

---

[26] G. Baum, "Baptism," in *Encyclopedia of Theology: The Concise Sacramentum Mundi*, K. Rahner, ed., (New York: Crossroad, 1982), 77.
[27] Richard P. McBrien, *Catholicism*, 2 vol. in 1 (Minneapolis: Winston, 1981), 738.
[28] Luther, *Works*, 53:103.
[29] Melanchthon expressed a similar view in *The Augsburg Confession*, art. IX.

But if one asks how an infant can exercise faith, the answer is that regeneration occurs at the moment when the invoked Word of God unites with the water and the infant responds to the Gospel with rudimentary faith. Baptism does not automatically regenerate (this would be the RC concept of *ex opere operato*). It must be combined with faith: "In baptism, children themselves believe and have faith of their own. God works this within them through the intercession of the sponsors who bring the child to the font in the faith of the Christian Church."[30]

Notice now, the introduction of *sponsors* to the baptismal event. Notice also, that God works faith into the infants through the "intercession" of the sponsors. Hence, the great concern of parents that their children be baptized, not just for the significance of the event itself, but also because they become responsible for the salvation of their children if indeed they are the intercessors through whom God will effect faith within their little children. Luther definitely instigated a reformation which led to Protestantism, but it seems at times he was only a stone's throw from the walls of the Vatican. These baptized infants must ratify their regeneration and rudimentary faith as they get older through repentance, mature faith, *and obedience*.

So let's get the picture here. An infant or little child is water baptized. As he grows up he is told that at water baptism he was regenerated and exercised an elementary faith in Christ because of the intercession of his sponsors, most likely his parents. Now, if he is truly elect, all this which occurred within him before he had any conscious awareness of what was going on will be confirmed by his repentance, mature faith, and obedience. Obviously, if he is not obedient, it proves

---

[30] Luther, *What Luther Says*, comp. E. M. Plass (St. Louis: Concordia, 1959), 51. So also with D. Hollaz (d. 1713) as cited by H. Schmid, *The Doctrinal Theology of the Evangelical Lutheran Church* (Minneapolis: Augsburg, reprint, 1961), 463-64, who said, "In infants, as there is not an earnest and obstinate resistance, the grace of the Holy Spirit accompanying Baptism breaks and restrains their natural resistance that it may not impede regeneration; wherefore their regeneration takes place instantaneously"; D. Bonhoeffer, *Cost of Discipleship* (London: SCM, 1959), 206; and F. Pieper, *Christian Dogmatics*, 3 vols. (St. Louis: Concordia, 1953), 3:264, 269-70.

that he was not truly elect and for some unknown reason his infant baptism did not "take." But the fires of hell await such a one. Hence, be obedient to make your calling and election sure. It all goes right back to a works-oriented approach to salvation, especially since through certain egregious sins one can lose this hard wrought salvation. To fall back on Philippians 2:13 at this point to try to prove that it is by God's grace that one is able to work out his own salvation is pure exegetical sophistry. The Church of England also teaches baptismal regeneration of infants. In *The Thirty-Nine Articles* (American Version, 1801), we read: "Baptism is . . . a sign of Regeneration or New-Birth, whereby, as by an instrument, they that receive Baptism rightly are grafted into the Church; the promises of the forgiveness of sin, and of our adoption to be the sons of God by the Holy Ghost, are visibly signed and sealed" (art. XXVII). And the priest, as prescribed in *The Book of Common Prayer*, prays just prior to baptism, "Give thy Holy Spirit to this child, that he may be born again, and be made an heir of everlasting salvation." After baptism, the priest gives thanks that God was pleased "to regenerate this infant with thy Holy Spirit, to receive him for thy own child, and to incorporate him into thy holy Church."[31]

Covenant Reformed

We must remember that many of the Reformed persuasion are determined to preserve their view of the sovereignty of God at all costs, even if that makes God directly responsible for sin and evil. As this relates to their soteriology, they are careful to argue for the position that God does everything in man's salvation (monergism) rather than including man in the process at any point (cooperation or synergism). Thus, it is very important in their system that regeneration precede repentance, faith, and justification.

Some of them believe in what we call *presumptive regeneration*, which says regeneration itself does not take place during infant

---

[31] *The Book of Common Prayer* (New York: Church Pension Fund, 1945), 270, 280.

baptism, but their baptism is a sign that they already possess the seeds of regeneration and faith. Their baptism is also a sign that God is dispensing grace in the covenantal community of the church. As such, the divine act of regeneration, which is not a conscious reality within the baptized, precedes the conscious response of faith and repentance.

Still others of this persuasion believe in *promissory regeneration* in which baptism is a sign and seal that the future regeneration will come to the baptized.

Calvin himself defined regeneration as the entire process of new birth, repentance, faith, justification, and sanctification. Regeneration for him was the umbrella over all the others. Regeneration began at water baptism but "does not take place in one moment or one day or one year." Instead it is accomplished "through continual and sometimes even slow advances."[32] He referred to the filling of the Holy Spirit in John the Baptist while the latter was still in the womb of his mother, thus proving that regeneration can take place in infants before they even hear the Word of God.[33] So he thought regeneration could take place in the womb or during early infancy. He paralleled circumcision and baptism, likening both of them to regeneration.

For the infants of believing parents, baptism connotes forgiveness of sins, union with Christ, and regeneration by the Holy Spirit. Infants cannot actually believe but they can receive the seeds of regeneration and sanctification.[34] For Calvin, baptism "is like a sealed document to confirm to us that all our sins are so abolished, remitted, and effaced that they can never come to his sight, be recalled, or charged against us."[35] If all this is true of an infant, one surely wonders why an adult baptized as an infant needs faith or justification. Sounds like it was all accomplished at their baptism when an infant.

The Scots Confession (1560), which was the first Reformed standard in English, leans toward *presumptive regeneration* when it says, "We

---

[32] Calvin, *Institutes*, III.3.9.
[33] Ibid., IV.16.19.
[34] Ibid., IV.16.17-20.
[35] Ibid., IV.15.1.

assuredly believe that by Baptism we are engrafted into Christ Jesus, to be made partakers of his righteousness, by which our sins are covered and remitted" (art. 21). On the other hand, *The Westminster Confession* (1647) leans toward *promissory regeneration* when it says baptism is "a sign and seal of the covenant of grace, of his engrafting into Christ, of regeneration, of remission of sins, and of his giving up unto God, through Jesus Christ, to walk in newness of life" (chap. 28.1). And W. G. T. Shedd (d. 1894) defended baptismal regeneration of infants from Luke 1:15, Acts 2:39, 1 Corinthians 7:14, and the parallel of OT circumcision with NT baptism of infants. "In the case of infant regeneration, there is an interval of time between regeneration and conversion. . . . The regenerate infant believes and repents when his faculties will admit of the exercise and manifestation of faith and repentance."[36]

Again, so much of this *ordo salutis* is an effort to make sure man has no part whatsoever in his salvation. In order to ensure this fact, regeneration as a sovereign and independent act of God in the individual must take place before repentance and faith. Thus, one is not regenerated because he believes; one believes because he has been regenerated. Shedd comments that "The Holy Ghost is not given as a converting and a sanctifying Spirit, until he has been given as a regenerating Spirit" (Matt 12:33; Jn 3:3).[37] J. Murray sums up the position of covenant theologians pretty well when he says, "Without regeneration it is morally and spiritually impossible for a person to believe in Christ, but when a person is regenerated it is morally and spiritually impossible for that person not to believe."[38] And

---

[36] W. G. T. Shedd, *Dogmatic Theology*, 3 vols. (Grand Rapids: Zondervan, reprint, n.d.), 2:508, n. 1. See also, Michael F. Bird, *Evangelical Theology: A Biblical and Systematic Introduction*, (Grand Rapids, MI: Zondervan Publishing, 2013) 762-763, and Wayne Grudem, *Systematic Theology: An Introduction to Biblical Doctrine*, (Grand Rapids, MI: Zondervan Publishing, 1994), 974-975.
[37] Ibid., 2:514.
[38] J. Murray, *Redemption Accomplished and Applied* (Grand Rapids: Eerdmans, 1955), 106.

L. Berkhof says, in no uncertain terms, that "a conversion that is not rooted in regeneration is no true conversion."[39]

In order to be fair, it must be stated that many modern Reformed theologians reject the concept of baptismal regeneration.[40] But they have retained the logic of saying that regeneration must precede faith.

Once again, R. C. Sproul is representative of this line of thinking:

> Remember that in Reformed theology's ordo salutis regeneration precedes faith. It does so with respect to logical priority not temporal priority. Reformed theology grants that God's act of regeneration and the believer's act of faith are simultaneous, not separated, with respect to time. The ordo salutis refers to logical dependency. Faith logically depends on regeneration; regeneration does not logically depend on faith. Again, the priority is logical, not temporal. Regeneration is the necessary condition of faith; faith is not the necessary condition of or for regeneration.[41]

Summary

Often, it appears that differences in theology or even theological systems hinge on the different ways key words are understood. Justification is a great example. It would seem that the Reformation hung on a difference in understanding of the meaning of "to justify." Regeneration is another term which is used in many different ways. Some groups want it to serve as an umbrella arching over the whole Christian experience. Others limit it to a two-tiered approach: presumptive or promissory regeneration at the water baptism of infants and full regeneration some time later in life. Still others narrow their understanding down to one instantaneous act of new birth which occurs at the moment of faith.

However, what is conspicuous by its absence in the foregoing discussions is a close look at the Scriptures themselves. We have

---

[39] L. Berkhof, *Systematic Theology* (Grand Rapids: Eerdmans, 1941), 485.
[40] Allen Mawhinney, "Baptism, Servanthood, and Sonship," *Westminster Theological Journal* 49 (Spring 1987): 47-48.
[41] Sproul, *Willing to Believe*, 193-4.

seen that Augustine arrived at his conclusions primarily through the influence of tradition and his own powers of logic. The Reformers cried *Sola Scriptura*, but they too had difficulty escaping the tentacles of RCC tradition.

Yet, without a solid foundation in the Scriptures themselves, is the building secure? Another way to envision Systematic Theology is as mighty river. But this river has two branches which feed it: Historical Theology and Biblical Theology. If there is pollution in one of these branches, then the main river is polluted as well. This is another way of saying that one's Systematic Theology is only as good as his Biblical Theology, since the latter is a building block of the former. Though Systematic Theology does incorporate General Revelation, its primary source is the Special Revelation of the Scriptures. Thus, solid exegesis of the Scriptures is paramount in developing a Systematic Theology which is comprehensive, consistent, coherent, and congruent. It only makes sense, then, to turn to the Scriptures to see regeneration in its biblical context.

Regeneration in the Bible

Titus 3:5

The NT uses a number of different words and images to convey the doctrine of regeneration. The noun *palingenesia* is used just twice: Matthew 19:28 and Titus 3:5. In Matthew, Jesus is speaking of the regeneration which will occur at His second coming. He refers to setting up His kingdom, placing the twelve over the twelve tribes of Israel, and rewarding those who have sacrificed for His cause. But in Titus 3:5, we have a direct reference to the rebirth of the believer: "Not by works of righteousness which we have done, but according to His mercy He saved us, through the washing of *regeneration* and renewing of the Holy Spirit." Of course, it is this reference to washing which convinces so many that the actual physical act of water baptism effects regeneration. But the near proximity of the reference to the Holy Spirit combined with other passages on the same subject help us understand that this regeneration is a ministry of the Holy Spirit, not something directly connected with water.

1 Peter 1:3, 23

Just as with the noun, the verb for regeneration (*anagennaō*) is used only twice in the NT: 1 Peter 1:3 and 23. The first verse says, "Blessed *be* the God and Father of our Lord Jesus Christ, who according to His abundant mercy has *begotten* us *again* to a living hope through the resurrection of Jesus Christ from the dead." Here it is the Father who does the begetting. In 1 Peter 1:23 we read, "Having been *born again*, not of corruptible seed but incorruptible, through the word of God which lives and abides forever." This time the focus is on the Word of God which is the tool used by God to give us new birth. But notice that in none of these four references (nouns and verbs) do we read about faith in connection with regeneration. Not that our faith is not involved, but there is nothing in these texts that would indicate that regeneration leads to our faith or that our faith leads to our regeneration. However, in this final reference in 1 Peter there is mention of the tool used by God to accomplish this regeneration: the Word of God. This would suggest that until one hears and understands the message, one cannot be born again. Of course, it must be asked how an infant could possibly hear and understand the message.

James 1:18

James 1:18 uses another verb (*apokueō*) to depict the new birth: "Of His own will He *brought* us *forth* by the word of truth, that we might be a kind of firstfruits of His creatures." The fact that this is not a reference to physical birth should be obvious from the instrument used: the Word of Truth. This is a spiritual birth, and it is accomplished through the agency of God's Word. Once again, we must ask how this would be accomplished in infants, since hearing and understanding are prerequisites for this rebirth if the agent of birthing is God's Word. It is passages like this which force those who practice infant baptism to reach out to far-fetched concepts like "seeds of faith" and the faith of the "sponsors" as explanations for how the new birth could be connected with God's Word in an infant.

The Tenses

Another aspect of the three verbs mentioned (1 Pet 1:3, 23 and Jas 1:18) is the tenses used. In James 1:18 and 1 Peter 1:3 we find the aorist tense. Though the aorist tense is really a nondescript tense as far as the aspect (*type* of action) of a verb is concerned, it is generally not one of the tenses used to describe a *process* or *ongoing* action. The aorist tense in 1 Peter 1:3 is found in a participle dependent on the understood present copula ("to be"). When the aorist participle is dependent on a present tense main verb, the action of the participle is antecedent to the action of the main verb. In other words, these Jewish believers of the diaspora had already been born again as Peter writes. Their birthing had already taken place.

The entire image of birthing should convey something that is not a process. Though, the gestation period can be described as a process, not so with birthing. Even though the event might take a day if we speak of a prolonged delivery, the birth itself is understood to be the consummation of the pregnancy, something that happens once, at a particular moment in time. In the case of 1 Peter 1:3 the aorist tense just says it happened and it happened at a time prior to Peter's writing. This picture is incongruous with any understanding of regeneration which spans several years of development.

The verb used in 1 Peter 1:23 also militates against any concept of process in the birthing of believers. This time the verb is in the perfect tense, which speaks of completed, past action with on-going results up to the present. The point here is that the action is complete and in the past. There is no process still going on in the life of the believers which could be described by a verb for regeneration.

John The Apostle

John 1:13

Though we do not have the preposition on the front of *gennaō* ("born") to indicate "again" (*ana* or *palin*), we do have reference to spiritual birth in this verse: "But as many as received Him, to them He gave the right to become children of God, to those who believe in His name: who *were born*, not of blood, nor of the will of the flesh, nor of the will of man, but of God." Here it refers to people who already exist receiving Christ and thus having the right to become children of God (1:12). People become children by birth, so the verb for birthing is used. Again, it is in the aorist tense, not a tense we would use to indicate a process. And if this verse teaches us nothing else, clearly regeneration is a work of God. Men may "receive" Christ, but it is a passive role on the part of man and an *active* role on the part of God. God becomes the divine obstetrician who very actively delivers the child. Whatever willingness of man is involved in "receiving" Christ, babies are relatively passive in the event of being birthed.

John 3:3-8

Of course, this is the best known passage for the concept of being "born again." Oddly enough, it has the least linguistic support for *rebirth* because the word for "again" (*anōthen*) probably means "from above" (3:31; 19:11, 23) as opposed to "again." Nevertheless, the same verb for birthing (*gennaō*) that we found in John 1:13 is used eight times in these verses. In each case, either the aorist or perfect tense is used, again emphasizing the fact that this birth is not a process.

One thing these verses also make clear is the connection between rebirth and the Holy Spirit (3:6-8). When connected with John 1:33 where John the Baptist predicted that the Messiah would be one who baptizes with the Holy Spirit, most expositors agree that the new birth effected by the Holy Spirit occurs at the time when the Holy Spirit baptizes the believer.

If this is the case, it may be important for answering the question about OT regeneration: OT saints were believers and possessors of eternal life, but they would not be regenerated in the same sense that believers from Pentecost on have been regenerated. By virtue of the New Covenant, we have the Holy Spirit living within us to quicken our consciences in a way unknown to the OT believer who relied more on the Law to spell out right and wrong. A man like David, who did have the Holy Spirit (though not as a seal until the Day of Redemption), appeared to have experienced the same kind of conviction for sin that we face today. Perhaps that is one reason he was a man after God's own heart.

1 John 5:1

Amazingly, some Reformed scholars are now resorting to 1 John 5:1 in support of their belief that *regeneration precedes faith* in the *ordo salutis*. A recent paper quotes John Piper as saying that 1 John 5:1 is the clearest text in the NT supporting the position that regeneration precedes faith.[42] The suggestion might not need to be addressed if it were not for the noted Reformed scholars cited in support: Stott, Ware, Frame, Murray, et al. The argument rides under cover of a misinterpretation of Greek grammar, namely the use of *participles* and the *perfect tense*.

Mounce, Wallace, Zerwick, and Moulton (all accomplished Greek grammarians) explain the basic force of the perfect tense as *completed action in the past with present results*. While the Greek verb translated "born" in 1 John 5:1 is in the *perfect* tense, the verb "believes" (see below) is a *present* tense participle. The Reformed scholars cited above argue that since the action of the main verb ("is born") is completed in the *past*, while the participle linked to the subject of the sentence is *present*, the action of the main verb ("is born/regenerated") must *precede* the "believing." So, they contend, regeneration must therefore *cause* and/or *result in* faith.

Granted, just as in English grammar, it is easy to get lost in Greek grammar. But the proposal needs to be examined further in order to expose the entire argument as based on a sophomoric error in Greek grammar. And before delving further, it should be noted that whereas some Reformed scholars employ the perfect tense of "is born" in 1 John 5:1 to support their understanding that regeneration precedes faith, *none* of the grammarians cited does so—they know better. So, what does 1 John 5:1 actually say?

---

[42] Matthew Barrett, "Does Regeneration Precede Faith in 1 John?" Paper presented at the 62nd Annual Meeting of the Evangelical Theological Society in Atlanta, GA, November 2011, quoting from John Piper, *Finally Alive* (Scotland: Christian Focus, 2009), 118. Also see Matthew Barrett, *Salvation By Grace: The Case for Effectual Calling and Regeneration*, (Phillipsburg, New Jersey, P&R Publishing, 2013)158-162, and John Piper, *Finally Alive*, (Fearn, Ross-Shire, Great Britain: Christian Focus, 2009) 118.

Whoever believes that Jesus is the Christ is born of God, and whoever loves Him who begot also loves him who is begotten of Him.

Πᾶς ὁ πιστεύων ὅτι Ἰησοῦς ἐστιν ὁ Χριστὸς, εκ τοῦ θεοῦ γεγέννηται, καὶ πᾶς ὁ ἀγαπᾷ τὸν γεγεννημένον ἐξ αὐτοῦ.

The subject of the sentence "whoever" is followed by a present participle in the Greek, here translated as "believes" (NKJV). Since the participle (ὁ πιστεύων) has what looks like an "o" in front of it, it is an "articular" participle which functions as an *adjective* connected to the impersonal pronoun (Πᾶς) and not as an *adverb* connected to the verb. The ESV reflects this by translating "Everyone who believes." Only if the participle were *not* preceded by the article could it then be connected to the main verb, "is born," and in some way describe or qualify the state, "born of God."[43] Thus, as an *adjectival* participle describing the *subject* of the sentence, it does not in any way specify the *results* of the main verb or what the main verb *causes*. Grammarians also speak of the particular verbal "aspect" the author wants to emphasize by using the perfect tense, whether *completed action in the past* ("has been born," an extensive perfect) or *present results* ("is born," an intensive perfect). We see this latter aspect emphasized in translations of Jesus' cry on the cross, *tetelestai*, a verb in the perfect tense. Most translators aptly put the emphasis here on the present

---

[43] There are eight ways an adverbial participle can describe the action of an independent verb: temporal, manner, means, cause, condition, concession, purpose, or result (Wallace, Grammar, 612). Take Ephesians 5:18-21, for example: The readers are told to "be filled" (main, finite verb). This main verb is followed by five participles (speaking, singing, making, thanking, and submitting). None of the participles has an article preceding it, so all of them must be adverbial participles describing the action of the main verb in some way. Of the eight options, the two that make the most sense are means or results: 1) Be filled by means of speaking, singing, making, etc.; 2) Be filled, with these results: speaking, singing, making, etc. So the participles are most likely telling the Ephesians how to be filled (means) or the results of being filled (result). But since they are all adverbial participles they are directly modifying the main verb, be filled.

results of the crucifixion by translating it in the *present*, "it is finished," although they *could* have put the emphasis on the *completed action in the past*, "it has been finished." Likewise, most translators of 1 John 5:1 emphasize the *present results of* the Greek perfect tense in John's use by rendering it in the *present*, "is born."

Finally, 1 John 5:1 is not specifically discussing the *original* faith of the current believer. A person who was born again in the past can be currently believing and demonstrating that faith by loving God and others who are born of God. But they can also be currently *dis*believing, and *not* loving God or others. John is concerned about *abiding* in faith. His point is that everyone who believes, at whatever stage of their faith journey (see 2:12-14), is still born of God and shows their pedigree (compare 3:9) by *abiding* in the love of God and others born of God. Since John is emphasizing a *general principle*, the participles "whoever believes" and "whoever loves" both exemplify a *gnomic* use of the present tense,[44] as they parallel "also loves" (gnomic present) in the last clause.

Throughout his paper Barrett confuses the grammar in claiming that regeneration actually *causes* faith. If this is what the verse says, it would support Reformed theology. But *cause* and *result* can only be predicated of an *adverbial* participle in relationship to the main verb. Unfortunately for his argument, the participles he cites are all adjectival. Consequently, the verse says nothing at all about believing as a *result* of, or *caused* by, the new birth (regeneration). To suggest that the new birth *causes* or *results in* believing is like saying *everyone running* (present participle) in a race *has been pinned* (perfect verb) with a race number and then claiming that being pinned with a number *caused* them to run the race. The entire paper is built on a simple mistake in Greek grammar. And it is not a debatable one.[45]

---

[44] Wallace, *Grammar*, 523.
[45] Although see, Thomas R. Schreiner, "Does Regeneration Necessarily Precede Conversion?" available online from 9Marks at: http://www.9marks.org/journal/does-regeneration-necessarily-preceed-conversion: accessed April16, 2018. Also see Robert W. Yarbrough, *1-3 John*, BECNT (Grand Rapids, Michigan, Baker, 2008), 270 for grammatical evaluations. Culver quoting Augustine says

Conclusion

We conclude that there is zero biblical support for placing regeneration before faith in the *ordo salutis*. And to say it takes *logical priority* without taking *temporal priority* is contradictory. The very word "priority" in this context speaks of time. It is a "temporal" word. Unless one switches the meaning of "priority" to "first in importance" (which is obviously not intended), then a statement about "logical priority" without "temporal priority" is nonsensical. And certainly in Historical Theology regeneration was seen to have *temporal priority* over faith, since infants were thought to be regenerated when water baptized. It was not until Reformed theologians realized how little biblical support there is for infant baptism that they began arguing for *logical priority* instead of *temporal priority*.

Sproul argues for *logical priority* because he sees the only other option as Pelagianism, semi-Pelagianism, or some form of what he calls *synergism* (God and man working together to effect salvation). "If we were to posit that faith precedes regeneration, then we would be assuming that unregenerate people, while still in an unregenerate state, have the moral ability to exercise faith.... This would involve an Arminian or semi-Pelagian view of the fall," he writes.[46] He cites writings from Chafer and Walvoord in which they eschew *synergism* but accuses them of *red herring* argumentation by focusing on who effects regeneration (God alone—*monergism*; or God and man working together—*synergism*). Rather he claims one is *synergistic* if faith precedes regeneration in the *ordo salutis*.[47] He accuses Walvoord and Chafer of being "vague" and "unclear" when they make statements like "regeneration is wholly a work of God in a believing heart." He thinks this is unclear because he understands the issue to be whether faith precedes regeneration or vice versa: "Is the heart

---

that Augustine's interpretation of I John 5:1 is, "Whosoever believeth that Jesus is the Christ *has been already* born of God." See, Robert Duncan Culver, *Systematic Theology; Biblical & Historical*, (Fearn, Ross-shire, Great Britain, Christian Focus Publications 2006), 698.

[46] Sproul, *Willing to Believe*, 194.
[47] Ibid., 196.

already believing, or is it believing because it has been regenerated? The answer to this question defines the difference between Calvinism and semi-Pelagianism."[48]

The problems here are multitudinous. The first is with the word *synergism*. Coming directly from the Greek word *sunergeō*, which means "to work together," the very definition of the word should be enough to cause any evangelical Protestant theologian to reject categorically a synergistic approach to salvation. Neither Chafer nor Walvoord would say that man and God work together to accomplish man's salvation (see Jn 1:13). How, then, can Sproul accuse them of that very thing? It is because in his understanding any ordo *salutis* which puts faith before regeneration is synergistic. How can this be, unless *faith* is understood to be a *work*? Of course, that is precisely what Sproul is suggesting because he thinks if man can believe prior to regeneration then man is *morally capable* of making a contribution to his own salvation. And if man is capable of making any contribution to the salvation process before regeneration, then his salvation is not all of God. Hence, it must be synergistic.

Is this biblical thinking? Absolutely not. This kind of ratiocination makes faith a work. The Scriptures contrast faith and works so often the concept hardly needs documentation. Could Ephesians 2:8-9 and Romans 4:4-6 be any clearer? If salvation is by faith, then *works are nowhere to be found* in the process. Yet to argue that faith prior to regeneration is synergistic would only be valid if faith is *equivalent* to works.

But what can we say about the statement that faith prior to regeneration presumes that man is *morally* capable of making a virtuous choice? That is what certain Reformed theologians contend is transparent from these words by the late John Gerstner:

> According to the Reformed doctrine, total depravity makes man morally incapable of making a virtuous choice. While Dispensationalism seems to go along with this idea to a degree, this

---

[48] Ibid. see also Matthew Barrett, *Salvation by Grace*, 125.

"totally depraved" man is nevertheless able to believe. We shall see that his faith precedes or is at least simultaneous with (and not based upon) his regeneration. As long as that doctrine is maintained, the nerve of total depravity is cut.... If the dispensationalist maintains, as he does, that man is morally able to respond to the gospel, then Dispensationalism does not believe that man is totally depraved after all.[49]

How can Walvoord and Chafer and Billy Graham—whom Sproul disparages as the most famous Dispensationalist of all—contend that man is totally depraved and that faith is prior to regeneration at the same time? The key is that they do not believe that man is capable of making a *moral* choice for God *on his own*. He needs "help," divine enablement. Chafer calls this enablement "divine persuasion." "The important truth to be observed in all of this is that, though divine persuasion be limitless, it still remains persuasion, so when a decision is secured for Christ in the individual he exercises his own will apart from even a shadow of constraint."[50] Billy Graham puts it this way: "The Holy Spirit will do everything possible to disturb you, draw you, love you—but finally it is your personal decision."[51]

So, here is what is comes down to. Both Reformed thinkers of the Sproul/Gerstner ilk and Dispensationalists like Chafer and Walvoord agree that a totally depraved human being is incapable of making a moral choice on his own. But the latter would call the divine enablement which makes man capable of such a choice "divine persuasion," while the former would call this divine enablement "regeneration." But our biblical theology has demonstrated that there is no biblical support for putting regeneration before faith. That is why some systematic theologians with Reformed leanings switch

---

[49] John H. Gerstner, *Wrongly Dividing the Word of Truth: A Critique of Dispensationalism* (Brentwood, TN: Wolgemuth & Hyatt, 1991), 109.
[50] Lewis S. Chafer, *Systematic Theology*, 8 vols. (1947-48; Grand Rapids: Kregel, 1993), 6:106-7.
[51] Billy Graham, *How to Be Born Again* (Waco, TX: Word, 1977), 168.

the order.[52] Their biblical theology demands it. But what about this concept of "divine persuasion"? Is it biblical?

R. C. Sproul realizes the argument comes down to this single point, precisely. Does God, in fact, draw/woo men to Himself, as John 6:44 appears to teach, or does He drag/force them into His kingdom in order to prove it is all of Him and none of them? Sproul argues that God drags men into His kingdom against their will.[53] He interprets the key verb of John 6:44 (*helkō/helkuō*) to mean "drag, force, or coerce." And Sproul seems to have biblical support for what amounts to Irresistible Grace. The verb *helkō* occurs only twice in the NT (Jas 2:6 and Acts 21:30). In both cases, believers are being dragged against their will into a hostile situation before and by unbelievers. The same is true of *helkuō* in its only non-Johannine use (Acts 16:19 where Paul and Silas are dragged before the authorities).

Sproul concludes that the use of *helkuō* in John 6:44 also means to "drag" in the sense of force. This is the exegetical fallacy dubbed by Moisés Silva as the "illegitimate totality transfer."[54] Just because the word means "drag against one's will" in James and Acts does not necessitate the same meaning in another context such as John 6:44. In Biblical Theology we seek to find John's meaning for the word in the context where he uses it. Other uses of the word in John would be more helpful than uses from writers such as James and Luke. John uses *helkuō* four other times in his gospel. John 12:32 is a context very much like John 6:44, so it would be begging the question to determine the meaning of John 6:44 from John 12:32. In John 18:10 we find Peter *drawing* his sword from its sheath in order to cut off the ear of the soldier. And in John 21:6, 7, the fishermen are *drawing* their nets with fish in them. The use of *helkuō* with inanimate objects or

---

[52] Demarest, Cross and Salvation, 291.
[53] Sproul, *Chosen*, 69-72.
[54] M. Silva, *Biblical Words and Their Meanings: An Introduction to Lexical Semantics* (Grand Rapids: Zondervan, 1983), 25-27. This term was coined originally by James Barr, *Semantics of Biblical Language*, (Oxford, Oxford University Press, 1961) 21.

subhuman creatures will probably not be determinative. How, then, can one decide the meaning of *helkuō* in John 6:44?

Sproul appeals to an article in Kittel to support his understanding that the word means "to compel by irresistible superiority."[55] We are not sure if this conclusion was a hasty reading on Sproul's part or not, but the article concludes just the opposite in regard to John 6:44. Albrecht Oepke[56] refers to two readings from 4 Maccabees and one from Jeremiah 31:3 to establish that in a familial context or a lover context *helkuō* means "to woo" or "to draw with love." In Jeremiah, it is God the Lover drawing His Love, Israel, with His lovingkindness, and in 4 Maccabees 14:13 and 15:11, it is a Jewish mother as she watches her seven sons martyred for their faith. In both cases the verb is used in connection with strong cords of love drawing the beloved to the one loving. Once again we see that context is king. John 6:44 speaks of people coming to Jesus only if His *Father* draws them. This is not a hostile context. It is the familial context, a context of love.

Why is this so important? Because love precludes force. Does any groom wish to drag, force, or coerce his bride to the altar? I think not. He may have sovereignly initiated the relationship, but then a period of courting and wooing took place in which the future groom *persuaded* his future bride of his many virtues.

We conclude that "divine persuasion" is exactly what the Bible depicts as the divine enablement necessary for a totally fallen being to believe in Christ for salvation. This is not *synergism*. God initiates the relationship, and God is the Persuader, the Wooer. Man is the responder. His ultimate faith is passive. He is a receptor, a receiver (Jn 1:12) of a divine gift. As Roy Aldrich argued long ago, *receiving* a gift can never be construed to be a meritorious work.[57] And never is this "divine persuasion" called "regeneration" in the Bible.

Millard Erickson came to this same conclusion in his study of Systematic Theology:

---

[55] Sproul, *Chosen*, 69.
[56] A. Oepke, "ἑλκυω," in *TDNT*, 1968 ed., VII: 503.
[57] Roy L. Aldrich, "The Gift of God," *Bibliotheca Sacra* 122 (July–September 1965): 252-53.

The conclusion here, then, is that God regenerates those who repent and believe. But this conclusion seems inconsistent with the doctrine of total inability. Are we torn between Scripture and logic on this point? There is a way out. That is to distinguish between God's special and effectual calling on the one hand, and regeneration on the other. Although no one is capable of responding to the general call of the gospel, in the case of the elect, God works intensively through a special calling so that they do respond in repentance and faith. As a result of this conversion, God regenerates them. The special calling is simply an intensive and effectual working by the Holy Spirit. It is not the complete transformation which constitutes regeneration, but it does render the conversion of the individual both possible and certain. Thus, the logical order of the initial aspects of salvation is special calling-conversion-regeneration.[58]

Robert Pyne expresses a similar understanding when he writes:

Many theologians, particularly those who are more Reformed, would insert regeneration between calling and faith. While there is clearly a divine work that comes before faith and is directed only toward the elect, it seems better to restrict oneself to more specific terminology in the description of that work. It may be argued (persuasively, in the opinion of this author) that regeneration takes place through the indwelling of the animating Holy Spirit. Since that indwelling comes through faith (Acts 2:38; Gal 3:2), it seems appropriate to regard regeneration as a consequence of faith, not as its cause.[59]

---

[58] M. J. Erickson, *Christian Theology*, 3 vols. (Grand Rapids: Baker, 1983-85), 3:933.
[59] R. Pyne, "The Role of the Holy Spirit in Conversion," *Bibliotheca Sacra* 150 (April 1993): 215, n. 29.

Summary

We have grappled in this discussion with one of the crucial differences between what is called Reformed Theology and Dispensational Theology, that is, regeneration as it relates to faith in the *ordo salutis* and the impact this *crux interpretum* has on one's understanding of Total Depravity. Both Reformed Theology and Dispensational Theology are systems of theology. By definition, a good system must have consistency, coherence, comprehensiveness, and congruity. Some doctrines, in any system, are deeply ingressive, that is, if one of these doctrines proves faulty, then the entire system is faulty and needs revision, at the least, or frank rejection.

We have also explained that Systematic Theology is only as good as the Historical Theology and the Biblical Theology on which it builds. If aspects of a system conflict with clear biblical data, then the system will have inconsistency, incoherence, incomprehensiveness, and incongruity. By their own admission, Sproul and Gerstner tell us that their view of Total Depravity governs the other four points of their Five Point Calvinism. But essential to their view of Total Depravity is their doctrine that regeneration must precede faith in the elect. If this crux interpretation falls, their understanding of Total Depravity is deficient. And if their understanding of Total Depravity is deficient, their entire five-point system is shaky, to say the least.

We have tried to demonstrate that the modern Reformed teaching that regeneration precedes faith developed in a world of infant baptism and baptismal regeneration. It was also more the result of human logic than biblical exegesis. Hopefully, we have shown that there is no biblical data to support the doctrine of regeneration prior to faith.

We have also tried to explain that the use of the pejorative term *synergism* to describe Dispensationalism is a misnomer, since no Dispensationalist would even suggest that man "*works* together with" God to accomplish his salvation. Faith is not a meritorious work, by definition. In essence the two are mutually exclusive. Furthermore, to speak of regeneration as the divine enablement required for a totally depraved being to believe for salvation is also a misconception. It is using biblical words in an unbiblical way. Is it not more biblical to stick to the biblical terminology for the work of the Holy Spirit or the Father in this divine enablement: calling, convicting, wooing, and persuading (Luke 14)? This kind of biblical data leads to good Biblical Theology. And good Biblical Theology helps build solid Systematic Theology.

Lordship Salvation

Much has already been said about subjects vital to the lordship salvation discussion. Especially crucial have been our investigation into the issues of assurance and the nature of saving faith. Since works have been taught as the way to heaven in mainstream Christianity since the end of the first century right on up to the cry of *sola fide* by the Reformers, it is fair to say that the lordship salvation approach to going to heaven has been a development since the Reformation.

We have traced this development of the claims of lordship salvationists to the roots planted, not by John Calvin, but by Theodore Beza. Because of his supralapsarian view of the divine decrees, he created the concept of limited atonement. That very doctrine led to his insistence that one not look to Christ for his assurance (because the professing believer might be reprobate and be looking to a Savior who did not die for him), but rather should look to the fruit of his own life. This kind of fruit inspecting became the battle cry of the English Calvinists and their Puritan strain of Christianity. When coupled with the amillennial interpretation of verses like Matthew 24:13, which says the elect must endure to the end in order to be saved, lordship salvationists insist that one be a "fruit inspector" until his last gasp in order to be assured of his salvation. In a conversation with this author D. Bock admitted that this might be the very case, i.e., that one cannot know that he will go to heaven when he dies until he dies. If that is so, then R. T. Kendall's observation that there is very little difference between the Arminians and the Calvinists, and even less difference between the Protestants and the Catholics in their soteriology, is absolutely correct. All must persevere in good works until they die to be ensured of entrance to heaven. Our good works become an integral part of the salvation equation.

Before proceeding further with distinctions, perhaps it would be beneficial to highlight the similarities. According to T. Lewellen,

> [G]reat essential agreement exists between proponents and opponents of lordship salvation. Both sides agree that regeneration, or the impartation of eternal life by the Holy Spirit to a sinner, is required for salvation. Both sides agree that regeneration produces a positional change: a Father-child relationship is established between God and the believing sinner. Both sides also agree that regeneration produces a constitutional change: a person receives the Holy Spirit and eternal life, which is God's quality of life placed within his soul. This constitutional change provides the possibility and the power for a superb transformation of character and conduct. Both sides agree that such transformation is expected, desired, demanded, and possible for the believer. Both sides also agree that Christians can sin, and sin severely.
>
> Both sides agree that sin in a believer is serious and brings on him or her the convicting work of the Holy Spirit and should result in confrontation and discipline by the church. And both sides agree that such disobedience can last for some period of time in a believer.... The truth is, lordship salvation does not teach that every professing Christian who sins is not a true believer. Likewise, Free Grace teachers do not affirm the salvation of everyone who claims to be a Christian.
>
> Undoubtedly, much of Christian history has taught that regeneration will produce some outward and visible change and that no change whatsoever may be evidence of a lack of true regeneration. But Free Grace teachers teach the same thing. The points of disagreement go back to the nature of faith and assurance. What the free grace position simply will not allow is that the change produced by regeneration is the grounds of or the evidence for assurance of genuine salvation.[1]

---

[1] Lewellen, "Lordship Salvation," 65.

The only addition this author might make to the above observations would be in the last sentence: "What the Free Grace position simply will not allow is that the change produced by regeneration is the *primary* grounds of or the *primary* evidence for assurance of genuine salvation." Good fruit in the lives of professing believers is certainly *secondary* or *corroborating* evidence that they are Christians. And there are many in the lordship camp who will agree with this statement of mine. The big problem, however, is their understanding of perseverance until the end of one's life. The moment they claim that only those who persevere until the end can be sure they are Christians, they not only steal assurance from the realm of possibility before death, but they also lift fruit inspecting up to the level of *primary* evidence. Any claim to rely first and foremost on the promises of God as their primary source of assurance is pure lip service. This should be intuitively obvious.

Since almost every subject we have covered relates to this subject of lordship salvation, we would need to repeat the entire exposition thus far to highlight the elements which answer this controversy. At this point in the course, then, I simply would like to zero in on the meaning of the term "Lord" in the NT and then turn to the Book of Romans for a closer look at its soteriology.

Kurios in the NT

The entire debate on "lordship salvation" hinges in part on presuppositions surrounding the term "Lord." It is assumed by everyone (to this author's knowledge) in the lordship camp to mean "Sovereign One." From this understanding comes the teaching that to accept Jesus as Savior and Lord means: 1) To trust Him to save the sinner from his sins; and 2) To submit to His sovereign control. J. V. Dahms is typical of those who teach total surrender in order to secure our salvation:

> That total surrender to God is the foremost requirement for human salvation in the OT economy accords with the NT emphasis on the primacy of repentance—that is, on "total surrender, total commitment

to the will of God"—if eternal life is to be inherited (e.g. Luke 24:47; Acts passim; Rom 2:4; 2 Cor 7:10; 2 Pet 3:9; Rev 16:9). Indeed, when repentance is distinguished from saving faith it is always mentioned first (Mk 1:15; Acts 20:21; Heb 6:1).

The priority of repentance with respect to human salvation accords with the fact that preeminence is given to the Lordship of Christ when the NT deals with what is required if one is to secure salvation (Acts 16:31; Rom 10:9; cf. Acts 2:36; 5:31; Rom 10:13; 1 Cor 1:2; 2 Cor 4:5; Phil 2:11; etc.).[2]

It will be noticed that Acts 2:36 is adduced as proof of Dahms' claims. We have referred to this passage before, but let's look at it again: "... is both Lord and Christ." This looks like a great proof-text for proponents of lordship salvation. Unfortunately, they have completely missed the background for Peter's sermon as it is grounded in Psalm 110.

David's Lord

Psalm 110 is the most quoted portion of the OT in the NT (33 quotes and/or allusions). It was used by Jesus in his confrontation with the Pharisees to stump them. "Whom do you say is the Messiah?" He asks His opponents. "The Son of David," they reply. But if the Messiah is the Son of David, how could David have called Him Lord, Jesus wants to know. The Pharisees walk away completely confused, to the point that they ask Him no more questions.

The reference Jesus is alluding to is Ps 110:1 which says, "The Lord said to my Lord, 'Sit at My right hand, Till I make Your enemies Your footstool.'" D. M. Hay remarks that "this pericope may be the only one in the entire synoptic tradition which can be regarded as directly expressing Jesus' understanding of messiahship."[3] The passages

---

[2] J. V. Dahms, "Dying With Christ," *The Journal of the Evangelical Theological Society* 36 (March 1993): 20.
[3] D. M. Hay, *Glory at the Right Hand: Psalm 110 in Early Christianity*, Society of Biblical Literature Monograph Series, no. 18, ed. R. A. Kraft (New York: Abingdon, 1973), 111.

involved (Matt 22:41-46; Mk 12:35-37; and Lk 20:41-44) highlight three points: (1) Jesus' opponents did not object to His use of the psalm as a messianic proof-text; (2) Jesus believed David wrote or at least spoke Psalm 110 through the superintendence of the Holy Spirit; and (3) Jesus thought of himself as the Messiah. What stumped them? Why didn't they just say, "Well, David easily could have called his own son Lord because He was the Messiah, the Savior of the world"? But they did not say that at all. Why not?

Although there are differences in contextual settings and slight variations in their use of the LXX, all three Synoptic writers appear to be in agreement on these three points. They will be examined together in the sense that Matthew will be the point of reference with the variations in Mark and Luke noted along the way.

Matthew is unique in stating it was the Pharisees whom Jesus interrogated in this pericope. In Mark it is not clear. Only a "great crowd" is specified, which could have included the Pharisees and Herodians (Mk 12:13), the Sadducees (Mk 12:18), and the scribes (Mk 12:28). Luke says even less than Mark, although he does suggest that the scribes have just been silenced (Lk 20:39-40).

Matthew's mention of the Messiah (τοῦ Χριστοῦ) did not seem to strike his audience as an unusual question. It certainly was not a common subject in Matthew. Outside the infancy narratives (five references), only two passages (Matt 11:2 and 16:16, 20) make reference to the Messiah before this one (in Mark only in 8:29 and 9:41; in Luke only in 3:15; 4:41; and 9:20). The subject of messianism was of some debate in Judaism. The number of messianic texts at Qumran which unambiguously point to an eschatological Messiah are seventeen, and perhaps twenty-one if terms like "Prince," "Scepter," "Branch," and "First-Born" can be included.[4] Earlier scholars like R.

---

[4] R. Price, *Secrets of the Dead Sea Scrolls* (Eugene, OR: Harvest House, 1996), 302, 516: *CD* 2:12; 6:1; 12:23; 14:19; 19:10; 20:1; *1QS* 9:11; *1Qsa* 2:12; 14:20; *1QM* 11:17; *1Q30* 1:2; *4Q252* 1 v.3; *4Q266* (Da) 18 iii. 12; *4Q267* (Db) 26; *4Q270* (De) 9 ii. 14; *4Q287* 10 13; *4Q375* 1 i. 9; *4Q376* 1 i. 1; *4Q377* 2 ii. 5; *4Q381* 15 7; *4Q458* 2. 6; *4Q458* 2 ii. 6; *4Q521* 2 ii. 41; 89; 93; *6Q15* (D 34; *11Qmel* 2:18; *1Qsb* 5:20, 27; *4Q161* 5-6 3; *4Q174* 1:1; *4Q175* 12; *4Q285* 42, 53, 4; *4Q369*.

E. Brown recognized two different messianic figures at Qumran.[5] But more recent apocalyptic scholars like J. J. Collins recognize four different types of messianic figures among the Qumran scrolls: a king, a priest, a prophet, and a heavenly figure.[6]

Apparently, this question was not much of a debate among the Pharisees. They did not respond to Jesus' question[7] about whose son the Messiah would be by retorting, "Which Messiah?" With what appears to be rapid repartee they acknowledged that the Messiah was to be from the line of David.[8] Jesus' reply left an obvious enigma. If

---

[5] See R. E. Brown, "The Messianism of Qumran," *Catholic Biblical Quarterly* 19 (January 1957): 53-82, for an excellent analysis of the two Messiahs, one from the line of Aaron and the other from the line of David. The Messiah from the line of Aaron was actually dominant over the one from the line of David (ibid.). But Brown also finds evidence for two Messiahs from the OT (Ezek 34:24 and 37:25 for the Davidic Messiah and Ezekiel 44-45 for the priestly). Likewise, the pseudepigrapha reveal the expectation of two Messiahs (see the Testaments of the Twelve Patriarchs). Against this view argues A. J. B. Higgins, "The Priestly Messiah," *New Testament Studies* 13 (January 1967): 211-39, whose view is heavily contingent on the Christian redaction of the Testaments of the Twelve Patriarchs.

[6] J. J. Collins, *The Scepter and the Star: The Messiahs of the Dead Sea Scrolls and Other Ancient Literature*, The Anchor Bible Reference Library, ed. D. N. Freedman (New York: Doubleday, 1995), 11-12. See also L. H. Schiffman, "Messianic Figures and Ideas in the Qumran Scrolls," in *The Messiah*, ed. J.G. Charlesworth (Minneapolis: Fortress Press, 1992), 118-19 and S. Talmon, "Waiting for the Messiah: The Spiritual Universe of the Qumran Covenanters," in *Judaisms and Their Messiahs at the Turn of the Christian Era*, eds. J. Neusner, W. S. Green and E. S. Frerichs (Cambridge: Cambridge University Press, 1987), 111-37.

[7] In Mark the scribes are the ones who teach that the Messiah is the Son of David. Luke just indicates the third person plural, "they," but it could be he is referring to the scribes who have just been silenced.

[8] Though the direct mention of *ho christos* occurs infrequently after the infancy narratives, there are numerous references to the Son of David (Matt 1:1, 20; 9:27; 12:23; 15:22; 20:31-32; and 21:9), which link Jesus with a messianic identity. It would seem even if two Messiahs were expected and the priestly Messiah were to be dominant in the eschatological age, during the "Times of the Gentiles" there was a greater focus on the political Messiah who could deliver them from foreign tyranny. However, Collins, 8-9, points out that the scrolls

the Messiah is to be the son of David, how can David (by the Holy[9] Spirit) address the son as his Lord?[10] To prove that David did address his son as Lord, Jesus quotes Psalm 110:1 from the LXX with only minor changes.[11] The argumentation stumps the Pharisees, for their concept of the Messiah was limited to that of a human being.[12] Here's the point: their messianic paradigm *did not include divinity* or any other kind of transcendent messianic figure. For David[13] to address

---

reflect hundreds of scribes, and there probably was not a scriptorium in the settlement. This means that most of the documents were written elsewhere. And Price (*Secrets*, 301) observes that the only unambiguous dual reference to the Messiahs of Aaron and of Israel was written by the sect at Qumran. It could be inferred from this that Qumran is the only place where more than one Messiah was expected. Price even suggests a messianic view which evolved from multiple Messiahs to one over the two centuries the sect may have been at Qumran (ibid., 302). On this issue, see also Emily Puesch, "Messianism, Resurrection, and Eschatology," in *The Community of the Renewed Covenant*, Christianity and Judaism in Antiquity Series, eds. E. Ulrich and J. VanderKam, no. 10 (Notre Dame, IN: University of Notre Dame Press, 1993), 237-40.

[9] Mark's account includes τῷ ἁγίῳ (cf. Mk 12:36), making it clear that the reference here is dative of means rather than sphere ("in the Spirit/spirit"). And R. H. Gundry notes that if the intention was to present David as having been caught up into heaven to overhear this conversation between Yahweh and the Messiah, then ἐν τῷ πνεύματι would have been followed by mention of a vision or audition (Ezek 11:24 LXX; 37:1 LXX; Rev 1:10; 4:2; 17:3; and 21:10) (R. H. Gundry, *Mark* [Grand Rapids: Eerdmans, 1993], 720).

[10] As mentioned in the previous chapter, the response of the Pharisees would have been different if they thought David was not the speaker (and most likely the author) and the Messiah the recipient of the oracle.

[11] All three Synoptics omit the article preceding κύριος. Matthew and Mark exchange ὑποκάτω ("under") for ὑποπόδιον ("footstool").

[12] L. Morris, *The Gospel According to Matthew* (Grand Rapids: Eerdmans, 1992), 564-65; D. A. Hanger, *Matthew*, Word Biblical Commentary, no. 35c, ed. R. P. Martin (Dallas: Word Books, 1993), 651; D. L. Bock, *Luke*, Baker Exegetical Commentary on the New Testament, vol. 3B, ed. M. Silva (Grand Rapids: Baker, 1996), 1639.

[13] Mark makes it very emphatic that David is the one who "spoke" (once with the aoristic εἶπεν and then with the historic present: λέγει) this psalm. Twice he uses αὐτὸς Δαυὶδ to emphasize His understanding that David spoke this psalm.

his own son as *lord* would have been a breach of ancient near eastern protocol.

The quandary faced by the Pharisees was simply this: on the one hand, they believed the Messiah would come from the line of David and would, therefore, be the "Son of David," and on the other hand, they believed τῷ κυρίῳ μου ("my Lord") in Ps 110:1 was a reference to the Messiah. *With their human concept of the Messiah, the Pharisees were nonplused.* That is why Jesus' argument-clinching question as to how the Messiah can be called Lord by David and also be David's son left them silent.[14] The only way out of the dilemma was to have a paradigm shift:[15] the Messiah must in some way be divine, or at the very least he must be superior to one of the greatest regal human beings of all time (David). That would be the only way the great King David could call his own son *Lord*.[16]

But the revelation granted to Peter by Jesus' heavenly Father (Matt 16:15-17) that the Messiah was to be the "Son of the living God" was not given to the Pharisees. They had no answer for him, as Matthew alone among the Synoptics makes clear (Matt 22:46). In fact, they were so embarrassed by their inability to solve this scriptural riddle, none of them dared ask him any more questions for fear of further embarrassment. They had hoped to stump him, but the tables were turned.

In summation, though the texts and contexts differ slightly, the Synoptics make the same points: (1) Jesus believed that David spoke Psalm 110 by means of the Holy Spirit; (2) Jesus believed τῷ κυρίῳ

---

[14] Some see this as an antinomy (Gundry, *Mark*, 721) and others as a haggadah (Bock, *Luke*, 1630).

[15] As D. L. Bock points out (ibid.), Jesus "breaks new ground in the thinking about who Messiah is."

[16] F. Neugebauer points out that in some respects the Jews saw the Messiah as David reincarnate: "But this meaning lies in the continuation between the first David and the son of David/Messiah, that is, the son of David is the new David, the last David, yes David redivivus" (F. Neugebauer, "Die Davidssohnfrage (Mark xii. 35-7 Parr.) und der Menschensohn," *New Testament Studies* 21 [October 1974]: 91). See also Jer 30:9: "But they shall serve the Lord their God, and *David their king* [italics mine], whom I will raise up for them" (NASB).

μου was a messianic reference; (3) Jesus believed the Messiah was both David's son and David's Lord; (4) David, by means of the Holy Spirit, claimed that someday all the enemies of the Messiah would be under his feet;[17] and (5) Jesus' audience did not refute His assertion that David was the author/speaker of Psalm 110 or that the psalm was messianic in character.

The importance of this passage must not be overlooked. The Jews of Christ's day did not have a concept of the Messiah which included divinity. This is precisely that which got Him crucified, as the trial narrative (Matt 26:63-65) indicates.

Jesus' "Blasphemy"

Once again using Matthew as a point of reference, the question from the high priest is whether Jesus was "the Christ, the son of the living God."[18] In Mark the question is whether He is the son of the

---

[17] D. L. Bock says the first verse of Psalm 110 makes three points: (1) the recognition of authority that David, the author-speaker, gives to this figure by acknowledging him as Lord, (2) the picture of this rule in the figure of sitting at the right hand, and (3) the declaration of the presence of his rule until all enemies are removed (Bock, *Luke*, 1638). He goes on to support the concept that the Messiah is presently reigning from the right hand of the Father, but acknowledges that Luke 20:41-44 does not develop this aspect of Psalm 110:1. Whether the psalm teaches a present reign or not is one of the issues of this study. It remains for further development of passages like 1 Corinthians 15:22-28 and those in Hebrews to make such a determination. Bock sees the messianic reign beginning at the resurrection-ascension and continuing to the end of the Millennium (ibid.). Others might see the reign of Christ beginning with the subjugation of his enemies at the Battle of Armageddon and the setting up of his Kingdom. In this sense he would rule *in the midst* of his enemies until the end of the Millennium when all his enemies would be destroyed.

[18] This question is particularly interesting in light of the Pharisaic response to the 'son of David' question. If the Pharisees lacked the concept of a divine Messiah, how is it that the high priest would be expecting a Messiah who would be the 'Son of God?' R. Gundry notes that divine sonship was attributed to the Davidic kings in 2 Samuel 7:14 and Psalm 2:7, and the Samuel passage was given a pre-Christian Jewish messianic interpretation in 4QFlor 1:10-12 (Gundry, *Mark*, 908). He also notes that "the Son of God" as used in 4QpsDan Aa = 4Q243 may

Blessed One, and in Luke the question is simply whether or not He is the Christ. Of course, the common denominator of all three questions is whether or not Jesus was the Christ, the Messiah. It is important to recognize Messiahship as the key point at issue, for Jesus' reference and identification with Ps 110:1 further underscores the fact that He interpreted the psalm messianically and viewed Himself as the Messiah. The variations in the questions between the Synoptics and the responses from Jesus can be explained by the different settings for the interrogations before the Jews. A variety of options have been proposed in an attempt to explain these differences, but the one set forth by D. L. Bock will suffice.[19] He suggests an initial inquiry before Annas which was recorded by Luke and John, followed by a two-part trial: an evening examination (Matthew and Mark) and an official morning trial (Luke). So a cursory questioning followed by two more detailed trials (one evening, the other morning) can explain the variations.

In the evening trial recorded by Matthew and Mark, Jesus simply agrees with the thrust of the question with either "You have said it" or "I am." But in the morning trial, he is resigned to the fact that they had their minds made up. It would do no good for him to respond to their question or to ask them questions in kind (Lk 22:67b-68). So rather than interacting with them in vain, Jesus seals his fate by references to Psalm 110:1 and Daniel 7:13.

In all three accounts the two messianic OT references are combined by Jesus. Psalm 110:1 does not mention "the Son of Man," and Daniel 7:13 does not mention "sitting at the right hand." But when Jesus puts them together, the high priest immediately tears his garments and accuses Him of blasphemy in Matthew and Mark's accounts. Luke omits this response from the high priest, but, again, Matthew and Mark may be covering the evening trial, while Luke was covering the morning confrontation.

---

also be a pre-Christian reference to the Messiah. And, according to M. Hengel, the Jewish view of the "Son of God" only signified divine appointment, not divine nature (M. Hengel, *The Son of God* [Philadelphia: Fortress, 1976], 21-56).
[19] Bock, *Luke*, 1779-80.

What did Jesus say which the high priest equated with blasphemy? As many point out, the Mishnah called for blasphemy when one uttered the holy Tetragrammaton (*Sanhedrin* 7.5).[20] But here, the only time Jesus comes close to this is when He replies to their question as to whether He is the Messiah (Mk 14:62) and says, "I am." But that would be too oblique to be a blasphemous utterance, and if it were, the high priest would have begun rending his clothes at that point, which precedes the references to Psalm 110:1 and Daniel 7:13. No, it was these references which evoked the summary accusation of blasphemy by the high priest. Gundry concludes that it was the self-elevation to a position equivalent to Yahweh which was the blasphemy.[21]

Again, we must point out that the Jews did not have a concept of the Messiah which was divine. Who would? Certainly, if the Messiah were from the line of David, He would be a man. But to also be divine would require something that never entered their minds: a God-man. What was missing, once again? It was the God aspect of the Messiah. It was no crime to claim to be the Messiah. But it was punishable by death to claim to be divine. This is the background for Peter's sermon

---

[20] Morris, *Matthew*, 685. But see D. R. Catchpole, *The Trial of Jesus*, Studia Post-Biblica, no. 18, ed. J. C. H. Lebram (Leiden: E. J. Brill, 1971), 132-35, for reasons why this was not the blasphemy in question.

[21] Gundry, *Mark*, 917: "We may best think that the high priest and rest of the Sanhedrin judge Jesus to have verbally robbed God of incommensurateness and unity by escalating himself to a superhuman level, by portraying himself as destined to sit at God's right hand and come with the clouds of heaven . . . ." See also Bock, *Luke*, 1798-800; D. L. Bock, *Proclamation from Prophecy and Pattern* (Sheffield: JSOT Press, 1987), 140-41, comes to the same conclusion, although he curiously thinks Luke's account makes no reference to Daniel 7:13 (Lk 22:69— Son of Man?) and sees the image of the Son of Man as a judge, whereas the Judge is clearly presented as the Ancient of Days who opened the books in Daniel 7:9-10. M. Hengel, *Studies in Early Christology* (Edinburgh: T & T Clark, 1995), 182, writes, "The 'one like a human' who comes with the clouds and is brought before the Ancient of Days *does not appear as judge* [emphasis added] but rather as the victorious party in a suit." Rather than a tie to judging, the Daniel reference for the Son of Man links Jesus with a kingdom, a dominion which is everlasting, which will not pass away and will not be destroyed (Dan 7:13-14).

in Acts 2 without which we cannot understand what he is saying in Acts 2:36.

Acts 2:36

Right in the midst of this great sermon Luke uses Psalm 110:1 to buttress Peter's claim that Jesus was the Lord and Messiah, His present session at the right hand of God in partial fulfillment of messianic promises given to David. But just as Daniel 7:13 is coupled to Psalm 110:1 in the trial of Jesus passages to supply the eschatological element, the juxtaposition of Joel 2 with Psalm 110:1 adds the authoritative element to Christ's session at the right hand of God, granting Him the right to dispense the Holy Spirit upon all mankind. Along with this comes the authority and right to save all who call upon His name (Acts 2:21). These ministries are present prerogatives not associated with any texts dealing with His priesthood, but rather with His Messiahship, His Lordship, His rule.

Although D. M. Hay thinks Jesus is *kurios* while He sits enthroned at God's right hand,[22] he considers this to be a *passive* lordship, certainly no threat to Caesar, and definitely not cosmological. However, H. Beitenhard contends that "*kurios* always contains the idea of legality and authority."[23] As gods these lords could "intervene in the life of men to save, punish or judge.... Therefore, they were called lords." One of the functions of a lord was "to save." This is certainly something Jesus is doing now. In further support of his contention, Beitenhard notes that the Jews would have pronounced the Tetragrammaton as *kurios* in their synagogues when orally transmitting the LXX. He proposes that early Christian scribes changed the Tetragrammaton in the text of the LXX to *kurios*. If so, it certainly helps interpret the meaning understood by the early Christians for the term *kurios*. *It was a substitute for God.* When the Christian community submitted itself to Christ as *kurios*, they also understood that he was ruler of the universe. Romans 14:9 says that Christ died and lived *again* (ἔζησεν,

---

[22] Hay, *Glory*, 71-72.
[23] H. Bietenhard, "κύριος," in *NIDNTT*, 1986 ed., 2:510-15.

ingressive aorist) that He might κυριεύσῃ (reign) over the dead and the living. This does not appear to be a *passive* Lord![24]

---

[24] Actually M. Saucy ("Exaltation Christology in Hebrews: What King of Reign?" *Trinity Journal* 14 [Spring 1993]: 61, n. 84), appeals to this verse to say this does not apply to "Christ's lordship until the occasion of the judgment (cf. v. 10)." But v. 10 does not mention the Judgment Seat of Christ or the Lord. Rather it is the judgment seat of God. M. Hengel uses this reference to the judgment seat of God and the reference to the Judgment Seat of Christ in 2 Corinthians 5:10 to show how interchangeable were the functions of the Father and Son on the throne (Hengel, *Christology*, 189). But Saucy cannot have it both ways. Either Romans 14:1-10 is not a context for the lordship of Christ's being postponed until the Judgment Seat (since God is on the throne here), or he must understand "Lord" to be an alternative for *Theos*. If the latter is the case, then Christ is ruling today, since God is ruling today. Does anyone want to say God is not ruling today since his enemies have not been completely subjugated? If one is not careful here, the conclusion is that both the Father and the Son are passive on the throne; that is, the one who is in charge of the universe is Satan.

Bietenard ("κύριος," 514-15) claims, "According to contemporary Jewish thought, the different spheres of the world in nature and history were ruled by angelic powers. Since Christ has now been raised to the position of κψριοσ, all powers have been subjected to him and must serve him (Col. 2:6, 10; Eph. 1:20f.) . . . . The Lordship of the messiah, Jesus, is a present reality. He is exercising in a hidden way God's authority and Lordship over the world and will bring it to a completion in the eschatological future." And W. Foerster ("κύριος," in *TDNT*, 1984 ed., 3:1139-95) cannot conceive of a passive lordship. "In the concept of the lord two things are conjoined in organic unity: the exercise of power as such, and the personal nature of its exercise, which reaches beyond immediate external compulsion into the moral and legal sphere" (ibid., 1040). He says its basic meaning is "having power." In regard to Jesus, Foerster asserts, "The name of κύριος implies a position equal to that of God," (ibid., 1089), and in regard to Psalm 110:1, "Session at the right hand means joint rule . . . He is the One who exercises God's sovereignty in relation to the world" (ibid., 1089-90).

M. Saucy ("Exaltation Christology," 59-61) tries to make the point that κύριος implies a certain passivity on the part of Christ in Hebrews. He argues that the reasoning which says κύριος overtook the term βασιλεύς because the latter was offensive to the Romans is specious. He may or may not be correct, but this argumentation completely misses the larger point. κύριος was a direct substitution made for Yahweh in the LXX. Whether this was accomplished by the Jews themselves long before Christ or by the early Christian scribes matters not. What is important is that κύριος was a substitute for something much higher

Hence, Peter's use of *kurios* in Acts 2:36 was the climax of a sermon designed to convince the Jews who crucified Jesus that He was more than just a man claiming to be the Messiah. He actually was God. He was *kurios*. The whole emphasis here is on divinity, not sovereignty. Of course, God is sovereign. But that is not the point. The point is simply to convince them that He was God. So it is, whenever the term "Lord" is used in reference to Jesus. "Our Lord and Savior" is our God and Savior. To believe in the Lord Jesus Christ is not a call to submission. It is a call to belief, a call to believe that: 1) Jesus was God (Lord); 2) He was the Savior (Jesus); and 3) He is the only Savior, the anointed One, the Messiah (Christ).

And so it is in Romans 10:9ff. "To call upon the name of the Lord" is not a statement of submission. It is just what it says: a call upon

---

than βασιλεύς because it became a substitute for the name of God. This is the "more than Messiah" concept suggested by D. L. Bock, "The Reign of the Lord Christ," 37-67, in *Dispensationalism, Israel, and the Church*, ed. C. A. Blaising and D. L. Bock (Grand Rapids: Zondervan, 1992), 53.

Saucy keeps using Christ's treatment (or lack thereof) of his enemies as a gauge to determine whether or not he is ruling today (does he want to make the same argument for God the Father?). He terms Christ's dealings with his enemies as "somewhat passive" in Hebrews 1-2. Though this overlooks his dealing with death and the devil (his two biggest enemies) in Hebrews 2, is his treatment of his enemies the final arbiter as to whether or not he is ruling? It must be remembered that, according to Beitenard, a lord was one who could intervene in the lives of men to save, punish, and judge. Hebrews certainly talks about the first two functions in regard to men. And other passages like 2 Peter 3:9 clarify why he has delayed his judgment, that is, so more men can be saved.

D. L. Bock ("Current Messianic Activity and OT Davidic Promise: Dispensationalism, Hermeneutics, and NT Fulfillment," *Trinity Journal* 15 [Spring 1994]: 64) states, "Jesus' salvific, ruling activity is as important as any rule over enemies.... Jesus is not reigning fully, since there is much more power Jesus will display in the future; but that is not to say he is not reigning at all." If the Lord Jesus is only partially restraining his enemies today, it is only because he is delaying the final climactic battle to give more men a chance to repent and be saved. And that is the emphasis of Hebrews (the salvation of men), as will be discussed further in the next chapter. The bottom line is this: just because Jesus does not presently *appear* to be Lord *of* all, does not mean that he is not Lord *at* all.

the name of the Lord. What is His name? Jesus Christ, the anointed Savior. And to acknowledge that He is Lord is to acknowledge that He is God. The entire argument of Romans reinforces this analysis.

The Argument of Romans

Virtually all expositors agree with the general flow of Romans. It starts with unbelievers and winds up with dedicated servants for the Lord. Somehow, sinners become saints, and the saints become dedicated servants. A typical outline adopted by many is: Sin ⇒ Salvation ⇒ Sanctification ⇒ Sovereignty ⇒ Service. It has been called "The Saga of the Sanctified Saint." Yet, as we read the section dubbed "Salvation" (an even more accurate term would be "Justification" since that is the term used as opposed to "salvation," which is never used in 3:21–4:25), the only noun or verb associated with justification in a causative way is either "faith" or "believe" (a combined total of 23x). Never is there any mention of repentance, turning, dedication, or commitment. Strange, if indeed any of the previously mentioned are requirements for justification.

We might conclude that Paul has no words in his vocabulary for dedication and commitment. That might explain the lack of wording to express this all important step in the salvation process for lordship salvationists. But this is not the case. Paul has much to say about commitment. But what Paul has to say about it is directed to those who are already justified. When we get to chapter five, the believers in Rome have already been justified (see 5:1). And all agree by the time we get to Romans 6:1-10, the subject is how to be delivered from the power of sin, not the penalty of sin. The penalty of sin was taken care of back in chapter four. But in order to live out the full "Saga of the Sanctified Saint," there must be a deliverance from the power of sin. Not surprisingly, it is here that we find the term Paul uses for dedication or commitment: *paristēmi*, which is translated as "yield" (KJV), "present" (NKJV; NASB), and "offer" (NIV). Interestingly enough, the term is found for the first time in Romans in 6:13 where believers who *have* died and risen with Christ (v. 8) are challenged to no longer *present* their members as instruments of unrighteousness to the Sin Nature, but to *present* themselves to God as being alive from the dead, and their members as instruments of righteousness to God. In a religious context, this is the word for making sacrifices (see BAGD, 628, 1d). And when it comes to oneself and his God, this is the word for making an all-out, one hundred percent surrender or yielding or dedication or commitment to the Lordship of that deity.

The order set forth in Romans (justification before dedication) is so important for understanding the victorious Christian life, I would like to suggest the following aphorism.

Dedication before Emancipation is Incarceration

One of my favorite stories on dedication and consecration to Christ comes from the lips of a pioneer missionary named Willard Clark. He was leaving his mission station in Africa to visit some of the native villages. And as he and his associates drove down a narrow pathway, they heard a scream in the underbrush. Taking his rifle, Clark began plunging his way through the underbrush until he came to a small clearing. There was a young African boy bleeding badly because he had just been severely mauled by an African lion. The lion was over on the side of the clearing waiting to pounce on the boy to finish him off when Clark raised his rifle and shot the lion dead, just as it was about to take its last leap.

They picked up the boy and took him back to the mission compound to care for him. After several weeks in the infirmary, the boy was strong enough to go back to his village in the bushland. Some months later, Clark was sitting on the open porch of his mission home rocking in his chair, enjoying the sunset and the cool evening breeze. But as he looked down the open pathway leading to the mission, he saw a procession approaching. As it came closer, he saw that it was this same young boy leading the procession. He came up to Clark's home and asked Clark if he recognized him. The missionary assured him he did. Then the young boy said, "Sir, I've come to give myself to you this day to become your servant for the rest of my life." Mr. Clark responded by saying, "This is not required of you. You don't need to do that." Then the boy said, "Sir, you do not understand the law of the jungle. The law of the jungle is this. If anyone has saved us from certain death, that life of ours belongs to the one who saved us. You saved me from certain death and according to our law of the jungle, my life belongs to you. I have come to give myself to you. These are my friends who are carrying all of my possessions." And his friends came up and put all the boy's possessions at the feet of the missionary. As Mr. Clark finished telling this experience in his life, he said, "There, for the first time, I think I began to realize what it must mean to Jesus Christ for a person to present himself and all that he has to the Lord."

Now, that is a beautiful story of dedication. But the question I want to ask is "Why?" Why did the little boy present himself and his goods to the missionary? You say, "Obviously, because the missionary saved his life." Yes, that is obvious. But was it out of his appreciation and love for the missionary? Oh, I am sure the little boy had a measure of appreciation for the missionary, a great deal, perhaps, but that is not why he became the life servant of the missionary. And do we suppose that the little boy had more love for the missionary after just this short acquaintance than for his own parents, people, and friends? Highly unlikely. Perhaps, he just wanted to come and live at the mission station rather than in the bush. But as another man's servant? Doubtful. No, the basis on which this life dedication was made was the law of the jungle. According to this law, the position of the little boy was the property of the man who saved his life. Regardless of the little boy's longing for his home, his own parents, his friends, the bush, according to the law of the jungle, his rightful position was at the side of the missionary. It was a matter of principle. His dedication was based on the principle of ownership set forth in the law of the jungle.

Now, I wonder what basis of appeal we usually hear when we are told to dedicate our lives to Christ. The lordship salvationists would tell us that this kind of commitment is part of true saving faith. Without this kind of commitment, our faith is an empty profession and will leave us grasping for God across a wide gulf between heaven and hell for eternity. But even those who are not lordship salvationists offer an appeal such as, "He gave His all for you; the least you can do is give your all to Him." Generally, the appeal comes right after a touching emotional story about Christ's love and sacrifice for us. And then, as the choir lifts the melodious strain of "I Surrender All," we are beckoned to the front to dedicate or rededicate or re-rededicate our lives to Him.

Why is it that these dedications do not seem to stick? Could it be because they are built on the wrong base? There is very little doubt that the born again Christian has a deep love and appreciation for what Christ has done for him. And in an emotional moment he may be very much moved to dedicate his entire life to Christ. But alas, the newly dedicated Christian soon discovers that sin still dwells in his members. He begins to feel like a hypocrite. He tells himself and others that he is sold out to Christ, he has given his all, but then he sees himself committing and struggling with the same old sins that have been his bugaboo for years. He swiftly realizes that his love for Christ, his gratitude for Christ, lofty motives though they be, are not lofty enough to lift him above the sea of sin in which he drowns daily. The temptation is to give up at best, or to even doubt one's salvation at worst.

What is wrong here? Wherein lies the failure? Quite simply, the failure probably lies in the pulpit. We Bible teachers are very explicit in our teaching of Romans 1-4. How carefully we paint the picture of that lugubrious monster called Sin, whose haunt is the verses of Romans 1-3. Then we open the door of hope in Romans 4 where we find the wall of the inner sanctuary lined with plaques containing promises concerning justification, redemption, and propitiation. This is all well and good. But here is where we can make a most serious error. Having ushered the new believer into the kingdom, we then skip Romans 5-11 and open the book of responsibility in Romans 12-16. Now that he knows the King, we tell the new Christian his responsibility to the King, to *present* or *yield* (*paristēmi,* 12:1; just as in 6:13 and 19, it is the next appearance of this word in Romans; its final appearance in this sense is in 14:10 in reference to the Judgment Seat of Christ) his body a living sacrifice, which is his reasonable service. Why is it reasonable? Why, of course, Jesus paid it all; all to Him I owe. And so, lest love's labors be lost, we urge the believer to dedicate his life to Christ out of love and gratitude for what Christ has done for him. The only teaching that could be worse than this would be to tell the unbeliever he must present his body a living sacrifice *in order* to be justified (precisely the position of lordship salvationists). But note: we skipped all the teaching of Romans 5-11.

I dare say, many reading this book have heard countless messages on salvation and dedication, but probably far fewer have ever heard any messages on emancipation, the theme of Romans 5-8. *Dedication before emancipation is incarceration.* It leads the believer into a prison of hypocrisy. We, meaning teachers and preachers, do God's sheep a great disservice by appealing for their dedication before explaining their emancipation from the Sin Nature. Until emancipation is understood, the sincere believer does not realize what he is dedicating to the Lord. He presents the Old Man to Christ, the self-life, thinking that his love for Christ will lead him to holiness and sanctification. It will not. Our love for Christ will not sustain us in Service. Why? Because we love sin more. Is that a shocking statement? Perhaps so, but it is true. And if you have ever been caught in the headlock of sin, you know whereof I speak. The headlock of sin negates our love for Christ as a powerful enough motive for victory. Oh, the *little* (are there such?) sins, yes. But I am talking about the headlock, the warden of Sin Prison. No matter how much you feel you love Christ, there are times when you and I love sin more than Christ. No, our love and gratitude for Him will never carry us through a life of dedication. Then what will? What *is* the basis for dedication? Where can I find a solid base for consecration? The answer, of course, is in Romans 6. So let us focus our lens at this point on Rom 6:12-14.

The theme of Romans 5-8 is "Sanctification." The theme of Romans 6 is "Freedom from Sin." There are five stair steps in Romans 6 that lead up to the plateau of freedom from sin: Know ⇒ Believe ⇒ Reckon ⇒ Present ⇒ Obey. The first three are in 6:1-11. First, we must *know* the facts of our identification with Christ. Then, we must *trust* in the truth of our identification with Him. Third, we must *appropriate* the reality of these identification truths. We must enter these truths into the credit column of our spiritual check book, and then start writing checks. Not until I have signed my name to one of these checks do I really believe and appropriate the fact that I have got the money in the bank. And it is not until temptation comes my way and my Sin Nature goes into rut like a big ten-point buck and I say, "Sorry, buck, but I am dead in the old realm of life where you ruled my life. According to my spiritual account, the Old Man I once was no longer exists, and I do not have to obey you because you have no authority in the new realm where I live today. My New Man is free from your domineering power. So, get lost." That is appropriating the truth of our position in Christ. Dead in the realm where the Sin Nature is king; alive in the realm where Christ is King.

The fourth step in our stairway of freedom from the Sin Nature is *paristēmi*: Yield, Present, or Offer. But before we get to that, I want to say one more word about "reckon." You see, the tense of this word is present, which in certain contexts speaks of continuous action. This stands in sharp contrast to the aorist tense, which has been used over and over again for our death and Christ's death to sin. He died on that cross once, for all time. And we died with Him, that is, our Old Man died, once, for all time. So, there was a point in time, specifically the point in time when we became believers, that our Old Man was crucified and buried with Christ. From that time on, we were and are dead to that old realm where our Old Man lived and the Sin Nature reigned. But . . . we must appropriate that fact continuously—daily. That is what the present tense is all about in this context. Every day we get up, we must reckon on the fact that our Old Man is dead. They say you can't keep a good man down. I'm not so sure that doesn't apply to a bad man as well. Our enemy, the Devil, wants to make us think we have never changed. He says, "You're no different than before you met Christ. You're not a new creature in Christ. You're the same Old Man you always were."

The Old Man is kind of like a Die Hard Battery. I bought a Sears Die Hard battery once. After several years of good service, I decided it was immortal. Then one day . . . no power. I couldn't even jump it. A friend, who knew more about cars than I, suggested that it was dead. He said you can't jump a dead battery. My Sears Die Hard, dead? I could scarcely believe it. That's the way we are with our Old Man. Christ has given us a new battery with unlimited power and a lifetime guarantee. But we refuse to believe our old battery is dead. God tells us in Romans 6 that our old battery is dead, but after all, we've been using it since birth and we refuse to believe it's no good. Of course, we are encouraged to use it by the flood of sales literature telling us how to discover hidden power in our old battery. But God says it will never work because it is dead. It's true. But your car will just sit there until you believe what He says and then appropriate it by switching the battery cables from the old battery to the new. Don't be a Sears Sucker. God, the Master Mechanic, says your Die Hard Battery is dead. Daily, moment by moment, as you face temptation, appropriate the fact, bank on the fact that the Old Man is dead and buried. The New Man lives in a brand new world (2 Cor 5:17). We have passed from death unto life (Jn 5:24). We have been delivered from the power of darkness and transferred into the kingdom of His beloved Son (Col 1:13). In this new world in which we live, in this kingdom of the beloved Son, the Old Man does not exist and the Sin Nature has no authority. We are out of its jurisdiction.

When we know these facts, believe these facts, and bank on these facts—then we are ready for Step Four: Dedication (*paristēmi*, Rom 6:13). You see, that is why 6:12 begins with "therefore." The word looks back to 6:1-11. It says, "On the basis of the facts of our position in Christ, our identification with Christ, our death in the realm where our Sin Nature had jurisdiction and our transfer into the realm where Jesus reigns—on the basis of these facts and your knowledge of, faith in, and appropriation of these facts you are ready to present or dedicate yourself to Christ as Lord of your life. Do you see the basis for consecration (dedication, presentation)? Romans 6:1-11 says nothing about our love or gratitude to Christ for what He has done for us. Those are wonderful motives, but they are not sufficient for life-time dedication. Romans 6:1-11 talks about our position in Christ. And it is our position in Christ, our freedom from the tyranny of the Sin Nature, which becomes a sound, lasting basis for Christian service. When the Christian offers himself for service on any other basis, he begs for trouble, for he is still under bondage to the Sin Nature. And in the midst of his Christian service he will find himself distraught at his inability to deal with his own life, let alone try to help others with theirs. He is in a prison of hypocrisy. *Dedication before emancipation is incarceration*. But once we understand and appropriate the truths of emancipation, then we are ready for presentation or dedication.

Romans 6:12-14 falls into two halves: 12-13a is the negative side, while 13b-14 is the positive side. Both the negative and positive sides have two parts. There are two negative prohibitions in 12-13a, one general and one particular. In general, "Stop allowing sin to reign in your mortal bodies with the result that you obey it in its lusts" (my translation). OK, let's nail down some of these words. Sin here is *hē hamartia*, so it refers to the Sin Nature. Remember, it is the Sin Nature we have been freed from as far as its reign over us. It has been deposed from its throne. However, the Sin Nature has not been destroyed or wiped out. It is still in us just waiting for the chance to take over full control of our lives once again. The word "reign" is *basileuō*, which refers to the reign or rule of a king over his kingdom. So the Sin Nature looks at your body as its kingdom—it wants to sit on the throne to rule. Now, we have all seen the little diagram of ego versus Christ sitting on the throne of our lives. Actually, when Christ is dethroned it is our Sin Nature which jumps up there as king to rule. So, when you sense that battle going on inside, it is a battle to decide who will rule in your life, who will sit on the throne in your life, Christ or your Sin Nature.

How will you know who is ruling? You can tell by the results. Verse 12b says the result of the Sin Nature's rule will be our obedience to our lusts. In his commentary, Newell brings out a good point here. He says the Sin Nature will rule through the lusts of the body.[25] The word *epithumia* ("lust") is not always a negative desire. The body has many normal, natural desires which are good and harmless. However, the Sin Nature can take these desires and pervert them. The desire for food, for sleep, for exercise, for sex, for drink—these are all basic, harmless desires of the body. But when the Sin Nature is in charge it can take any one or all of these and pervert them for evil. And when one of these has you or me in its grip, then we can be assured the Sin Nature is sitting on the throne of our lives. Like a wicked king, it

---

[25] William R. Newell, *Romans: Verse by Verse* (Chicago: Moody Press, 1938), 228.

makes us cower and bow down in slavish obeisance to its perverted desires and commands. But notice we do not have to let it reign. Why? Because of all that has been said in 6:1-11. One Christian leader said, "There is no known sin in the Christian life which is not voluntary sin." I respond, "Oh, no. It was involuntary. I just couldn't help it." "Yes, I believe you couldn't help it. But Christ could." As one little girl said, "When sin knocks on your door, send Christ to answer." Christ died a substitutionary death for us. We all believe that, if we are born again. But what we fail to realize is that Christ wants to live a substitutionary life in us as well. The victorious Christian life is a substitutionary life. We must substitute the Christ-life for the self-life. "When sin knocks on your door, send Christ to answer." When I am obedient to an evil lust, it is usually because I choose to be so. It is because I chose to do it eagerly because I love it so much, or it is because I am trying to battle it with the self-life rather than the Christ-life.

Getting rather particular now, Paul says, "and do not present your members as instruments of unrighteousness to sin" (6:13a). Further expanding on the meaning of this word for "yield" or "present" or "offer," *paristēmi* literally means "to stand beside." It is as though Christ and the Sin Nature are asking for volunteers to step forward. If I choose Christ then I go stand alongside of Him. It is like the old song, "Who is on the Lord's side? Who will serve the king? Who will be His helpers, other lives to bring? Who will leave the worlds side? Who will face the foe? Who is on the Lord's side? Who for Him will go?" And when a church has an altar call, this is what they are asking one to do. Come down front to say, "I will be on the Lord's side. I present my body for His battle, His service, His disposal." So, this word means to put something at the disposal of another.

Specifically, Paul says, "Don't put your members (that is the members of your body) at the disposal of the Sin Nature as instruments of unrighteousness." The word "instruments" (*hopla*) means "weapons." So clearly, we have warfare imagery here. Revolting, isn't it, to realize that our bodies which God created and called good can become instruments or weapons for evil when presented to an evil king like the Sin Nature? The stomach can become a garbage dump for all sorts of refuse. The eye can be used as a spy satellite to invade and scan virgin territory as yet uncaptured by the evil one. The hand can become a thief to rob, a club to beat, a murderer to kill. And the tongue can work like a bayonet to stick and stab, to whip and wound innocent victims. Sobering, isn't it, to realize what a good thing can become when at the disposal of an evil tyrant like the Sin Nature? However, we do not have to do this. Why not?

"But" (*alla*) expresses strong contrast to introduce the positive side (Rom 6:13b-14): *On the* contrary, we should present ourselves to God. Why should we dedicate our lives to Him? Is it because we love Him so much for what He has done for us? No. I hope you do love Him for that, but our basis for dedication is our freedom from the prison where the Sin Nature was warden. We have been set free. It is because of our *position* in Christ, not our love for Christ that we should offer ourselves to Him.

Suppose a ship was at sea and it was discovered that the captain was a crook. The crew throws the crooked captain into the brig. The first mate is appointed captain of the ship until they reach port. Now, to whom should the crew members present themselves? To the old crooked captain who keeps yelling out for their allegiance or the first mate, the acting captain? They very well may have built up a tremendous loyalty and love for the old captain. Oh, he has his faults, to be sure, but after all, he is a good sort in a lot of ways. He pays well, feeds us well, can hold his liquor well. Why should they present themselves to the new captain? Why? You know why. It is because by position the crew members are under the employ of the ship owners back on land. By position, they should be loyal to whoever is acting on behalf of the owners of the ship. The old captain was not doing this. He was a crook. So the crew members should present themselves as loyal members to the new captain, not because they love the new captain more than the old, not because the new captain will pay them better, but because in their position as employees of the ship owners they should serve whoever is acting on behalf of the owners. The basis for their presentation is not their gratitude, but their position.

Andrew Murray states, "A superficial acquaintance with God's plan leads to the view that while justification is God's work, by faith in Christ, sanctification (growth) is our work, to be performed under the influence of the gratitude we feel for the deliverance we have experienced and by the aid of the Holy Spirit. But the earnest Christian soon learns how little gratitude can supply the power."[26] He goes on to explain that sanctification, just like justification, is by faith in Christ. Christ is our substitute in death and Christ is our substitute in life. Preaching substitutionary death without substitutionary life is like leaving your own newborn baby in the incubator when you leave the hospital. Miles Stanford writes, "The love motive from which to live the Christian life is good, it is high, but it is not adequate.... As growing Christians, it is time for us to see the necessity of going beyond the love motive to the life motive."[27] "For me to live is Christ...." (Phil 1:21). "I am crucified with Christ, nevertheless I live, yet not I, but Christ lives in me" (Gal 2:20).

On this solid basis, we are to present, dedicate, yield, or consecrate ourselves to God. And it is important to understand what we are presenting to the Lord. We are to present ourselves "as alive from the dead." These are very important words. Unless we present ourselves as those that are alive from the dead, we will be presenting the dead man, the Old Man. We will not accomplish anything for the Lord because the Lord cannot use a dead man. The Old Man, the self-life has nothing to offer Christ. It will only meet failure and frustration. More and more dedications will seem necessary. This person will wear the carpet out with rededications, but no progress will be made until he presents himself as alive from the dead, in other words, until he knows, believes, and reckons on his identification with Christ and presents the New Man, the New Creature in Christ.

J. C. Metcalf sees both the problem and the answer when he says, "The modern teaching of consecration, which is tantamount to consecration of the 'old man,' seeks to bypass the death sentence, and, therefore, only leads to frustration and failure. When, however, you and I are prepared in simple humility to make the fact of our death with Christ our daily basis of life and service, there is nothing that

---

[26] Andrew Murray, *Abide in Christ* (London: James Nisbet & Co., 1888), 65.
[27] Stanford, *Green Letters*, 52.

can prevent the uprising and outflow of new life, and meet the need of thirsty souls around us."[28]

And H. Duncan echoes this thought when he writes, "God asks us to present our bodies as living sacrifices unto Him (Rom 12:1).... Notice this exhortation comes after Rom 6. There is a reason for this order—crucifixion comes before consecration. Un-crucified self refuses to be consecrated. This is why so many people, with all sincerity, walk down the aisles again and again, consecrating uncrucified self to God."[29] Duncan is right on target when he observes that all out dedication or consecration is mentioned in Romans 12:1 and that this important exhortation comes long after the truths of Romans 6:1-11. In fact, Romans 12:1 begins with the words: "I beseech you, therefore, brethren, by the mercies of God, that you *present* your bodies a living sacrifice."

Each word is important, but notice that the exhortation is to "*brethren*." Commitment truth is truth for Christians, not non-Christians. It is truth about the Walk, not truth about the Way. It is not truth about evangelism; it is truth about discipleship. And the word "*therefore*" is also significant. It is telling us that it is on the basis of all the truths he has presented thus far that he makes his appeal. This includes all the Sanctification truth of Romans 6–8 as well as the Eternal Security truth of Romans 9–11. Not until the believer knows how to be free from the *power* of the Sin Nature (Romans 6–8) and how secure he is in Christ (Romans 9–11) is he really ready to go all out in Christian service (Romans 12–16).[30]

And of course, here in Romans 12:1 we find the next occurrence of *paristēmi*. Remember the last one? Romans 6:13 (Sanctification truth). And the next one? Romans 14:10 (Service truth and the Judgment Seat of Christ). Isn't it interesting that the concept of discipleship, or all-out commitment to Christ, is something associated with this word *paristēmi* (dedication, consecration, presentation, commitment)? Never is it associated with the Great White Throne Judgment on

---

[28] J. C. Metcalf, quoted in Stanford, *Green Letters*, 52-53.
[29] H. Duncan, quoted in Stanford, *Green Letters*, 53-54.
[30] See *Portraits of Righteousness*, for a full exegetical exposition of Romans 5-8.

unbelievers. The believer, who is going to heaven, is asked, "What did you do with the life, the gifts, the opportunities I gave you?" In other words, "Where is your commitment?" But that question is to heaven-bound people. The unbeliever is never asked, "Why didn't you commit your whole life to me?" *Lordship salvationists have it all backwards.* But that should not surprise us.

As S. Lewis Johnson taught his students, "If you are not accused of cheap grace and antinomianism when you present the gospel, then you are not presenting Paul's gospel, for that is exactly what he was accused of (Rom 6:1)." Would we ever accuse the lordship salvationists of cheap grace? I seriously doubt it. But that should not be cause for rejoicing on their part. It should be cause for serious doubt whether they are presenting the gospel of Paul. Wherever the true gospel of Free Grace is presented, there will always be those who have trouble believing it, simply because it flies in the face of everything that makes sense to the carnal mind.

How can we overstate the importance of the truth of Romans 6? Some think the identification truths of Romans 6 are too deep for the new Christian to understand, just like some think prophecy is too deep to understand. Paul spent three weeks with the Thessalonians, and during those three weeks he grounded them in the details of prophecy. Why? Because our blessed hope is half the answer to solving the misery in our condition on earth. But the other half is positional truth. If Paul grounded new Christians in prophetic truth, you can be sure he grounded them in positional truth. This is preventative theology. This tells us how we can be free from domination by the Sin Nature. It all hinges on our death, burial, and resurrection with Christ—our *position* in Christ. These are some of the first facts a new Christian should learn. If he does not, he may lose years never knowing that, although the Sin Nature is still in his life, he is free from its rule and does not have to obey it. When he realizes and appropriates this truth, he is ready to present or dedicate or consecrate his life and his limbs to the Lord. But not before. *Dedication before emancipation is incarceration.*

We have seen four of the five steps in the stairway to freedom from the Sin Nature: Know ⇒ Believe ⇒ Reckon ⇒ Present. What is the basis for our presentation? Not our love for Christ. We love sin *more* at the time we chose to do it. Not our gratitude to Christ. We are basically ingrates in response to God's grace. But the basis for our dedication of life and limb is our position in Him. Positional truth. That is the platform for all spiritual growth.

Martina Navratilova, a tennis icon retired from the women's circuit, defected from Communist Czechoslovakia to become an American citizen. Let's suppose sometime after her citizenship became official she was approached by an undercover agent and asked to spy for Mother Czechoslovakia. At that point Martina would have a decision to make. Let's suppose she does make her decision. She should not let this former government rule in her life. And the way the Czech government will not reign as king in her life will be to refuse to put her time and talents at the disposal of that government.

Now the question is, why shouldn't she spy for Czechoslovakia? Why shouldn't she put her time and talents at the disposal of the government of Czechoslovakia? The normal answer that would be given as we speak of the spiritual life in most of our circles today is, "Well, because of her love for America. Look at how much more money she can make here. Look at the freedom she enjoys." Yet the fact is she might love Czechoslovakia more than America. After all, she grew up there and her family is still there. It is her homeland and she still speaks Czech when she wants to. Deep down in her heart, there is every possibility that she loves Czechoslovakia more than America. If it is her love which is to be the basis for her decision on becoming a spy, there is no telling what may happen.

The basis upon which this woman must reject Czechoslovakia's claim to reign and rule in her life and must not put her talents and time at their disposal—the basis for that is her position. And her position is that of a citizen, a subject of the United States government. It is as she recognizes her position as an American citizen and accepts that position that she must refuse the attempt of the Czech government to rule and reign in her life and must not put her time and talents at their disposal.

Now, that is exactly the situation of the believer. Before I became a child of God, I lived in the kingdom of darkness. Sin ruled and reigned in my life. Then I was converted, born again into the kingdom of God's dear Son. I became a citizen of God's kingdom. Now here is the Sin Nature, the former king, still seeking to rule and reign in my life. The Sin Nature has not been eliminated or eradicated. It still wants to rule and reign in my life. But I am told in Romans 6:12-14 not to let the Sin Nature, that former governing force, have rule over my life and body. Why not? It is not because I do not love certain forms of sin. The basis for my refusal to let the former king rule in my life is my *position* in Christ. I am no longer a citizen of the kingdom where the Sin Nature rules. I am a citizen of the kingdom where Christ rules. It is on the basis of my new position that I must say, "I can no longer let the Sin Nature rule and reign in my life and, therefore, I cannot put my life and limbs at its disposal any longer." Again, the unambiguous basis for this decision is my position in Christ.

Positional truth is not peripheral; it is fundamental. It is not optional; it is essential. This is one of the first things a new Christian must learn. *Dedication before emancipation is incarceration.* But when this truth is known, believed, and counted on as true, then the believer is ready to sing:

> Take my life and let it be,
> Consecrated Lord to thee;
> Take my hands and let them move,
> At the impulse of thy love,
> At the impulse of thy love.

Infants and "Heathen"

Infants

This is a subject we cannot ignore. With abortion, infanticide, and infant starvation so rampant on our planet, we must ask the question as to what happens to these children after they die. As ministers of the gospel, we will be faced with this question. Of course, the world likes to point out the apparent inconsistency of a loving God and all the suffering in the world. There is no suffering which grips the heart more than the suffering of innocent people, especially children. So what does the Bible say?

Most evangelicals retreat to 2 Samuel 12 where David is suffering the aftermath of his affair with Bathsheba. She has born him a child, although the text does not mention the age of the child. Presumably, the child is quite young, if not a new born. There is little reason to think that the Lord would wait long before sending Nathan with his prophecy of discipline. He explains how the sins of David have caused the enemies of the Lord to speak evil of Him because of His anointed's selfishness with Bathsheba. His sins resulted in the death of Bathsheba's husband, Uriah the Hittite. So, the Lord struck the child of David, but spared the life of David.[1]

---

[1] This passage has interesting implications for the subject of divine discipline. We can all understand the deserved suffering which comes to us as a result of our own sins. It would make sense for David to die because of his adultery and murder. But no, David's son reaped the judgment of his father's sins.

When David says he could go to his dead son, but his dead son could not come back to him, many think this must be a reference to life after death.[2] The implication, then, is that child is in heaven. Why? Because we all believe that David went to heaven after he died. And if David says he is going to go to be with his dead son, then his dead son must be in heaven as well.

On the other hand, this passage could simply be saying that David's child is dead and buried. He is in the ground. Someday, David will die and go into the ground as well, however, the child will not be coming back from the dead to rejoin David in this life. This is the approach taken by E. Merrill, former head of the OT department at Dallas Seminary. As Merrill puts it, "David attested to the irrevocability of death—its finality renders further petition absurd. I will go to him, David said, but he will not return to me. This reflects his conviction that the dead cannot return to life as it was. Rather, it is the living who go to the dead."[3]

Others point out the contrast between David's reaction after Absalom's death and that of the child. Perhaps he kept weeping for Absalom because he feared his son would not share eternal life with him. But he stopped weeping when the child died because he was sure he would enjoy eternal life with this child.

Of course, this raises the question of Ecclesiastes 12:7, where we read that at death the body will go to the earth from whence it came, and the spirit will go to God who gave it. This describes the death of a believer. Does David have implications in his statement of ultimate destiny beyond the grave? It is difficult to be sure. But is this the only passage pertinent to this question? No.

There are other passages which address the issue of infant salvation. In Matthew 18 Jesus tells His disciples to allow the little children to come to Him since "of such is the kingdom of heaven." Though this could simply refer to the fact that one must have a child-like trust to enter heaven (Matt 18:1-5), it can also mean that there are

---

[2] Demarest, *Cross and Salvation*, 305, for example.
[3] E. Merrill, "2 Samuel," in *The Bible Knowledge Commentary*, ed. J. F. Walvoord and R. B. Zuck (Wheaton, IL: Victor, 1988), 468.

so many children in heaven, the whole place could be characterized as a childlike place. Zane Hodges has even suggested that after the separation of the sheep and the goats, only children are left alive (physically) to populate the kingdom. "And these shall go away into everlasting punishment, and these into eternal life" (Matt 25:46). In other words, if all the unbelievers are gone, and all the believers are gone, who is left to populate the Millennium? One possible answer is the children younger than the age of accountability. The children are left because they have yet to make a decision. How could they? They have not reached an age where the Lord will hold them accountable.

Other passages which imply an age of accountability include Deuteronomy 1:29 and Numbers 14:29, both dealing with the Wilderness Wanderings. The children were not considered responsible for the lack of faith of their fathers. Hence, they were exempt from the punishment of the parents: "Your children who do not yet know good from bad—they will enter the land. I will give it to them and they will take possession of it" (Deut. 1:29). Then the age of responsibility was given as twenty:

> The carcasses of you who have complained against Me shall fall in this wilderness, all of you who were numbered, according to your entire number, from twenty years old and above. Except for Caleb the son of Jephunneh and Joshua the son of Nun, you shall by no means enter the land which I swore I would make you dwell in. But your little ones, whom you said would be victims, I will bring in, and they shall know the land which you have despised. But as for you, your carcasses shall fall in this wilderness. (Num 14:29-32)

This concept of accountability is also established in Jonah 4:11, the last verse in the book. It says there were 120,000 people that did not know their left hands from their right. The implication is that these were innocent people, because they did not know any better. But it would conflict with texts like Romans 1 and Psalm 19 to say that a whole city of adults were not spiritually accountable for the revelation they had received of God in nature. Thus, the best interpretation here is that this is the number of children. God does not want any children to perish (Matt 18:14). He is especially concerned about innocent lives. We can debate texts such as 2 Samuel 12, Matthew 18-19, Numbers 14, and Jonah 4, but the main reason I find in Scripture for believing infants who have died are in heaven is based on the character of God. We know that His very nature is love (1 Jn 4:8). Just as God cannot lie because He is truth, He cannot do anything unloving because He is love. And love is doing what is in the best interests of the one loved. But we also know that God is just: "For all His ways are just; a God of truth and without injustice; righteous and upright is He" (Deut 32:4). This means He will do what is *right* for each person. Is it *right* to hold people accountable before the age of accountability, which differs for each child? Obviously not.

This is Paul's implicit concern in Rom 5:13-14 for "those who have *not* sinned according to the likeness of the transgression of Adam" (emphasis added). I conclude that children who have died *before* they are capable of responding to the light God has brought them (Jn 1:9) will be in heaven. Does this salvation bypass the blood of Christ? Of course not. These children are *not* held accountable for *personal sin like Adam* (Rom 3:19-20; 5:13-14), but the blood of Christ *is* applied to their *original sin in Adam* (5:18). The work of the cross transcends time and space.

If you take the Augustinian view that these children are born with *vitiam* (a sinful nature and the physical death sentence) and *reatus* (the guilt and condemnation that would send them to hell), then the blood of Christ is applied to them retroactively. Or, as I currently hold based on the work done by Ken Wilson (reference my prior discussion of this and his dissertation), children are born with *vitiam* but not *reatus* (physical death and a sinful nature but no condemnation or guilt), then these children would die before the guilt of personal sin could alienate them from God and would, therefore, go to be with their Maker. If this latter view gives you heartburn, it is a good indication of how deeply the roots of Augustinianism run in Western Christianity. None of the church fathers before Augustine held his view. And, unbelievably, much of his support came from the observation that babies squirm when brought near to the baptismal font! Surely this proves them guilty.

"Heathen"

Do these same principles apply to the "heathen" that have never heard? How could a loving God send people to eternal damnation if they never had a chance to respond to the gospel? Can they be saved like the OT saints without actually hearing about Jesus (see Rom 3:21-26)? We hear these kinds of questions over and over again. There seems to be a growing tendency toward inclusivism in both Protestant[4] and Catholic[5] circles based on the simple assumption that a loving God would not create a person and hold him accountable for a message he never heard. What does the Bible say?

Light Received Brings Light

This basic principle is crucial to understanding the heathen question. In Matthew 13 Jesus begins His ministry of parables to His disciples, immediately following the "unforgivable" sin of Matthew 12. In that passage the Pharisees accuse Jesus of healing the paralytic by the power of Beelzebub. In other words, they attribute His great miracle done by the power of the Holy Spirit to the power of the devil. The purpose of these miracles was to bear testimony to the person and message of Jesus Christ. The strategy was working. The common people said, "Isn't this the son of David?" By that question, they were calling Jesus the Messiah, for it was well-known that the Messiah would be the son of David (remember the answer of the Pharisees when Jesus asked them who the Messiah would be in Matthew 22). So they were ready to receive Him. But the Pharisees, who held the power among the common people, were afraid of losing their power. So, they

---

[4] For a Reformed approach, see N. Punt, *Unconditional Good News* (Grand Rapids: Eerdmans, 1980); for an Arminian approach, see C. Pinnock, "An Inclusivist View," in *More Than One Way?* ed. Okholm and Phillips (Grand Rapids: Zondervan, 1995), 119. This has been republished, *Four Views on Salvation In A Pluralistic World*, (Grand Rapids, Michigan, Zondervan, 1995).

[5] For a Catholic approach, see K. Riesenhuber, "The Anonymous Christian According to Karl Rahner," in *The Anonymous Christian*, ed. Anita Roper, trans. Joseph Donceel (New York: Sheed and Ward, 1966), 171.

put doubt into the minds of the people. They said this miracle might have been done by the devil's power. In reply, Jesus accused them of blasphemy against the Holy Spirit. By discrediting His miracle, they were destroying His credibility before the people. So this is when He turned to a ministry of parables instead of miracles.

In His omniscience Jesus knew the majority of the Pharisees would never trust Him as their Savior or Messiah. In an act of mercy, He chose to keep on revealing truth to those who had ears to hear and to conceal truth from those who did not have ears to hear. The Pharisees did not have ears to hear. So, these stories with their veiled truth would keep the unbelieving Pharisees from receiving more light for which they would be accountable at the Judgment. On the other hand, Jesus could keep on revealing more light to those who did believe in Him and had ears to hear. When asked why He was suddenly teaching in parables, Jesus replied:

> Because it was given unto you to know the mysteries of the kingdom of heaven, but to them it has not been given. For whosoever has, to him more shall be given, and he shall have abundance; but whosoever does not have, even what he has will be taken away from him. Therefore, I speak to them in parables, because seeing they do not see, and hearing they do not hear, nor do they understand. (Matt 13:11-13)

Do you see how *light received brings light, but light rejected brings night*? In order to avoid heaping more judgment on the unbelieving Pharisees, Jesus lowers the wattage of His light bulb (you see, there will be degrees of suffering in the Lake of Fire), but through the parables He could keep on teaching His disciples—they got more light.

Light for Every Man

Jesus is the light of the world. And He "gives light to every man coming into the world" (Jn 1:9). This accords with Psalm 19 and Romans 1 where we learn that just the design and fingerprints left in creation tell us about a Supreme Being. That is why the Mesopotamians began astrology. As they looked out at their post-diluvian world they found their fate lay at the feet of the Weather God. Everything for them was dependent on weather patterns. A flood could wipe out their crops. A drought could do the same. Life and death was beyond their control. Everything was chaotic. They could not control Mother Nature. There was no order to their universe, except in the stars themselves. As they saw the constellations maintaining their patterns and repeating their positions in the heavens, there was order, there was design. This could only mean one thing. The stars themselves must be supreme beings, gods. So they worshipped the stars. Their ziggurats were their churches. The Tower of Babel was a ziggurat built to worship the stars, to burn incense to the Sun goddess (Ishtar) on the top floor.

Of course, the Mesopotamians stopped one step short. They saw the design in the universe but failed to recognize that the stars which made up the design were not divine. Rather, a Grand Designer put the stars in place. The constellations pointed to a designer far greater and more intelligent than tiny little Homo sapiens who lived and died by the vicissitudes of the weather. It is this revelation of His hand in creation which is the light given to every man or woman above the age of accountability. This light speaks of a Supreme Being.

But once a man has received this light, he must decide what to do with it. Remember the principle: light received brings more light. If this man sees this light and receives it, that is, believes a Supreme Being must exist, the next step is to "grope." This is a reference to Acts 17:27 where it says that man can grope for God. If he gropes, this is evidence of a positive response to the light which has been given to him. So, God gives him more light. Light received brings light.

What is this additional light? We do not know. It could be any number of things. Cornelius was groping. God brought Peter to him. At the very least, we can say that more light of some sort will be given. We accept that no man can exercise saving faith without the persuasive, convicting, and calling ministry of the Holy Spirit. No man comes unto Christ unless the Father draws him.

The Name of Christ

God has promised a Redeemer since Adam and Eve, and those who trust this promise are saved. One thing is certain today: Jesus is His name. Whatever and however additional light is given, once one has heard the Name and is past the age of accountability he must believe in this "named" Messiah. There is no other name ("identity") by which we can be saved (Acts 4:12; Jn 14:6). So how do we reconcile this with all the people who have never heard of Jesus?

First, even today people may be justified by faith if they trust in the Messiah as God has revealed Him but haven't yet been told His name. This may well have been the case with Cornelius before visions provided more light (Acts 10). Moreover, Revelation 14:6-7 says,

> Then I saw another angel flying in the midst of heaven, having the everlasting gospel to preach to those who dwell on the earth—to every nation, tribe, tongue, and people—saying with a loud voice, "Fear God and give glory to Him, for the hour of His judgment has come; and worship Him who made heaven and earth, the sea and springs of water.

This message is given toward the end of the Tribulation Period. Let us notice two important aspects of this message:

1. The message goes to every nation, tribe, tongue, and people; everyone hears.
2. The message centers on the creative work of God.

These points are important for our understanding of the heathen question. First of all, no one is left out. God sees that the message gets to everyone. There will be accountability. And secondly, He calls their attention to that which they have observed. It is a call to worship "Him who *made* heaven and earth. . . ." They have had the same light every man has received: a Supreme Being who created the heavens and the earth. Now, they are called to accountability by that Supreme Being.

But this message of accountability is also called a "gospel," that is, "good news." It is good news because now they are called to worship the God of creation. They have a choice. If they choose to worship Him, then they have responded to the light they have been given. The result? More light, the light of Jesus Himself. Just a few verses later we are reading about the "Lamb" and "the faith of Jesus."

Summary and Conclusion

These same principles can be applied to our present time before the Tribulation. If someone responds to the light they have been given by God, they will receive more light. That can come in the form of a missionary, an angel, Jesus, or probably several other ways of which we are not aware.

As a youth pastor for Scofield Memorial Church in the 70's, I took a group of kids into the jungle of Mexico to visit a mission run by a Dr. Dale. He is one of only three people I have known with three Ph.D. degrees. His father started this mission, which ministers to the Aztec Indians. The mission headquarters was inland at a fork in the river—a day's walk from three different Aztec villages. There was no horseback riding, since the Aztecs still remember through their oral tradition the stories of Cortez and his men as they came on horses and slaughtered their ancestors. To reach the villages Dr. Dale had to do what all the Indians did—walk.

Dr. Dale told us how the mission began, with a story similar in many respects to the Cornelius story. His father had actually begun as a missionary on the coast of the Gulf of Mexico. One day, an Aztec Indian walked right out of the jungle and told an amazing story. He said a very bright light appeared one evening in their village. A person spoke from within the light in their own tongue and told them to send someone to the coast where they would find a white man who would tell them about the God of the heavens and the earth. Dr. Dale's father led this man to Christ and spent six months teaching him about Christianity. Then he sent him back to tell his people.

A year later, the same man returned to the coast. He said he was unable to adequately explain his new faith to his people. He wanted Dale to come back with him. Unwilling to leave his family, Dale moved his whole missionary effort inland. This entire mission began with light to one man that culminated in the name of Jesus, and the good news spread to an entire people group.

Salvation only *begins* with justification by faith in God for His free gift of life—His promised redemption through blood. Those who trust the promise but die before hearing the Redeemer's Name in this life— just as all OT saints—will be judged by the light they *have* received. However, the Lordship of Jesus Christ is fully consummated only *after* His return to earth, and a full view of salvation must incorporate this truth: The fullness of our salvation includes a co-inheritance with Jesus as Lord, and the fullness of that inheritance depends in turn on our ongoing faithfulness to light received in this life.

Our God has not left us without witness to His saving intent (Acts 14:17); it is to this end that God has spoken and still speaks (Heb 1:1-2). In order to be saved, each person who reaches the age of accountability must receive God's free gift by trusting His promise of redemption. He loves everyone He ever created. And He is just; He will do right by each person—the blood of Christ avails as a ransom for *all* sin. So, if someone does not respond to the light he has been given in nature concerning a Supreme Being, he is without excuse. But if he responds to this light, God is faithful—He will bring him more light. If this person keeps responding to the light God brings him, he will ultimately come face to face with the Lordship of Jesus Christ even if he is not made aware of the specific name of Jesus before he dies.

Divine Sovereignty and Human Responsibility

There are very few subjects in the Christian realm as controversial and divisive as divine sovereignty and human responsibility. There was a time in the seventies that I would have listed the charismatic issue as the most divisive in Christendom. No longer. Some of those who wish to promulgate the good news of sovereignty treat it just that way, as though it were the gospel.

The issues at stake are not trivial. Perhaps, that is why the emotional storm whirling around these issues ranks as a Grade 5 hurricane. Entire houses and buildings are leveled by this storm. Lives are lost in its wake. Like most divisive issues, there are two poles: 1) Those who claim the sovereignty of God is undermined if man has any part in the salvation process; and 2) Those who say the personhood of man is undermined if sovereignty is stressed to the point that human choice is eliminated. So, one group says the personhood or attributes of God are at stake, while the other group says the personhood or attributes of man are at stake. It would be nice to find some sort of middle ground, but then that is why this has been such a divisive issue for centuries. That middle ground is hard to find.

Nevertheless, we need to arrive at some sort of working solution to the dilemma which will allow us to function in the ministry. Though we may have to arrive at the conclusion that the subject is one of the mysteries which belongs to God (Deut 29:29), we need some sort of understanding to use as a working basis when we share the gospel, when we comfort the bereaved, when we teach the Scriptures, and when we encourage our missionaries. What can we say?

Determinism versus Indeterminism

For believers in a Supreme Being who has conveyed certain moral absolutes to our finite world, *indeterminism* is not a viable option. Indeterminism says there are no efficient moral causes. As such, everything that happens is the product of chance. This is both the basis for and the downfall of the theory of evolution. The claim is that life began by spontaneous generation through the chance coalescence of certain chemicals necessary to form a DNA chain.

Dr. Frank Salisbury of Utah State University once estimated the chances of forming a specific DNA molecule. For his estimate he assumed that life already existed. Obviously, the chances of spontaneous generation of life from *inanimate* matter are even more remote. He also assumed the existence of 10^{20} hospitable planets like the earth, which is many more planets, hospitable or inhospitable, than most astronomers think exist. He allowed 4 billion years for this DNA molecule (not even a cell) to come into being. He concluded that the probability of just one molecule coming into existence on just one of these planets was one chance in 10^{415}. Even if the universe were packed full of hospitable planets with no space between them, the chances are still only one in ten.[1]

Yet, if someone persists by saying, "Well, there is always that chance . . . ," consider the work of Emile Borel, one of the world's great experts on mathematical probability. He actually formulated a basic law of probability which says that the occurrence of any event where the chances are beyond one in 10^{50} is an event which we can state with certainty will *never* happen—no matter how much time is allotted, no matter how many conceivable opportunities could exist for the

---

[1] Will Durant, "The Reformation," in *The Story of Civilization*, vol. 6 (New York: Simon & Schuster, 1957), 490, emphasis added.

event to take place. In other words, life by chance is mathematically impossible on earth or anywhere else.[2]

The late Carl Sagan went one step further.[3] He estimated the chance of life evolving on just planet earth. He concluded the chances were one in $10^{2,000,000,000}$, a number so large that it would take 6,000 average sized books just to write it out and far, far beyond the limits of Borel's law of probability. Nevertheless, cynics like Sagan prefer to put their trust in the theory of evolution rather than the God of creation. George Wald, a Nobel prize-winning biologist from Harvard, said, "One only has to contemplate the magnitude of this task to concede that the spontaneous generation of a living organism is impossible. Yet, here we are—as a result I believe, of spontaneous generation."[4] At least he had the honesty to explain his conclusion:

> The reasonable view was to believe in spontaneous generation; the only alternative, to believe in a single primary act of supernatural creation. There is no third position. For this reason many scientists a century ago chose to regard the belief in spontaneous generation as a philosophical necessity.... Most modern biologists, having viewed with satisfaction the downfall of the spontaneous generation hypothesis, yet unwilling to accept the alternative belief in special creation, are left with nothing.[5]

Thus, it is important to recognize that those who believe indeterminism do just that; they *believe*. The "chance" world-view is a religion, a faith. But as already noted from some of its own adherents, this faith defies reason. Faith without reason is fanaticism. Christianity is

---

[2] E. Borel, *Probabilities and Life* (New York: Dover, 1962), chapters one and three.
[3] C. Sagan, ed., Communication with Extra-Terrestrial Intelligence (Boston: MIT Press, 1973), 46.
[4] G. Wald, "The Origin of Life," in *Physics and Chemistry of Life*, by the editors of *Scientific American* (Simon & Schuster, 1955), 9.
[5] Idem., "Innovation in Biology," *Scientific American* 99 (September 1958), 100, emphasis added.

not fanaticism. As we look out at the universe and see order, design, and defined patterns, we realize that this did not happen by chance. Why? Because it defies the second law of thermodynamics, which says everything tends toward disorder—chaos. Order defies disorder; design contradicts chaos. Only a Supreme Being could bring order out of chaos. Only a Divine Designer could override the observable second law of thermodynamics. Chance could never do it, no matter how much time is allotted.[6]

So, for the reasonable person indeterminism is not a statistically viable option. Determinism is the only other choice. Determinism accepts efficient causes. There is cause and effect in the universe. Design does not happen by chance. Design is determined by a Designer. But within the world of determinism there is what we might call "hard" determinism and "soft" determinism; or alternatively, "absolute" determinism and "relative" determinism. What do we mean by all this?

Hard Determinism

Regarding Evil

Hard determinism takes man completely out of the equation. The sovereignty of God is presented in such a way that He is responsible for everything. He causes everything; therefore, He is responsible for everything. He is the first and final efficient cause for everything that happens. Though lip service may be paid to human choice, it is just that—lip service.

Jonathan Edwards argued: If every event has a cause, then so do free human choices; God is the First Cause of everything; therefore, God must be the cause of our free choices.[7] In essence, he used God

---

[6] See, *Signs of Intelligence: understanding intelligent design*, eds. William A. Dembski and James M. Kushiner, (Grand Rapids, MI. Brazos pres. 2001) and Robert J. Spitzer, *New Proofs for the Existence of God: Contributions of Contemporary Physics and Philosophy*, (Grand Rapids MI., Eerdmans Pub. 2010)
[7] J. Edwards, "Freedom of the Will," in *Jonathan Edwards*, eds. Clarence H. Faust and Thomas H. Johnson (New York: Hill and Wang, 1962), 305.

to eliminate freedom. This is precisely where hard determinism loses its ball in the weeds. According to this view, a person is not the efficient cause of his moral actions. God becomes the *efficient* moral cause with the human being only the instrumental moral cause. In other words, man becomes God's tool to effect evil in the world.

Such a view should be morally repugnant to anyone without blinders. God is directly responsible for all the evil in the universe. I find it ironic that those whose view of sovereignty effectively rejects human choice consider it blasphemous to think man could contribute anything at all to the salvation process. Yet in the same breath, they can make God directly responsible for evil and sin. That is what I call true blasphemy. Yes, God is sovereign—absolutely. But He is also light; in Him is no darkness at all. God could not produce or directly cause sin if He wanted to, just as He cannot lie. His ontology forbids it. It is simply not in His make-up.

Another serious problem this view causes for Christians is that it completely removes human responsibility. After all, if man is only the agent, the instrument, then how can he be held responsible? When a murder takes place we do not hold the gun or the knife responsible. We do not put guns and knives on trial. They are not the *efficient* moral causes; they are the *instrumental* moral causes. The guns and knives may have been used to commit evil, but they were only instruments. They had no choice in the matter. It is the human wielding the gun or knife who is responsible. By analogy, God in this view must be the efficient moral cause of evil.[8]

Consequently, if the human is only the instrument in the act

---

[8] As Gordon Clark affirms, "I wish very frankly and pointedly to assert that if a man gets drunk and shoots his family, it was the will of God that he should do it . . . " He goes on to assert, "Let it be unequivocally said that this view certainly makes God the cause of sin. God is the sole ultimate cause of everything. There is absolutely nothing independent of him. He alone is the eternal being. He alone is omnipotent. He alone is sovereign. (*Religion, Reason, and Revelation*, [Philadelphia, PA: Presbyterian & Reformed, 1961], 221). Also, " God wills all things that come to pass . . . God desired for man to fall into sin. I am not accusing God of sinning; I am suggesting that God created sin." (R.C. Sproul, *Almighty Over All* [Grand Rapids: Baker Book House, 1999], 54).

of evil he cannot be held responsible. The efficient cause using the instrument is responsible for the evil. Of course, this is the conclusion of the cynics in this world as they look at the concept of a loving God in a world with too many Hitlers, Stalins, and Mao Zedongs. If such a God is in control, then either He is not loving or His powers are weak. Better to simply say He does not exist. Or, if such a God does exist, we don't want to have anything to do with Him. We conclude with Norman Geisler that hard determinism makes God immoral and man amoral.[9]

Regarding Love

Hard determinism also has implications for the love of God. Whereas the Arminian says God elects men *based on* His foreknowledge, the hard determinist says God elects men *in spite of* His foreknowledge. In other words, the former believes God looks down the corridors of time and knows (foreknowledge) who is going to believe in Jesus. *Based on* this foreknowledge, He then elects those who are going to believe in Jesus (1 Pet 1:1-2). One problem with this view is that it makes God's election contingent on man's choices when John 1:13 tells us that we were not born of the will of man. We will clarify the role of man's will below. But if the Arminian view has problems, it seems to me that in their effort to preserve their view of the sovereignty of God the hard determinists have created even greater problems. According to them, God elects men *in spite of* His foreknowledge. In other words, regardless of the desires or choices of man, God elects some and reprobates others. He does this *in spite of* His prior knowledge that the elect do not even want to know Him. He drags them kicking and screaming into the kingdom. He forces them against their will.

Although we all can probably relate to this imagery to some degree since many of us probably stubbornly resisted God's call for some time before trusting Christ, there is a great deal of difference between

---

[9] N. Geisler, "God Knows All Things," in *Predestination and Free Will*, eds. D. Basinger and R. Basinger (Downers Grove, IL: InterVarsity, 1986), 75.

coercion and persuasion. We have already seen (pp. 253-254) how R.C. Sproul teaches the meaning of *helkuō* in John 6:44 is to "drag" instead of to "draw." We have also seen how he misleadingly refers to Kittel to support his view, when in fact Kittel says just the opposite. The key, as usual, is context. In a hostile environment such as persecution, the verb does mean to drag (such as into a court of law). However, in a love context (such as a father or mother for her children or a lover for his beloved) the verb invariably means to draw or woo.

C. S. Lewis once described his own conversion in terms of having been brought "screaming and kicking into the kingdom." However, he went on in *The Screwtape Letters* to say, "The Irresistible and the Indisputable are the two weapons which the very nature of [God's] scheme forbids Him to use. Merely to override a human will . . . would be for Him useless. He cannot ravish. He can only woo."[10] And again in *The Great Divorce*, Lewis clarifies his understanding: "There are only two kinds of people in the end: those who say to God, 'Thy will be done,' and those to whom God says, in the end, 'Thy will be done.' All that are in Hell, choose it. Without that *self-choice* there could be no Hell."[11]

Herein lies the rub. For God to drag us kicking and screaming into His kingdom is a violation of the love principle—force is not love. As Lewis said, "He cannot ravish." Nor does He want to. One of the reasons for creating man was to answer the question concerning God's character, "Is God worthy of being loved?" The only way to answer that question was *to give man a choice*. That is precisely why we see God and Satan contending for the allegiance of Job. When Lucifer rebelled he opened both the love aspect and the sovereignty aspect of God's character to question. In God's genius both questions can be answered with the same response: obedience to His commands. "He who has My commandments and keeps them, he it is who loves Me . . . " (Jn 14:21). Deuteronomy 8:2 says God tested the Israelites in the Wilderness for forty years to see what was in their hearts, that is, to see if they would keep His commandments. Deuteronomy

---

[10] C. S. Lewis, *The Screwtape Letters* (New York: Macmillan, 1961), 38.
[11] Idem., *The Great Divorce* (New York: Macmillan, 1945), 69, emphasis added.

11:1, 13, and 22 make loving God synonymous with keeping His commandments. So, love and obedience walk hand in hand. But so do sovereignty and obedience. When I submit to God's commands, I am saying, "Yes, Lord, You are my Lord, my King, my Master—You are Sovereign." However, we love Him because He first loved us—He took the initiative (1 Jn 4:10, 19).

Throughout the OT we get a picture of God's jealousy and anger at Israel when she chooses to worship other gods. If the Israelites were not free moral agents, there would be no cause for this jealousy and anger. God could simply force them to do what He wanted. But no, that way He would never know if they loved Him. I sometimes ask a husband if he chose his wife. Often, he responds with a smile and says, "No, she chose me." What he is saying is that their marriage was a reciprocal decision born of mutual love. No man wants to drag his bride kicking and screaming to the altar. If she does not love him, he would rather find someone who does. God is the same way. True love cannot use force.

Someone will surely object by saying that if a child is so immature that he does not realize playing with fire will hurt him, then the loving father will pull him away from the fire against his will. This is still love. Or the drowning man may kick, scream, and even fight against his savior, but it is still love on the part of the savior to pull him out of the water. However, this opens up another problem. In the case of mankind it is not a single individual who is at stake in this matter of election. It is the entire human race with billions and billions of people. Scripture claims that God loved the *whole* world. Even John Calvin recognized the meaning of "world" as all of mankind.[12] If a man walked by a lake and saw one person drowning, we would certainly question his love if he did not make an effort to save the person drowning. But if he walked by a lake and saw five people drowning, selected two to save, and left the rest to drown when he was perfectly capable of saving them as well, then we should also question his love. For if he has the ability to pull an unlimited

---

[12] See again, Calvin's *Institutes*, 3.1.1; Commentaries, 3.139; also his comments on John 1:29, Romans 5:15, and 1 John 2:2.

number of drowning people out of the lake against their wills, sees five drowning, but only pulls out two, then his omnibenevolence (He is not a respecter of persons, Rom 2:11; and He loves the whole world, Jn 3:16) is open to question.

This is why the hard determinist is forced to interpret "world" in John's writings as "the [limited] world of the elect." It is because he has no way to deal with the reprobate and maintain the omnibenevolence of God. God cannot love everyone in the world or He would save them all since He is omnipotent and can pull people kicking and screaming into the kingdom. Of course the other alternative for a hard determinist is to become a universalist. That would be the only way to preserve the character of God's love.

Vessels of Wrath

But what about Romans 9:22-23, objects the hard determinist, which says God has prepared vessels of wrath for destruction in contrast to the vessels of mercy which He has prepared for glory. So let's look at this passage in context to see how some translators may have inadvertently or otherwise muddied the waters:

> [14]What shall we say then? Is there unrighteousness with God? Certainly not! [15]For He says to Moses, "I will have mercy on whomever I will have mercy, and I will have compassion on whomever I will have compassion." [16]So then it is not of him who wills, nor of him who runs, but of God who shows mercy. [17]For the Scripture says to Pharaoh, "For this very purpose I have raised you up, that I may show My power in you, and that My name may be declared in all the earth." [18]Therefore He has mercy on whom He wills, and whom He wills He hardens. [19]You will say to me then, "Why does He still find fault? For who has resisted His will?" [20]But indeed, O man, who are you to reply against God? Will the thing formed say to him who formed it, "Why have you made me like this?" [21]Does not the potter have power over the clay, from the same lump to make one vessel for honor and another for dishonor? [22]What if God, wanting to show His wrath and to make His power known, endured with much longsuffering the vessels of wrath prepared for destruction, [23]and that He might make

known the riches of His glory on the vessels of mercy, which He had prepared beforehand for glory.

Before we can understand this particular passage we need to get the overall context. At the end of Romans 8 Paul claimed that nothing could separate one of God's children from the love of God in Christ Jesus. The imaginary objector says, "Wrong. Look at Israel. They were chosen, but now God has rejected them." So, Romans 9-11 tries to answer this objection.[13] It concludes by saying, "The gifts and calling of God are irrevocable" (Rom 11:29). In Romans 9 the focus is on divine sovereignty: the People of Election (1-5); the Principle of Election (6-13); and the Privilege of Election (14-33).

We first need to remember that the emphasis in Romans 9 is on election, not reprobation. The emphasis is on His mercy, not His justice. Another question in the mind of the objector besides what happened to Israel is, "How can a righteous God associate with these scummy Gentiles?" So after propounding the incredible privileges of the Jewish people simply because they are part of the chosen nation of Israel (People of Election, vv. 1-5), Paul goes on to discuss the Principle of Election (vv. 6-13). The first thing he says is that God's promises (God's Word) are not lost or have not gotten off course (*ekpiptō* is used of a ship getting off course). He never intended to include each and every one of Abraham's children just because they were his physical seed. To prove his point he cites Ishmael and Esau, both the seed of Abraham, but neither one was included in the kingdom program. Paul is trying to establish the Principle of Election here, and that principle is that God elects (chooses a people for Himself for spiritual reasons, not physical). Does this seem unfair? Paul anticipated that kind of reaction. So, in 9:14-29 he defends God's right to elect whomever He wishes. As the Creator it is His privilege. So we call this section the Privilege of Election.

There are two objections raised against the Principle of Election in 9:14-29. In 9:14, the objector simply says, "God is unfair." Paul says,

---

[13] See Arnold Fruchtenbaum, *Israelology: The Missing Link in Systematic Theology*, (Ariel Ministries Inc., 1989).

"No way." Actually, the fact of the matter is this, if God were only just and not also merciful, we would all be destroyed. For there is none righteous, no, not one. If we got what we deserved, then God would be just. Actually, the only "injustice" with God is His mercy. His mercy stops the guillotine of God's justice. "Mercy triumphs over judgment" (Jas 2:13). The quote on His mercy here comes from Exodus 33 (Mt. Sinai) after the Israelites have made the golden calf. They all deserve to be wiped out. This is clearly speaking of temporal judgment, not eternal destiny. But instead God shows mercy. And 9:16 makes it clear that human will and human works can make no demands on God's mercy. God sovereignly bestows His mercy as He sees fit. That is His right, His prerogative, His privilege.

God had mercy on the Israelites, but not on the Egyptians. He hardened Pharaoh's heart. This hardening of Pharaoh's heart is something I want to come back to, but for the moment, we can simply say that in Pharaoh's case justice was carried out. Pharaoh got what he deserved. That was justice. In Moses' case and in the case of the Israelites who were allowed to live, they got "injustice"—they got mercy, something they did not deserve.

But now we get the objector's second objection (9:19). In the first one, he said God is unfair. In this one, he says God is responsible for sin. The argument goes something like this:

> If God hardened Pharaoh's heart, then how can God hold Pharaoh responsible in the final judgment for his actions and his disbelief? Actually, God is responsible. Since He's the most powerful force in the universe, no one can oppose His will. And if God wills my mind to be hardened, then He's responsible, not I.

Does this sound familiar? God is being accused of being a "hard" determinist. This sounds exactly like the view of E. H. Palmer is his defense of Dortian (Five Point) Calvinism:

> Foreordination means God's sovereign plan, whereby He decides all that is to happen in the entire universe.... He decides and causes all things to happen that do happen.... He has foreordained

everything . . . : the moving of a finger, the beating of a heart, the laughter of a girl, the mistake of a typist—even sin.[14]

So, if God has so willed it and His will is irresistible, then God is responsible for sin and all the evil in the world. This is the thinking of the objector in v. 19.

What is Paul's answer? Actually, the answer comes in the next chapter, but for the time being Paul does not answer the objector. Instead, he admonishes him for his brashness in even asking such a question or for bringing God down to his own level. Does a pot have the right to question how it is being made? The potter has the sovereign right to make the pot anyway he sees fit and can use it for whatever he wishes. If he wants to use one vessel as a dog dish and another as a salad bowl, that is his privilege. The pot has nothing to say about it (vv. 20-21).

Then Paul applies the analogy to God's relationship with men. Some are prepared for glory and some for destruction. In short, let God be God. It is blasphemous for us to challenge Him. Actually, the man in v. 19 is saying, "We humans have a better sense of fairness than You, God." In so saying, we have tried to place ourselves above God. It is really man saying to God, "Look, God, step down from that throne a bit. I have a few things I want to say to You, a couple of questions I want to ask. Sit down here—I want to give you the third degree. Now tell me this: what right do You have making me this way?"

Paul's immediate reaction is that of the parent who has just been reprimanded by his impudent, disrespectful child. He wants to grab him by the throat and say, "Listen to me, you little squirt. I'm your father, and you're just a little child. You have no right to talk to me that way." Of course, that is a small scale model of what is taking place when the created being confronts the Creator. Paul concludes that we have no right to question God's ways with us, whereas God, on the other hand, has every right to do with us as He pleases.[15]

---

[14] E. H. Palmer, *Five Points of Calvinism*, 25.
[15] See the interchange in the book of Job. God asks Job 70 questions in 38:1-42:6, to reveal Job's ignorance and God's wisdom.

And in 9:25-29, Paul says, "None of this present setting aside of the Jews in favor of the Gentiles should surprise you. It was all clearly prophesied by Hosea and Isaiah. As a matter of fact, if God had acted in justice (v. 29), the Jews would have been wiped off the map like Sodom and Gomorrah long ago. God owes nothing to the Jews. Indeed, it is only by His mercy and grace they still exist." That is what Isaiah concludes.

So, this certainly looks like "hard" determinism here, doesn't it? But we must point out once again, the emphasis here is not on God's rejection, but on His election; not on His reprobation, but on His mercy. He has mercy on whom He has mercy, and He has compassion on whom He will have compassion. Yes, but isn't the objector right? How can Pharaoh be blamed if God hardened Pharaoh's heart? How can Esau be blamed if God rejected him even before he was born? And what about these vessels of wrath prepared for destruction. How does this harmonize with a God who claims to love all without respect of persons?

Pharaoh's Heart

We cannot understand the hardening of Pharaoh's heart without looking at the story in Exodus. What is generally overlooked in this discussion is that many times in Exodus it says Pharaoh hardened his own heart (Ex 8:15, 32; 9:34). Sometimes it just says Pharaoh's heart became hard (Ex 7:13, 22; 8:19; 9:7, 35). And then it says God hardened or would harden his heart (Ex 4:21; 7:3; 9:12; 10:1, 20, 27; 11:10; and 14:4, 8, 17). How can we harmonize these statements?

First of all, we must remember that Pharaoh had known Moses and the God of the Jews long, long before the plagues began. Pharaoh was a man who had already rejected the Lord many times before Moses asked for their release.

Secondly, we must acknowledge a moral law that applies to all men, not just Pharaoh. This law states that moral convictions, if not acted upon, become weaker and weaker, until at last the heart of man becomes altogether callous. The NT speaks of this process as the "searing of the conscience," (I Tim 4:2) a process by which the conscience, a facet of the heart, is covered with scar tissue and made insensitive. It is interesting to read the Exodus account to see how many times Pharaoh said, "I have sinned ... make supplication for me ... your God is righteous." He was convicted of his sin, of God's power to save him, and seemed to make a sincere repentance. But Pharaoh was like so many "foxhole" Christians who only repent under duress. As soon as the crisis was over, back he jumped on the throne. And each time Pharaoh did this, his heart got a little harder. Pharaoh hardened his own heart through his actions and decisions.

But the text also says God hardened Pharaoh's heart. How so? Through His mercy. You see, God could have been just and dispensed with Pharaoh immediately. He did not have to mess around with ten plagues. But in His mercy, He gave Pharaoh a chance to repent after each plague. Each time he waited for a sincere about-face from Pharaoh. And that is just like the God we know. Chance after chance He gave Pharaoh, patiently enduring his blasphemy and treachery, as Rom 9:22 says, yet each time Pharaoh insincerely repented his heart got a little harder. "Because the sentence against an evil work is not executed speedily, therefore the *heart* of the sons of men *is fully set* in them to do evil" (Eccl 8:11). How did God harden his heart? Only indirectly through His mercy did God harden Pharaoh's heart. In one place (Ex 9:16), God tells Pharaoh He has *allowed* him to remain (NASB) for His ultimate glory. God could have rightfully cut him off long before. So, it is only through His long-suffering and mercy that God allowed Pharaoh's heart to become hard.

Before we leave Pharaoh, it is necessary to observe the word used for "raised up." It is the verb *exegeira*, which does not mean to "create" or "fashion." Sanday and Headlam point out that in this context it means God lifted Pharaoh to a prominent state in history.[16] This passage says nothing about being created to go to hell.

In his hard determinism John Calvin used this passage to support his views of the reprobate which God created to go to hell. In his comments on v. 22 Calvin said: "Paul's second answer shows briefly

---

[16] W. Sanday and A. C. Headlam, *A Critical and Exegetical Commentary on the Epistle to the Romans*, International Critical Commentary (Edinburgh: T. & T. Clark, 1902), 256.

that, although the counsel of God is incomprehensible in regard to predestination, yet His unimpeachable equity is to be seen as clearly in the destruction of the reprobate as in the salvation of the elect."[17] And in order to emphasize that God is the efficient moral cause of evil and men are only instruments, Calvin says, "Paul has used the word *vessels* in a general sense to mean *instruments*. . . . for the Lord uses us as instruments. . . ."[18] And to reinforce his understanding of double predestination, he says:

> Although Paul is more explicit in this second clause [v. 23] in stating that it is God who prepares the elect for glory, when before [v. 22] he had simply said that the reprobate were vessels prepared for destruction, there is no doubt that the preparation of both is dependent on the secret counsel of God. Otherwise, Paul would have said that the reprobate yield or cast themselves into destruction. Now, however, he means that their lot is already assigned to them before their birth.[19]

No wonder Will Durant summarized his overview of John Calvin's doctrine of double predestination by saying, "We shall always find it hard to love the man who darkened the human soul with the most absurd and blasphemous conception of God in all the long and honored history of nonsense."[20] Calvin's determinism is so hard that God is the only efficient moral cause[21] in the universe. All other creatures, including Satan, are just instruments in His hand:

---

[17] J. Calvin, *The Epistles of Paul to the Romans and Thessalonians*, Calvin's New Testament Commentaries, ed. D. W. Torrance and T. F. Torrance, trans. R. MacKenzie (Grand Rapids: Eerdmans, 1960), 210.
[18] Ibid., 211.
[19] Ibid., 212, emphasis added.
[20] Will Durant, *The Story of Civilization*, "The Reformation," VI (New York: Simon and Schuster, 1957), 490.
[21] Calvin's successor in Geneva, Theodore Beza did Calvin one better, or one worse, depending on one's perspective. He declared election "ground zero." God's decree to elect some and reprobate others preceded His decree to create man in the first place. Why would God create someone He had already decided

All external circumstances which contribute to the blinding of the reprobate are the instruments of His wrath. Satan himself, who works inwardly with compelling power, is God's minister in such a way that he acts only by His command.... Paul does not inform us that the ruin of the ungodly is foreseen by the Lord, but that it is ordained by His counsel and will. Solomon also teaches us that not only was the destruction of the ungodly foreknown, but the ungodly themselves have been created for the specific purpose of perishing (Prov. 16.4).[22]

Sanday and Headlam are more fastidious with the text. They correct Calvin when they write: "The Apostle says nothing about eternal life or death.... He never says or implies that God has created man for the purpose of his damnation."[23]

Self-Destruction

If there ever was a passage which looks like double predestination, this one is it. But Calvin assumes way too much when he states (see above) "their lot is already assigned to them...." The Greek is very illuminating: Whereas many English translations use the verb "prepared" in both 9:22 and 23, these are two different verbs in the original: *katērtismena* and *proētoimasen*. Moreover, the two verbs are in different tenses and voices, and only the latter has a prepositional prefix (*pro-*) to indicate sequence ("beforehand").

Again, it is helpful to remember that the emphasis of the passage is on God's mercy, not His wrath, and certainly not reprobation. Let me

---

to condemn for eternity? To demonstrate His justice before the universe, claimed Beza, as he echoed the teaching of his mentor. After all, how could God really prove His justice if He never sentenced anyone for sin? See Walter Kickel, *Vernunft and Offenbarung bei Theodor Beza*, in *Beirtäge zur Geschichte und Lehre der Reformierten Kirche*, 25 (Neukirchener Verlag des Erziehungsvereins GmbH Neukirchen-Vluyn, 1967), 100–67. A chart of Beza's system has been translated and attached at the end of Appendix B.

[22] Ibid., 207-8, emphasis added. Note how Calvin is really arguing for supralapsarianism, as Kickel claims (ibid., 148).

[23] Sanday and Headlam, *Romans*, 258.

explain how that works in these verses. In v. 23 Paul speaks of "vessels of mercy which He prepared beforehand for glory." In this case, the verb is third person singular, aorist *active*, indicative. This means that the subject of the verb, God, was actively involved in this preparation of the vessels of mercy ahead of time. He was the direct agent, the efficient cause. But in v. 22, the verb is completely different—it is a plural, *middle/passive*, perfect participle that agrees with "vessels." It is describing the *current state* (signified by the perfect tense) of these vessels. The middle/passive voice is highly significant. First of all, it tells us that God was not directly involved in this process at all.[24] He is not the subject of this verb, and the verb is not active voice. Conspicuously, there is no outside agent acting on vessels until the following verse.

On the contrary, the middle voice indicates action in which the recipient participates. The closest concept we have in English to help understand this is the idea of doing something for oneself or to oneself. For example, if I say "I washed my hands," that would be a verb in the middle voice, since the action of washing was done by me to myself, together with soap and water. In this case the vessels of wrath *incurred wrath as a result of their own actions*. But another important factor in regard to the vessels of wrath is the lack of any indication of God's prior action. While God "pre-prepared" vessels of mercy for glory, He *endured* vessels of wrath "who prepared themselves." Translating this verb "prepared" as in 9:23 implies that God "pre-prepared" the vessels of wrath just as He did the vessels of mercy. Not so! Nothing was done in eternity past to ensure the fate of these vessels. They did this to themselves in time.

Dan Wallace[25] gives several reasons why he does not think

---

[24] If one were to insist the participle is *passive*, indicating *agency*, it does not necessarily change the meaning. Quite often the passive does not have an *external* agent. If I say, "I am whipped," that is passive, but there is no external agent. I could have done it to myself.

[25] Daniel B. Wallace, *Greek Grammar Beyond the Basics: An Exegetical Syntax of the New Testament* (Grand Rapids, MI: Zondervan Publishing House, 1996), 417-18.

κατηρτισμένα is in the middle voice. We shall discuss these in a moment, but first one must see the theological persuasion Wallace has imported into his grammar in numerous places, not the least of which is Rom 9:22. Wallace gives evidence of a belief in hard determinism when he says, "... this view [middle voice for κατηρτισμένα] ignores the context in which *God's predetermining will for both kinds of vessels is asserted* (vv. 20-23)" (italics mine). This is none other than double predestination, a conclusion all hard determinists must come to if they are intellectually honest. At least Thomas Schreiner comes out and admits to the same: "... double predestination cannot be averted."[26] And earlier in his discussion Wallace claims: "Is not the *destiny* of the vessels (one for honor, one for dishonor) entirely *predetermined* by their Creator?" (italics mine). In as much as predeterminism was imported into Christianity via Athens and Augustine, perhaps one should be on guard when grammatical evidence is marshalled by one promoting a theological position (remember Sanday and Headlam's observation that nothing in Romans 9 points to eternity,[27] a point of view initiated, once again, by Augustine). Finding such a view of God, a view (that claims God created the vast majority of humans to torture forever in hell just so the vessels of mercy could better appreciate God's mercy towards them) so repugnant none other than John Stott became an annihilationist. On this passage he wrote: "Certainly God has never 'prepared' anybody for destruction; is it not that by their own evildoing they prepare themselves for it?"[28]

As for the grammar, it reminds me of the evolution debate in which competent scientists assess the same data and utilize that which supports the position they already affirm before the data is analyzed. Wallace says the direct middle (a reflexive use in which the subject of the sentence is acting upon himself--"I wash my hands of this whole affair") is quite rare in the NT (and by implication the odds of κατηρτισμένα being middle voice are slim indeed). Yet no less

---

[26] Thomas R. Schreiner, *Romans*, ECNT (Grand Rapids: Baker Books, 1998), 522.
[27] *Romans*, 258, although they seem to contradict themselves on 262.
[28] John Stott, *Romans* (Downers Grove, IL: InterVarsity Press, 1994), 272.

than A. T. Robertson said, "Sometimes, indeed, it is difficult to tell whether a verb is middle or passive...."[29] Indeed, as already said, in all the Greek tenses save the aorist and the future it is always an open question whether we have middle or passive. "The dividing line is a fine one at best."[30] Only the context and the verb-idea can decide."[31] Thus, as usual, we find that context is king. Wallace could be guilty of an invalid totality transfer (just because a word means such-and-such five times it must mean such-and-such in its next usage). It is almost like saying the optative mood is rare in the NT and therefore when one sees an optative it bears no exegetical significance. This kind of exegetical error diminishes context.

As for the direct middle Robertson lists an entire page of examples.[32] He even includes παρασκευάσεται (prepare himself) from 1 Corinthians 14:8, a strikingly similar use to what we have in Romans 9:22, although it is a different verb. This use would mitigate against Wallace's "idiomatic argument." And Wallace's second argument that there are no uses of the middle voice in the perfect tense in the NT is another example of an invalid totality transfer. It's like Sproul's argument that because ἕλκω always means "to drag or to draw" in every NT usage other than John 6:44, it must mean "to drag or to draw" in John 6:44. Again, context is diminished, as we have demonstrated in our discussion of ἕλκω in our chapter on "Regeneration."

Then Wallace tells his readers that κατηρτισμένα with its perfect tense suggests a "done deal." That would be true if the participle is being used as an extensive perfect with the emphasis on the completed action in the past. However, since this is a participle and not a finite verb, it is more likely to be speaking of a state of being with the emphasis on the present results. It functions as a predicate adjective with the copulative understood: "vessels of wrath *that are* fit (κατηρτισμένα)

---

[29] A.T. Robertson, *A Grammar of the Greek New Testament in the Light of Historical Research* (Nashville, TN: Broadman Press, 1934), 816.
[30] Moulton, *Prol.*, p. 162.
[31] Robertson, *Grammar*, ibid.
[32] Robertson, *Grammar*, 807.

for destruction." Numerous commentators understand it this way and like to translate it "ripe" or "ready" (cf. Weiss, Cranfield, Stott). However, some like Schreiner[33] are so eager to support their view of double predestination, they ignore the verb form (middle/passive) and call it a "divine passive," meaning God is the one who did the preparing for destruction. Forget the fact that God is conspicuous by his absence in this verse when juxtaposed to his clear presence in v. 23 as the one that prepared the vessels of mercy. At any rate, Wallace's entire point on the lexical nuance of κατηρτισμένα and the completed action of the perfect is, like so many of these things, the interpreter's call.

Wallace's last appeal is to context. He goes back to v. 20 to point out the potter's sovereign will over how he makes his pots. He uses this to support his double predestination: "Is not the *destiny* of the vessels . . . entirely *predetermined* by their Creator?" (italics mine). He then transports the idea of eternal destiny from the pots to the people, completely ignoring that God's activity in v. 22 is not preparing vessels for destruction; it is enduring with much longsuffering vessels fit for destruction. Now if God is the one preparing these vessels for destruction (presumably over a number of years), why would he need endurance and longsuffering? After all, he is the one preparing these vessels he has destined for eternal torture. On the other hand, if the vessels have "done it to themselves" or are "fit" for destruction because of a life-time of impenitence and sin, now that would require endurance and longsuffering, just as God endured Pharaoh's insincere repentance time after time. Just as Pharaoh hardened his own heart directly by his obduracy and deceit and God indirectly so by enduring him through plague after plague (Eccl 8:11), so God allows the non-elect to create their own cauldron of debauchery and duplicity.

Interesting in his discussion on context that Wallace completely side-steps the obvious change in the verbs from κατηρτισμένα to προητοίμασεν. The contrast begs discussion. Whereas the second verb has the prefix προ-, the first does not. This suggests that God

---

[33] Schreiner, *Romans*, 522

was active "prior to" in a way he was not active in the first verb. Of course, the second verb is active indicating that God, the subject, acted on the vessels of mercy, the direct objects. The middle/passive form of κατηρτισμένα removes God from any direct activity in the "preparation" of the vessels of wrath. In fact, just to translate as κατηρτισμένα "prepared" is misleading. It is translated "prepared" one other time (Heb 10:5) out of thirteen uses, so that is a possible translation. However, when the English reader sees the word "prepared" in back to back verses connected by a consecutive καὶ (and), he would assume the same Greek word is behind the English, thus lending more credence to double predestination. But this is precisely what Paul does not do, that is, use the same words. Why? Could it be that he has a contrast in mind, a contrast between the vessels of wrath and the vessels of mercy with regard to the actors on the stage.

In conclusion, we find all of Wallace's arguments on behalf of double predestination far from convincing.

This brings us back to the meaning of "wrath." We have already seen in Romans that wrath does not refer to eternity.[34] In Romans 1:18 the wrath of God *is being revealed* against the impiety and unrighteousness of men who hold back the truth in unrighteousness. We discovered that this wrath is defined by the three statements in vv. 24, 26, and 28 where "God gave them up" to the control of their Sin Natures. It is this kind of wrath which the life of Christ will save them from (see 5:9) as they learn to let Him live his substitutionary life in them. They are already justified (see 5:1 and 9), but they have not yet been saved from the power of the Sin Nature (wrath) to a full inheritance. So the vessels in 9:22 have tested God's patience with their stubbornness in sin. Being given every opportunity to repent, they persistently defy the truth and are ultimately turned over to the control of their Sin Natures; they are vessels of wrath incurred by sinful works of the flesh. Charles Hodge says, "They are fit for destruction,"

---

[34] See Romans 13:4 for the temporal and human aspect of wrath on earth.

which involves temporal punishment/death or (for believers) loss of inheritance.

Even this word "destruction" does not categorically mean eternal damnation. It is the same destruction that most of the world will experience during the last half of the Tribulation Period. In 1 Corinthians 5:5, this same word is used for the incestuous brother who has been turned over to Satan for the *destruction* of his flesh. Nevertheless, his spirit will be saved, yet so as by fire. So here is a believer headed for heaven who suffers temporal destruction and loss of reward. So also in 1 Thessalonians 5:2-3 we read: "For you yourselves know perfectly that the day of the Lord so comes as a thief in the night. For when they say, 'Peace and safety!' then sudden *destruction* comes upon them, as labor pains upon a pregnant woman." Again, this is temporal destruction. As always, context is the key (the use of this word in 2 Thess 1:8-9 is eternal: "those who do not obey the gospel of our Lord Jesus Christ. These shall be punished with everlasting *destruction* from the presence of the Lord and from the glory of His power," but notice how clear this is from the context).

I once saw a great illustration of this verse. My elders and I went to an Oiler-Cowboys exhibition game in the Astrodome. There were five of them. I had the inside seat, which means there was an elder on the aisle, four elders next to him, then there I was, on the inside. Next to me were a couple of men I did not know. I introduced myself to them, and they asked why I had come. It seemed like a silly question, so I just said I came to see Landry and the Cowboys (the Oilers were not much of a team at the time). One of them proudly said they had come to see the Cowboys' cheer leaders. We all kind of laughed. Well, after the game started, they began ordering beer. It was kind of funny watching the five elders passing the beer down the aisle. By half-time these guys were well on their way to inebriation. Then a couple of very pretty girls came and sat in the two empty seats in front of us. These boys quickly introduced themselves. When the game began again, they continued to order beer. They were royally drunk somewhere into the third quarter. Then, they became gross and obnoxious with the girls in front of us. People were staring at them from a radius of about five seats. Everyone agreed—they were fit for destruction! But they had done it to themselves. All we did was pass the beer!

Conclusion

Hard determinism may be apparent from a superficial view of Scripture, but a deeper look reveals another picture. God is love. He wants to be loved. By withholding the capacity to choose from His creation, He calls for worship by robots who cannot voluntarily choose to love. To be sure, this is one viable view of sovereignty. A person could make ten computers and program them such that at the snap of his fingers they sing "Glory to the Creator," and we could say that their creator is sovereign over them.[35] But is there any love relationship here? I don't think so. Cooperative determinism offers a much higher view of sovereignty.

Soft Determinism

Another approach which incorporates more of the biblical data than hard determinism is what we might call *soft* or *cooperative* determinism. This is not Arminianism or Pelagianism. Those systems might be dubbed "self-determinism." In soft determinism man is still totally depraved. There is no prevenient grace to offset the effects of Adam's fall. There is no spark of good within man, which he can fan into a fire of righteousness acceptable to God. But soft determinism does not leave man totally out of the salvation equation. He still has the capacity to choose, to seek, to grope (Acts 17). There is a difference between saying, "None seeks after God," and "None can seek after God." But in saying this it does not mean he can find God or make a saving decision for God on his own. He needs God's persuasive power (Jn 6:44). This is why we call it cooperative determinism. Instead of dragging man kicking and screaming into the kingdom, the Holy Spirit draws into the kingdom those who respond to His persuasion.

---

[35] For a recent critique of Determinism see John C. Lennox, *Determined to Believe? The Sovereignty of God, Freedom, Faith & Human Responsibility*, (Grand Rapids, MI: Zondervan, 2017).

We might use a similar illustration to explain cooperative determinism. In this view of sovereignty the Creator creates ten people (entities with the capacity to interact with Him, to love Him, and to obey Him—none of which animals are able to do). He could then reveal Himself to them as their Creator and seek their worship. In fact, He might even ask them to sing, "Glory to the Creator" out of their gratitude for the gift of life. Some may choose to do so; the rest may say, "Hey, I didn't ask to be born, and I am not singing any song of gratitude." But as these rebellious creatures walk away, the Creator can pursue them and reveal more of Himself to them. After learning more, a couple of them repent of their ingratitude, turn around and worship the Creator. But the Creator still pursues the ones who have yet to respond to Him in a positive way. After extensive persuasion, many of these do come back to the Creator. Some never do, but it is not because the Creator did not try to reveal Himself to them. Yet in His greatness, the Creator is able to use even the lives of those who have rebelled against Him to accomplish His overall plan for human history. A Creator who is sovereign over these kinds of creatures, it seems to me, is much more sovereign *and* beneficent than One who is a computer programmer.

But this still does not answer a basic question. How can there be any cooperation when the election of God takes place before a person's birth? Even if we concede that the issue with Jacob and Esau in Romans 9 was not eternal destiny[36] (the issue was who would mediate God's redemptive purposes), Scripture still teaches that God chose a people for Himself (election) before the foundation of the world (Eph 1:4). It even says we were "chosen *in Him*" before the foundation of the world. How can we be "in Him" before we are "in Him"? The "in Him" concept is outlined in Romans 6, and it clearly deals with our baptism into Christ's death, burial, and resurrection. And it is accomplished by the baptism (the dipping into) of the Holy

---

[36] As Sanday and Headlam observe, "The absolute election of Jacob,—the 'loving' of Jacob and the 'hating' of Esau,—has reference simply to the election of one to higher privileges as head of the chosen race, that the other. It has nothing to do with their eternal salvation" (*Romans*, 245).

Spirit, something which only began after Pentecost, A.D. 33 (or 29, if you prefer). So how can we be "in Him" before His birth, the cross, the baptism of the Holy Spirit, and our own birth?

A suggested answer to this dilemma and to the controversies surrounding the decrees of God (supra–, infra–, etc.) may be in the ontology of God, the makeup of God. He is three, but also one. "The Lord our God, the Lord is one." Because He is one, all His attributes are part of His indivisible essence. Thus, His election and His foreknowledge are one and coextensive. This may well be the meaning and implication of 1 Peter 1:2, which says "elect *according to* the foreknowledge of God the Father." He has not chosen us *based on* His foreknowledge or *in spite of* His foreknowledge, but *in accordance with* His foreknowledge. In commenting on this verse, J. Walvoord wrote:

> The word "elect" . . . teaches not the logical order of election in relation to foreknowledge, but the fact that they are coextensive . . . . the whole process of the divine purpose, election, and foreknowledge are all eternal . . . . all aspects of the eternal purpose of God are equally timeless.[37]

Or as N. Geisler expresses it:

> [T]here is no chronological or logical priority of election and foreknowledge . . . . Whatever he forechooses cannot be based on what he foreknows. Nor can what he foreknows be based on what he forechose. Both must be simultaneous and coordinate acts of God. Thus God knowingly determined and determinately knew from all eternity everything that would come to pass, including all free acts. Hence, there are truly free actions, and God determined they would be such. God then is totally sovereign in the sense of actually

---

[37] L. S. Chafer and J. Walvoord, *Major Bible Themes* (Grand Rapids: Zondervan, 1980), 233.

determining what occurs, and yet humans are completely free and responsible for what they choose.[38]

We could just as easily have said that believers were chosen in Christ from eternity future. His omniscience allows God to view time from the beginning, or the end, or all at once. He is not bound by our limited dimensions. And His omnipresence allows Him to transcend time and space, so He is at the beginning and at the end or both simultaneously. So much of our confusion on these issues probably stems from our finite limitations. Even the concept of foreknowledge is an accommodation for our human limitations. We could just as well talk about the *post*knowledge of God. He simply knows *eternally* and *simultaneously* without any necessity of succession in thought.

Conclusion

It must be admitted in the final analysis that discussions concerning the *ordo salutis* are only attempts to elucidate the inscrutable interface between limited thinkers constrained by time and space and the Creator who is not thus bound.[39] But when we try to bind God's eternal acts to our boundaries of time and logic, we turn something mysterious into nonsense. To hold to hard determinism and in the same breath talk about the validity of human choice is nonsense. Granted, the scriptural juxtaposition of divine sovereignty and human responsibility is a mystery, but as Geisler points out, a mystery may go *beyond* reason but a mystery is not *contrary* to reason. That which is *contrary* to reason we call a *contradiction*, not a mystery. J. I. Packer's

---

[38] Geisler, "God Knows," 70-71. Norman Geisler, *Systematic Theology*, (Minneapolis, Minnesota, Bethany House, Pub. 2004) vol. 3, 86. See also *Divine Foreknowledge Four Views*, eds. James K. Beilby & Paul R. Eddy, (Downers Grove, Ill. InterVaristy Press, 2001) and D.A. Carson, *Divine Sovereignty & Human responsibility Biblical Perspectives in Tension*, (Atlanta, Georgia. John Knox Press, 1981).

[39] See Hugh Ross, *Beyond The Cosmos: the extra-dimensionality of God*, (Colorado Springs, CO. Nav Press, 1996)

attempt[40] to explain divine sovereignty and human responsibility as an antinomy (two incontrovertible truths that are inexplicable) is a contradiction simply because of his limited view of sovereignty, that is, a deterministic God, who is sovereign over beings without the capacity to choose. Human responsibility assumes choice. So Packer's antinomy is a feeble attempt to harmonize No-Choice with Choice. No Choice + Choice = Nonsense, i.e., a contradiction, not a mystery. A mystery is incomprehensible, but not contradictory. Soft determinism allows the two truths to coexist compatibly or cooperatively without any resulting contradiction.

---

[40] J. I. Packer, *Evangelism and the Sovereignty of God* (Chicago: Inter-Varsity Press, 1961), 18-24.

Universalism

Ever since Rob Bell's book *Love Wins*[1] there has been a growing interest in universalism. Simply stated, one view of universalism is that all of God's created angels and humans will spend eternity with him. This would not exclude animals and goldfish, but neither does it include them. It does, however, include the fallen angels and the devil. Some universalists would exclude the latter two. However, to be consistent with their own arguments the devil and his fallen angels should be included. After all, if love wins over evil, then the originators of evil (the devil and his angels) must be included, or evil wins.[2]

At the root of this discussion is one's view of God and whether or not one attribute wins out over another (love over justice, for example). Much of universalism is a counter to the abhorrent view

---

[1] Robert H. Bell, Jr., *Love Wins* (New York, N.Y.: HarperCollins Publishers, 2011). It might be worth noting that none of the ideas in *Love Wins* is unique to Bell. They can all be found in Thomas Talbott's book referenced below and written over ten years before *Love Wins*.

[2] From the very outset we should have a problem with universalism if it is going to include the devil and his angels. Why? Because much is made in the New Testament about the second person of the Godhead becoming a man in order to provide salvation for men. A man had to die in order to pay the penalty for fallen man. If the fallen angels are going to be saved, then the second person of the Godhead would have to become an angel (a God-angel) and die in their place. But it is pretty clear from Hebrews that Christ is only going to die once. There is no alternate provision of a God-angel to die a substitutionary death for the fallen angels.

of God espoused by the double predestination of Augustine, Calvin, Beza, Perkins, the Westminster Confession, and their ilk (see the appendix on "Another Tale of Two Cities"). In its most repugnant form, God is said to have elected some to spend eternity with him and selected others to torture for eternity. It's difficult to get hard and fast figures on the number that are elect, but it is a clear minority. After all, many are called but few are chosen. So, in this view, God will torture the vast majority, say ninety percent, of the people he has created for all eternity. And this decision to torture them was made before he created them or before they had done anything culpable in his sight (sin). Some if not most Augustinian/Calvinists will object to the word "torture" because it so tarnishes the image of God. But we read in Revelation 14:10-11, "He shall be tormented with fire and brimstone in the presence of the holy angels and in the presence of the Lamb. ¹¹ And the smoke of their torment ascends forever and ever . . . " Tortured, tormented—what's the difference?

This view of God has driven many from the Christian faith. Others have simply rejected the theology that would create such an ungainly God, to put it mildly. Talbott says the Augustinian/Calvinistic God created a black hole of depression for him. He realized that his own parents were more omnibenevolent than Augustine's God. But if the teachings of Calvinism caused him to stare at the black hole, his research into the respected Church Fathers and leaders of the Reformation pushed him right into the hole. It wasn't until he began reading the words of George MacDonald that he got out of the hole.[3]

The universalists claim the Bible presents God as a God of love, mercy, and forgiveness. Mercy triumphs over judgement (Jas 2:13). Such a God is completely incapable of the treachery of torturing his own creation forever in hell or the lake of fire. And if he is, this is not the kind of God we wish to worship. One former pastor, who claimed to lean toward universalism, said the concepts of universalism freed him up from some of his doubts about God's character and enabled

---

[3] Thomas Talbott, *The Inescapable Love of God* (Universal Publishers/uPUBLISH.com, 1999), 12-15.

him to worship in a fresh and liberated way. He left his long-time ministry over this issue.

This is a topic not in wide-spread discussion when I wrote *FGS* twenty years ago. Because of its emergence, we decided it would be good to add this study. Our procedure will be much like our other studies. We will look at this doctrine from a historical perspective first. Then we will look at the Scriptures: Historical Theology + Biblical Theology = Systematic Theology.

Universalism in History

According to Talbott, the early Church Fathers were universalists. He claims it was Augustine that introduced exclusivism with his emphasis on double predestination and the separation of the elect from the non-elect. He thinks Origen (d. 254) was the greatest theologian between Paul and Augustine, and Origen was a universalist. He makes reference to Clement of Alexandria (d. 215), the mentor of Origen, and Gregory of Nyssa (d. 395). Of these, the teachings of Origen, who believed that the devil might eventually be saved, were the most influential. Numerous supporters of the final salvation of all men and angels were to be found in the postapostolic church. Origen's theology was not declared heretical until the fifth ecumenical council in 553.[4]

Augustine himself admitted that many, if not the majority, of early church fathers were universalists: "There are very many (*imo quam plurimi*, which can be translated "majority") who though not denying the Holy Scriptures, do not believe in endless torments."[5] A quick snapshot of the most influential early Christian Universalists, from Patristics scholar Ilaria Ramelli, certainly reinforces Augustine's admission:

> The main Patristic supporters of the apokatastasis [restoration] theory, such as Bardaisan, Clement, Origin, Didymus, St. Anthony, St.

---

[4] http://www.theopedia.com/universalism#note-0, Accessed June 6, 2017.
[5] Augustine, *Enchiria, ad Laurent.*

Pamphilus Martyr, Methodius, St. Macrina, St. Gregory of Nyssa (and probably the two other Cappadocians), St. Evagrius Ponticus, Diodore of Tarsus, Theodore of Mopsuestia, St. John of Jerusalem, Rufinus, St. Jerome and St. Augustune (at least initially) . . . Cassian, St. Isaac of Nineveh, St.John of Dalyatha, Ps. Dionysius the Areopagite, probably St. Maximus the Confessor, up to John the Scot Eriugena, and many others, grounded their Christian doctrine of apokatastasis first of all in the Bible. - Ramelli, Christian, Doctrine, 11.[6]

Nothing in the later Nicene Creed (381) precludes the possibility that all will be saved. It is not until the Athanasian Creed (500), that the phrase "they that have done evil, into everlasting fire" is introduced in creedal form.

Though scholars more qualified than I might debate over some of the above, we have to admit that quite a number of early church fathers believed in universalism. But they ran into a stone wall in the person of Augustine. With his change in theology around 412 he introduced determinism to his soteriological philosophy. I say philosophy because his determinism came from the pagans: the Stoics, the Neoplatonists, and the Manichaeans. It did not come from the Bible. With his view of double predestination God divided mankind into two groups: the elect and the non-elect. With this understanding the majority of people will go to hell. Although Origen himself died in the third century, as we have already pointed out, he was not branded a heretic until the sixth century. Slowly, the deterministic approach of Augustine took over, especially in the West.

Whether biblical or not, Augustine's approach fell right into the hands of the civil powers (Popes and kings). It is fairly easy to manipulate the masses when their souls are hanging over the jaws of hell. Thus, most Christians in the West since Augustine have been motivated by fear instead of by love. Campus Crusade for Christ

---

[6] Matthew Distefano, "Indeed Very Many: Universalism in the Early Church," April 10, 2017, accessed June 6, 2017, http://www.patheos.com/blogs/unfundamentalistchristians/2017/04/indeed-many-universalism-early-church/.

helped start a great revival in America in the 1960s. Their gospel tract, "The Four Spiritual Laws," came from the west coast to the east like a warm refreshing rain. Why? Because the first law claimed, "God loves you and has a wonderful plan for your life." Prior to that some door-to-door evangelists used to begin their gospel presentation by saying to a startled homeowner, "Do you know that you are a miserable sinner bound for hell?" No wonder so many of them had the door slammed in their faces. It has often been said that the most famous sermon ever given in America was by Jonathan Edwards, the title of which is "Sinners in Hands of an Angry God." Here is an excerpt from the sermon:

> The God that holds you over the pit of hell, much as one holds a spider, or some loathsome insect over the fire, abhors you, and is dreadfully provoked: his wrath toward you burns like fire; he looks up on you as worthy of nothing else, but to be cast into the fire; you are ten thousand times more abominable in his eyes, than the most hateful venomous serpent is in ours.[7]

It is easy to see how the harsh Augustinian view of God has created an atmosphere in which universalism with its positive message of love can flourish. But just reacting to the errors of Augustine doesn't make universalism right. Could it be the universalists have swung the pendulum from one extreme to the other, both approaches missing the biblical balance between love and justice. We think so. So, now let us take a look at some Biblical Theology.

Universalism in the Bible

At the outset of this discussion, we would like to set forth a hermeneutical principle, that of going from the clear to the unclear. In other words, if we can find a clear passage that teaches a doctrine,

---

[7] Jonathan Edwards, "Sinners in the Hands of an Angry God," reprinted in Ola Elizabeth Winslow, *Jonathan Edwards: Basic Writings* (New York: The New American Library, Inc.), 159.

it is better to begin with that passage and interpret less clear passages in light of the clear one. This is called by some the analogy of faith. An example would be the warning passage in Hebrews 10:26-39. Those who take a Reformed approach to Hebrews tell us that this passage has language so strong it must be referring to eternal condemnation.[8] They say this is the benchmark for the other warning passages. If this one is clearly eternal condemnation, then the other warning passages are interpreted in light of this clear message. Analogy of faith would indicate that all of the warning passages deal with the threat of eternal condemnation.

Another example would be Ephesians 2:8-9, which Protestant scholars generally agree clearly teaches that salvation is by faith alone without any meritorious works. With this clear passage as a benchmark other passages like Romans 2:6-11, which might seem to teach salvation by works, are interpreted. The assumption here is that if both books are from God and even the same human author, that he won't contradict himself. So, we start with a clear passage and interpret the unclear passages with the clear passage as a benchmark. So, let's go right to the clearest passage that mitigates against universalism.

Revelation 20:10

> [10] The devil, who deceived them, was cast into the lake of fire and brimstone where the beast and the false prophet are. And they will be tormented day and night forever and ever.

The importance of this passage cannot be overstated. Here we are told that the devil is thrown into the lake of fire with the beast and the false prophet. Like most passages, context is king. The questions we must start with are when did the beast and the false prophet get thrown into the lake of fire, and how long have they been there? In Revelation 19:20 we are told that the beast and the false prophet will be thrown into the lake of fire at the end of the Battle of Armageddon.

---

[8] Scot McKnight, "The Warning Passages of Hebrews: A Formal Analysis and Theological Conclusions," *Trinity Journal* 13 (Spring 1992):22-59.

So much for the when. Now how long have they been there before the great white throne judgment of Revelation 20? Revelation 20 tells us that after winning the battle of Armageddon the Messiah sets up shop in Jerusalem and reigns for a thousand years.

Although amillennialists do not take the thousand years literally, they must deal with the fact that a thousand years is mentioned six times in Revelation 20:1-6. Never has any number been repeated so many times in the Bible in such close context and been taken figuratively; the usage is always literal. In Revelation 20:10 the final judgment has come, what v. 11 calls a "great white throne" judgment. This judgment takes place a thousand years after the beast and the false prophet were thrown into the lake of fire. If that is so, we can deduce a couple of things. First, since both the false prophet and the beast are viewed in Revelation as real people, then annihilationism[9] must not be true, at least for them, since they had been there 1000 years and not been burned up.

The second deduction we can make concerns how long they will be in the lake of fire. The verse says "forever and ever." For universalism to be true, "forever and ever" cannot mean forever and ever in the sense of linear time going into the future. That is pretty much the point of universalism, namely, that an all-loving God could not torture his creation for an eternity. So, they work hard to show that the word *aiōn* does not mean eternity.[10] They say it means "a period of time." Though the word *aiōn* by itself can refer to a period of time and not eternity, the phrase *aiōnas tōn aiōn* (the age of ages) without exception means linear time in the future forever. That's why translators translate *aiōnas tōn aiōn* as "forever and ever," when literally the words say, "age of the ages."

So, we are suggesting that universalists are facing a theological cul-de-sac. This text is so clear that they must do some pretty creative

---

[9] John Stott became an annihilationist toward the end of his life for many of the same reasons people become universalists. See his defense in "John Stott's Response to Chapter 6," in David L. Edwards with John Stott, *Essentials: A Liberal-Evangelical Dialogue* (London: Hodder & Stoughton, 1988), 306-31.
[10] Talbott, 86-90.

things to avoid the obvious meaning. What do they do? They say the beast and the false prophet are not real people. If they're real people, case closed. Therefore, they claim that the beast and the false prophet are institutions, and these institutions are done away with. One is the political system of a one world government that is shattered by Jesus when he defeats the antichrist. The second is the religious system headed up by the false prophet, which could be worldwide.[11] There are serious problems with doing this:

1. The text uses personal pronouns for the beast and the false prophet, like "he" and "him" and "his" (19:20).
2. The false prophet is said to perform miracles to deceive the people. Religious systems don't perform miracles. That is very far-fetched. No twelve-year-old reading this text would come up with that.
3. It is said that the beast sets up his image for people to worship. People don't worship political systems. In 2 Thessalonians 2:4 the beast sets himself up as God. Even in the Roman era when people were expected to call Caesar "Lord," they didn't address the Roman Empire as Lord.
4. In 19:20 we are told that the false prophet and the beast were thrown "alive" into the lake of fire. We don't speak of political systems and religious systems as "alive."
5. In 2 Thessalonians 2:3 the beast of Revelation is called a "man of sin" and "the son of perdition." How on earth can this be understood to be a political system? It refers to an individual.
6. Jesus spoke of the beast of Revelation as the "abomination of desolation" spoken of by Daniel. Daniel predicted two abominations, the first being a foreshadowing of the second. The first was a real person, Antiochus Epiphanes (circ. 160 BC). His blasphemous acts were predicted by Daniel and fulfilled to the letter. In fact, the fulfillment was so accurate, biblical critics

---

[11] Gregory MacDonald, *The* Evangelical *Universalist* (Eugene, OR: Cascade Books, 2006), 129.

claim that Daniel must have been written after the fact, *ex eventu* prophecy, or prophecy that is not prophecy; it's history. But those who believe the Bible understand Daniel to be a prophet. If he wasn't, then Jesus was wrong because Jesus called him a prophet (Matt 24:15).[12] If Jesus was wrong, then he is not God. And if he is not God, he's not our Savior. But Daniel also said that Antiochus Epiphanes was just a foreshadowing of the ultimate abomination of desolation that would commit sacrilege in the place of worship for the Jewish people during the Tribulation. Antiochus Epiphanes was a real person in the foreshadowing of the ultimate abomination of desolation. There are no hermeneutical rules with which I'm familiar that would say that the second abomination of desolation will not be a real person.

We could go on and on with arguments against the beast and the false prophet being institutions. The point is, if they're real people, then they were thrown into the lake of fire and not annihilated. Revelation 20:10 tells us that they will have been there a thousand years and would be there forever and ever.

This one clear text should be all we need to dismiss universalism. And I don't do this lightly. I find no personal pleasure in thinking about people spending eternity separated from their creator with all the torture and angst and suffering that must entail, suffering I'm sure we can only imagine. That's why when John wrote Revelation he called the ultimate destiny of the unbeliever a lake of fire. Fire is not much of a threat to an immortal body (unbelievers exist forever, so their bodies must not be corruptible). Therefore, the lake of fire must simply be symbolic of the worst kind of suffering John can imagine.[13]

Whenever I read the story of Calvin's execution of the Servetus at the stake in Geneva, my stomach turns. They burned him to death with green wood to prolong his agony. It took three hours[14] for his

---

[12] Or Matthew is wrong about what Jesus said. Either way we have problems.
[13] See, "The Metaphorical View" by William Crockett in, *Four Views of Hell*, ed. William Crockett, Grand Rapids, MI. Zondervan Publishing, 1992) 43-77
[14] Talbott, 25.

body to give up the ghost. This is the fruit of Augustine's focus on the elect. And how can we forget or even imagine the torture in England when people were burned to death for having an English Bible. One Englishwoman was pregnant and the torture of the fire was so great her baby delivered right in the midst of her burning. A bystander rushed into the flames to save the baby, but the sheriff overseeing the event grabbed the baby and threw it back into the fire.[15] It's hard to imagine anything worse, but that's what John was trying to do when he talked about the lake of fire.

Ephesians 1:10 and Colossians 1:19-20

> [10] that in the dispensation of the fullness of the times He might gather together in one all things in Christ, both which are in heaven and which are on earth—in Him.

> [19] For it pleased the Father that in Him all the fullness should dwell, [20] and by Him to reconcile all things to Himself, by Him, whether things on earth or things in heaven, having made peace through the blood of His cross.

The issue in these two passages, which were written about the same time from the same place, deals with the reconciliation of all things in heaven and on earth either in Christ or to himself. That argument is that "all things" either means "all things," or all things means "all things." How can "all things" mean "some things," or "almost all things"? So, if "all things" means "all things," then this must include unbelieving humans, the fallen angels, and the devil.

But if Revelation 19:20 tells us that two human beings, the beast and the false prophet, were thrown in the lake of fire and not annihilated and would suffer there forever and ever (Rev 20:9-10), then here are two people not included among the "all things." Furthermore, if the devil himself is thrown into the lake of fire to suffer there for eternity

---

[15] Michael Farris, *From Tyndale to Madison* (Nashville, TN: B&H Publishing Group, 2007), 59-60.

(Rev 20:10), then he is not included in the "all things." We are also told that an "everlasting fire [is] prepared for the devil and his angels" (Matt 25:41). It is hard to imagine that another everlasting fire is prepared for the devil other than the lake of fire where he will be cast according to Revelation, so the everlasting fire and the lake of fire must be the same fire. But this fire will contain not just the devil, the beast, and the false prophet, but also the devil's angels. Now we have a lot more people (humans + angels) not included in the "all things" to be reconciled. Consequently, we can conclude that "all things" in Ephesians 1 and Colossians 1 does not really mean "all things." And although it might be argued that what Paul means by "all things" is not exactly clear, it cannot be argued that what John meant by the devil, the beast, and the false prophet is not perfectly clear, as argued above. Thus, we are making the less clear more clear by what is clear.

1 Corinthians 15:22

[22] For as in Adam all die, even so in Christ all shall be made alive.

Here the argument revolves around the parallelism between "in Adam all die" and "in Christ all shall be made alive." If the "all" affected by Adam refers to all mankind, then the all affected by Christ should also refer to all mankind. It seems pretty obvious. However, "in Christ" is a stock Pauline phrase for believers "in Christ." In 1 Corinthians 12:13 it says, "For by one Spirit we were all baptized into one body." The body refers to the body of believers, or as Ephesians 1:22-23 says, the church. In 1 Corinthians 1:2 we read, "To the church of God which is at Corinth, to those who are sanctified in Christ Jesus." The position of unbelievers, according to Ephesians 2:1, is "dead in trespasses and sins." But once they believe, their new position in heavenly places is "in Christ." So, in Christ is a technical phrase for believers who have been baptized by the Holy Spirit into the body of Christ, the church. It does not refer to all mankind.

Another way to understand "all shall be made alive" is similar to Daniel 12:2, where it says those who sleep in the dust of the earth "shall awake." Among those who shall awake are both believers and unbelievers: "some to everlasting life, some to shame and everlasting contempt." In other words, the "shall awake" would refer to the resurrection of believers and unbelievers. The "shall be made alive" of 1 Corinthians 15:22 could be read the same way: the ultimate resurrection of believers and unbelievers, or all mankind.[16]

1 Peter 3:18-20

> [18] For Christ also suffered once for sins, the just for the unjust, that He might bring us to God, being put to death in the flesh but made alive by the Spirit, [19] by whom also He went and preached to the spirits in prison, [20] who formerly were disobedient, when once the Divine longsuffering waited in the days of Noah, while the ark was being prepared, in which a few, that is, eight souls, were saved through water . . .

Here the argument is that unbelievers get a second chance after death to receive Christ.[17] After all, he went and preached to those in prison. What was he preaching to them, if not offering them a way out of prison? And so, if these people got a second chance, so does everyone who has rejected or will reject Christ in this life. And who in his right mind would reject Christ after experiencing the separation from God and the extreme suffering of hell, whatever that looks like? Thus, all men and angels will be reconciled to God, or so goes the argument. Where is the fly in this exegetical ointment? It's in the "by whom" beginning verse 19. What is the nearest antecedent for "whom"? Of course, it is "the Spirit." It is through the agency of the Holy Spirit that Jesus preached to the spirits in prison. But there is nothing in the text to tell us that the preaching was in the next life. In prison can simply refer to the state of these unbelievers when Peter was writing. Noah was a preacher of righteousness. He probably preached the entire time he was building his ark because undoubtedly people

---

[16] See John 5:28-29 for this inclusive concept.
[17] Bradley Jersak, *Her Gates Will Never Be Shut*, (Eugene, OR: Wipf & Stock, 2009), 17. He claims the Greek makes this very clear. Quite the opposite.

asked him on a regular basis why he was building a ship so far from the sea and when it had never rained. Just as he does today, the Holy Spirit, the Spirit of Christ, preaches through men to other men. Noah, a man, preached to the men and women of his generation. Because they did not listen to him, they died and their spirits went to hell. The preaching wasn't to them in the next life while they were in hell. No, the preaching was in this life while Noah was building the boat.

That's why this text mentions the "Divine long-suffering waited in the days of Noah while the ark was being prepared." "Long-suffering" could be just God's grieving over the sinfulness of mankind, impatiently waiting until Noah had finished the boat to bring the universal flood. But it also could refer to God's long-suffering while Noah preached to them, giving them every opportunity to respond to his message. The word long-suffering is a compound word in Greek: makrō + thumia, long + (heat, wrath, rage). So, another way to put this is that God was slow to anger, that he had a long fuse. So, the sinfulness of mankind during Noah's day made God angry, and his wrath was going to come, but the fuse was 120 years long.

Universalism is not Hinduism, but they have something in common. I once asked a former Hindu what's the appeal of Hinduism is. He said it is the ultimate system of non-accountability. In other words, with karma and reincarnation a person always gets another chance. So, both systems offer at least one more chance for salvation after our physical death. But the Bible says, "It is appointed for men to die once, and after this the judgment" (Heb 9:27).

Romans 5:18

> [18] Therefore, as through one man's offense judgment came to all men, resulting in condemnation, even so through one Man's righteous act the free gift came to all men, resulting in justification of life.

Here is another passage where the universalists like to talk about the word "all." Thomas Talbott goes on for pages intertwining this passage with 1 Corinthians 15:22 (see above) to show that "all" means "all." We have explained that throwing the devil, the false prophet, and the beast into the lake of fire forever and ever destroys all (no pun intended) these "all" arguments, unless, of course, you interpret this unholy trinity as something other than real persons.

On the other hand, Talbott does not do his homework on the word translated "condemnation" in Romans 5:18. If he did, he would discover that the word does not mean eternal condemnation. Neither this "condemnation" nor its opposite "justification of life" refers to a courtroom verdict.

Paul's word for a courtroom judgment or verdict is *krima* (5:16a), but the word used here is *katakrima*. Notice that those four letters ("kata") prefixed to *krima* take us out of our Position and into our Condition, making it the death sentence handed down (*katakrima*, 5:16a, 18a) after our guilty verdict (*krima*, 5:16a). By "death sentence" we mean not only physical death (5:12) but also the life that we inherited from Adam: enslaved by sin, resulting in moral defeat, misery, and despair for the believer who chooses to live self-sufficiently by the flesh. It is a life that is behaviorally indistinguishable from a nonbeliever "in Adam."

Likewise, *dikaiōsin zōēs* (righteous living), the term that parallels *katakrima* in 5:18, also signifies Condition, not Position; and the preposition *eis* (with a view to) in front of *dikaiōsin zōēs* indicates that "righteous living" is the intended goal of our justification.[18] The reversal secured for us by Christ's work in 5:18 thus leads to the intended goal of sanctification: a righteous life for believers that will maximize their glory for God. However, the next verse shows that this Condition will prevail over the Old Identity in Adam ("sinners," 5:19a; see 5:12c) only when the New Identity in Christ is fully realized ("righteous ones," 5:19b) in "the many" who receive the abundance of the free gift of grace and of righteousness (5:15, 17) by faith (1:17; 3:22). Thus, the sequential conjunctions in 5:18-21 trace the logical sequence of Adam's work and Christ's work, respectively, to show

---

[18] The phrase *dikaiōsin zōēs* ("acquittal of life") is very likely a *genitive of result*. See J. H. Moulton and G. Milligan, *Vocabulary of the Greek New Testament* (Peabody, MA: Hendrickson, 1997), 328 [hereafter MM], where it is defined as "a process of absolution, carrying with it life."

how the new Condition can be lived out despite the fact that believers in this life still carry with them the sinful trappings from their old identity in Adam.[19]

The point we are making is that Romans 5:18 is not even talking about eternal condemnation or its opposite, positional justification. Paul left that subject in Romans 4. "Therefore, having been justified . . . " (5:1) moves the reader away from the subject of justification (Rom 4) into the subject of sanctification (Rom 5-8).

Matthew 25:46

> [46] And these will go away into everlasting punishment, but the righteous into eternal life."

To begin this discussion, we must point out that the words "everlasting" and "eternal" are the same Greek word: *aiōn*. This would appear to be a clear passage pointing toward eternal punishment for the goats and eternal life for the sheep in this parable. Again, going from the principal of the clear to the unclear, most interpreters think the meaning of "eternal life" is clear: life with God forever in linear time going forward. If that's what eternal life means, then eternal punishment should also refer to punishment without God forever in linear time going forward. However, some want to look at the word "eternal" (*aiōn*) again, and argue that it just means an age or period of time. Again, context is king. When we look at this word "eternal" in John 3:16, it must refer to linear time going forward forever because it is contrasted with the words "shall not perish."

But they also go into a discussion of the word for punishment, which is *kōlasin*. Talbott quotes William Barclay, who writes, "*Kōlasis* is never used of anything but remedial punishment in all Greek secular literature."[20] But then he goes on to explain that the etymology of the word was of pruning trees to make them grow better. Now Barclay

---

[19] See *Portraits of Righteousness* for a full discussion of this pericope (Rom 5:12-21) and its significance for sanctification.
[20] Talbott, 91.

may refer to this, but that information really came from Moulton and Milligan and the Greek papyri.[21] However, they don't say the word means to prune trees but rather that it means "restraint," especially in its only other NT usage in 1 John 4:18. Again, Talbott is not doing his homework carefully.

Of course, what the universalists must do with an age of punishment after death is pretty much exactly what the Catholics have done with purgatory traditionally.[22] The Catholics say it is a place where the elect that are not perfected in Christ's love go, to have their sins purged away so they're fit for heaven. The big difference, of course, would be the Catholics say purgatory is for believers, while the universalists say their purgatory is for unbelievers, the devil, and his fallen angels. It is suggested that the fires of hell and/or the lake of fire are there as a purgation or cleansing. Some even go so far as to say that the Lord himself is a consuming fire and therefore these people are purged by the very presence of the Lord himself.[23] How this view would fit in with the idea of spiritual death as separation of the human spirit from God while at the same time being purged of any vestiges of sin in unbelievers by the presence of the Lord, I will leave for the reader to figure out.

In a face-to-face interview with Thomas Talbott, he explained that nothing about hell, the lake of fire, or outer darkness is punitive. It is all healing. For him, hell, the lake of fire, and outer darkness are three different places where the suffering gets progressively worse in their remedial methods. Each is intended to bring the unbeliever to repentance so he can receive the salvation of Jesus. If an unbeliever hardens his heart in hell, then he is thrown into the lake of fire. If he continues to harden his heart in the lake of fire, he is thrown into outer darkness. The increased suffering in each of these places is

---

[21] "κόλασιν," Moulton and Milligan, *The Vocabulary of the Greek Testament* (London: Hodder and Stoughton, 1963), 352.
[22] We realize Pope Benedict II changed the meaning of purgatory to more of an internal suffering. But, strangely, he kept the idea of an indulgence to get people out of purgatory once a year (Jersak, 138).
[23] Ibid., 139.

designed to break the will of the impenitent person or angel. But now Talbott faces a conundrum. According to him, the unbeliever uses his free will to resist God. But if he persists in this resistance while in outer darkness, then God will intervene and coerce his will to effect repentance. Aha. In the final analysis, Talbott is condoning the very system he set out to resist, that is, a God that forces people into his kingdom against their will, or as R. C. Sproul puts it, he drags them kicking and screaming into his kingdom.[24] In other words, Talbot winds up right back where he started with a deterministic God, only in this case God has determined that all his created people (humans and angels) will be reconciled to himself, even if it requires force for the hard-headed.[25]

Daniel 12:2

> ²And many of those who sleep in the dust of the earth shall awake, Some to everlasting life, Some to shame and everlasting contempt.

The word for "everlasting" in Hebrew is 'ôlām. Obviously, the context of this passage is eschatological. For a dispensationalist, this is the resurrection of Old Testament believers after the Tribulation Period (12:1), a time of trouble such as the world has never seen. As we often find in prophecy, we see a couple of mountain peaks without seeing the valley in between. According to Revelation 20:11-15, all unbelievers are raised at the same time, after the Millennium. They stand before the great white throne where the books are opened and they're judged according to their deeds. But that is the second mountain peak. The first one was the resurrection of Old Testament believers to be rewarded according to their deeds so they could go into the Millennium to serve the Lord alongside New Testament

---

[24] R. C. Sproul, *Chosen by God* (Tyndale, 1994), 69-72.
[25] A personal interview with Thomas Talbott on August 1, 2017. By the way, he had no answer for the problem of providing a salvation plan for the angels through a second *kenosis* (emptying) of Christ to become a God-angel to die in place of the angels. He had not even thought about the issue.

Universalism

saints coming from the rapture and from the martyred saints during the Tribulation. But we are concerned in this current study with the meaning of "everlasting," ʻôlām. The universalists again want to argue that ʻôlām just refers to an age, a period of time, just as they argue for *aiōn* in the NT.

But there's a major problem here not addressed by the universalists I've read. This same word for everlasting (ʻôlām) is used in Daniel 7:14 and 7:27 regarding God's kingdom; it is said to be an everlasting (ʻôlām) kingdom. Virtually all interpreters agree that this kingdom is the eternal state. When coupled with Revelation 21 and 22, it is life within New Jerusalem forever and ever. God's kingdom is one that will last forever and ever; it's a kingdom that is everlasting. But you can't have it both ways: the word ʻôlām can't mean forever and ever in Daniel 7 and then just be a period of time in Daniel 12. Furthermore, to state the obvious, the word ʻôlām is used in parallel in Daniel 12:2. Does anyone really want to say that those raised to everlasting life won't live with God forever and ever? Well, if everlasting means forever and ever in 12:2b, then it has to mean forever and ever and 12:2c. Otherwise, Daniel is writing nonsense.

Of further note is the fact that some universalists want to use Daniel 12:2 with its parallel uses of ʻôlām to help them interpret Matthew 25:46 and the parallel uses of *aiōn*.[26] In other words, if ʻôlām means "the age to come" in both uses in Daniel 12:2, then they say that is support for *aiōn* meaning an "age to come" in both uses of Matthew 25:46. Again, the meaning of "age to come" just does not fit ʻôlām in Daniel 7, something that they failed to notice or failed to discuss. In either case Daniel 12:2 actually supports just the opposite of what the universalists are trying to claim for Matthew 25:46. All four words (ʻôlām ... ʻôlām; *aiōn* ... *aiōn*) mean eternal time in the sense of linear time going forward forever and ever.

Of course, one has to wonder what the universalists have in mind when they talk about an "age to come." Since they're amillennial, the age to come for them should be the eternal state of the New

---

[26] Nik Ansell, "Hell: the Nemesis of Hope?" in *Her Gates Will Never Be Shut* by Bradley Jersak (Eugene, OR: Wipf & Stock, 2009), 203, note 43.

Jerusalem. Surely they think the eternal state is eternal. The only way out of this would be to argue that *aiōn* in Matthew 25:46a refers to a "period of time" in which the condemned will be purged of their sins by the presence of the Lord. The parallelism of 25a and 25b would then demand that the sheep enjoy life for a "period of time." Do they really want to say the believers enjoy life for only a period of time? Unlikely.

Isaiah 60 and Revelation 22

The argument here is that the Spirit and the Bride at the end of Revelation 22 are inviting unbelievers just mentioned as being outside the New Jerusalem to come and drink of the water of life freely. They liken these people to all the nations coming into the city in Isaiah 60. But dispensationalists would take Isaiah 60:1-18 as the millennial period. There are many unbelievers in the Millennium. They will stage a final rebellion against Christ at the end of the Millennium. But in Revelation 22 the invitation from the Spirit and the Bride comes after Jesus has said he's coming quickly. We are at the end of the book. These visions have been given to stir up current readers of the book. The fact that this program is imminent is a call to unbelievers of every generation to receive the free gift of eternal life. To apply this invitation to unbelievers who have died and been resurrected standing outside the gates does all kinds of violence to the order of the text.

Bradley Jersak wrote a whole book trying to establish post-mortem salvation for unbelievers (*Gates*, see footnote 15). He draws pages of parallels between Isaiah 60 and Revelation 21-22. As an amillennialist he understands all of Isaiah 60-66 as referring to the eternal state of the New Jerusalem. It is interesting, then, to read his comment on Isaiah 65:20:

> No more shall an infant from there live but a few days,
> Nor an old man who has not fulfilled his days;
> For the child shall die one hundred years old,
> But the sinner being one hundred years old shall be accursed.

If this is the eternal state, how is there reproduction (infants) and death (child shall die)? Jersak's comment: "Isa 65:20 is a real pickle."[27] In the hermeneutical circle the parts have to add up to the whole. And when you have the whole, it will help explain the parts. But if one part is out of sync with the whole, then perhaps you don't have the whole, and you better start over.[28] Isaiah 65:20 certainly doesn't fit into an understanding of the eternal state, but it could fit quite nicely into an understanding of the Millennium where you have both infants and death.

Another Gospel

In this respect, the Roman Catholics and the universalists have something in common: suffering before glory. The Protestants also see suffering before glory (1 Pet 1:3-12), but the suffering is on earth for believers, who will then be rewarded in the next life (glory) according to their response to their suffering while still alive on this earth (see Rom 8:17ff). But for the Roman Catholics and the universalists there is suffering in this life and the next for what could be the majority of people ever created.

The Roman Catholic believers that have not been perfected in Christ's love go to purgatory to suffer an appropriate length of time to purge the vestiges of sin from their lives when they died physically. The universalists see unbelievers going to a place of suffering also to be purged of their sins and unbelief. In both cases, these people from their respective purgatories don't get into heaven or the New Jerusalem until they have suffered for their sins.[29] The Roman Catholic sufferers have already believed, but their gospel is Belief + Suffering = Salvation (those few perfected in Christ's love while still living in the flesh get to go straight to heaven). Their belief was while alive on earth, but it is still part of the salvation equation. The universalist gospel is the

---

[27] Ibid., 174.
[28] See E. D. Hirsch, Jr., *Validity in Interpretation* (Yale University Press, 1967). See his discussion on heuristic genres versus intrinsic genres (68-126).
[29] The apparent general assumption is that no one is bad enough to go to eternal hell and no one is good enough to go directly to heaven.

same: Belief + Suffering = Salvation. In their case the belief is in the next life. But it is the same gospel as the Catholics: Belief + Suffering = Salvation. If I am not mistaken, that is another gospel than the one preached by Paul to the Galatians and everyone else. It is a long way from Faith Alone in Christ Alone.

Syllogisms

Most of my citations are from Thomas Talbott and Gregory McDonald because they were the two most cogent authors among the universalists I read. Gregory MacDonald is a pseudonym, obviously playing off the name of George McDonald, who was the defrocked Scottish theologian who opened the eyes of Talbott to universalism. But both McDonald and Talbott are Christian philosophers first and exegetes second. As philosophers they love syllogisms.

Syllogisms became popular among theologians during the days of Theodore Beza at the Geneva Academy as a way of adapting Aristotelian logic to theology.[30] Sometimes they were used to try to give people assurance of their salvation: Major premise: Everyone who believes in Jesus Christ will have eternal life; Minor premise: I believe in Jesus Christ; Conclusion: therefore, I have eternal life. The logic of syllogisms is inescapable; however, the conclusions are not always palatable. In such cases, you can usually find a fatal flaw in one of the premises.

Talbott claims that he ran into syllogistic reasoning in the "argument from evil" against the existence of God while a first-year student in college. His philosophy professor said: Major premise: God is all-powerful. Therefore, he has the power to get rid of evil in the world; Minor premise: God is all-loving. Therefore, he should want to get rid of evil in the world. There is only one Conclusion: Because there is evil in the world, an all-powerful, all-loving God does not

---

[30] See Walter Kickel, *Vernunft und Offenbarung bei Theodor Beza*, Beiträge zur Geschichte und Lehre der Reformierten Kirche 25 (Lemgo, Germany: Neukirchener Verlag des Erziehungsvereins GmbH Neukirchen-Vluyn, 1967), 61-66.

exist. Einstein used the same kind of reasoning to argue that God exists as a Supreme Intelligence, but is not a personal God. Why? Because there's too much suffering and evil in the world for an all-powerful, all-loving God to exist.

We digress from our primary subject to answer this "argument from evil" only because it has been used as a recruiting tool to atheism. There are problems with this syllogism on at least two levels. First, yes, we believe that God is omnipotent, or all-powerful. But sometimes God's power is limited by God's purpose. Shadrach, Meshach, and Abed-Nego are a case in point. When asked to bow down to Nebuchadnezzar, they refused and their response was:

> O Nebuchadnezzar, we have no need to answer you in this matter. [17] If that is the case, our God whom we serve is able to deliver us from the burning fiery furnace, and He will deliver us from your hand, O king. [18] But if not, let it be known to you, O king, that we do not serve your gods, nor will we worship the gold image which you have set up" (Dan 2:16b-18)

These servants of God do not question God's power (God . . . is able). But they are not sure of his purpose, so they're committed to dying if necessary to fulfill God's providential purpose for their lives. The Hebrew here is helpful. The NKJ translates the Hebrew as though Shadrach, Meshach, and Abed-Nego are convinced that God will deliver them (and he will deliver us). If so, then verse 18 makes no sense. However, the *waw* beginning the clause, "And from your hand He will deliver us, O king" can just as easily be translated "then," which I would suggests makes much more sense. God is able. If it serves his purpose to deliver us, then he will. But if not, then we are ready to die before we commit idolatry. We don't question God's power, but sometimes we don't know his purpose. The second limits the first. This shouldn't be hard to understand. There are all kinds of limitations on God's omnipotence. He cannot lie. He cannot make square circles. And he cannot undermine his own purposes.

Secondly, the atheist or the deist questions whether God is all-loving. But they have a narrow understanding of love. It is precisely because God is all-loving that evil is in the world. You see, an all loving God wants to love and be loved. That is part of the fulfillment of love. We suggest that one of the great purposes (a metanarrative) for the human race is to the answer the question raised by the rebellion of Lucifer as to whether God is worthy of being loved. That's why many have suggested that the Bible is one great love story. And that's why God's love language is obedience. But, in order to show love, one must have the choice not to love. God's desire to be loved could never be satisfied by robots. Only people created in his image with the free choice to obey or not to obey could demonstrate their love for him. But giving people the free choice to obey or not to obey also opens the door to evil. He could only eliminate evil by removing free choice or by destroying this world and all its inhabitants. Thus, an all-loving God and the existence of evil in the world are not a contradiction.

Now, as a Christian philosopher, Talbott has created his own syllogistic type of reasoning to help explain different approaches to the nature of God:

1. It is God's redemptive purpose for the world (and therefore his will) to reconcile all sinners to himself.
2. It is within God's power to achieve his redemptive purpose for the world.
3. Some sinners will never be reconciled to God, and God will therefore either consign them to a place of eternal punishment, from which there will be no hope of escape, or put them out of existence altogether.

Obviously not all three of these propositions can be true, and yet each one appears to have some biblical support. Different approaches to theology will adopt two of the propositions and throw out the one that does not fit their scheme. Here is Talbot's summary of these different positions:

> The Augustinians, because they believe strongly in the sovereignty of God's will (proposition (2)) and the doctrine of eternal punishment

(proposition (3)), finally reject the idea that God wills the salvation of all (proposition (1)); the Arminians... reject proposition 2; and the Universalist, because I embrace both one and two, finally reject proposition three.[31]

According to Talbott, every theologian must reject one of these three propositions. Much of his thinking about Christianity is based on this claim.

However, what if one of the propositions simply isn't correct? That could change things considerably. Notice I did not say "false." Talbott has already argued that not all three propositions can be true; one has to be false. But what if one is simply incorrect? If so, then the entire discussion is moot. I would say his first proposition is incorrect. He claims that God's redemptive purpose and God's will are the same. Furthermore, he says it is God's will to reconcile all sinners to himself. But here he makes the classic mistake made by so many theologians when they do not distinguish between God's providential will and his preferential will. There is a distinction in the Greek language between the word *boulēma* and *thelēma*. The latter refers to one's desire while the former speaks of one's predetermined decision, depending, of course, on the context.

For example, in the Garden of Gethsemane Jesus prays "not my will but yours be done." An examination of the text shows that when the translators translated the word "will" used by Jesus in reference to his own will, it is the Greek word *thelēma* (Luke 22:42) It means his wish or desire. Nevertheless, he yields to his Father's *boulēma* (Luke 22:42), which was the predetermined decision to sacrifice his son. As both God and man Jesus did not want to be separated from his father with whom he had perfect fellowship from eternity past. Nevertheless, he subjugated his desire to the Father's predetermined decision.[32]

---

[31] Talbott, 43-47.

[32] Another interesting use of the verb *boulomai* is found in a verse universalists like to use to support their point of view, 2 Peter 3:9, "The Lord is not slack concerning *His* promise, as some count slackness, but is longsuffering toward us, not willing that any should perish but that all should come to repentance."

The primary text supporting the first proposition that it's God's will to redeem all mankind comes from 1 Timothy 2:4, which says God "desires all men to be saved." Which word do you think is used there, *boulēma* or *thelēma*? It is *thelēma*. It is not God's predetermined will or decision to save all men; it is his desire. To turn his desire into his predetermined will would require force. Because he has created free moral agents whom he will not force, God's desires are not always met. To give another example, I'm sure it was God's desire that Adam and Eve not eat at tree of the knowledge of good and evil. But of their own free will they chose to do so. God was not going to force them to do the right thing. Principle: God's desires can be thwarted by the free will man. Hence, Talbott's first proposition that it is God's purpose and therefore his will that all men be saved is simply incorrect. If that is incorrect, then much of his Christian philosophy is incorrect as well.

Conclusion

Though we sympathize with the desire of universalists to exalt the love of God above all of God's other virtue, all sorts of problems usually result from such an unbalanced approach (cf. the Calvinists' exaltation of the sovereignty of God above all other attributes). But even the approach of the universalists to the love of God narrows their understanding to one which would deny the existence of evil in the universe. *Au contraire*, it is his love which allows for evil in the universe. Without allowing his creatures to have volition, or the capacity to choose, he would never experience love. Robots don't love. A divine micromanager of the universe can only be sovereign over robots.

We also find the universalists failing for a lack of adequate exegesis. They must turn people into institutions and assign inconsistent meanings to key terms. And, not to be unexpected,

---

The word "willing" is the participle *boulomenos*, meaning it is not God's predetermined decision that any should perish. This might have something pretty important to say about double predestination as taught by the Augustinians.

their amillennialism forces them into contradictory interpretations of eschatological passages. Also, by eliminating the Millennium, they have no escape from the sinister view of double predestination that assigns 90% or more of all humanity to be tortured forever. There may well be more people born into the Millennium than have lived throughout all the millennia of human history so far. With Christ sitting on his throne in Jerusalem for those thousand years, it is hard to see more than 10% of humanity rebelling against him.

For these reasons and many more, we regretfully must reject universalism as a viable option for biblical soteriology.

APPENDIX A

Sōzō and the Hermeneutical Circle

Systematic Theology versus Biblical Theology

It is important when one begins a study in Systematic Theology to understand the tension with Biblical Theology. Whereas the latter takes a specific book and tries to determine the theology taught in that book, the former tries to take into account the entire teaching of God's Word on a particular doctrine. We might call Biblical Theology the "worm's view" and Systematic Theology the "bird's view." Of course, it should be intuitively obvious that a proper system cannot be constructed without an accurate understanding of the theology of each book of the Bible as it stands on its own. The problem lies in the fact that no one person lives long enough to master the theology of each book of the Bible. Hence, systems of theology are developed before all the homework has been done. Each system seems to have some holes in it somewhere. That may sound discouraging or disillusioning to the beginning student, but from another point of view, the statement is encouraging. If mankind could completely systematize theology, that would be another way of saying that mankind can put God in a box, that the finite can fathom the infinite, that the ways of God are not mysterious after all.

Nevertheless, some attempt at systematizing theology must be undertaken or the minister of God is left floating on a shifting sea of spiritual understanding and is easily blown about by every wind of doctrine. And so, we search for a system that will answer as many of our questions as possible. But that is the most we can say for our system. It will never answer all of our questions. It will never be without its difficulties. But hopefully, we can arrive at a system which will answer more of our questions than any other. If we find a system that answers more questions than the one we presently adhere to, we should switch.

The Terms

In this study, we are exploring "salvation." That is what soteriology is, the study of salvation. But before we can study "salvation," we need to understand our terminology. What are the terms involved, and what do they mean in the NT as a whole? The Greek word for "salvation" is σωτηρία or *sōtēria*. The Greek word for "to save" is σωζω or *sōzō*. It is important for us to study these words in their context so we can formulate an understanding of them before we import them into a system of theology.

Sōzō

The way we do this kind of study is with our concordance. We become lexicographers, that is, dictionary makers. At least we will pretend to be such in our study of these two words. The way we do this is by categorizing the various uses we find for the word in question. Take *sōzō* for example. The first use we find of this word in the NT is in Matthew 1:21 where it is said that Jesus "will save His people from their sins." Surely we would categorize this use as some sort of "spiritual salvation." But the very next occurrence of the word does not reveal a context of spiritual salvation at all. This is Matthew 8:25 where the disciples cry out in the midst of a dangerous storm on the Sea of Galilee, "Lord, save us! We are perishing!" Obviously, this salvation is not spiritual; it is physical. So we have a second category: physical salvation. If we were entering this word in a dictionary, we would have two broad categories at this point: spiritual salvation and physical salvation. But what about our third use, Matt 9:21? Here, we read about the woman with an issue of blood. She says to herself, literally, "If only I could touch His garment, I would be *saved*." Is she thinking about spiritual salvation? Unlikely. The context demands some sort of physical salvation, but probably not from physical death. The context demands physical healing from her physical malady. For this reason, the NKJV correctly translates this, "I shall be made well." But how should we categorize the usage? Under our broad categories, it aligns with physical salvation. But since it is not salvation from physical death, it must form a second subcategory under the broader category. In other words, the broad category of physical salvation now has two subcategories: 1) from physical disease; and 2) from physical death.

As we continue in our concordance study of σῴζω, we realize that further uses in Matthew 9 are connected to the woman who needed physical healing. But when we get to Matthew 10:22 the picture gets a bit fuzzy. This is a context of persecution. Only those who endure until the end will be saved. But does this mean only those who are willing and able to hold strong to their faith in the face of persecution and perhaps martyrdom are truly Christians and will go to heaven? Or could this refer to the persecution of believers just prior to the return of Christ to set up the millennial kingdom? Here, one's theological presuppositions imposed upon the text have a major influence. If one has a strong Reformed theological perspective, he might opt for a meaning which is spiritual, that is, only those who persevere until the end will go to heaven. But if one is premillennial in his approach, he might decide this refers to physical salvation from the Tribulation Period or deliverance at the Judgment Seat of Christ.

So far, we have seen four different contexts. In Matthew 14:30 Peter calls out to the Lord to save him from physical drowning. Here, then, we see another use which we would put into the category of physical salvation from death. And so it goes. Each time we encounter a use we have seen before, we place that occurrence into that specific category. When we discover uses we cannot categorize as we have been doing we establish a new category or subcategory. Matthew 16:25 is just such a usage. It is so important for our study that we will defer discussing it until later. But as we progress through the concordance, it is surprising how often this word σωζω is used for meanings far afield from the spiritual salvation which opens the doors of heaven to a forgiven sinner.

Sōtēria

Is the same thing true of the word for salvation, σωτηρία? It appears to be so. In Luke 1:69-71, we find two uses of "salvation" which are definitely referring to eternal life. But in Acts 7:25, the use of "salvation" is a reference to deliverance of the Jews from slavery in Egypt. Luke uses this word again (the noun—he has already used the verb for physical salvation in v. 31) in Acts 27:34 to refer to physical salvation of the 276 people on the ship who needed physical nourishment to survive. And Paul seems to have a couple of uses in Philippians which do not appear to refer to reception of eternal life. For example, Phil 2:12 tells his readers to work out their own salvation with fear and trembling. Most interpreters prefer not to relate this usage to reception of eternal life because of the obvious connection with works, although others would argue that these works are simply evidence of their possession of eternal life. Dispensationalists understand the salvation mentioned in 1 Thessalonians 5:9 as deliverance from the Tribulation Period. And what about salvation in 1 Peter 1:5 and 9? The word for "born again" (αναγεννάω/*anagennaō*) is only used three times in the NT, and two of them occur in close context right here in 1 Peter 1:3 and 23. The tenses of these verbs (aorist and perfect, respectively) make it clear that these readers of Peter had already been "born again" by the time they received his letter. That was no longer an issue. What can we make, then, of the meaning of "salvation" in this context? Whatever it is, it certainly does not fit into the category of reception of eternal life.

Is James any different? In James 1:16-18, James addresses people whom he calls his "beloved brethren." He says they have been begotten by the Word of Truth. Surely he speaks of people who have received eternal life. Then in James 1:19, he addresses the same group (the "beloved brethren") and tells them if they clean up their act and receive the implanted Word with meekness, they can have "salvation." Does this refer to eternal life? It seems they already had that. Perhaps it only comes to those who maintain the gift they received (1:16-18) through a life of good works. That is precisely what many groups teach and believe. Others get out of the difficulty by suggesting that James must be talking about living a good life as proof that one is a true possessor of eternal life, not just an empty professor. That is convenient, but is that what the text is saying? It certainly appears that σωτηρία, like σώζω, is also used in a wide variety of ways in the NT.

It is very important in our study of "salvation" that we use our biblical theology to under gird our systematic theology. If we do not we will be guilty of imposing our theological views upon the text or letting our systematic theology override our biblical theology. In good exegesis, the parts must add up to the whole, and then the whole will help us understand the parts (this is called the hermeneutical circle). But if one part is out of sync with the whole, then our understanding of the whole is faulty. We must always be ready to adjust our understanding of the whole to correspond with and complement our understanding of the parts. They are *mutually informing*.

Sōzō and the Hermeneutical Circle in Romans 10:9-10

Let us take another classic text to illustrate: Romans 10:10. Here we are told that with the heart one believes unto righteousness and with the mouth one confesses unto salvation. The word "unto" is *eis*, which usually has a goal in mind, that is, "with a view to." So this text really does say that one confesses with the mouth "with a view to" or "with the goal in mind" of salvation. This leaves the obvious dilemma: what if one does not confess with his mouth? Can he go to heaven? If one is honest with the text, he must admit that to be saved one must confess with his mouth. To explain the dilemma as "evidence of salvation" simply circumvents the problem.[1] In Romans 10:10, one absolutely must confess with his mouth to be saved. Of course, this transparent understanding of the text has led most evangelists to the declaration that men and women must respond to an invitation to come to the front and confess Christ with their mouths if they wish to go to heaven.

---

[1] Wallace, *Greek Grammar Beyond the Basics*, 686.

But for those who can free themselves of the shackles of traditional thinking long enough to explore new solutions to old problems, confession with the mouth is certainly a work. Circumcision was identified as a work by Paul. What are some of the characteristics of a work? Observable by the naked eye; accomplished by physical means; performed by a human agent. All these are true of circumcision, but they are also true of confession with the mouth. If circumcision is a work, then so is confession with the mouth. But that means we must perform a work in order to be saved. Since we do not believe in salvation by works (Eph 2:8-10), there must be another explanation. Either confession with the mouth is not a work or it could be that the salvation to which Paul refers in this passage is not reception of eternal life. Perhaps it is in one of the other categories we have already observed to be beyond the scope of the spiritual salvation which gives us eternal life, or perhaps it is in a new category, one which we have yet to observe until now.

One way to find out is to use our concordance again to look up other uses of σῴζω and σωτηρία in Romans (biblical theology). The first use we find of the verb σῴζω and σωτηρία is in Romans 5:9. It is used again in the next verse. And in both verses we find that the readers have already been justified (v. 9) and reconciled (v. 10), but they have not yet been "saved" (vv. 9 and 10). In both verses, the justification is in the past and the reconciliation is in the past. These past tenses (aorist participles) place the action of these verbs before the action of the main verbs —"shall be saved." Both main verbs are in the future tense. These people have been justified and reconciled, but they have not yet been saved. If they died before receiving the Book of Romans, they would go to heaven because they had been justified and reconciled. But they would not be "saved." So once again we are faced with the likelihood that just as in Romans 10:10 "saved" in Romans 5:9-10 might something other than the salvation which takes someone to heaven when they die. What could it mean?

We need to look for other clues. Perhaps it would help to ask ourselves what the Romans were to be saved from. Romans 5:9 tells us exactly what they will be saved from: wrath (*orgē*). But what is that? Does not wrath refer to God's judgment on unbelievers for eternity? This is lexically possible, but the key question is to establish the meaning of "wrath" in Romans. So once again, we search in our concordance for the first use of wrath in Romans to see if it gives us any clues. And it certainly does. The first use of wrath in Romans is found in Romans 1:18. There it tells us that the "wrath" of God "is revealed" from heaven against all ungodliness and unrighteousness of men who hold back the truth in unbelief. The important factor to notice is the present tense of "is revealed" (*apokaluptetai*). This wrath is presently being revealed from heaven against the ungodliness and unrighteousness of mankind. This is not referring to something that will take place at the Great White Throne (as a matter of fact, there is no use of *orgē* in the NT which links it directly with the Great White Throne). It is in no way connected with eternal judgment. This is a present time judgment.

Specifically, this wrath is defined in the rest of Romans 1 as three stages of God's giving sinful man over to the control of his sinful nature as he descends the staircase into the basement of depravity. The phrase *paredōken autous ho theos* (God gave them up/over) defines these three stages in vv. 24, 26, and 28. The bottom of the basement is to have a mind that is *adokimos*, "disapproved" or "unable to tell right from wrong." It is total control by the sin nature. That is wrath in Romans 1:18ff. So let us try it out in Romans 5:9 to see if it makes any sense. "Much more, then, having now been justified by His blood, we shall be saved from wrath [the control of our sinful nature] through Him." Does that make sense? Perhaps. But does it fit the rest of the context? In Romans 5:10, it says that we were reconciled (past tense) through the death of His Son, but we shall be saved (future tense) through His life. If the meaning of wrath in Romans 5:8 is adhered to, then the saving in Romans 5:9 must also refer to being saved from the tyranny of the sin nature in our lives. And this does make sense. We were saved from the penalty of sin by His death, but we shall be saved from the power of sin by His life. We gained eternal life as He became our substitute in death, but we shall enjoy an abundant life as He becomes our substitute in life. "I have been crucified with Christ; it is no longer I who live, but *Christ lives in me.* . . ." (Gal 2:20). The hardest thing for a non-Christian to believe in is the substitutionary *death* of Christ, but the hardest thing for a Christian to believe in is the substitutionary *life* of Christ. Romans 5:10 is about His substitutionary life. In this "swing section" of Romans the author is turning away from his focus on justification from the penalty of sin to salvation from the power of sin. And being saved in this section is to be delivered from the tyranny of the sin nature in one's life (the wrath of Rom 1:18).

Could this meaning of "saved" fit in Romans 10? In Romans 5, being saved was an advance in the Christian life over being justified. Being justified delivers one from the penalty of sin; being saved delivers one from the power of sin. Could these definitions work in Romans 10? Maybe. If one looks at v. 9 as an equation, it would look like this: Belief+ Confession = Salvation. The verse also makes it clear that belief is a matter of the heart, whereas confession is a matter of the mouth. One is internal, while the other is external. One is spiritual, the other physical. But v. 10 explains that it is the internal transaction of belief that results in righteousness. This righteousness (*dikaiosunē*) is the same righteousness accorded to Abraham in Romans 4:3 (Gen 15:6), *dikaiosunē*. "Abraham believed God, and it was accounted [imputed = *elogisthē*, the aorist tense of *logizomai*] to him for righteousness." Paul has already established that imputed righteousness is the direct result of faith and faith alone. The verb form for all this is "to justify" (*dikaioō*—can you see this is the same root as *dikaiosunē*?). By faith and faith alone, one is justified or credited with the righteousness of Christ. It is a matter of the heart.

But with the mouth confession is made "with the goal of" (*eis*) salvation. Once again, let us suspend our ingrained presupposition that salvation or being saved must be equivalent to justification or the transaction which would put us in heaven if we died. Let us assume for the sake of argument that this salvation is a step beyond justification, just as it was in Romans 5:9-10. Let us adopt the same definition we discovered in the context of Romans 5, that is, to be saved is to be delivered from wrath, the tyranny of the sin nature in one's life (Rom 1:18). If this is so, obviously deliverance from the penalty of sin is a prerequisite for deliverance from the power of sin. In other words, justification must precede sanctification. No one will be sanctified who has not already been justified. With this understanding in mind, Romans 10:9-10 tells us that one believes in his heart in order to be justified—delivered from the *penalty* of sin—and he confesses with his mouth in order to be sanctified, or saved, or delivered from the *power* of the sin nature in his life. We would propose that this understanding makes sense and fits the following context.

Paul himself wants to prove this point, and he calls upon Scripture to achieve his goal. He equates "calling upon the name of the Lord" with confession with the mouth. We know this because of the common understanding that if A = B and B = C, then A = C. In v. 10 he said that "confession with the mouth" (A) leads to "salvation" (B), and in v. 13 he says that being "saved" (B) comes from "calling upon the name of the Lord" (C); therefore, A = B, B = C, and A = C: Confession with the Mouth = Calling upon the Name of the Lord.

But notice from the progression in vv. 14-15a that calling upon the name of the Lord is a separate, distinct, and subsequent act to believing. This becomes transparent if we follow the progression in reverse: 1) After the sending comes the preaching; after the preaching comes the hearing; 3) after the hearing comes the believing; and 4) after the believing comes the calling upon. The acts here are sequential. The calling upon and the believing are not identical acts, nor are they concomitant. After one believes, he can then call upon the name of the Lord (confess with his mouth the Lord Jesus). But this leaves the obvious question of whether one can believe and *not* call upon the name of the Lord.

In order to answer this question, we once again retreat to our concordance to find other uses of "calling upon the name of the Lord." And we discover from its usage in Acts 7:59; 9:14, 21; 1 Corinthians 1:2, and 2 Tim 2:22, that to "call upon the name of the Lord" is to openly, publicly identify with or to worship Him. Saul of Tarsus found believers because he asked where they were meeting. He was told they were "calling upon the name of the Lord" over at the house of Festus. So, off he went to find them and persecute them. What we discover, then, from Romans 10:9-10 is that calling upon the name of the Lord (confession with the mouth of the Lord Jesus) is open, public identification with Jesus Christ as one's personal Lord and

Savior. And Paul explicitly states that this is an integral step in one's deliverance from wrath, or the power of the sin nature in one's life. The power of Satan is in darkness. But when one comes to the light (Eph 5:11-14), the darkness is dispersed, and the power of the enemy and his accomplice (our sin nature) is defeated. In the terms used in Romans 5:9 and 10:9-10, the justified believer is then "saved."

Now the point of this entire exercise is to expand our understanding of the terms *sōzō* and *sōtēria*. We have done this by studying the words in their immediate contexts. And we have applied the hermeneutical circle to our study. If any part of the text does not harmonize with our understanding of the whole, we must revise the whole until all the parts synchronize. If we want to be accurate in our soteriology, the study of *sōtēria*, then it behooves us to be accurate in our understanding of its uses in the NT. Our aim is to arrive at our systematic theology by harmonizing the results of our biblical theology. What we will discover is that this so great salvation revealed in the NT is far greater than we ever imagined. This salvation has the power to deliver people from sin and death in this life to a full inheritance in the next.

Sōzō and the Hermeneutical Circle and James 2:14-26

There may be no text which has caused more difficulty for the early Reformers like Martin Luther than James 2:14-26. He was so excited about the salvation by faith he discovered as he translated Romans from the Greek that the writings of James threw him for a complete loop. He never wholeheartedly accepted the "right strawy epistle" into the canon of Scripture, for in his mind James was teaching salvation by works. And it is not hard to see why he adopted this understanding of the text. After all, in the very first use of *sōzō* (Jas 1:21) in the book, it looks like works are the way to heaven—the text tells us if we will "clean up our act" (set aside the excess wickedness—*ruparian* actually refers to ear wax) and become meek students of the Word, our soul can be saved. Obviously, we have to get rid of the evil in our lives. Then we can receive the Word with the right attitude; and only then can our soul be saved. Does not this sound like a works approach to going to heaven? Of course it does.

The next use of *sōzō* (2:14) then appears to clinch the deal. The setting is that of a man who claims to have faith but does not have any works to go along with his faith. Surely his faith alone cannot save him, can it (the question is asked with the Greek interrogative *mē*, which expects a negative answer)? The rest of chapter two would seem to indicate, in no uncertain terms, that a man is justified by both faith and works. It would even seem to imply that his faith is not complete without works. This teaching is so obvious from the text that Luther simply concluded that both Paul (Romans 4) and James (James 2) could not be right, so he tossed out James. But the councils which met after Luther did not agree with him. James was added to the canon. That implies, of course, that somehow the two points of view can be harmonized. In most evangelical circles James 2:14-26 is explained as "evidence of faith." In other words, if one *really* has faith, he will also have works. If one does not have works, he never really believed. He is a (false) professor of Christianity, but not a possessor. Just as a fruit tree will produce fruit if it is alive, so a true believer must be producing fruit if his faith is real.[2] Otherwise, his apparent faith is a false profession. C. Ryrie's footnote on James 2:14 in his *Ryrie Study Bible* labels this kind of faith "spurious," which means fake or false. And, as noted, most evangelicals are comfortable with this approach to the passage.

However, what about the hermeneutical circle? Does the whole explain all the parts? Do all the parts add up to the whole? The presupposition most interpreters bring to this text is that "save" means to go to heaven. With that understanding imposed upon James 2:14, the teaching of the text either means we must add works to our faith in order to go to heaven (which is what Luther thought the text was saying), or the text must be talking about genuine faith versus false faith (as Ryrie explains it). But are there some details of this text which are not in sync with the whole? I think so. For example, let us take the word "dead" in v. 17. If I were to take you to the wax museum of the Presidents at Disney World as your guide, and upon entering the museum looked at you and said, "OK, gang, look at the dead Presidents." Would that statement make any sense to you? It

---

[2] Wallace, *Greek Grammar Beyond the Basics*, 219.

shouldn't. Why? Simply because these Presidents were never alive. We don't use the word "dead" of things that were never alive, that are fake, false, or spurious. We use it of things that were alive, but now are dead. If I took you into a morgue and said, "Look at all the dead people," you would understand that statement. It makes sense. Why? Because these are real people who were once alive, but now they are dead. This is the major point of our passage, and it just does not fit the oft-proposed explanation of false faith versus genuine faith. However, as we shall see, it does harmonize nicely with faith that was once alive but now is dead.

If we discover one detail out of sync with the proposed whole, the hermeneutical circle requires us to look for a new understanding of the whole passage. We must keep looking for an explanation for the whole which will satisfy all the parts. As we saw in Romans 10:9-10, our concordance is our best friend. So, let us take our concordances to see where else we find this word *sōzō*. We have already seen two of these uses (1:21; 2:14). But the word also shows up in James 4:12; 5:15; and 5:20. In all five of these uses, "brethren" are being addressed. Since the three most important rules of Bible study are "context, context, context," the fact that all five times the word is used it is found in a context of admonition to "brethren" may be important. If, as some suggest, the audience to which James writes consists throughout of believers and unbelievers—all of whom he addresses as brethren since he may not be able to distinguish the genuine from the false brothers—then there is no special significance to James addressing brethren in these five passages. But if it could be demonstrated that he is addressing *only* believers in one of these five uses of *sōzō*, that might prove very significant for the interpretation of the other uses. And this is precisely the case in James 1:16-21.

Here James speaks to his "beloved brethren." And he speaks of the Father of lights who gives only perfect gifts. This Father has *already* given them birth by the Word of truth. In fact, James includes himself among those who have received this glorious gift of spiritual birth when he says "us." No doubt the "beloved brethren" of James 1:16 have been "born again." They have already received a spiritual birth. But in v. 19, the same group of "beloved brethren" is addressed again.

This time they are told not only to be quick to hear, slow to speak, and slow to wrath, but they are also told to clean up their act and receive the engrafted Word with meekness. Why? Because this Word has the potential to save their *psuchas*, whatever that is. And whatever it is, it must not refer to going to heaven since these people have already received the spiritual birth of James 1:18. For the moment, we will suspend the investigation of what this Greek term might mean. We will simply concur that it could not possibly refer to some aspect of going to heaven for two reasons: 1) these people are already born again, so they don't have to do anything to receive that gift; 2) other parts of Scripture teach us that we cannot work our way to heaven.

As we look at the uses of *sōzō* in James, there is another one which might be similar to James 1:21 since it is found in a like phrase: σώσει ψυχὴν αὐτοῦ (*sōsei psuchēn autou*), "will save his_???"(Jas 5:20). Ostensibly, this would also appear to be a passage dealing with evangelism, since the KJV, the NKJV, and others translate this word *psuchēn* as "soul." But the context does not support such an interpretation if it is true that we can neither work our way to heaven nor lose our ticket to heaven once it has been received. Why? Because it is the *brethren* to whom this passage has been addressed (v. 19). The passage speaks of one of these brethren going astray. There is no reason, whatsoever, to think the make-up of these brethren has changed since chapter one. So we may well have a use of *sōzō* very similar to James 1:21. Or, even if the nuance varies somewhat, we should still be able to agree that the passage is not dealing with evangelism.

As we move to the end of the text we find the word *sōzō* again in James 5:15. This time the translators choose "restore" or "heal" to convey the meaning. Why not "save"? Because it is apparent to them that, again, the brethren are addressed and a church member that is sick is calling for the elders of the church to pray for healing. This is not a passage about evangelism or going to heaven.

Besides James 2:14, this leaves only James 4:12 among the uses of *sōzō* for us to interpret. It says there is only one Lawgiver who is able to "save and destroy." Though this usage could refer to the fact that only God is able to send people to heaven or hell, I would suggest that such an interpretation does nothing to advance the argument of the passage in context. Again, it is the *brethren* who are addressed. And they are told not to judge each other. To do so is to take the place of God, to make themselves judges of the law and thereby put themselves above the law. There is only one Lawgiver. He is trying to motivate them to stop judging each other. How does it motivate brothers, who have already received the free gift of eternal life, to tell them not to judge other brothers because God is able to send some to heaven and others to hell? This would be relevant only if we believed we can lose our salvation. But if one holds to eternal security, then these words, even as a parenthetical addition, are gratuitous. But there *is* a time when brothers *will* be judged by this Lawgiver. At that time, He will examine their works and determine which shall last for eternity and which will not. Those works that do not stand the test of fire are "destroyed." Those that last forever are "preserved" or "saved." Now, we are getting somewhere. It fits the argument of the text quite well to remind brothers that we should not judge one another's works since we are not able to make these works stand the test of fire. Only God can do that, and He will—at the Judgment Seat of Christ. So for now let us stop judging each other, brethren. I think this understanding makes the best sense here. But again, even if some other meaning is in view, James is still addressing brethren, so it is unlikely that he is trying to motivate them with a reminder about heaven and hell.

This brings us full circle back to James 2:14. But let us look back over the terrain we have covered and observe something about the use of *sōzō* in James. In all four of the uses observed so far, brethren/believers have been addressed. This has led us to conclude that the issue at stake in these exhortations has not been going to heaven. Whatever the meaning of *sōzō* in these passages, the one thing they all have in common is that they are not giving instructions on how to get to heaven. What then are the chances that the only other use in the recorded writings of James will deal with how to go to heaven? Slim at best.

The next important step in figuring out the meaning of James 2:14 is . . . you guessed it . . . *context* (surprise). It is amazing how seldom we hear a clear discussion of context in the interpretation of this passage; and in this case, both the near and remote contexts are extremely important. Starting with the remote context, we look at the thrust of the book in general. From the prologue (1:2-18) on, the main thrust appears to be the value of trials in the life of a Christian. The book seems to be a manual on the Christian *walk*, not the *way*. James wants his readers to know how to triumph in the midst of their trials in the Christian life. After stating the value of such trials in the prologue, he offers a thematic statement for the letter in James 1:19—be quick to hear, slow to speak, and slow to wrath. These three qualities are the virtues needed in the midst of a life of trials, if one is to glean the multifaceted value that trials can offer the believer. So the body of the letter is designed to instruct the Christian on these three qualities: 1) Quick to Hear (1:20-2:26); 2) Slow to Speak (3:1-18); and 3) Slow to Wrath (4:1-5:6).[3] Thus, the passage in question (2:14) comes right in the midst of a section on how one should be quick to hear the still, small voice of God in the midst of his trials. He must learn to be a good listener. For James, a good listener is more than just a hearer of the Word; he is also a doer of the Word. When one is depressed over the trials that have hit in life, it is time to go *do something*. Specifically, James suggests visiting a widow or an orphan in their distress. We will find happiness in our *doing* (οὗτος μακάριος ἐν τῇ ποιήσει αὐτοῦ ἔσται, "this one will be happy in his doing," 1:25). Specifically, find someone who may have it worse than you do, like a widow or an orphan. Ironically, by trying to help them in their distress you may find yourself better able to persevere in the midst of your own trials.

So it is important to realize that in this overall section on becoming a good listener in the midst of trials, James has already set the stage for doing good works long before he gets to James 2:14. And in his teaching on good works, James in no way suggests that they will help us get to heaven. Quite the contrary, for those who already have new life (1:18) he suggests that these works will help us "produce the righteousness of God" (1:20) in this life.

When James hits chapter two, his theme has not changed. He still wants to teach them about being good listeners in the midst of their

---

[3] See, Zane C. Hodges, "Light on James 2 from Textual Criticism," *Bibliotheca Sacra* 120 (1963): 341-50

trials so they can hear God's voice speaking to them. But there is a common blemish in Christian assemblies which can deprive them of ever becoming good listeners. What is that blemish? It is being a respecter of persons (προσωπολημψίαις/ *prosōpolēmpsiais*; this word literally, when broken down into its parts, means "to receive the face," and thus came to mean "to receive or take something at face value," a word found uniquely in religious circles in all of Greek literature). These believers were judging each other (κριταὶ διαλογισμῶν πονηρῶν, "judges with evil thoughts," Jas 2:4). James goes through a number of reasons why they should not do this, but he comes to the climax of his argument at the end of the section (vv. 12-13). He says they should so speak and so do as those who are *about to be judged* by the law of liberty. When will that be?

Again, the rest of the book helps to answer this question. In James 4:11-12 he again urges them to stop judging each other. His reasoning is that it is God who will someday judge His family. But when? In James 5:8 he tells us that the coming of the Lord is near. Because of that imminent coming, believers should not murmur and grumble at each other. The Judge stands before the door. Here James is serving as the Roman Lictor, a person whose job it was to announce the entrance of the judge. The setting is one in which the plaintiffs are sitting around the courtroom grumbling at the defendants, the accused. Suddenly, the Lictor comes into the room and shouts, "Silence! Behold, the judge stands at the door!" The judge is about to enter the room to begin trying cases. So be quiet. Of course, James is using this imagery common in his day to refer to The Judge, the Lord Jesus Christ, who is about to come to judge His own. So what does James have in mind back in James 2:12-13 when he says the believers are not to judge each other since they are about to be judged by the law of liberty? It is the judgment of the Lord Himself, who stands before the door. At His return, believers will be judged. In light of that impending Judgment Seat of Christ, we should not be judging each other during this age.

But James goes on in James 2:13 to say something else about this impending judgment. He says that judgment will be without mercy on those who have shown no mercy. It is the same picture we were given by the Lord in the Gospels that if we are not forgiving on

Sōzō and the Hermeneutical Circle

earth, we will not find forgiveness in heaven (Matt 18). This is not a statement about our position, but one about our condition. We are His servants who cannot lose our eternal standing with Him. But if in the midst of our service we are judgmental and unforgiving of our fellow students, then He will be unforgiving of us. Without going into all those passages, it speaks of the negation of much of our service for Him, as far as accruing any glory for Him, if we have done it with a judgmental, self-righteous attitude. If we minister His Word, it will not return unto Him void, but we will not have brought personal glory to Him in our service. All of this will show up at the Judgment Seat of Christ.[4]

So, this is the near context of James 2:14, the very two verses preceding the passage in question. But before we jump into it, perhaps a word needs to be said about James 3:1. Once again, the subject of judgment pops up. The section is about learning how to be slow to speak. It is about tongue control. How can we hear God's voice in the midst of our trials if we are talking? James begins by warning the would-be teachers in the congregation. In an assembly where many different speakers (1 Cor 14) could step up to speak, he cautions them against competitiveness. He actually cautions them against teaching at all. It is not something to be rushed into. Why? Because teachers will receive a stricter judgment—they receive more light and will be held responsible for the greater light they have received (Jn 15:22). But the question I raise is "when"? When will they be judged? Some might suggest on earth by other believers. Probably true, but that is the very thing that James has argued against in this book. We should not be judging each other. There is also the problem of self-condemnation, which comes to the teacher who has failed to live up to the very standard he teaches. But surely, in light of all the other passages we have referenced on judgment in this book, the judgment in view here is God's judgment. Once again, when will Christian teachers be judged? At the Judgment Seat of Christ, of course. So is it not interesting that the two verses immediately preceding James

---

[4] See 1 Corinthians 3-4, 9:24-27, 2 Corinthians 5:9-10, Romans 14:10, and 1 John 2:28.

2:14-26 deal with the Judgment Seat of Christ, as well as the verse immediately following? Would it not be fair to think that the subject matter between these verses might deal with the Judgment Seat of Christ as well? And I would propose to you, that is exactly what James has in mind. Now then, we are ready for the passage.

It is important to observe the word ὄφελος/*ophelos* in James 2:14. This is the normal word for "profit." It is found in what we shall discover is another strategic passage for soteriology, Matthew 16:26, when the question is asked what profit does a man receive if he gains the whole world, but loses his own life. It is apparent that when the Lord returns for His own and asks for an accounting of what they have done with their lives and the gifts and talents He has given them He would like to see a profit on His investment. In Matthew 25, the servants who were faithful invested that which their master had given them so that they had a profit to give Him when He returned. But to the unfaithful servant the master said the money which had been given to this servant should at least have been given to the bankers so he could have drawn interest on what was his. In other words, he was looking for a profit. Would it be too much of a stretch to suggest that this is precisely the meaning of this word for profit in James 2:14? Once again we must remind ourselves that James has the Judgment Seat of Christ in mind. To be sure, the one who has no works to add to his faith offers little profit to those around him (the brother or sister in need of daily provisions, the widows, the orphans), and there will be little profit for him at the Judgment Seat of Christ.[5] And what we are going to suggest in James 2:14-26 is that faith without works offers no profit for the Lord, either.

---

[5] For those who want to argue that James could not have had the Judgment Seat of Christ in mind since his letter was written before 1 or 2 Corinthians and Romans where this time of judgement is explicitly revealed, we reply with all the verses on judgment in the Book of James previously mentioned. James 5:8-9 speak of imminent judgment from the Lord (*kurios*). Just because the exact phraseology βήματος τοῦ Χριστοῦ (Judgment Seat of Christ, 2 Cor 5:10) is not used does not mean the same concept is not in his mind. This phrase is not used in 1 Corinthians 3 either, but most dispensationalists agree that the concept there is the Judgment Seat of Christ.

Let us assume for the sake of argument that what James has in mind in this passage is in fact the Judgment Seat of Christ. If that is the whole, do the parts add up? Is there anything out of sync? We have already seen that the assumption that this passage is trying to compare genuine faith with false faith does not fit all the details of the text. Therefore, *that guess* must be wrong—it is an incorrect understanding of the whole. So we try again. Let us try the Judgment Seat of Christ. If someone were to show up at this judgment seat, he would certainly have faith. Without faith, he would not have shown up there to begin with. But now that he is there, the Lord is going to judge the act-intention complexes of his life, or his works and their motives. But what if he looks at the Lord and says, "I have faith, but I do not have any works." Can that kind of faith save him? Well, if this passage is not using "save" in the sense of getting into heaven, then the confusion of a works-oriented approach to getting into heaven is not in the picture. But 1 Corinthians 3 does present a picture at the Judgment Seat of Christ of our works being tested by fire. Those done for the glory of Christ are preserved as gold, silver, and precious stones. In other words, these works are preserved for eternity. But works done for our own glory will be burned up as wood, hay, and stubble. They are destroyed, as we inferred from James 4:11-12. And so, if a man has done no works for the glory of Christ, then none of the works of his life will be saved, but he will be in heaven. He would have arrived there by faith, without works, but nothing is preserved (as "profit") to bring glory to Christ in His kingdom.

But how does this approach explain the meaning of "faith without works is dead" any better than the genuine faith versus false faith approach? Well, let's remember what we are proposing. Things that are dead were once alive. We propose that the problem facing James' readers was that partiality, materialism, and contempt for others had eroded their faith.[6] They were in something of a state of paralysis regarding good works. As they sat around in this state of paralysis,

---

[6] The context of 2:14-26 is 2:1-13 where James charges his brothers with showing partiality. He also confirms that his brothers have a faith like his in our glorious Lord Jesus Christ.

they grew more and more self-centered and complacent. We could very well describe their faith as "dead." This does not mean they did not have any faith. Nor does it mean that their faith was false. It simply means they had lost their fire or fervor for Christ.

If we were to visit a Christian youth group and upon leaving I said to you, "Man, is that a dead youth group." What do you think I am trying to say? Am I saying there are no born-again Christians in the group? I don't think so. No, I am trying to say that the group is not on fire for Christ. They are dead, lifeless, inactive. To fire up their faith, they need to get active again. In other words, they need to add some works to their faith. Let's see if this meaning holds up as we work through the text. But to do this let's jump over the objection involving the demons[7] for a moment to pick up on this discussion of "faith without works is dead" as it relates to Abraham and Rahab.

Certainly, the text indicates that Abraham was justified by works. This is the obvious and plain meaning of the text. It was another reason Martin Luther disliked this book. Paul said we are justified by faith without works, but James says we are justified by faith plus works. To understand this text, we must observe that there are two points of reference in the text as it pertains to the life of Abraham. One is in Genesis 15, while the other is in Genesis 22. In Gen 15:6 Abraham believed and it was reckoned unto him for righteousness. This is the same passage Paul refers to in Romans 4:3 to prove that Abraham was justified by God without any works at all. It was his faith that was reckoned for righteousness. At this point in his life, it might be argued

---

[7] If the understanding that the passage deals with heaven or hell can be set aside, then there is another more plausible way to understand the mention of the demons. This text is best explained by recalling James' opening question of the value of claiming to have faith without works. This imaginary objector to what James is trying to teach about the relationship between faith and works is saying works do not matter. "I believe, and that is all that counts." No, says James. Demons hold to some orthodox theology; they believe in one God just as you dead-faith Christians do. But even their faith shows more life than yours. They at least tremble. A healthy faith will have works. Works do matter. Anyone with faith alone has a diseased faith. The faith of demons is healthier than yours in the sense that it shows more life than yours. At least they tremble.

that Abraham already had a personal relationship with Yahweh. But all interpreters agree that he had one after this point. Yet the Genesis 22 account comes approximately twenty-five years later. And after Genesis 22 we do not hear much about Abraham. His willingness to sacrifice Isaac stands as the high point of his faith. No longer do we read about the kind of failures he had with Pharaoh, Hagar, and Abimelech. And the emphasis James brings to this event in Genesis 22 is Abraham's work, not his faith. When James wants to refer to the faith of Abraham, he goes back to Genesis 15. But here James is saying that Abraham's willingness to sacrifice his son was a work which brought to him justification and a mature faith (ἐκ τῶν ἔργων ἡ πίστις ἐτελειώθη, "his faith was made complete by his works"—the Greek verb *teleioō* does not speak here of perfection as much as completion or maturity[8]).

The justification James refers to does not come until Abraham marches up Mt. Moriah with Isaac. But Paul says Abraham was justified twenty-five years before when he simply believed. Perhaps James will give us another clue as to what he means. It comes at the end of v. 23 when it says Abraham was called a friend of God. This word for friend (*philos*) is a word which speaks of emotional love. And no wonder Abraham was said to be a friend of God. He put his love for God before his love for his own son. And it is interesting that three of the major religions of the world—Judaism, Christianity, and Islam—call Abraham a friend of God. How does this help us solve the justification puzzle? We must remember what the word "justify" means *to declare righteous*. When these three religions of the world call Abraham a friend of God, they are declaring him righteous. They are saying, "This man must be a believer in God because his love for Him is so apparent from his willingness to sacrifice his own son." But

---

[8] It must be remembered that this term in its verbal or adjectival form has been used many other times in this book, most notably in the introduction (1:3-4), which sets the tone for the entire book. This is again a book not about the *way*, but a book about the *walk*. It is a book about faith which is tested through trials. As we endure these trials our faith is matured or made complete. Of course, this is exactly what James is talking about in the life of Abraham.

who is it that is declaring Abraham righteous after the Isaac affair? Is it God? No. It is men. Remember, as men we can see the fruit; only God can see the root. God declared Abraham righteous in Genesis 15 because he could see the faith of Abraham in his heart. But men cannot see into the heart. It was not until they saw the works of Abraham that they could declare him righteous.

Apparently, then, what we have here are two levels of justification: one before God by faith, and another before men by works. God can declare us righteous when He sees our faith; men declare us righteous when they see our works. Does this harmonize with Paul? Sure it does. If we look in Rom 4:2, we will even see that Paul acknowledges the type of justification James underscores. He says if Abraham was justified by works, and he was, he would have something to boast about, but not before God. Paul uses the first class conditional construction in this verse to indicate the reality of justification by works, but he makes it very clear that this justification is not before God. No, it could only be before men. Justification before God is by faith and faith alone, as Paul develops in the rest of Romans 4.

James wants to discuss the quality of faith that endures in the midst of trials. This kind of faith is not the faith of the baby Christian. It is the faith of the mature Christian. And it is only after persevering with good works, in the midst of the trials of our Christian life, that our faith can be declared mature. Our works cooperate with our faith in this sense, to develop it and bring it to maturity.

But where does Rahab fit in? And why bring up Rahab, of all people? The contrast is too obvious. Abraham was the father of the Jews, male, and moral. But Rahab was a woman, a Gentile, and immoral. It is a merism, a figure of speech in which the opposites are mentioned with the effect of including the whole (night and day, head to toe, heavens and earth, etc.). If the principle James is teaching applies to these opposites, Abraham and Rahab, then this principle will apply to *all of humanity*.

The key to understanding Rahab is to compare what James says about her to what Hebrews 11 says about her. In Hebrews 11 the emphasis is on faith. And again we must remember that the emphasis of James is on works. In Hebrews 11:31 Rahab *receives* the spies by faith, but in James 2:25, she *sends them out another way*. In Hebrews 11:31 only God can see the faith of Rahab. The spies were probably shaking in their boots wondering if she really believed their report. How would they know? The Gestapo knocks on Rahab's door to ask if there are any spies in the house. The spies are up on the roof, but they can hear Rahab interacting with the Gestapo. What will she tell them? They wonder. Have they been set up? Was she on their side or not? They only knew the answer to these questions when Rahab misdirected the Gestapo. Then they could run out, give Rahab a hug, and tell Joshua that there is a believer in Jericho because she sent them out another way. She should be spared. They are convinced that she is a believer in their message because of her work, that is, when she sent them out another way. And so they declare her righteous. She is justified before men by her works.[9] To summarize, only God could see her faith when she received the spies. At that very moment, He could declare her righteous, but no one else could. However, when she sent the Gestapo out the other way, the spies could go to Joshua and declare her righteous based on what they could see, her works. In this sense, and in this sense only, Rahab was justified by works.

James wraps it all up with a final illustration. He wants to find some sort of illustration where he can show the relationship between faith and works. He chooses the human being with his body and spirit, his material part, which is visible and his immaterial part, which is invisible. Preachers are always looking for a good illustration, and it looks like James is on to a good one. Works are visible; faith is invisible. So how do we draw the parallel? Why, we parallel the visible with the visible and the invisible with the invisible, of course; the body with works, and the spirit with faith. Right? Wrong. James does just the opposite, and this is extremely important to notice if we are going to understand what he is trying to teach us about the relationship between faith and works.

James says the body without the spirit is dead. In other words, if we pull the spirit out of the body, the body goes limp, lifeless. If we want

---

[9] Notice also that her faith that worked saved the physical lives of the spies and of Israel.

the body to show any life, we have to put the spirit back into the body, much as God breathed the spirit of life into the elements which went to make up Adam. How does this illustrate the relationship between faith and works? James parallels our faith to the body, and our works to the spirit. In other words, if we separate works from our faith, it goes lifeless and limp. It is dead. If we want to bring our faith back to life, we must add works to our faith. Works act like a shot of adrenaline to our faith. They fire it up. They give it vim and vigor. They bring it to life. There is nothing here at all about that which is genuine and that which is false. The entire illustration of the body being brought to life by the spirit is meaningless if it speaks of a false faith becoming genuine when we add works to it. That would be heresy.

From these discussions on the uses of the terms sōzō and *sōtēria* within the hermeneutical circle we can see that context is king when it comes to understanding the meaning of salvation in the Bible. We must be careful not to carry our preconceived notions of the meaning of these important theological words into the text.

APPENDIX B

Another "Tale of Two Cities"

Introduction

It was the best of times. It was the worst of times. The best of times in Athens, but the worst of times in Jerusalem. Alexander the Great found no more worlds to conquer, but when his four generals split up his kingdom, the Seleucids in Syria and the Ptolemys in Egypt used Palestine as their football field in their effort to control the Mediterranean world. The Golden Age of philosophy had flourished in Athens for over two hundred years when Antiochus Epiphanes stormed into Jerusalem and committed the original abomination of desolation spoken of by Daniel the Prophet. Even in the Babylonian deportations Nebuchadnezzar had not so desecrated the holy temple of the Jews. Yes, it was the best of times in Athens, but the worst of times in Jerusalem.

The dream of Alexander the Great, who had studied at the foot of Aristotle for three years, was to "Hellenize" the known world. He was so convinced of the superiority of Greek philosophical thinking that he carried copies of *The Odyssey* and *The Iliad* with him as he swept over the Medo-Persian Empire faster than a hawk dive-bombs a field mouse. He wanted each of his conquered countries to experience the wisdom of Athens. Greek became the *lingua franca* of his realm. East met West, and the resulting union was a marriage that has had more impact on Western Civilization than Newton's discovery of the laws of motion.

What we are talking about is the ripple effect of two thinkers from Athens as their philosophies landed in the sea of Judaeo-Christian thought like two meteors into the Mediterranean. Those thinkers were Plato and Aristotle. Ralph Stob, a Christian philosopher, has observed: "This element of the Greek spirit had great influence on ... the Christian movement in the first three centuries. At the same time it was the factor which was operative at the bottom of some of the heresies which arose."[1] Or as Marvin Wilson puts it, "Westerners have often found themselves in the confusing situation of trying to understand a Jewish Book through the eyes of Greek culture."[2] Dom Gregory Dix goes so far as to say that the miscegenation of early Christianity with Greek philosophy has led to a "spiritual schizophrenia in the process."[3] What we would like to do in this study is to outline the salient points of the philosophies of Plato and Aristotle which influenced Western Christianity and then illustrate these influences, specifically through the doctrine of Double Predestination.

Plato (d. 347 BC)

Plato bought into the dualistic philosophy of the Persians (Zoroaster), which recognized the ongoing struggle between the impersonal forces of good and evil. However, Plato's twist was to relegate everything good to the spiritual world. Everything evil was in the material world. Only in the spiritual world could we find the perfect ideals of which their inferior, material replicas are made. And in this spiritual world we also find immortal souls which preexist their union with material bodies.

When an immortal soul does enter a material body, good mixes with evil, and suffering begins for the immortal soul. The goal of human life becomes the release of this entrapped soul to reenter the

---

[1] Ralph Stob, *Christianity and Classical Civilization* (Grand Rapids: Eerdmans, 1950), 49.
[2] Marvin Wilson, *Our Father Abraham* (Grand Rapids: Eerdmans, 1989), 167.
[3] Dom Gregory Dix, *Jew and Greek* (London: Dacre, 1953), 14.

world of ideals, the perfect and good spiritual world. So, just as his dualism (good versus evil) is a metanarrative[4] for the entire universe, so it is for man. Man's body is a prison for his soul. This immortal soul is incarcerated in a defective, crumbling pot of clay. Salvation is not something one gains until death, when the soul is freed and able to float upwards into that celestial realm of goodness and perfection. This dualistic view of man is at the very root of salvific doctrine in Western Christianity.

Werner Jaeger goes so far as to say that "the most important fact in the history of Christian doctrine was that the father of Christian theology, Origen, was a Platonic philosopher at the school of Alexandria. He built into Christian doctrine the whole cosmic drama of the soul, which he took from Plato, and although later Christian fathers decided that he took over too much, that which they kept was still the essence of Plato's philosophy of the soul"[5]

Plato's soteriology was far, far from that taught in the OT. Most OT readers have to work hard to think of an OT promise of salvation in heaven for man's soul after death (it is in there, but most folks do not know where). The salvation emphasis in the OT was longevity in the land. God's fellowship and blessings were something to be savored and enjoyed in the historical context of this world. As Wilson points out,

> Certainly, the godly of the Old Testament could never have brought themselves to sing such patently foreign and heterodox words as the following, which may be heard in certain churches today: "This world is not my home, I'm just a-passin' through," or "Some glad morning when this life is o'er, I'll fly away," or "When all my labors and trials

---

[4] A way of explaining the purpose and flow of human history. See Stanley J. Grenz, *A Primer on Postmodernism* (Grand Rapids: Eerdmans, 1996), 44-46. He explains the metanarrative as a system of myths (narratives) which, though unprovable, exercises a force and offers the principal means by which an individual human society or society as a whole can explain its existence.

[5] Werner Jaeger, "The Greek Ideas of Immortality," *Harvard Theological Review* 52 (July, 1959): 146.

are o'er, and I am safe on the beautiful shore." To any Hebrew of Bible times this kind of language would be unrealistic and irresponsible, a cop-out—seeking to abandon the present, material world, while focusing on the joys of the "truly" spiritual world to come.[6]

Now despite the claims of Jaeger that Origen of Alexandria was most responsible for inculcating Platonism into Christianity, this author believes the Bishop of Hippo had far more influence than Origen. And Augustine did not get his Platonism from Origen. It came from the influence of Plotinus and Neo-Platonism. Therefore, in order to trace the influence of Athens on Jerusalem, the next link in the chain is Plotinus.

Plotinus (d. AD 270)

This man of brilliance and mysticism is considered by some to have been the most influential man since the Apostles on Western Christianity. He is known as the Father of Neo-Platonism. After growing up and studying philosophy in Alexandria and Persia, he settled in Rome, where he began a school. He was said to have been a man without enemies, greatly beloved for his divine wisdom. He himself made no attempt to perpetuate his wisdom, but Porphyry, his disciple and biographer, edited and organized his scattered lectures. These became known as *The Enneads*, which were translated by Marius Victorinus and studied diligently by Augustine. Augustine actually credits Plotinus for getting him on the road to truth and, eventually, of his conversion to the Orthodox Church.[7] Says Michael Azkoul:

---

[6] Wilson, *Abraham*, 168-69. It must be observed that Wilson is referring to OT believers. Obviously, there is some NT emphasis on the temporary trials of this world as opposed to the glory that shall be revealed in the sons of God when Christ returns (cf. Rom 8:17ff).

[7] In the *Confessions*, VII, Augustine makes clear his dependence on Plotinus and *The Enneads*.

In the case of Augustine ... his attraction to Platonism—specifically Plotinus of Lycopolis (204-270) and his school (Neo-Platonism)—was very serious, perhaps fatal. He did more than accessorize his theology with it. From this Greek philosopher and his *Enneads*, more than any other, Augustine borrowed the principles to develop his Christian version of Greek philosophy.[8]

It has been said that Augustine was Christianity's first writer of introspection, as witnessed by his *Confessions*. Perhaps, but it was the mysticism of Plotinus and his elevation of contemplation to the status of a productive principle which was Augustine's inspiration for his *Confessions*. Augustine even compared the writings of Plotinus with the Holy Scriptures.[9] He both paraphrased and quoted freely from Plotinus. So influential was Plotinus that W. R. Inge claims:

> Plotinus gave an impetus to this fusion [the coalescence of Greek philosophy into a theocentric system of religious discipline], for the victory of his philosophy was so rapid and overwhelming that it absorbed the other schools, and when Neoplatonism captured the Platonic academy at Athens, ... it reigned almost without a rival until Justinian closed the Athenian schools in 529.
> ... Even Augustine recognized that the differences between Platonists and Christians were slight, and the church gradually absorbed Neoplatonism almost entire [sic].... It is no paradox to say with Eucken that the pagan Plotinus has left a deeper mark upon Christian thought than any other single man.[10]

While Inge no doubt overstates his case, nevertheless we cannot be hasty in dismissing his claims. For many would ascribe such

---

[8] Michael Azkoul, *The Influence of Augustine of Hippo on the Orthodox Church*, Texts and Studies in Religion 56 (Lewiston, NY: Mellen, 1990), 129.

[9] Apud Platonicos me interim, quod sacris nostris non repugnet, reperturnum esse confideo (*Contra Acad.* III, xx, 43 PL 32, 957).

[10] W. R. Inge, "Plotinus," *Encyclopedia Britannica* 18 (Chicago: Encyclopedia Britannica, 1955), 81.

sweeping influence to Augustine, and if Augustine's primary source was Plotinus, then the implication is obvious.

According to Plotinus, the Supreme Being is the source of all life, and is therefore absolute causality. This Supreme Being is moreover, the Good, insofar as all finite things have their purpose in it, and ought to flow back to it. The human souls which have descended into corporeality are those which have allowed themselves to be ensnared by sensuality and overpowered by lust. They must turn back from this; and since they have not lost their freedom, a conversion is still possible. Here, then, we enter upon the practical aspect of his philosophy.

Along the same road by which it descended the soul must retrace its steps back to the Supreme Good. It must first of all return to itself. This is accomplished by the practice of virtue, which aims at likeness to God, and leads up to God. In the ethics of Plotinus all the older schemes of virtue are taken over and arranged in a graduated series. The lowest stage is that of the civil virtues; then follow the purifying; and last of all the divine virtues. The civil virtues merely adorn the life, without elevating the soul. This is the purpose of the purifying virtues, by which the soul is freed from sensuality and led back to itself, and thence to the Supreme Being. By means of ascetic observances the man becomes once more a spiritual and enduring being, free from all sin.

But there is still a higher attainment; it is not enough to be sinless, one must become "God." This is reached through contemplation of the Supreme Being, the One—in other words, through an ecstatic approach, the soul may become one with God, the fountain of life, the source of being, the origin of all good, the root of the soul. In that moment, it enjoys the highest indescribable bliss; it is as it were swallowed up of divinity, bathed in the light of eternity. Porphyry tells us that on four occasions during the six years of their correspondence Plotinus attained to this ecstatic union with God.

As Porphyry set out to popularize the teachings of Plotinus, he emphasized the religious side of Neo-Platonism. The object of philosophy, according to Porphyry, is the salvation of the soul. The origin and the cause of evil are not in the body, but in the desires of the soul. Hence, the strictest asceticism (abstinence from meat, wine, and sexual relations) is demanded, as well as the knowledge of God. He became an enemy of Christianity in his writing *Against the Christians*. Here he does not attack Christ, but he does denounce the practice of Christianity current in his day. By 448 his works were condemned.

Augustine (d. 430)

The Platonists

When Augustine began reading *The Enneads* in the late fourth century, they opened his eyes to the "invisible things" (*Confessions*, VII, 20). When it comes to the Platonic principles, it must be stated that Augustine held the Christian philosophy to be the highest of the philosophies, since it rested on faith, while the Greek philosophies relied upon reason. But he also saw them as preparatory for the coming of Christianity. Once here, the Christian philosopher could "spoil the Egyptians" just as Moses did when he left bondage in Egypt. Rational inquiry was to be pursued in order to grasp by reason what was already held by faith. Platonism was "the handmaiden to faith." Therefore, Augustine did not seek to know in order to believe, but rather he believed in order that he might know (faith seeking reason).[11] There were certain matters in which reason could precede faith (*ipsa ratio antecedit fidem*—reason itself precedes faith), such as in physics or mathematics.

For Augustine, God was the Platonic Good. Augustine thought of the material world as a hazy copy of the World of Ideals, the spiritual world. Indeed, all phenomena are but contingent ektypes (*ek* =

---

[11] Augustine anticipated the Anselmian "fides quaerens intellectum" (faith seeking understanding), and he quoted Isaiah on behalf of this proposition— "fides quaerit, intellectus invenit; propter quod aut propheta: Nisi credideritis non intelligentis" (Isa 7:9): "Faith seeks; reason finds; because of which even the prophet *says*: If you will not believe, you will not understand." The quote from Isaiah is his Latin translation of the Septuagint. It does not come from the Vulgate.

"out of" or "from" in Greek) of the eternal Ideas. Again, since there are some created and material things superior to others and some things below which more greatly resemble things above, Augustine's universe is a hierarchy or ladder of beings leading to Him Who is the Supreme Being. The ascent to God begins with a "turning" to Him, a "turning" which necessarily involves divine illumination. Of course, the limitation of our ascent is not merely the limitation of our created nature, but also the result of our moral and spiritual condition.

At this point, Augustine introduces his version of the Platonic memory. Memory according to him is the soul's ability to recall the past, the bringing forward what has been stored within our being. Memory is the storehouse of knowledge which, with the intellect's *a priori* categories, brings the truth of the world external to it. Memory is the *sine qua non* of all knowledge, whether intellectual or sensory. The intellect, unlike the sense, is fed by two streams: from the soul and, indirectly, from the world of phenomena. The intellect, stamped or "impressed" with the divine Ideas, beckons us to contemplate the soul and the heavenly realm to which it is akin. When the intellect or reason concerns itself with the physical world, it produces "science" *(scientia)*; but when it searches the realm of the spirit, it uncovers "wisdom" *(sapientia)*. Inasmuch as both *scientia* and *sapientia* comprehend some aspect of the truth, they both, to some degree, require illumination. The higher we ascend on the scale of being, the greater the "light" given to the soul.

Now where, we must ask ourselves, do these concepts appear in Scripture? Alas, they do not. But the long arms of Plato have reached forward through the centuries and through his resurgent disciples like Plotinus to embrace the Bishop of Hippo. In fact, this new strain of Platonism in the church was so evident in Augustine that Michael Azkoul claims,

> [Augustine's] philosophical religion is a perversion of the Christian revelation. He is also responsible, in large measure, for the division between East and West; and, indeed, even for the Occident's loss of the patristic spirit . . . . There is good reason that Orthodoxy has never recognized him as a Father of the church—his latter-day champions

notwithstanding; and, certainly not a "super-Father," as he has been known in the West since the Carolignian period. He is surely not the apex of the patristic tradition; in fact, he was the beginning of something new.[12]

Augustine's life quest was to experience the mystical union resulting from a beatific vision of the Good, just as Plotinus claimed to have done. Plotinus was convinced that during this mystical state we actually have an experience of formless intuition. This mystical ascent seems to those who pass through it to be a progressive stripping off of everything that is alien to the purest nature of the soul, which cannot enter into the Holy of Holies while any trace of earthliness still clings to it. He describes this holy ascent as "a flight of the alone to the Alone."

Plotinus acknowledged that such an ascent was a rare experience indeed. It is the consummation of a life-long quest of the highest, to be earned only by intense contemplation and unceasing self- discipline. Hence, the necessity of asceticism. Augustine, as Bishop of Hippo, set up a school for young aspirants, who were willing to mortify their bodies for the prize of the goal of holy ascent. Augustine himself never experienced the mystical union described by Plotinus, though he yearned for it his entire Christian life.

In order to be fair, we must not credit Augustine with imbibing all of Plato's philosophy. E. Portalié enumerates the Platonic theories which the Bishop of Hippo rejected: eternity of the world, emanationism, pantheism, autosoterism, the pre-existence and the transmigration of the soul, and polytheism.[13] But he also lists those doctrines of Plato which Augustine always approved and appropriated: philosophy as *amor sapientiae* (the love of wisdom), with God and the soul as its object; the idea of the Good, the doctrine of "illumination" and the distinction between "intellection" (knowledge of eternal things) and "science" (knowledge of temporal things), corresponding to Plato's

---

[12] Azkoul, *Influence of Augustine*, ii-iii.
[13] E. Portalié, "Augustine," in *Dictionnaire de Théologie Catholique* I (Paris: n.p., 1909): 2268-2472.

double-tiered reality; and, of course, the theory of eternal ideas or Forms which Augustine placed in the Essence of God.

A.H. Armstrong called Augustine "the first Christian thinker whom we can place among the great philosophers."[14] Augustine the philosopher believed truth came by rational inquiry, but Augustine the theologian also believed that faith certifies reason's discoveries. Another way of putting this is that faith leads to understanding, or, Christianity supplies the "faith" and Platonism satisfies the reason. The confidence he placed in Plato, Aristotle, Plotinus, Porphyry, and the like was not shared by the earlier Fathers. They may have taken elements, but never principles from the Greeks. At best certain elements from the philosophers could decorate the temple of truth, but never form its foundation.

Augustine's dependence on reason explains why his writings chase rabbit trails of the mind far from the halls of revelation. It seems strange that one who believed so thoroughly in the depravity of man and the corruption of human reason would, at the same time, depend so completely upon his own reason to ratify truth. It was centuries after his death before Augustine became the theological master of the West.[15] But he has had such an impact on Western Christianity that, as Hermann Reuter observed, Augustinianism prepared the West for division with the East.[16] B. B. Warfield agreed, saying, "But it was Augustine who imprinted upon the Western section of the Church a character so specific as naturally to bring the separation of the

---

[14] A. H. Armstrong, "St. Augustine and the Eastern Tradition," *Eastern Churches Quarterly* V, 7-8 (1963): 161.

[15] See H. Leibscheutz, "Development of Thought in the Carolingian Empire," *The Cambridge History of Later Greek and Early Medieval Philosophy*, ed. A. H. Armstrong (Cambridge: n.p., 1967), 571-86.

[16] Hermann Reuter states: "Augustin hat die Trennung des Occidents und des Orients verbereits, eine bahnbrechende Wirkung und den ersteren ausgeuebt" (Augustin thoroughly prepared the split between the West and the East; he was the initial pioneer and the foremost influence in this development) in *Augustinische Studien* (Gotha: n.p., 1887), 229.

Church in its train."[17] And, as Armstrong remarks, the *sine qua non* of Augustinianism is Neo-Platonism.[18]

To trace all or even the majority of Augustine's influence on the West would span far beyond the scope of this study, but one of his salient doctrines will be examined: Double Predestination. We will see that behind this difficult doctrine, to put it mildly, lies an elitism implicit within Augustine's theology, an elitism which finds its identity in the elect.

Double Predestination

In Augustine's mind his doctrines of "original sin," "irresistible grace," and "double predestination" were organically linked. We have written on his doctrine of "irresistible grace" in a previous article.[19] The grace referenced in Augustine which is irresistible is not the grace of regeneration, which he believed was bestowed at water baptism, nor the grace of an efficacious call, but rather the grace (gift) of perseverance. It was this grace that God irresistibly foisted on the elect so that, for them, apostasy was impossible. Of course it was impossible, since Augustine defined the elect as those who persevere in their loyalty to Christ until the end of their lives (*à la* Matt 24:13). Because the Scriptures were refracted by Augustine through the prism of the Platonists, God's light was bent toward the elite. And because of their emphasis on the contemplative life (mysticism) and self-denial (asceticism) as twin engines which power the flight of the soul out of its corporeal prison into the presence of the Supreme Good, "heaven" was inaccessible to the masses. After all, how could illiterate people (the masses) ever hope to enjoy a life of study and contemplation (reason plus revelation)? And among the contemplative still fewer could qualify for heaven based on the austere requirements of asceticism (all sex = sin, either venial or mortal). Augustine did allow

---

[17] B. B. Warfield, *Calvin and Augustine* (Philadelphia: n.p., 1956), 307.
[18] Armstrong, "St. Augustine," 161, 167.
[19] David R. Anderson, "The Soteriological Impact of Augustine's Change from Premillennialism to Amillennialism," *Journal of the Grace Evangelical Society* 15 (Spring-Autumn, 2002).

for sexual relations between a husband and wife as a necessary evil for the propagation of the race, but his Manichaean background never left him in this area. For the Manichaeans, sex was always evil. So for Augustine. Plotinus himself so abhorred his body that he never bathed so as to not give any honor or attention to the body, while at the same time making it all the more repugnant (not to mention pungent). The point here is that Neo-Platonism fostered an elitism which manifested itself in Augustine through his understanding of the elect.

While all baptized were regenerated by the Holy Spirit, only those who persevere until the end of their lives will prove to be the elect, the few. Again we quote from Azkoul, a former student at Calvin College until he began his study of Augustinianism:

> Also, predestination is inseparable from Augustine's doctrine of irresistible grace. Grace for him is a divine but created force, whereby God compels the will of man from evil to good and negates the consequences of "original sin" in those who are baptized. The grace of the Sacrament of Baptism is given to "many" while on the "few" is imposed irresistibly "the grace of perseverance" which denies apostasy to the elect. Saving grace is compulsory, because, if freely given, the wicked nature of man would reject it. The Reformation will adopt Augustine charitology as its own.[20]

The "elect" become the focal point of Augustinian theology. To understand this it may help to remember the passage of Augustine from the Manicheans to the Academics to the Platonists to Christianity. He spent nine years as a "hearer" (*auditor*) in the Manichaean philosophy, a combination of Zoroastrianism, Buddhism, and Christianity. The Manichaeans distinguish between the "sons of mystery" and "the sons of darkness," with the latter obviously being outside the realm of Manichaean enlightenment. But within the ranks of their own members, the "sons of mystery" were divided between the "elect"

---

[20] Azkoul, *Influence of Augustine*, 181.

and the "hearers." Mani proclaimed salvation through knowledge (*gnōsis*), which itself was achieved through ascetic practices. The Elect were sealed with a threefold preservative: 1) Purity of the mouth—abstinence from meat and alcohol; 2) Purity of life—renouncing physical property and physical labor; and 3) Purity of heart—forsaking sexual activity.

Few of us are able to cast away the baggage of our past. These Manichaean distinctions are easily transferred to the world of Christianity, especially since the word "elect" is a biblical term. But the distinction between the regenerate (the baptized) and the elect (those who are compelled by the gift of perseverance) is the creation of Augustine. No doubt his ascetic background originated with Manichaeism and was perpetuated by Plotinus and Porphyry. This is a salvation for only the "few," the "elect," the "sons of God," who slowly but surely distance themselves from material things. By grace, the grace/gift of perseverance, the Elect escape the bondage of the flesh.

Tied in closely with election and perseverance is predestination. Ferdinand Prat[21] claims that Augustine changed his exegesis of Romans 9 in 397. He began to see Jacob and Esau as types of two different sets of people, the Elect and the Reprobate. By adopting the hermeneutics of Tyconius,[22] which utilized typology extensively instead of allegory, Augustine began finding types all over the Bible. Regardless of the fact that Romans 9 never mentions hell, Hades, heaven, eternal, judgment, condemnation, or the like, Augustine reads eternal bliss and eternal condemnation right into the passage.

And within Romans 8 Augustine equated God's knowledge with God's will, that is, God's foreknowledge is tantamount to predetermination. Hence, it is predetermined before the foundation of the world that those whom God chose (the Elect) would spend eternity with Him and those He passed over (the Reprobate) would spend eternity without Him. Of course, Augustine is left with the same dilemma that the Reformers who copy his system will inherit—

---

[21] Ferdinand Prat, *The Theology of St. Paul*, trans. J. L. Stoddard 1(Westminster, 1952), 450.
[22] Anderson, "Soteriological Impact," 4.

how does Augustine's idea of double predestination exonerate God from evil? All Augustine's sophistry could not answer this dilemma, nor could that of the Reformers. Alas, the omnibenevolence of God becomes the foil in double predestinarian guise. As we shall see, Theodore Beza simply punted on the idea of omnibenevolence. He elevated the hatred of God to the same level as the love of God, calling both virtues and evoking equal glory to God from each.

His Influence in the West

Although Augustine was praised by Pope Celestine as a man of great learning and a doctor of the Faith, Augustine still lived in the shadow of the Fathers. St. Jerome did not mention him in *De viris illustribus*. St. Gennadius of Marseilles shows little knowledge of what Augustine had written. Sulpicius Severus ignored Augustine altogether in his biography of St. Martin of Tours, but in the same work he showed great appreciation for the works of Sts Cyprian, Ambrose, Jerome, Paulinus and John Cassian. Nor did Sts Nicetas of Remesiana, Valerian of Cimiez, Peter Chrysologus of Ravenna reveal any hint of Augustinian influence in their writings.

Those who opposed the teachings of Augustine were formidable, among which were St John Cassian, Sts Vincent of Lerins, Hilary of Arles, Honratus and Gennadius of Marseilles, Faustus of Riez, and Arnobius the Younger. Cassian was his most powerful contemporary, who claimed that Augustine's new and dangerous opinions were unknown to the Fathers and at variance with accepted interpretation of the Scriptures. In reaction to Augustine's doctrines on irresistible grace and double predestination Cassian accused him of transposing grace and liberty, realities of the spiritual order, to the rational plane, where grace and liberty are transformed into two mutually exclusive concepts. Cassian's voice was drowned out by the din of the Pelagian/Augustinian controversy, but that of St. Faustus of Riez (d. 485) was not.

Faustus opposed both the autosoterism (you can save yourself) of Pelagius and the double predestination of Augustine. He preached the doctrine of *meritum de congruo et condigno*, that is, grace is commonly imparted but not imposed. He also took predestination to be a parody of the pagan notion of fate. Under his leadership the Council of Arles condemned predestinationism. And in 530 the Council of Valence rejected double predestination.

However, during the so-called "Carolingian Renaissance" the star of Augustine began to rise. Among the Frankish intellectuals, Augustine became the greatest of the Fathers (*doctor super omnes*). Charlemagne slept with a copy of *The City of God* under his pillow. At the Benedictine Monastery of Corbie (near Amiens), Ratramnus affirmed double predestination and also concluded that the Eucharist was simply a memorial (based on the metaphysics of Augustine, which separated material and immaterial entities). One of his disciples, Gottschalk of Mainz (d. 869) claimed to be the true heir of Augustine. He defended double predestination, was condemned at the Council of Mainz (848), was vindicated at Valence (855), and finally opposed again in 856 until an "exhausting compromise" was reached at the Council of Douzy.

From this point on, there were disagreements on what Augustine meant, but no disagreement in the West that he was the greatest of the Fathers. Anselm, Aquinas, Bonaventure, and the Reformers would drape themselves in the mantle of Augustine. And, as we have seen, Augustine was heavily influenced by Plato. But before we jump from the double predestination of Augustine to that of the Reformers, we need to stop long enough to take a glimpse at the influence of Aristotle on the historical theology of Western Christianity. Aristotle entered the church through Thomas Aquinas, and it was the principles of logic taught by Aristotle which the Reformers utilized to try to justify double predestination.

Aristotle (d. 322 BC)

Aristotle was the son of the court physician to the king of Macedon. At the age of seventeen he went to Plato's Academy in Athens, where he remained for twenty years as a student and then a teacher. After the death of Plato he spent the next twelve years away from Athens, serving for three of these years as the tutor to the son of Philip II of Macedon, Alexander the Great. In 335 he returned to Athens to open a new school called the Lyceum, where he taught for the next twelve years. Upon the death of Alexander anti-Macedonian feelings threatened the school, forcing Aristotle to flee to Euboea, where soon afterward he died.[23]

Though he was a student of Plato, Aristotle reacted to the concept of the unseen world of ideas being more real than the world of the five senses. Reality for him was what he could observe right in front of him. The unseen world would require revelation for validation. Not so with the empirical world of nature. Reason and logic alone could mine the diamond fields of nature. He is sometimes called the Father of the Scientific Method, and was the first to classify the physical world into specific fields of biology, zoology, and physics. He is also known as the founder of logic, and his syllogistic reasoning and "four causes" were utilized heavily by the Reformers to buttress their approach to predestination.

A syllogism contained a Major Premise, a Minor Premise, and a Conclusion. Knowledge can be *deduced* by syllogistic reasoning as described in *Prior Analytics*. The Reformers relied heavily on this type of reasoning in order to give assurance of election to church members: Major Premise—Believe on the Lord Jesus Christ and you will be saved; Minor Premise—I have believed on the Lord Jesus Christ; Conclusion—I am saved.

The "four causes" of Aristotle were used by him to explain change in nature: 1) Material Cause—the matter from which something has evolved; 2) Formal Cause—that which gives shape and structure to that which is changing; 3) Efficient Cause—that which imposed the form on the matter; and 4) Final Cause—the end to which that substance emerges and which requires the efficient cause to act in a determinate way. These will be honed and applied by Theodore Beza to theology in order to under gird his supralapsarianism (God decreed to elect some and reprobate all others before the creation and fall of man) and double predestination to the glory of God. In doing so he used both the inductive and deductive logic of Aristotle.

---

[23] Paul D. Feinberg, "Aristotle," *Evangelical Dictionary of Theology*, ed. Walter A. Elwell (Grand Rapids: Baker, 1984), 75-78.

The writings of Aristotle were lost to western thinkers for centuries after the Fall of Rome. But during the twelfth century scholars discovered a mother lode in Spain. Here in the libraries of Toledo, Lisbon, Segovia, and Cordoba Arabic translations of books that Europeans had long talked about but never read were found. Ptolemy's *Almagest*, the lost key to astronomy and astrology; Galen's *On the Art of Healing* and *On Anatomical Procedures*, the first scientific medical textbooks; Euclid's *Elements of Geometry*; Archimedes' treatises on mathematical engineering; and, best of all, the vast corpus of Aristotle's works—*Metaphysics, Physics, On the Heavens, History of Animals, On Generation and Corruption, De Anima* (Aristotle's famous treatment of the soul), *Nicomachean Ethics,* and *Politics.* Two more works attributed to Aristotle were also found, although it was discovered at a later date that these belonged to Neo-Platonists: *Theology of Aristotle* and the *Book of Causes.* Taken together, these books were the greatest discovery in Western intellectual history.[24] It became the joint task of scholars from Europe and Africa (Christian, Jewish, and Muslim) to translate these books into Latin. Here is an excerpt of what they read after translation into English:

> The evidence of the senses further corroborates [the sphericity of the earth]. How else would eclipses of the moon show segments shaped as we see them? As it is, the shapes which the moon itself each month shows are of every kind . . . but in eclipses the outline is always curved; and, since it is the interposition of the earth that makes the eclipse, the form of this line will be caused by the form of the earth's surface, which is therefore spherical. . . . Hence one should not be too sure of the incredibility of the view of those who conceive that there is continuity between the parts about the pillar of Hercules [the Straits of Gibraltar] and the parts about India, and that in this way the ocean is one.[25]

---

[24] Richard E. Rubenstein, *Aristotle's Children* (New York: Harcourt Books, 2003), 16.

[25] Aristotle, *On the Heavens* (*De Caelo*), J. L. Stocks, trans., in *Works*, 1 (Chicago: Encyclopedia Britannica, 1952), 2.14, 297b.24-298a.20.

No wonder these men were bug-eyed over this treasure trove of knowledge. The church was in shock. Ever since the start of European universities, the Queen of the Sciences had been theology. But with Aristotle *redivivus* there emerged a new interest in the physical world. Along with this information came the realization that Aristotle accumulated his wealth of knowledge apart from any assistance from the church or the Bible, using human logic, reason, and observation as his guide. Here the church was not an authority. This was no minor matter, for at this time the church enjoyed a position of unchallenged power and authority, dominating European thought and culture.

Some welcomed this new font of wisdom. Peter Abelard (d. 1142) went so far as to imply that whatever could not be proven true through logic was considered false. Unfortunately, when one leans upon reason solely and independently of revelation, and makes reason the final arbiter of truth, a very strange thing begins to happen: reason reasons out revelation altogether. This is what slowly took place on the European stage between the 1200s and the 1700s.

Thomas Aquinas (d. 1274)

In the 1200s Thomas Aquinas (d. 1274) sought to accommodate the work of Aristotle with the church and make room for both to coexist under the blessing of church authority. His work, known as Thomistic Scholasticism, brought resistance from the church initially because of its dependence on Aristotle. In 1277 several of his propositions were condemned in Paris and Oxford, but in 1323 he was canonized. In the sixteenth century Thomism was the leading light of the RCC. He was made a Doctor of the Church in 1567, and in 1879 Pope Leo XIII commended his work for study. It is because of his influence on the Reformers and in particular their adoption of Aristotle's syllogistic reasoning and his "four causes" that Thomas Aquinas is included in our discussion.

Aquinas sought to unite reason-based and revelation-based thinking into a new and acceptable whole. He did this by dividing life into two distinct realms: the realm of Nature and the realm of

Grace. In the lower realm of Nature (which included science, logic, and things having to do with the natural, temporal world) man's intellect and independent reason operated quite well on their own. Reason was seen as a reliable guide to truth in this realm. Revelation, on the other hand, was necessary for understanding the upper realm of Grace, which included such things as theology, prayer, worship, God, angels, and things pertaining to the eternal supernatural world.

Aquinas did not think of the realm of Nature and the realm of Grace as oppositional. He believed the realm of Nature should be subjected to the authority of the church. But by simply placing the material world in a category of its own, even though initially connected to the realm of Grace, over time the distinction became so great in people's minds that the connection disappeared altogether.

The "Enlightenment" was a celebration of human reason, and it rose like a beast out of the sea of the "Dark Ages," an age when revelation reigned supreme. The celebration of human reason is the cornerstone of modernism, where there is a blatant disregard for revelation and a high regard for reason; where Nature is the sole, impersonal, guiding intelligence of the universe; where the Word of God is considered as relevant as the proclamations of Zeus; where human reason is the sole measurement of ethics, morality, and freedom. Despite the protestations of postmodernism against the omnipotence of human reason, the stronghold of reason over divine revelation remains as powerful as ever.[26]

We are now ready to jump forward to the Reformers in order to see how the influence of Plato and Aristotle converged at the Geneva Academy through their dependence on Augustine and Aristotelian logic.

---

[26] See Christian Overman, *Assumptions That Affect our Lives* (Louisiana, MO: Micah Publishing, 1996), 106-07.

The Reformers

John Calvin (d. 1564)

Although John Calvin is often thought of as Augustine's alter-ego, most of the Reformers were Augustinian in background. Martin Luther, for example, was an Augustinian monk. John Calvin followed Augustine almost exclusively in his typological dependence on Romans 9 to support his double predestination. But as Sanday and Headlam point out, the loving of Jacob and the hating of Esau "has reference simply to the election of one to higher privileges as head of the chosen race, than the other. It has nothing to do with their eternal salvation."[27] And again, "The Apostle says nothing about eternal life or death. He says nothing about the principles upon which God does act; ... He never says or implies that God has created man for the purpose of his damnation."[28] Calvin and his followers never consider that the initial use of "wrath" in Romans occurs in Rom 1:18 and deals with God's anger against man's sin in time instead of eternity. This may well be its use throughout Romans, including Rom 9:22 ("vessels of wrath").

It should be apparent that this hermeneutical approach to Romans came directly from Augustine. Like so many others of his time Calvin had been studying Augustine for quite some time before dedicating his talents to Christian theology. He had only been a believer for four years when he published the first edition of his *Institutes* (1536). He claimed that his theology was thoroughly Augustinian. Of course, he differed from Augustine in his understanding of justification and the sacraments, but with regard to predestination and his preoccupation with the elect and getting one's soul to heaven, he adopted Augustine almost wholesale. He taught a clear double predestination and supralapsarianism.[29] He said God caused the Fall of Adam and so

---

[27] William Sanday and Arthur Headlam, *The Epistle to the Romans*, ICC (Edinburgh: T. & T. Clark, 1968), 245.
[28] Ibid., 258.
[29] Calvin, *Institutes*, III, 21, 5.

"arranged" it in His decree of predestination "for His own pleasure."[30] So did his successor at the Geneva Academy.

Theodore Beza (d. 1605)

Beza succeeded Calvin in Geneva. His supralapsarianism emphasized that Christ died only for the elect. Although Calvin certainly subscribed to the double predestination of Augustine, Beza brought it to the forefront of his theology. He even developed a chart (see end of this Appendix) which elevated the hatred to God to the same level as the love of God, making them both equal attributes of God which brought equal glory to God. As we shall see, he utilized the "four causes" of Aristotle to arrive at his conclusion, but the roots of his double predestination went back to Augustine and Neo-Platonism. So through Beza, Plato and his student Aristotle met once again at the Geneva Academy.

By the time of Beza, the preoccupation of the Reformed church was to find out whether or not one was a member of the elite group, the elect. Assurance was separated from faith so that one could no longer find assurance of his salvation by looking to Christ, since Christ only died for the elect, and the person in question might very well be one of the reprobate. This began the great fruit-inspecting industry of the Reformed Church.

From the chart in the Appendix we can see that the just and merciful God decrees to elect some and reprobate others before the creation and fall of man. This is called supralapsarianism. Limited atonement is a corollary of supralapsarianism deduced from the decree of election and reprobation before the creation of man. If, it is reasoned, God's first decree was election and reprobation, then the death of Christ could only have been for the elect. That is called Limited Atonement. It does not come from Scripture; it comes from reason and logic.

---

[30] Ibid., III, 23, 7. Notice his appeal to Augustine for support. Compare Opuscules, Sp. 2054: "Cependant je recognoy ceste doctrine pour mienne, qu'Adam est tombé non seulement par la permission de Dieu, mais aussi *par le secret conseil d'iceluy* . . . ." (Adam fell not only by the permission of God, but also by the secret counsel of His will) [emphasis mine].

Moses Amyraut, who studied at the Geneva Academie under Beza, spent his career trying to convince Dortian Calvinists that Calvin did not teach Limited Atonement.[31]

Beza, in fact, seems to have gotten lost in the maze of human logic and reasoning. Building from a Platonic *à la* Augustinian base in order to determine who the elect might be, he incorporates the logic of Aristotle to help make this determination. He employs syllogistic and dialectical reasoning, as well as inductive and deductive logic. He takes Aristotle's "four causes" (material, formal, efficient, and final) and creates subcauses[32] to keep God from being the author of evil.

Beza realizes he not only is in danger of making God the author of evil, but his supralapsarian approach (people are damned before they are created) presents a potentially repugnant concept of the Creator. So he works hard to make man the efficient cause of sin, while God is the deficient cause (permissive will). He works deductively, starting with the attributes of God (He is merciful and just) and extrapolates from there, all leading to the ultimate glory of God. The glory of God means the open, public, manifestation of His attributes. If His justice is going to be manifested, God must do something just which can be observed. So He chooses to justly condemn the reprobate.[33]

No question that God's justice demands judgment of sin and

---

[31] Brian Armstrong, *Calvinism and the Amyraut Heresy* (Madison, WI: University of Wisconsin, 1969), 210-14.

[32] See Walter Kickel, *Vernunft und Offenbarung bei Theodor Beza*, Beiträge zur Geschichte und Lehre der Reformierten Kirche 25 (Lemgo, Germany: Neukirchener Verlag des Erziehungsvereins GmbH Neukirchen-Vluyn, 1967), for a full discussion of Beza's dependency on Aristotelian logic along with his own developments in addition to the "four causes": 61-68, 159-66. There were *causa prima* and *causa secunda*; direct causes and indirect (three types) causes; *causa efficiens* and *causa deficiens* (*permissio volens*, permissive will) and *causa finalis*.

[33] Kickel rightly observes, "dass das ganze System Bezas hinfällig ware, wenn zugegeben werden müsste, dass Gott seine Vorsätze ändern kann" (that the entire system of Beza was weak, since it must be allowed that God can change his decree), 166. He argues that the immutability of God precludes His changing what He has decreed.

condemnation of unbelievers. The rub comes in His decree to condemn the reprobate before He creates them. Beza realizes this decree before creation presents an image of God problem, but it is a dilemma from which he could not extricate himself. Nor could his followers, like William Perkins. Arminius would try, but he simply swung the pendulum to the opposite extreme.

William Perkins

Perkins defended his theology in a book called *A Golden Chain*. Since he was trained at the Geneva Academy under Beza, the subtitle of his book should come as no surprise:

> "A GOLDEN CHAIN: or, THE DESCRIPTION OF THEOLOGIE: Damnation, according to Gods word. A view whereof is to be seen in the Table annexed Hereunto is adioyned the order which M. Theodore Beza vsed in comforting afflicted consciences."

Like the theology of his predecessor, the most obvious feature of *A Golden Chain* is the centrality of the doctrine of double predestination.[34] Perkins defines predestination as "that by the which he hath ordained all men to a certaine and everlasting estate: that is, either to salvation or condemnation, for his owne glory."[35] Perkins quotes Augustine no less than 588 times with Chrysostom coming in second with 129 references.[36] He completely mistranslates Rom 9:22 when he says, "Moreover, every man (as Paul avereth) is unto God, as a lumpe of clauy in the potters hand: and therefore God according to his supreme authoritie 'doth make vessels of wrath. . . .'"[37]

Perkins writes about four degrees of God's love: effectual calling, justification, sanctification, and glorification.[38] Notice how

---

[34] R. T. Kendall, *Calvin and English Calvinism to 1649* (Oxford: Oxford University Press, 1979), 55.
[35] Ibid.
[36] Ibid., 54.
[37] Perkins, *Works*, 2:694.
[38] Ibid., 2:78

conveniently he slips "sanctification" into the mix, when Rom 8:30 quite obviously omits sanctification in its "golden chain." It is, in fact, conspicuous by its absence. Perhaps God does not guarantee progressive sanctification as the champions of an amillennial interpretation of Matt 24:13 presume. As Kendall observes, "The horror of horrors for a disciple of Perkins is the thought that he could be a reprobate."[39] The reprobate man is born into the world already doomed, no matter what he does in his lifetime. It does him no good to make his calling and election sure; his lot is unalterably fixed and decreed by God, whose right it is to take the lump of clay from which man is to be created and "make him a vessel of dishonor." All such interpretations of Rom 9:22 fail to observe that the verb they keep translating as active (*katērtismena*) is not active at all, but rather a middle/passive participle. God does not act upon these vessels in any way, shape, or form. By contrast God does act upon the vessels of mercy in the very next verse; He prepares these for glory.

Jacob Arminius (d. 1609)

Although Arminius studied under Theodore Beza and was an admirer of William Perkins, it is surmised that he never agreed with their understanding of the decrees of God or their resulting double predestination. Arminius's contention was that God only predestines believers. You might say he leaves off the right hand side of Beza's chart on predestination. Arminius saw four decrees:

1. God appointed Jesus Christ to be our Mediator and Redeemer;
2. God decreed to receive into favor those who repent and believe and leave in sin all unbelievers;
3. God decreed to administer in a sufficient and efficacious manner all means which were necessary for repentance and faith;

---

[39] Kendall, *Calvin*, 67.

4. God decreed to save those who He knew from all eternity would believe and persevere and to damn those He likewise knew who would not believe and persevere.[40]

Arminius remains consistent in his thesis that "election of grace is only of believers,"[41] for predestination "is the decree of the good pleasure of God in Christ, by which He determined within Himself from all eternity to justify believers."[42] If a person believed and persevered, he was elect; if he did not believe and persevere, he was not elect. From the above it can be seen that both the mainline Reformers and Arminius made perseverance a requirement for election. The difference was that the Calvinists said lack of perseverance proved the professing Christian was not elect after all, even if he did have temporary faith, while Arminius said lack of perseverance could cause a believer to lose his salvation. In either case, the one who did not persevere until the end (Matt 24:13) was not elect.

The position taken by Arminius might be argued to be more biblical in that one cannot find any biblical support for the use of the word "predestination" in connection with unbelievers. However, his understanding of faith differs very little from that of the Calvinists.[43]

The Synod of Dort (1618-1619)

The year after Arminius died his followers preserved his teachings in the Remonstrance of 1610. His five points were:

1. God has decreed Jesus Christ as the Redeemer of men and decreed to save all who believe on Him;
2. Christ died for all but only believers enjoy forgiveness of sins;
3. Man must be regenerated by the Spirit;
4. Grace is not irresistible;

---

[40] Jacobus Arminius, *Works of Arminius*, i., 589f.
[41] Ibid., iii, 583.
[42] Ibid., ii., 392.
[43] See Kendall, *Calvin*, 141-150, for a lengthy discussion of this claim.

5. Perseverance is granted through the assistance of the grace of the Holy Spirit, but whether one can fall away from life in Christ is left open.[44]

In November of 1618 the Synod of Dort began the first of 163 sessions, which resulted in what is known as the Five Points of Calvinism. Though not in the order popularly referenced under the acronym TULIP, here is the Synod's response to the Remonstrance:

1. God's eternal decree of predestination is the cause of election and reprobation, and that this decree is not based upon foreseen faith;
2. Christ died for the elect only;
3. Men by nature are unable to seek God apart from the Spirit;
4. Grace is irresistible[45];
5. The elect will surely persevere in faith to the end.[46]

Though the discussion between the Arminians and the Calvinists will probably continue unabated until Jesus comes, the point at issue here is double predestination and its perseverance in the annals of church history, especially in Western Christianity. The supralapsarian position of Beza (God decreed double predestination before the creation and fall of man) certainly was maintained by the Synod of Dort.

---

[44] The full text of the Five Articles of the Remonstrants (also the Canons of Dort) are given in Peter Y. DeJong (ed.), *Crisis in the Reformed Churches: Essays in commencement of the great Synod of Dort, 1618-19* (Grand Rapids: 1968), 207ff.

[45] It is interesting that modern day exponents of these five points explain irresistible grace as an extension of the efficacious call of God: "In addition to the outward general call to salvation which is made to everyone who hears the gospel, the Holy Spirit extends to the elect a special inward call that inevitably brings them to salvation" [David N. Steele and Curtis C. Thomas, *The Five Points of Calvinism* (Philadelphia: Presbyterian & Reformed, 1975), 18]. Augustine linked "irresistible" to the gift of perseverance.

[46] DeJong, *Crisis in the Reformed Churches*, 229-62.

The Westminster Assemblies (1643-49)

The primary focus here was not soteriological but ecclesiastical. Nevertheless, there was quite a discussion over the order of the decrees and universal versus limited atonement. Limited atonement won the day, and the wording regarding the decrees was such that either a supra- or infralapsarian could agree.[47]

Regarding double predestination, their *Confession of Faith* (III. iii, 9) says some are "predestinated unto everlasting life, and others fore-ordained to everlasting death." Those who are not elected to eternal life were passed by and ordained to dishonor and wrath to the praise of God's glorious justice. The number of both the elect and the reprobate "is so certain, and definite, that it cannot be either increased, or diminished."

Summary

From the foregoing we can see that the Reformers capitalized on both revelation and reason. Following the lead of Augustine, they combined the revelation of Scripture with the reason of the Greek philosophers, namely Plato and Aristotle. As Alister McGrath notes, "Theology was understood to be grounded upon Aristotelian philosophy, and particularly Aristotelian insights into the nature of method; later Reformed writers are better described as philosophical, rather than biblical, theologians."[48] In search of Augustine's elect, the Reformers refined the doctrine of double predestination with the syllogistic reasoning and causality of Aristotle. In this quest they have obviated any possibility of assurance of salvation before physical death, since one must persevere in the faith until the end of his life to either find out (Calvinism) or determine (Arminianism) whether he is elect or not.

---

[47] B. B. Warfield, *The Westminster Assembly and its Work* (1931), 56.
[48] Alister E. McGrath, *Christian Theology: An Introduction,* 2nd ed. (Malden, MA: Blackwell, 1997), 74.

Beza's Double Predestination[49]

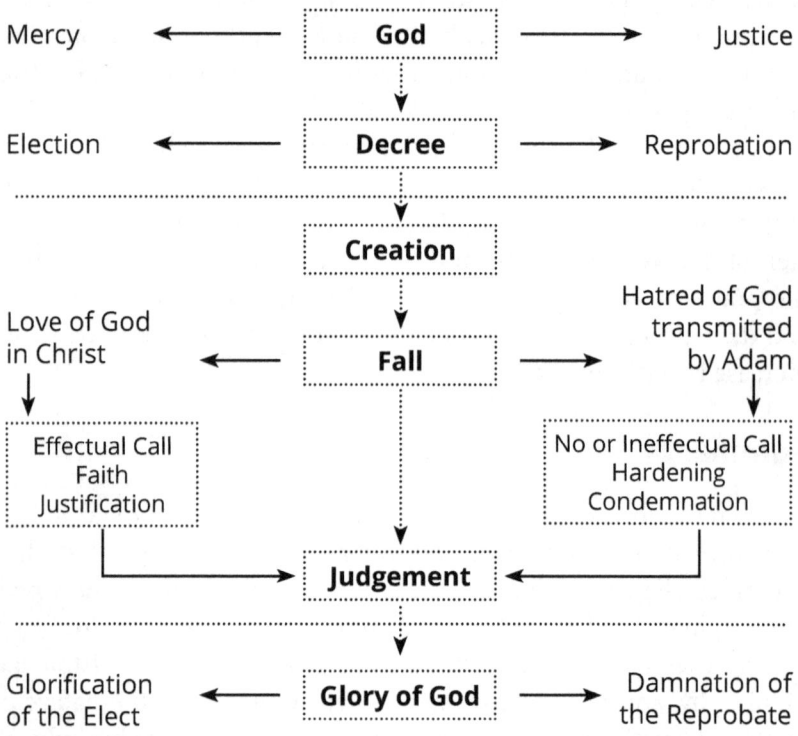

---

[49] In *Summa totius Christianismi*, Quellenverzeichnis Nr. 6. Translation mine.

Further Reading: Selected Bibliography

Books

Anderson, David R., and James S. Reitman. *Portraits of Righteousness: Free Grace Sanctification in Romans 5–8*. Liberty University Press, forthcoming.

Badger, Anthony B., *Confronting Calvinism: A Free Grace Refutation and Biblical Resolution of Radical Reformed Soteriology*, Lancaster, PA: Createspace, 2013.

Baird, S. J. *The First Adam and the Second: The Elohim Revealed in the Creation and Redemption of Man*. Philadelphia: Lindsay and Blakiston, 1860.

Baltzer, K. *Das Bundesformular*. Neukirchen: Neukirchen Verlag, 1964.

Barrett, C. K. *From First Adam to Last: A Study in Pauline Theology*. New York: Charles Scribner & Sons, 1962.

Bock, D. L. "A Theology of Luke-Acts." In *A Biblical Theology of the New Testament*, eds. R. B. Zuck and D. L. Bock, 87-166. Chicago: Moody Press, 1994.

Brown, C., ed. *The New International Dictionary of New Testament Theology*. Grand Rapids: Zondervan, 1975; Exeter: Pasternoster Press, 1975. S.v. "Death," by W. Schmithals; and "Life," by H.-G. Link.

Calderstone, P. J. *Dynastic Oracle and Suzerainty Treaty: II Samuel 7, 8-16*. Loyola House of Studies, 1966.

Carson, D. A. *Exegetical Fallacies.* 2d ed. Grand Rapids: Baker Books, 1996.
Chamberlain, W. D. *The Meaning of Repentance.* Grand Rapids: Eerdmans, 1943.
Clements, R. E. *Abraham and David.* Naperville, Ill.: Alec R. Allenson, Inc., 1967.
―――. *Abraham and David: Genesis 15 and Its Meaning for Israelite Tradition.* Studies in Biblical Theology, 2d. no.5. London: SCM Press, 1967.
Craigie, P. C. *The Book of Deuteronomy.* The New International Commentary on the Old Testament. Grand Rapids: Eerdmans, 1976.
Demarest, B. *The Cross and Salvation.* Wheaton: Crossway Books, 1997.
Dillow, Joseph. *Reign of the Servant Kings.* Hayesville, NC: Schoettle, 2002.
Driver, S. R. *A Critical and Exegetical Commentary on Deuteronomy.* Edinburgh: T. & T. Clark, 1895.
Eichrodt, W. *Theology of the Old Testament.* 2 volumes. The Old Testament Library. Translated by J. A. Baker. Philadelphia: The Westminster Press, 1961.
Elwell, W., ed. *Evangelical Dictionary of Theology.* Grand Rapids: Baker Book House, 1984. S.v. "Federal Theology," by G. N. M. Collins and "Imputation," by R. K. Johnston.
Farris, T. V. *Mighty to Save: A Study in Old Testament Soteriology.* Nashville: Broadman, 1993.
Feinberg, J. S. "Salvation in the Old Testament." In *Tradition and Testament: Essays in Honor of Charles Lee Feinberg,* 39-77. Edited by J. S. Feinberg and P. D. Feinberg. Chicago: Moody Press, 1981.
Fensham, F. C. "Father and Son as Terminology for Treaty and Covenant." In *Near Eastern Studies in Honor of W. F. Albright,* 121-35. Edited by K. Goedicke. Baltimore: Johns Hopkins Press, 1971.
―――. "Ordeal by Battle in the Ancient Near East and the Old Testament." In *Festschrift for Eduardo Volterra.*
Frankena, R. "The Vassal-Treaties of Esarhaddon and the Dating of Deuteronomy." In *Oudtestamentische Studien.* Edited by P. A. H. De Boer. Leiden: E. J. Brill, 1965.
Güterbock, H. G. *Siegel aus Bogasköy.* Berlin: Im Selbstverlage des Herausgebers, 1940.

Hillers, D. R. *Treaty Curses and the Old Testament Prophets*. Biblica at Orientalia 16. Rome: Pontifical Biblical Institute, 1964.

Hoffner, H. A., Jr. "Propaganda and Political Justification in Hittite Historiography." In *Unity and Diversity*, 49-64. Edited by Hans Goedicke and J. J. M. Roberts. Baltimore and London: The Johns Hopkins University Press, 1975.

Hodges, Z. C. *Absolutely Free!* Grand Rapids: Zondervan, 1989.

Hughes, P. E. *The True Image: The Origin and Destiny of Man in Christ*. Grand Rapids: Eerdmans, 1989.

Kaiser, W. C., Jr. *Toward an Old Testament Theology*. Grand Rapids: Zondervan, 1978.

Keil, C. F. and Delitzsch, F. *The Books of Samuel*, 2 volumes. Translated by J. Martin, Commentary on the Old Testament, 10 volumes. N.p.; reprint, Grand Rapids: Eerdmans, 1982.

Kitchen, K. A. *Ancient Orient and Old Testament*. Downers Grove: InterVarsity, 1966.

Kline, M. *The Structure of Biblical Authority*. Revised ed., Grand Rapids: Eerdmans, 1975.

Kline, M. *Treaty of the Great King*. Grand Rapids: Eerdmans, 1963.

Korosec, V. *Hethitische Staatsverträge: Ein Beitrag zu ihrer juristischen Wertung*. Leipzigerrechts wissenschaftliche Studien, 60. Leipzig: Verlag von Theodreicher, 1931.

Luther, M. *What Luther Says*. St. Louis: Concordia, 1959.

MacArthur, J. F. *The Gospel According to Jesus*. Grand Rapids: Academie Books, 1988.

McCarthy, D. J. *Old Testament Covenant: A Survey of Current Opinions*. Richmond, VA: John Knox Press, 1972.

McCarthy, D. J. *Treaty and Covenant: A Study in Form in the Ancient Oriental Documents and in the Old Testament*. Analecta Biblica, 21. Rome: Pontifical Biblical Institute, 1963.

Noth, M. "God, King, and Nation in the Old Testament." In *The Laws in the Pentateuch and Other Studies*, 145-78. Translated by D. R. Ap-Thomas. Edinburgh and London: Oliver and Boyd, 1966.

Pentecost, J. D. *Things to Come*. Grand Rapids, MI: Zondervan, 1969.

Postgate, J. N. *Neo-Assyrian Royal Grants and Decrees*. Rome: Pontifical Biblical Institute, 1969.

Price, R. *Secrets of the Dead Sea Scrolls*. Eugene, OR: Harvest House Publishers, 1966.

Pritchard, J. B., ed. *Ancient Near Eastern Texts relating to the Old Testament*. 3d ed., with supplement. Princeton University press, 1969.

Quek, S.-H. "Adam and Christ According to Paul." In *Pauline Studies*. Edited by D. A. Hagner and M. J. Harris, 67-79. Exeter: The Paternoster Press, 1980; Grand Rapids: Eerdmans, 1980.

Quell, G. "κύριος, The Old Testament Name for God." In *Theological Dictionary of the New Testament*, 1984, edition.

Sailhamer, J. H. "Is There a 'Biblical Jesus' of the Pentateuch"; and "The Theme of Salvation in the Pentateuch." In Sailhamer, J. H. *The Meaning of the Pentateuch*, 460-536; 562-601. Downers Grove, IL: InterVarsity, 2009.

Schaff, P. *History of the Christian Church*. 5th ed. Vol. 2, *Ante-Nicene Christianity*. N.p.: Charles Scribner's Sons, 1910; reprint, Grand Rapids: Eerdmans, 1967.

Scroggs, R. *The Last Adam: A Study in Pauline Anthropology*. Philadelphia: Fortress Press, 1966.

Shank, R. *Elect in the Son*. Springfield, MO: Westcott, 1970.

―――. *Life in the Son*. Springfield, MO: Westcott, 1961.

Spurgeon, C. H. *Spurgeon's Expository Encyclopedia*. Vol. 7. Grand Rapids: Baker, 1978.

Steinmetzer, F. X. *Die babylonischen Kudurru (Grenzsteine) als Urkudnenform*. Paderborn: Verlag von Ferdinand Schöningh, 1922.

Thompson, J. A. *Deuteronomy: An Introduction and Commentary*. Tyndale Old Testament Commentaries. InterVarsity, 1974.

Thompson, J. A. *The Ancient Near Eastern Treaties and the Old Testament*. London: Tyndale, 1964.

Tozer, A. W. *I Call It Heresy!* Harrisburg, PA: Christian Publications, 1974.

Weinfeld, M. *Deuteronomy and the Deuteronomic School*. Oxford: Clarendon Press, 1972.

Wiseman, D. J. *The Alalakh Tablets*. London: The British Institute of Archaeology at Ankara, 1953.

Woolf, B. L. *Reformation Writings of Martin Luther*. London: Lutterworth Press, 1952.

Wright, G. E. "The Lawsuit of God: A Form-Critical Study of Deuteronomy

32." In *Israel's Prophetic Heritage*. Edited by B. W. Anderson and W. Harrelson. New York: Harper and Row , 1962.

Periodicals

Allis, O. T. "Thy Throne, O God, is for Ever and Ever." *Princeton Theological Review* 21 (1923): 237-39.

Barrosse, T. "Death and Sin in Saint Paul's Epistle to the Romans." *Catholic Biblical Quarterly* 15 (1953): 438-59.

Ben-Barak, Z. "Meribaal and the System of Land Grants in Ancient Israel," *Biblica* 62 (January 1981): 73-91.

Best, E. "Dead in Trespasses and Sins (Eph. 2.1)." *Journal for the Study of the New Testament* 13 (1981): 9-25.

Black, C. C. II. "Pauline Perspectives on Death in Romans 5-8." *Journal of Biblical Literature* 103 (1984): 413-33.

Braswell, J. P. "The Blessing of Abraham versus the Curse of the Law: Another Look at Gal 3:10-13." *Westminster Theological Journal* 53 (1991): 73-91.

Clines, D. J. A. "The Psalms and the King." *Theological Student's Fellowship Bulletin* 71 (Spring 1975): 1-6.

Combrink, H. J. B. "Some Thoughts on the Old Testament Citations in the Epistle to the Hebrews." *Neotestamentica* 5 (1971): 22-36.

Cooke, G. "The Israelite King as Son of God." *Zeitschrift für die alttestamentiche Wissenschaft* 73 (161): 202-25.

Daniel Lee. "A Reassessment of the Meaning of the Abrahamic Covenant for Evangelical Theology." *Ouodibet Journal* vol. 6 no.3 (July – September 2014).

Danker, F. W. "Romans 5:12: Sin Under Law." *New Testament Studies* 14 (1968): 424-39.

Dorsey, D. A. "The Law of Moses and the Christian: A Compromise." *Journal of the Evangelical Theological Society* 34 (September 1991); 321- 34.

Fensham, F. C. "Common Trends in Curses of the Near Eastern Treaties and Kudurru Inscriptions compared with Maledictions of Amos and Isaiah." *Zeitshcrift für die alttestamentliche Wissenschaft* 75 (1963): 155-75.

————. "Maledictions and Benediction in Ancient Near Eastern Vassal-Treaties and the Old Testament." *Zeitschrift für die alttestamentliche Wissenschaft* 74 (1962): 1-9.

Fitzmyer J. "ἐφ' ᾧ in Romans 5.12," *New Testament Studies* 39 (1993): 321-39.

Gordis, R. "The 'Begotten' Messiah in the Qumran Scrolls." *Vetus Testamentum* 7 (1957): 191-94.

Gerstenberger, E. "Covenant and Commandment." *Journal of Biblical Literature* 84 (1965): 33-51.

Harner, P. B. "Exodus, Sinai, and Hittite Prologues." *Journal of Biblical Literature* 85 (1966): 233-36.

Hill, A. E. "The Ebal Ceremony as Hebrew Land Grant?" *Journal of the Evangelical Theological Society* 31 (December 1988): 399-406.

Hooker, M. D. "Adam in Romans 1." *New Testament Studies* 6 (1960): 297-306.

Huffmon, H. B. "The Treaty Background of Hebrew YADA'." *Bulletin of the American Schools of Oriental Research* 181 (1966): 31-37.

Johnson, S. L. Jr. "Romans 5:12—An Exercise in Exegesis and Theology" In *New Dimensions in New Testament Study*, ed. R. N. Longenecker and M.C. Tenney, 298-316. Grand Rapids: Zondervan, 1974.

Jones, B. W. "Acts 13:33-37: A Pesher on II Samuel 7." *Journal of Biblical Literature* 87 (Spring 1987): 321-27.

Kaiser, W. C., Jr. "The Old Promise and the New Covenant: Jeremiah 31:31-34." *Journal of the Evangelical Theological Society* 15 (1972): 11-23.

Katz, P. "The Quotations from Deuteronomy in Hebrews." *Zeitschrift für die neutestamentliche Wissenschaft* 49 (1958): 213-23.

Kaufman, S. A. "The Structure of the Deuteronomic Law." *Maarav* 1/2 (1978-79): 105-58.

Korosec, V. "The Warfare of the Hittites—From the Legal Point of View." *Iraq* 25 (1963): 159-66.

Loewenstamm, S. E. "The Divine Grants of Land to the Patriarchs." *Journal of the American Oriental Society* 91.4 (1971): 509-10.

Lopez, Rene, "Israelite Covenants in the Light of Ancient Near Eastern Covenants," *CTS Journal* 9 (Fall 2003): 93.

McCarthy, D. J. "Covenant in the Old Testament: Present State of Inquiry." *Catholic Biblical Quarterly* 27 (1965): 217-41.

———. "Notes on the Love of God in Deuteronomy and the Father-Son Relationship Between Yahweh and Israel." *Catholic Biblical Quarterly* 27 (1965): 144-47.

———. "Three Covenants in Genesis." *Catholic Biblical Quarterly* 26 (1964): 179-89.

Mendenhall, G. E. "Ancient Oriental and Biblical Law." *Biblical Archaeologist* 17 (May 1954): 50-76.

———. "Covenant Forms in Israelite Tradition." *Biblical Archaeologist* 17 (September 1954): 50-76.

Milne, D. J. W. "Genesis 3 in the Letter to the Romans." *Reformed Theological Review* 39 (1980): 10-18.

Muilenburg, J. "The Form and Structure of the Covenantal Formulations." Essays In Honor of Miller Burrows, reprinted from *Vetus Testamentum* 13 (1963): 380-89.

Parunak, H. V. "A Semantic Survey of *niham*." *Biblica* 56 (1975): 512-32.

Thompson, J. A. "Covenant Patterns in the Ancient Near East and Their Significance for Biblical Studies." *Reformed Theological Review* 18.3 (October 1959): 65-75.

———. "The Significance of the Near Eastern Treaty Pattern." *Tyndale House Bulletin* (1963): 1-6.

Tucker, G. M. "Covenant Forms and Contract Forms." *Vetus Testamentum* 15 (1965): 487-503.

Weaver, D. "The Exegesis of Romans 5:12 among the Greek Fathers and Its Implication for the Doctrine of Original Sin: The 5th-12th Centuries (Part 2)." *St. Vladimir's Theological Quarterly* 29 (1985): 133-59.

———. "The Exegesis of Romans 5:12 among the Greek Fathers and Its Implication for the Doctrine of Original Sin: The 5th-12th Centuries (Part 3)." *St. Vladimir's Theological Quarterly* 29 (1985): 231-57.

Wedderburn, A. J. M. "The Theological Structure of Romans 5:12." *New Testament Studies* 19 (1973): 332-54.

Weinfeld, M. "Berit-Covenant vs. Obligation." *Biblica* 56 (1975): 120-28.

———. "Covenant Terminology in the Ancient Near East and Its Influence on the West." *Journal of the American Oriental Society* 93 (1973): 190-99.

———. "Deuteronomy—The Present State of Inquiry." *Journal of Biblical Literature* 86 (1967): 249-62.

———. "The Covenant of Grant in the Old Testament and the Ancient Near East." *Journal of the American Oriental Society* 90 (1970): 184-203.

Wiseman, D. J. "Abban and Alalah." *Journal of Cuneiform Studies* 12 (1958): 124-29.

———. "The Vassal-Treaties of Esarhaddon." *Iraq* 20 (1958): 1-99 + 53 (plates).

Yadin, Y. "A Midrash on 2 Sam. vii and Ps. 1-11 (4QFlorilegium)." *Israel Exploration Journal* 9 (1959): 95-98.

Unpublished Materials

Merrill, E. H., interview by author, 15 March 1994, Dallas Theological Seminary, Dallas.

Shank, R., interview by author, 7 April 1976, Conroe, Texas.

Weinfeld, M., interview by author, 24 February 1998, Hebrew University, Jerusalem.

Wilkin, R. N. "Repentance as a Condition for Salvation in the New Testament." Th.D. diss., Dallas Theological Seminary, 1985.

Subject-Author Index

A
abiding, 190, 202, 223, 249
ability, 8, 42, 44, 46, 47, 49, 50, 51, 52, 56, 124, 196, 231, 250, 304, 382
Abraham, 3, 27, 57, 61, 62, 67, 70, 73, 84, 138, 146-150, 154, 161, 163, 306, 358, 370, 371, 372, 376, 378, 404, 407
Abrahamic Covenant, 61, 146, 148, 150, 153, 407
accountability, 50, 289, 290, 293, 294, 296, 336
Adam, 3, 34, 35, 37-42, 49, 56-59, 62, 67, 68, 71, 87, 88, 103, 115, 190, 195, 290, 293, 319, 334, 337, 338, 348, 374, 394, 395, 402, 403, 406, 408
Alexander, Archibald, 174, 175
amillennial, 1, 9, 14, 20, 22, 23, 24, 28, 29, 214, 217, 232, 258, 341, 398
Amyraldianism, 86
Amyraut, Moise, 86, 89, 93, 94, 396

anger, 65, 75, 78, 80, 156, 158, 304, 336, 394
anthropology, 33, 103
antinomianism, 17, 284
apostasy, 26, 119, 136, 152, 200, 385, 386
Apostolic Fathers, 76, 128
Aquinas, Thomas, 210, 235, 236, 389, 392, 393
Aristotle, 375, 376, 384, 389, 390, 391, 392, 393, 395, 396, 401
Arminian, vii, xi, xiii, 24, 26, 31, 35, 51, 104, 123, 216, 231, 250, 291, 302
Arminius, Jacob, 24, 91, 220, 231, 397, 398, 399
Assurance, 12, 13, 19-22, 24, 28, 29, 104, 106-109, 143, 168, 171, 172, 174, 208-228, 258-260, 344, 390, 395, 401,
atonement, 35, 66, 75, 76, 80, 82, 86, 87, 90, 91, 92, 93, 94, 95, 98, 103, 128, 193, 218, 233, 258, 395, 401

Augustine, 1, 3-23, 25, 27, 28, 29, 31, 32, 42, 43, 44, 46, 51, 87, 88, 89, 91, 100, 101, 104, 105, 118, 128-131, 133, 145, 168, 172, 208, 209, 211, 212, 214, 217, 219, 232-236, 243, 249, 250, 290, 314, 325-328, 333, 378-389, 393, 394, 395, 397, 400, 401

B

Babylon, Babylonian, 58, 67 146, 147, 149, 155, 375

baptism, 9, 42, 88, 100, 103, 118, 119, 128, 129, 130, 131, 144, 145, 155, 160, 161, 162, 189, 232, 233, 234, 235, 236, 237, 238, 239, 240, 241, 242, 243, 244, 250, 256, 320, 321, 385

baptismal regeneration, 88, 120, 232, 235, 237, 239, 241, 242, 256

belief, 2, 16, 101, 130, 131, 136, 137, 161, 162, 164, 167, 175, 179, 181-185, 189, 211, 222, 234, 247, 271, 299, 314, 343, 344, 358

believe, 11, 12, 19, 21, 32, 34, 45, 46, 48, 59, 67, 68, 72, 88, 92, 95, 96, 97, 98, 104, 120-124, 127, 130, 133 -135, 137, 143, 144, 162-164, 166, 167, 169, 172, 173, 175, 176, 179, 180, 182, 184, 185, 186, 188, 191-194, 196, 203, 209-211, 214, 215, 222, 223, 225-228, 230, 231, 234, 235, 238-241, 245, 251, 252, 254, 255, 256, 271, 272, 276-278, 280, 288, 292, 294, 299, 302, 326, 332, 334, 344, 345, 346, 355-359, 370, 381, 398, 399

believer, 12, 13, 21-24, 28, 30, 36, 48, 49, 82, 92, 97, 100, 105, 106, 109, 114, 115, 116, 118, 119, 121, 122, 137, 141, 142, 143, 145, 157, 163, 188, 195-198, 203-207, 209, 211, 212, 215, 220, 222, 223, 224, 227, 242, 243, 246, 249, 258, 259, 275, 276, 283-286, 288, 318, 337, 360, 361, 365, 371, 373, 394, 399

Berkhof, L., 101, 173, 174, 178, 242

Beza, Theodore, 23, 86, 89, 90, 91, 93, 218, 219, 231, 258, 311, 312, 325, 344, 388, 390, 395, 396, 397, 398, 400, 402

biblical theology, 14, 28, 56, 252, 253, 355, 356, 360

blessing, 61, 62, 63, 69, 111, 114, 123, 161, 162, 186, 392

blood, 59, 62, 67, 68, 77, 81, 95, 131, 158, 159, 175, 197, 245, 290, 296, 333, 353, 357

Bock, D. L., 60, 61, 72, 114, 126, 127, 142, 181, 258, 264, 265, 266, 267, 268, 271, 403

body, 4, 6, 9, 26, 33, 34, 39, 42, 47, 69, 70, 83, 87, 115, 163, 188, 275, 276, 279, 280, 286,

Subject-Author Index

288, 332, 333, 334, 365, 373, 374, 376, 377, 380, 386
born again, 87, 118, 120, 121, 129, 141, 167, 182, 188, 222, 228, 233, 235, 239, 244, 245, 246, 249, 275, 280, 286, 354, 362, 363

C

Cain, 60
call upon, 231, 269, 271, 359
calling, 19, 24, 118, 120, 121, 123, 124, 126, 129, 155, 159, 160, 163, 203, 213, 214, 216, 226, 233, 239, 255, 257, 291, 293, 306, 359, 363, 388, 397, 398
Calvin, 1, 14, 15, 16, 17, 18, 19, 20, 21, 22, 23, 25, 28, 29, 86, 89, 91, 92, 93, 94, 98, 106, 107, 114, 127, 131, 132, 133, 139, 145, 167, 168, 171, 211-219, 221, 231, 240, 258, 304, 310, 311, 312, 325, 332, 385, 386, 394-399
Calvinist(s), 23, 30, 31, 35, 46, 51, 52, 54, 86, 97, 107, 171, 219, 220, 232, 258, 325, 348, 396, 399, 400
carnal, 4, 5, 20, 47, 48, 49, 200, 214, 284
Cassian, John, 45, 46, 327, 388
Catechism, 102, 107, 132, 170, 237
Chafer, Lewis Sperry, 31, 86, 126, 132, 173, 198, 209, 230, 250-252, 321

choice, 1, 122, 251, 252, 294, 297, 300, 301, 303, 322, 323, 346
chosen, 28, 51, 58, 61, 218, 237, 253, 254, 306, 320, 321, 322, 325, 340, 394
commitment, 132, 167, 168, 170, 171, 175, 176, 177, 178, 179, 260, 272, 273, 274, 283, 284
condemnation, 41, 87, 88, 97, 115, 158, 182, 205, 207, 290, 329, 336, 337, 338, 367, 387, 397
condition, 9, 27, 29, 30, 41, 84, 85, 92, 93, 106, 116, 128, 132, 134, 143, 144, 149, 154, 165, 178, 200-203, 242, 248, 284, 367, 382
confession, 13, 66, 107, 119, 130-132, 168-170, 193, 194, 197, 200, 221, 234, 237, 240, 241, 325, 356, 358, 359, 401
conscience, 49, 56, 236, 309
contrition, 119, 131, 132
conversion, 44, 105, 119, 123, 128, 130, 132, 133, 134, 177, 189, 229, 233, 235, 241, 242, 249, 255, 303, 378, 380
council, 15, 16, 17, 28, 46, 101, 102, 236, 361, 389
Covenant, 120, 121, 145, 146, 148, 149, 150, 153, 154, 163, 239, 246, 264, 404, 405, 408, 409
covenantal, 152, 240

crucified, 56, 89, 160, 162, 266, 271, 277, 282, 283, 357
Cursed Generation, 158
curses, 27, 64, 79, 146, 147, 151, 163

D
Davidic, 61, 72, 146, 149, 150, 163, 263, 266, 271
day of the Lord, 2, 159, 318
death, 9, 10, 12, 13, 16, 17, 23, 28, 34, 35, 36, 38, 39, 40, 41, 42, 59, 65, 66, 67, 69, 70, 74, 79, 80, 81, 82, 85, 87, 89, 90, 92, 95, 96, 98, 100, 101, 103, 113, 119, 130, 144, 151, 156, 188, 190, 191, 193, 194-197, 199, 202, 208, 218, 226, 231, 237, 260, 268, 271, 274, 277, 278, 280, 282, 284, 287, 288, 290, 293, 312, 318, 320, 324, 332, 333, 335-337, 339, 343, 353, 357, 358, 360, 377, 384, 389, 390, 394, 395, 401
dedication, 272-274, 276, 278, 279, 281, 283, 285
deliver, 42, 60, 71, 263, 345, 360
deliverance, 10, 35, 62, 144, 156, 272, 282, 353, 354, 358, 360
deliverer, 57, 59
Demarest, Bruce, 17, 102-104, 107, 118, 124, 126, 129, 132-134, 141, 174, 175, 176, 234, 253, 288, 404

depravity, 8, 33, 46, 50, 51, 53, 54, 56, 58, 122, 231, 235, 251, 252, 357, 384
destroy, 9, 27, 31, 153, 202, 363
destruction, 26, 27, 210, 305, 308, 309, 311, 312, 314, 316-319
determinism, 298, 300, 301, 302, 309, 310, 311, 314, 319, 320, 322, 323, 327
Dillow, Joseph, 18, 19, 21, 22, 24, 172, 177, 213, 216, 217, 219, 404
discipleship, 199, 201, 202, 203, 283
dispensationalism, 3, 31, 67, 114, 230, 251, 252, 256, 271
Divine Sovereignty, 297, 299, 301, 303, 305, 307, 309, 311, 313, 315, 317, 319, 321, 322, 323
Dortian, 30, 31, 86, 97, 98, 107, 231, 307, 396
double predestination, 46, 88, 89, 90, 91, 311, 312, 314, 316, 317, 325, 326, 327, 348, 349, 385, 388, 389, 390, 394, 395, 397, 398, 400, 401
drawing, 27, 53, 253, 254

E
ears to hear, 292
elect, 9, 10, 11-14, 17, 18, 19, 20, 21, 23, 24, 25, 29, 35, 52, 54, 77, 86, 89, 90-98, 101, 104, 120, 122, 129, 130, 131, 208,

209, 212-221, 224, 227, 234, 238, 239, 255, 256, 258, 302, 305, 306, 311, 316, 321, 325, 326, 327, 333, 339, 385, 386, 387, 390, 394, 395, 396, 399, 400, 401
election, 11, 18, 22, 24, 40, 52, 93, 121, 124, 126, 213, 216, 217, 219, 232, 239, 302, 304, 306, 309, 311, 320, 321, 387, 390, 394, 395, 398, 399, 400
endurance, 316
endure, 29, 30, 63, 159, 258, 353, 371
enthronement, 71
eternal destiny, 192, 208, 211, 307, 316
eternal life, 11, 13, 14, 36, 63, 68, 69, 92, 100, 103, 108, 110, 113, 114, 117, 121, 137, 138, 143, 157, 164, 184, 185, 190, 196, 223, 224, 225, 226, 228, 246, 259, 261, 288, 289, 312, 338, 342, 344, 354, 355, 356, 357, 364, 394, 401
eternal security, 24, 31, 97, 124, 167, 192, 193, 194, 195, 196, 197, 198, 199, 202, 203, 205, 208, 209, 216, 364
evidence, 2, 24, 25, 26, 32, 53, 67, 68, 95, 108, 138, 147, 177, 181, 189, 196, 201, 216, 217, 222, 223, 226, 230, 259, 260, 263, 293, 314, 354, 355, 361, 391

evil, 34, 38, 44, 54, 56, 57, 69, 87, 89, 108, 123, 239, 279, 280, 281, 287, 301, 302, 308, 310, 311, 324, 327, 344, 345, 346, 348, 360, 366, 376, 377, 380, 386, 388, 396
Exegesis, 39, 61, 408, 409
expiation, 75, 218

F
faith, 6, 11, 12-18, 20-29, 45, 57, 62, 63, 68, 77, 84, 87, 88, 92, 93, 95, 101, 104-110, 114, 115, 117, 119, 120-123, 126, 127, 128, 130, 131-136, 138, 142, 143, 150, 154, 156, 160, 163-190, 200, 203, 204, 209-221, 226, 227, 231-242, 244, 247, 249, 250, 251, 252, 254, 255, 256, 258, 259, 261, 272, 274, 278, 281, 282, 289, 293, 294, 295, 296, 299, 325, 329, 337, 353, 358, 360, 361, 362, 368-374, 381, 384, 395, 398, 399, 400, 401
faithfulness, 4, 29, 138, 149, 150, 153, 227, 296
fatalism, 87, 88
federal headship, 36, 41
fellowship, 27, 34, 37, 66, 67, 82, 135, 136, 137, 139, 143, 144, 153, 154, 159, 161, 162, 163, 164, 165, 186, 187, 199, 200, 202, 203, 204, 205, 225, 347, 377

flesh, 2, 4, 10, 43, 44, 47, 49, 53, 70, 100, 101, 103, 108, 114, 131, 175, 200, 219, 245, 317, 318, 335, 337, 343, 387
foreknowledge, 92, 302, 321, 322, 387
forensic, 8, 9, 14, 16, 22, 41, 82, 105, 107, 111, 112, 114
forgiveness, 65, 92, 103, 104, 115, 120, 123, 129, 132, 135, 169, 200, 211, 234, 237, 239, 240, 325, 367, 399
Fredriksen, Paula, 4, 6
free gift, 14, 143, 201, 203, 228, 296, 336, 337, 342, 364
free grace, vii, ix, xi, xii, xiii, xiv, xv, 19, 41, 100, 123, 143, 170, 172, 178, 179, 221, 222, 223, 259, 260, 284
Free Will, 88, 302
fruit, 2, 18, 20, 23, 24, 28, 108, 127, 128, 131, 133, 134, 136, 142, 144, 145, 162, 212, 214, 215, 220, 221, 222, 223, 226, 227, 231, 233, 258, 260, 333, 361, 372, 395

G

generation, 26, 56, 62, 63, 145, 149, 150, 151, 153, 154, 155, 156, 157, 158, 159, 160, 161, 162, 163, 165, 298, 299, 336, 342
Gentile(s), 47, 49, 61, 63, 83, 126, 155, 161, 162, 186, 263, 306, 309, 372
Gerstner, J., 67, 132, 251, 252, 256
gifts, 18, 79, 148, 203, 237, 284, 306, 362, 368
glorification, 33, 118, 119, 121, 122, 124, 126, 129, 233, 397
glorified body, glorified, 39, 48, 70, 121, 122, 138,
God, 3, 7-11, 13, 14, 16, 17, 19, 21, 23, 25, 26, 27, 29, 33-39, 42-70, 74-83, 87-109, 112-127, 129, 133-138, 140-164, 166, 168, 169, 170, 173, 175, 176, 179, 180, 182, 188-200, 203-207, 210-341, 344-348, 351, 356, 357, 358, 363, 364, 365, 366, 367, 370, 371, 372, 373, 374, 377, 378, 380-390, 393, 394, 395, 396, 397, 398, 399, 400, 401, 402, 405, 406, 407, 408
God the Father, 80, 192, 196, 271, 321
gospel, 10, 35, 42, 49, 59, 61, 62, 64, 68, 92, 105, 117, 121, 126, 128, 134, 135, 136, 156, 163, 167, 169, 173, 183, 186, 210, 225, 233, 252, 253, 255, 284, 287, 291, 294, 297, 318, 328, 343, 344, 400
Gottschalk, 46, 91, 389
Grace, 1, 11, 19, 52, 56, 59, 63, 68, 77, 86, 89, 125, 143, 172, 178, 203, 204, 221, 223, 226, 229, 231, 232, 234, 247, 251,

253, 259, 385, 386, 393, 399, 400, 403
grant, 44, 138, 146, 147, 149, 150, 151, 153, 154, 155, 163
Great White Throne, 54, 113, 156, 157, 283, 357
guilt, 42, 44, 75, 76, 82, 88, 104, 118, 160, 290

H

hamartiology, 33
hardening, 49, 159, 307, 309
heart, 26, 36, 40, 49, 51, 52, 54, 61, 62, 70, 78, 80, 85, 117, 120, 121, 122, 130, 142, 148, 153, 154, 169, 179, 180, 183, 187, 189, 206, 210, 219, 234, 236, 246, 250, 285, 287, 307, 308, 309, 310, 316, 339, 355, 358, 359, 372, 387
heathen, 65, 287, 291, 294
heaven, xiii, 2-8, 9, 12, 13-17, 23, 26-30, 33, 47, 56, 58, 63, 68, 69, 74, 87-91, 93-95, 97, 100, 101, 102, 106, 112, 116, 122, 123, 125, 129, 138, 140, 144, 145, 156, 160, 190, 194, 200, 201, 208, 209, 217, 218, 224, 226, 233, 236, 237, 258, 259, 264, 268, 274, 284, 288, 289, 290, 292, 294, 318, 333, 339, 343, 353-358, 360, 361, 363, 364, 365, 367, 369, 370, 377, 385, 387, 394
Hebrew, 27, 60, 61, 65, 70, 72, 75, 77, 138, 147, 153, 162, 202, 340, 345, 378, 408, 410
hell, 25, 26, 27, 33, 70, 87, 88, 89, 90, 91, 156, 160, 192, 193, 218, 237, 239, 274, 290, 310, 314, 325, 327, 328, 335, 336, 339, 343, 363, 364, 370, 387
hermeneutical circle, 180, 343, 355, 360, 361, 362, 374
high priest, 76, 78, 186, 266, 267, 268
Historical Theology, 31, 43, 209, 243, 250, 256, 326
Hodge, Charles, 24, 174, 175, 216, 317
Hodges, Z. C., 77, 137, 157, 167, 171, 173, 174, 175, 182, 183, 184, 222, 223, 224, 289, 365, 405
holiness, 14, 24, 45, 57, 58, 84, 120, 132, 200, 216, 276
holy, 18, 25, 29, 39, 45, 48, 52, 61, 64, 66, 70, 77, 78, 83, 106, 108, 109, 114, 115, 117, 119, 120, 121, 122, 138, 144, 145, 159, 160-164, 193, 198, 199, 212, 221, 226, 237-241, 243, 246, 252, 255, 257, 259, 262, 265, 266, 269, 282, 291, 292, 293, 319, 320, 321, 326, 334, 335, 336, 379, 383, 386, 400
Holy Spirit, 18, 25, 29, 39, 48, 52, 61, 70, 83, 106, 108, 109, 114, 115, 117, 119, 120, 121,

122, 138, 144, 145, 159, 160-164, 193, 198, 199, 212, 221, 226, 237, 238, 239, 240, 243, 246, 252, 255, 257, 259, 262, 265, 266, 269, 282, 291, 292, 293, 319, 321, 334, 335, 336, 386, 400

human nature, 34

humanity, 3, 34, 35, 42, 44, 82, 349, 372

I

identity, 57, 65, 115, 155, 263, 294, 338, 385

Immortality, 377

Imputation, 38, 404

Inability, 46

Indeterminism, 298

infant(s), 9, 39, 87, 88, 100, 118, 120, 129, 130, 131, 233, 234, 235, 237-242, 244, 250, 256, 287, 288, 290, 342, 343

infralapsarianism, 91

infusion, 17, 102, 115, 116

inheritance, 138, 201, 202, 296, 317, 318, 360

J

Jesus Christ, 14, 44, 59, 74, 75, 77, 79, 81, 83, 85, 87, 89, 91, 93, 95, 97, 113, 128, 132, 133, 135, 160, 164, 189, 197, 228, 241, 244, 271, 272, 274, 291, 296, 318, 344, 359, 366, 369, 390, 398, 399

Jewish, 4, 10, 57, 64, 72, 73, 113, 151, 154, 157, 158, 159, 161, 162, 165, 245, 254, 266, 267, 270, 306, 332, 376, 391

John the Baptist, 134, 144, 145, 151, 158, 159, 160, 162, 163, 240, 246

judgment, 19, 20, 27, 48, 54, 56, 57, 79, 93, 108, 112, 113, 135, 153, 154, 156, 157, 158, 160, 161, 162, 199, 202, 203, 213, 214, 226, 270, 271, 287, 292, 294, 307, 330, 336, 337, 356, 357, 366, 367, 368, 369, 387, 396

Judgment Seat of Christ, 113, 156, 157, 202, 203, 270, 275, 283, 353, 364, 366, 367, 368, 369

justification, justify, 8, 9, 13-18, 20, 22, 23, 24, 33, 50, 51, 63, 82, 83, 99, 100, 101, 102, 104, 105-124, 126-131, 133, 156, 165, 168, 172, 176, 177, 208, 211, 212, 214, 216, 232, 233, 234, 236, 237, 239, 240, 242, 272, 273, 275, 281, 282, 296, 336, 337, 338, 356, 358, 371, 372, 389, 394, 397, 399

K

Kendall, R.T., 21, 23, 168, 170, 171, 177, 178, 215, 218, 220, 231, 258, 397-399

kingdom, 2, 4, 7, 28, 51, 52, 54, 101, 108, 114, 129, 134, 140, 144, 145, 160, 163, 201, 205, 233, 235, 243, 253, 268, 275,

278, 279, 285, 286, 288, 289, 292, 302, 303, 305, 306, 319, 340, 341, 353, 369, 375

L

Ladd, George Eldon, 76, 78, 81, 111, 112, 113, 115, 132, 166

law, 6, 47, 49, 52, 62, 63, 80, 81, 103, 112, 144, 154, 164, 171, 172, 203, 211, 220, 222, 273, 274, 298, 299, 300, 303, 309, 328, 364, 366

legalism, 66, 205, 207, 220

liberty, ix, 205, 207, 366, 388

license, 15, 16, 104, 107, 212

light received, 292, 293, 296

Light Received, 291

Lordship of Christ, 132, 261

lordship salvation, 125, 171, 258, 259, 260, 261

love of God, 77, 83, 101, 196, 249, 302, 306, 348, 388, 395

Luther, Martin, 8, 9, 14, 16, 22, 92, 105, 106, 107, 115, 119, 120, 131, 132, 139, 145, 169, 210, 211, 237, 238, 360, 361, 370, 394, 405, 406

Lutheran theology, 171

M

MacArthur, John, 107, 125, 126, 167, 170, 171, 173, 174, 177, 215, 220, 221, 222, 405

maturity, 2, 17, 84, 121, 371, 372

McKnight, S., 25, 26, 27, 28, 30, 329

Melanchthon, Philipp, 9, 14, 106, 168, 169, 237

Mercy Seat, 64, 76, 77

Messiah, 59, 60, 68, 71, 72, 134, 150, 159, 160, 161-163, 183, 188, 246, 261-269, 271, 291, 292, 294, 330, 408

messianism, 262

millennium, 2-5, 10, 12, 27, 29, 30, 85, 157, 266, 289, 340, 342, 343, 349

monergism, 239, 250

moral, 17, 45, 66, 102, 103, 104, 123, 201, 203, 231, 250, 252, 270, 298, 301, 304, 309, 311, 337, 348, 372, 382

mortal, 16, 34, 70, 101, 119, 279, 385

Mosaic Covenant, 146, 149, 150, 153, 154, 162, 163

Moses, 26, 57, 64, 66, 72, 146, 164, 305, 307, 309, 381, 396, 407

Murray, J., 24, 216, 241, 247, 281, 282

mysticism, mystical 84, 85, 378, 379, 383, 385

N

natural, ix, 15, 47, 48, 50, 238, 279, 393

Nicodemus, 182, 188, 189

non-elect, 18, 23, 95, 234, 326, 327

O

obedience, obey, 34, 56, 58, 64, 81, 125, 148, 149, 150, 153, 168-172, 174-179, 187, 188, 218, 220, 221, 224, 238, 277, 279, 284, 303, 304, 318, 320, 346

Old Man, 276, 277, 278, 282

omnipotence, 196, 345, 393

ontology, 301, 321

ordo salutis, x, 118, 121, 123, 124, 125, 127, 129, 231, 233, 235, 241, 242, 247, 250, 251, 256, 322

Origen, 3, 5, 326, 327, 377, 378

original sin, 39, 40, 41, 87, 88, 118, 234, 290, 385, 386

P

Paul, 9, 18, 19, 21, 24, 36, 38, 39, 41, 46-49, 52, 53, 61-64, 66, 75, 76, 77, 80, 81, 83, 84, 85, 99, 108, 110-113, 117, 126, 129, 135, 156, 157, 164, 171-173, 175-177, 198, 201, 203, 213, 215, 216, 227, 253, 272, 280, 284, 290, 306, 308-313, 317, 322, 326, 334, 337, 338, 344, 354, 356, 358, 359, 360, 361, 370-372, 387, 390, 397, 406, 407

Pauline, 113, 157, 334, 403, 406, 407

Pelagianism, Pelagius, 39, 42-46, 51, 103, 235, 250, 251, 319, 388

penalty, 33, 37, 45, 66, 95, 96, 118, 180, 193, 194, 272, 324, 357, 358, 359

penance, 16, 101, 119, 130, 131, 132, 139

Pentecost, 145, 149, 154, 160, 163, 164, 246, 321, 405

perfection, 101, 148, 371, 377

Perkins, William, 23, 24, 90, 91, 219, 220, 231, 325, 397, 398

perseverance, vii, viii, xiv, 11, 12, 13, 18, 22-25, 31, 98, 107, 123, 124, 126, 172, 195, 214, 216, 217, 220, 227, 232, 260, 385-387, 399, 400

personal sin, 36, 39, 41, 290

persuasion, persuade, 23, 54, 163, 175, 177, 180, 185, 220, 239, 240, 252-254, 303, 314, 319, 320

Plato, 4, 44, 376, 377, 382-384, 389, 390, 393, 395, 401

Plotinus, 378-380, 382, 383, 384, 386, 387

position, 3, 9, 13, 23, 29, 44, 77, 84, 85, 89, 92, 93, 106, 107, 116, 123-125, 133, 134, 170, 171, 178, 184, 200, 201, 203, 211, 220, 222, 239, 241, 247, 260, 268, 270, 274, 276-278, 281, 284-286, 299, 314, 334, 367, 392, 399, 400

post-apostolic, 105, 129, 131

power of sin, 33, 66, 272, 357, 358

predestination, 46, 52, 87, 89, 91, 92, 93, 129, 168, 218, 233, 302, 311, 314, 376, 385, 386, 387, 388, 389, 390, 394, 395, 397, 398, 399, 400
premillennialism, premillennial, ix, xii, xiii, 1, 2, 3, 10, 12, 14, 28, 149, 217, 353, 385
preservation, 120, 121, 122, 195, 196
promise, 6, 29, 59-62, 71, 73, 132, 136, 148, 149, 150, 157, 190, 210, 211, 293, 296, 347, 377
promises of God, 223
propitiation, 75, 76, 77, 80, 92, 95, 96, 102, 197, 275
Protestant(ism), 22, 23, 99, 126, 138, 166, 217, 221, 235, 238, 251, 329
psalms, 71, 72, 407
punishment, 26, 45, 57, 66, 87, 158, 289, 318, 338, 339, 346
Puritan, 23, 170, 171, 220, 221, 258

Q

Qumran, 155, 262, 263, 264, 408

R

Rahab, 370, 372, 373
ransom, 81, 82, 296
rapture, 2, 3, 157, 341
receptivity, 169, 170
reconciliation, 82, 83, 91, 92, 333, 356
Redeemer, 70, 80, 81, 115, 293, 296, 398, 399
redemption, redeem, 4, 56, 80, 81, 86, 90, 114, 176, 241, 246, 348, 403
Reformation, 9, 29, 106, 132, 167, 170, 171, 210, 211, 242, 258, 298, 311, 325, 386, 406
Reformers, 7, 8, 14, 15, 22, 29, 99, 101, 105, 107, 117, 131, 167-170, 178, 243, 258, 360, 387-390, 392-394, 399, 401
Reformed theology, 107, 122, 133, 169, 230, 231, 232, 242, 249
regenerate, 13, 14, 25, 35, 48, 122, 133, 134, 182, 185, 210, 227, 238, 239, 241, 387
regeneration, 9, 17, 25, 49, 50, 88, 101, 102, 118, 119-124, 126, 128-131, 133, 134, 182, 222, 230-247, 249-252, 254-256, 259, 260, 385
Reign, 18, 19, 22, 24, 172, 177, 213, 216, 219, 270, 271, 404
relationship, 27, 51, 63, 65, 66, 82, 105, 112, 115, 135-139, 143-147, 151-154, 159, 161-165, 167, 176, 181, 183, 186-188, 199, 200, 202-205, 249, 254, 259, 308, 319, 370, 371, 373, 374
remission, 67, 144, 162, 241

repentance, 119-140, 142-145, 151, 152, 153, 155, 160, 162, 163, 165, 189, 204, 221, 232, 233, 234, 238, 239, 240, 241, 255, 260, 261, 272, 310, 316, 339, 340, 347, 398

reprobate, reprobation, 18-22, 29, 213-216, 219, 221, 258, 305, 306, 309-312, 390, 395-398, 400, 401

responsibility, 297, 299, 301, 303, 305, 307, 309, 311, 313, 315, 317, 319, 321, 323

restoration, 105, 205, 326

resurrection, 2, 4, 7, 69-71, 135, 185, 244, 266, 284, 320, 335, 340

revelation, 2, 3, 5, 56, 72, 75, 97, 136, 140, 156-158, 178, 199, 201, 204, 243, 294, 301, 325, 329, 330-334, 340-342, 393

rewards, 17, 101, 102, 147, 149, 150, 201, 202, 204, 205

righteous, 2, 6, 8, 9, 12, 14, 16, 17, 23, 29, 45, 50, 71, 80, 87, 99, 100, 101, 102, 104, 105, 106, 107, 109, 110, 111, 112, 113, 114, 115, 116, 122, 130, 135, 137, 158, 159, 177, 191, 197, 208, 211, 222, 234, 237, 290, 306, 307, 310, 336, 337, 338, 367, 371, 372, 373

Roman Catholic(ism), RCC, 5, 7, 13, 14, 15, 16, 17, 21, 22, 26, 99, 100, 101, 102, 107, 110, 114, 117, 118, 119, 130, 132, 177, 209, 212, 215, 216, 217, 232, 234-237, 243, 263, 291, 343, 392, 407, 408, 409

rule, 5, 7, 55, 56, 58, 70, 72, 150, 189, 266, 269, 270, 271, 279, 284, 285, 286

Ryrie, Charles, 50, 126, 132, 167, 173, 361

S

sacrifice, 62, 65, 67, 70, 75, 76, 78, 84, 93, 155, 193, 194, 199, 275, 276, 283, 347, 371

salvation, vii, x, xi, xiii, 7, 8, 11-14, 21-24, 26, 28-30, 33, 35, 37, 42, 44, 45, 54, 55, 57, 58, 62, 63, 66-68, 71, 87, 90-95, 106, 108, 109, 110, 118-120, 122-132, 144, 156, 161, 162, 166, 168, 171, 172, 175, 178, 180, 192, 193, 196, 197, 199, 201-204, 208-212, 215, 216, 221, 223, 227, 231-241, 250, 251, 254-256, 258-261, 271, 272, 275, 276, 288, 290, 296, 297, 301, 311, 319, 320, 324, 326, 329, 336, 339, 340, 342-344, 347, 352-356, 358-360, 364, 374, 377, 380, 387, 394, 395, 397, 399-401

sanctification, sanctified, 14, 15, 17, 18, 22, 33, 38, 58, 83, 84, 85, 95, 101, 102, 104-107, 114, 119, 120-124, 126, 129, 132, 144, 156, 165, 176, 195, 200, 201, 212, 219, 234,

236, 240, 276, 281, 282, 334, 337, 338, 358, 359, 397, 398
Satan, 6, 34, 35, 38, 55, 56, 94, 197, 270, 303, 311, 312, 318, 360
Second Adam, 57, 71
security, 20, 70, 193, 194, 195, 199, 208, 214
seed, 57, 59, 60, 61, 62, 149, 150, 161, 163, 189, 244, 306
separation, 35, 36, 39, 56, 69, 155, 157, 199, 230, 289, 326, 335, 339, 384
Shank, R., 24, 145, 216, 406, 410
Shedd, W. G.T., 241
sin, 9, 16, 22, 29, 33-42, 45, 48, 49, 50, 56, 62, 65, 66, 67, 74-76, 78, 82, 85, 88, 90, 95, 101, 104, 105, 116, 121, 122, 126-128, 131-133, 141, 144, 152, 156, 180, 191, 193-195, 197, 200, 204, 218-220, 224, 233, 237, 239, 246, 259, 272, 275-277, 279, 280, 285, 286, 291, 296, 301, 307, 308, 310, 312, 316, 317, 325, 331, 337, 339, 343, 357, 358-360, 380, 385, 394, 396, 398
sinfulness, 36, 42, 66, 85, 140, 336
soul, 33, 34, 47, 70, 153, 154, 168, 174, 259, 311, 360, 363, 376, 377, 380, 381-383, 385, 391, 394

sovereignty, 55, 122, 124, 239, 270-272, 297, 300-304, 306, 319, 320, 322, 323, 346, 348
spirit, 8, 19, 21, 41, 45, 47, 48, 49, 52, 69, 83, 100, 108, 114, 120, 122, 130, 131, 145, 160-163, 198-200, 214, 215, 234, 239, 241, 243, 246, 259, 264, 321, 334-336, 342, 399, 400
spiritual, 3, 4, 5, 11, 12, 23, 25, 29-31, 34-39, 42, 48, 62, 66, 119, 122, 129, 141, 174, 189, 190, 200, 209, 234, 244, 245, 276, 277, 285, 306, 339, 352-354, 356, 358, 362, 363, 376-378, 380-382, 388
Sproul, R.C., 30, 51, 107, 108, 230-232, 242, 250-254, 256, 301, 303, 315, 340
Spurgeon, C.H., 127, 133, 406
supralapsarianism, 89, 91, 94, 218, 219, 231, 390, 394, 395
Synod, 46, 86, 89, 92, 93, 231, 399, 400
systematic theology, 14, 28, 229, 355, 360

T
temporal, 8, 9, 27, 70, 118, 124, 134, 151-154, 157, 158, 160, 162, 199, 202, 203, 242, 248, 250, 307, 317, 318, 383, 393
Torah, 57, 66, 112, 154
transgression, 41, 290
tyranny, 47, 156, 263, 278, 357, 358

U

unbeliever, x, xiii, 25, 36, 42, 48, 49, 50, 51, 52, 121, 137, 142, 143, 186, 204, 222, 276, 284, 332, 339, 340
unfaithfulness, 151, 153, 202
ungodly, 83, 112, 201, 312
union with Christ, 109, 111, 124, 129, 234, 240
unregenerate, 35, 46, 47, 48, 49, 50, 51, 122, 124, 133, 134, 231, 250
unrighteousness, unrighteous, 6, 45, 47, 71, 104, 156, 272, 280, 305, 317, 357

V

victory, 63, 85, 143, 276, 379
volition, 179, 348

W

Warfield, B.B., 169, 170, 384, 385, 401
Wesley, John, 104, 145
will, 1, 2, 7, 12, 13, 15, 17, 20, 22, 26, 27, 28, 30, 32-35, 39, 43, 44, 45, 47, 49, 50-53, 55, 59, 60, 62-64, 67-71, 74, 78, 82, 83, 86-89, 91, 92, 95, 96, 100, 101, 103, 105, 108, 109, 113, 119-122, 124, 125, 128, 133, 135-139, 141-144, 149, 150, 153, 154-159, 167, 169, 170, 172-175, 177, 178, 182, 185, 187, 189, 190-192, 194, 198, 200-204, 206, 208, 209, 212-215, 217, 220, 222, 226, 230, 234, 236, 238, 240, 241, 243-246, 252-254, 256, 258, 259-262, 265, 267, 268, 270, 271, 274, 276, 278-282, 284, 285, 287, 288, 289, 290, 292-298, 301-305, 307-309, 312, 314, 316, 317, 318, 324-327, 329, 330, 332, 334, 335, 337-348, 352, 353, 355-358, 360-373, 381, 385-387, 390, 391, 395, 396, 400
will of God, 33, 125, 261, 301
works, 13, 17, 22, 44, 45, 56, 62, 77, 84, 87, 100-102, 106-110, 112, 118, 128, 135, 136, 138, 140, 168-172, 175-177, 185, 186, 197, 202, 206, 210, 211, 219, 221-223, 227, 231, 233, 238, 239, 243, 251, 255, 256, 258, 259, 307, 312, 313, 317, 329, 354-356, 360, 361, 364, 365, 368-374, 381, 388, 391, 396
wrath, 26, 47, 75, 76, 77, 78, 80, 145, 153, 154, 155, 156, 157, 158, 159, 160, 162, 197, 305, 309, 312, 313, 315, 317, 328, 336, 356, 357, 358, 360, 363, 365, 394, 397, 401

Z

Zwingli, 22

Scripture Index

Old Testament
Genesis
1-11 58
1 5
3:14-19 35
3:15 .... 59, 60, 61
12:1-3 61
12:7 61
15:6 62
31:3 150
41:8 35
Exodus
4:21 309
7:3 309
7:13 309
7:22 309
8:15, 32 309
8:19 309
9:7 309
9:12 309
9:16 310
9:34 309
9:35 309
10:1, 20, 27 309
11:10 309
14:4, 8, 17 309
12:27 75
20:12 69
25:17-20 77
Leviticus 65
Numbers
14:29 289
Deuteronomy
1:6-18 64
1:29 289
4:23-31 .... 149, 153
4:24 27
8:2 303
25:1 111
30:1-10 150
Ruth 58
1 Samuel
8:14 147
2 Samuel
7:14 266
15:4 111
1 Kings
3:6 148
8:23 148
9:4 148

11:4	148
11:11	150
11:35	150
14:8	148
15:3	148
17:17	69

2 Kings
4:32	69
Job	58
19:25-27	70
42:6	152

Psalms
1-11	410
2:7	266
110:1	70, 261, 264, 265, 266, 267, 268, 269, 270
16:9-11	70
19:1-4	47
90:4	5

Ecclesiastes
8:11	310, 316
12:1-8	69
12:7	288

Isaiah
6:9-	142
6:10	142
26:19	71
53:6-7	74
59:6	50
60:1-18	342
65:20	342, 343

Jeremiah
5:7-9	78
8:6	152
30:9	265
31:3	52, 153, 254
31:9	153
31:19	152
31:31-	408

Ezekiel
36:25-27	160

Daniel
7:9-	268
7:13	267, 268, 269
7:14	341
9:26	72
12:2	334, 340, 341
12:2-3	71

Hosea
11:1-8	78
11:8-9	78

Joel
2:38	114

Jonah
3:5	136
3:5-10	152
4:11	289

Habakkuk
2:4	63

Zephaniah
1:14-18	157

Malachi
3:1	159
4:1	27
4:1-5	160

New Testament

Matthew
1:21	352
3:7	158
8:25	352
9:13	135

Scripture Index

10:22 353
12:41 136
14:30 353
16:25 353
16:26 368
19:27-30 201
19:28 243
24:3 25
24:6 25
24:13 ..... 10, 11, 25, 29, 30, 31,
            209, 213, 232, 258
25:34 201
25:46 .... 338, 341, 342

Mark
1:15 134
2:17 135
10:45 81
14:24 218

Luke
1:15 241
1:69-71 354
2:25 163
5:32 135
10:25 138
11:32 136
14:23 201
15:4-7 137
17:3-4 139
17:13 .... 19, 214
20:39-40 262
20:41-44 .... 262, 266
22:42 347
22:67 267
22:69 268
24:44-47 127
24:47 .... 127, 135, 261

John
1:1-2 88
1:3 200
1:7 .... 134, 163
1:9 .... 200, 290, 292
1:12 .... 175, 178, 182, 254
1:12-13 175
1:13 .... 245, 246, 251, 302
1:25-33 159
1:29 .... 74, 218, 304
1:33 246
2:1-2 96
2:2 92
2:11 167
2:23 .... 180, 182, 187, 188
2:23-25 ...... 180, 182, 183, 185
2:25 188
3:3 241
3:3-8 246
3:5 233
3:16 .... 9, 48, 92, 95, 96, 97,
            305, 338
3:19-21 49
4:8 290
4:10 304
4:19 304
5:1 247
5:13 224
5:24 .... 226, 278
5:28-29 335
5:34 134
5:35 134
5:35-40 178
5:36-47 134
6:26 183
6:29-47 163

6:44 .... 51, 52, 53, 253, 254, 303, 315, 319	2:38 255
6:60-66 184	2:39 241
6:65 53	2:40 160
8:56 62	2:41 164
10:29 196	2:44 .... 163, 164
10:37-38 186	2:47 164
12:32 253	3:17 164
12:40 142	3:19 .... 126, 142, 162, 164
12:42 188	3:19-20 161
13:8 204	4:4 .... 163, 164
14:6 294	4:6 154
14:16 198	4:12 .... 163, 294
14:21 .... 55, 187, 303	5:31 261
15:6 202	7:2 61
15:14 187	7:2-3 147
15:15 188	7:3 148
15:22 367	7:25 354
16:7-11 48	8:2 163
16:8-11 49	8:13 189
17:6 .... 96, 97	8:15-17 119
17:9 97	10:43 .... 162, 163
17:11 198	11:21 .... 126, 162
18:10 253	13:33-37 408
19:38-39 188	13:39 164
20:29 186	14:15 126
20:30-31 186	14:17 296
20:31 .... 166, 182	15:19 126
21:6 253	16:19 .... 51, 253
21:7 253	16:31 .... 126, 175, 176, 261
Acts	17:27 .... 52, 293
2:1 241	17:30 135
2:21 269	20:21 .... 135, 261
2:26-35 70	21:30 .... 51, 253
2:36 .... 160, 261, 269, 271	27:34 354
2:37 164	**Romans**
	1:5 158

1:16-5 37	5:12-14 38
1:18 ..... 37, 156, 157, 158, 317, 357, 358, 394	5:12-21 .... 37, 41
	5:13-14 290
1:18- 47	5:15 .... 178, 304
1:18-20 .... 47, 50	5:15-16 203
1:28 .... 46, 47	5:15-21 41
2:5 .... 156, 157	5:18 .... 336, 337, 338
2:5-10 157	5:18-21 37
2:6-11 329	5:19 115
2:11 305	6:1 284
2:13 113	6:1-10 .... 85, 116, 272
2:14-16 47	6:1-11 .... 278, 283
3:9-12 50	6:10 194
3:10-18 191	6:12-14 .... 276, 279, 286
3:11 52	6:13 .... 278, 281, 283
3:19-20 290	6:23 190
3:21 .... 37, 52	8:2 144
3:21- 291	8:8 53
3:24-25 77	8:17 .... 138, 203, 343, 378
3:25-26 95	8:30 398
3:26 112	8:31 196
3:28 171	8:33 113
4:2 372	8:33-34 115
4:3 .... 62, 116, 358, 370	8:38-39 196
4:4-6 251	9:22 .... 305, 310, 314, 394, 397, 398
4:16 62	
4:21 196	9:22-23 305
5:1 113	10:9 .... 261, 271
5:1-11 83	10:9-10 ...... 188, 355, 359, 362
5:8 .... 197, 357	10:10 .... 355, 356
5:9 .... 197, 356, 357, 360	10:14 173
5:9-10 .... 356, 358	11:29 .... 203, 306
5:10 .... 357, 358	12:1 283
5:12 .... 38, 88, 407, 408, 409	13:4 317
5:12- 338	13:13-14 43
5:12-13 41	14:1-10 270

14:9 269
14:10 .... 283, 367
15:18 171
1 Corinthians
1:2 .... 84, 200, 334, 359
1:30 81
2:10-3 47
2:10-11 49
2:15 48
3:1-3 47
3:2 202
3:12-15 202
3:13 202
3-4,9:2 367
3-4,9:24-27 367
5:5 318
5:7 75
5:11 143
6:11 .... 110, 113
6:19- 97
6:19-20 80
7:22-23 80
9:26-27 217
10:12 .... 12, 226
12:13 334
13:2 175
14:8 315
15:3 74
15:22 .... 334, 335, 336
15:22- 266
2 Corinthians
3:16 142
3:18 .... 116, 200
4:3-6 49
4:5 261
5:10 .... 270, 368

5:17 278
5:18-20 83
5:21 .... 116, 191
Galatians
2:16 112
2:20 .... 138, 282, 357
3:2 255
3:3 203
3:8 61
3:10-13 407
3:11 .... 63, 112
3:13 80
3:16 61
4:4-5 81
4:7 138
5:1 205
5:4 203
5:6 175
5:21 201
Ephesians
1:3 .... 85, 200
1:4 320
1:6 205
1:7 82
1:10 333
1:14 199
1:20 270
1:22-23 334
2:1 .... 36, 334
2:6 85
2:8 251
2:8-9 .... 54, 329
2:8-10 .... 206, 356
2:10 138
2:12 36
2:13-18 83

4:17-19 49
4:18 36
4:30 198
5:5 201
5:11-14 360
5:18-21 248

Philippians
1:21 282
1:27 33
2:11 261
2:12 .... 13, 354
2:12-13 .... 44, 100, 108
2:13 .... 100, 239

Colossians
1:13 278
1:14 82
1:19-20 333
2:5 175
2:6 270
2:10 270
3:1 85
3:24-25 201

1 Thessalonians
1:10 .... 156, 157, 158
2:16 .... 156, 157
4:13-18 157
5:1-11 157
5:2-3 318
5:9 354
5:23 33

2 Thessalonians
2:3 331
2:4 331

1 Timothy
2:4 348
2:6 82

2:14 38
4:2 309

2 Timothy
2:12-13 203
2:22 359
4:10 227

Titus
2:14 81
3:5 .... 118, 233, 243
3:7 110

Philemon
24 227

Hebrews
1:1-2 296
1:13-2 85
2:8 85
2:10 138
2:17 76
4:1 203
4:9 206
6:1 .... 135, 261
6:4-5 .... 18, 213
6:4-6 .... 19, 204
7:25 197
7:27 194
9:5 77
9:12 194
9:27 336
10:4 193
10:5 317
10:10 .... 83, 194
10:10- 195
10:11 194
10:12 194
10:14 .... 84, 95
10:26 .... 26, 27

Reference	Pages
10:26-39	162, 329
10:30	27
10:38	63
10:39	27, 138
11:7	117
11:8	62
11:19	62, 70
11:26	72
11:31	372, 373

James

Reference	Pages
1:16	362
1:16-18	141, 354
1:16-21	362
1:18	244, 245, 363
1:19	354, 365
1:21	360, 363
2:4	366
2:5	201
2:6	51, 253
2:12-13	366
2:13	307, 325, 366
2:14	361, 363, 364, 365, 367, 368
2:14-26	180, 360, 361, 368
2:20	180
2:22	84
2:25	373
3:1	367
4:11-12	366, 369
4:12	362, 363
5:8	366
5:8-9	368
5:15	362, 363
5:19	141, 142
5:19-20	141
5:20	141, 363

1 Peter

Reference	Pages
1:2	245
1:3	244, 245, 354
1:5	354
1:18-19	81
1:23	244, 245
3:18-20	335

2 Peter

Reference	Pages
1:10	219
2:1	97, 98
2:4	97
3:9	135, 271, 347

1 John

Reference	Pages
1:1-2	88
1:1-4	225
1:3	200
1:9	200
2:1	96
2:1-2	96, 197
2:2	96, 304, 367
3:19-21	49
3:36	157
4:8	290
4:10	77, 304
4:18	339
4:19	304
5:1	226, 247, 249
5:13	223, 224, 225, 226

Jude

Reference	Pages
9	26
24	196

Revelation

Reference	Pages
3:5	204
3:19	136
5:9	97
6:16-	157

9:20-21 140	20:11-15 340
14:3 97	21:7 201
14:4 97	22:17 178
14:6-7 294	22:19 204
14:10 158	
14:10-11 325	**Apocrypha**
19:20 .... 329, 333	**4 Maccabees**
20:1-6 330	14:13 254
20:10 .... 329, 330, 332	15:11 254

Scripture index created by Gracelife.org Scripture Indexing Tool, http://www.gracelife.org/resources/bibletools/

www.ingramcontent.com/pod-product-compliance
Lightning Source LLC
Chambersburg PA
CBHW032029150426
43194CB00006B/202